Strategic Studies Institute Book

CONFLICT MANAGEMENT AND "WHOLE OF GOVERNMENT": USEFUL TOOLS FOR U.S. NATIONAL SECURITY STRATEGY?

Volker C. Franke
Robert H. Dorff
Editors

April 2012

*****

Comments pertaining to this report are invited and should be forwarded to: Director, Strategic Studies Institute, U.S. Army War College, 45 Ashburn Drive, Bldg. 47, Carlisle, PA 17013-5046.

*****

All Strategic Studies Institute (SSI) publications may be downloaded free of charge from the SSI website. Hard copies of this report may also be obtained free of charge while supplies last by placing an order on the SSI website. SSI publications may be quoted or reprinted in part or in full with permission and appropriate credit given to the U.S. Army Strategic Studies Institute, U.S. Army War College, Carlisle Barracks, PA. Contact SSI by visiting our website at the following address: *www.StrategicStudiesInstitute.army.mil.*

*****

The Strategic Studies Institute publishes a monthly e-mail newsletter to update the national security community on the research of our analysts, recent and forthcoming publications, and upcoming conferences sponsored by the Institute. Each newsletter also provides a strategic commentary by one of our research analysts. If you are interested in receiving this newsletter, please subscribe on the SSI website at *www.StrategicStudiesInstitute.army.mil/newsletter/.*

ISBN 1-58487-524-0

CONTENTS

FOREWORD

On February 25, 2011, Kennesaw State University (KSU) and the Strategic Studies Institute (SSI) of the U.S. Army War College, conducted a symposium entitled "Conflict Management: A Tool for U.S. National Security Strategy." This symposium was the first collaboration between KSU and SSI, and it was conducted in the inaugural year of KSU's new Ph.D. program in International Conflict Management (INCM). In addition to the focus on conflict management, the symposium was designed to examine one of the ongoing research interests in the SSI academic engagement series, the role of "whole of government" (WoG) efforts in addressing contemporary national and international security challenges and opportunities. Three symposium panels addressed the following topics: "Responding to New Foreign Policy and National Security Threats," "WoG Prospects and Challenges," and "WoG Lessons from Iraq and Afghanistan." The symposium discussions ranged from the conceptual to the practical, with a focus on the challenges and desirability of interagency cooperation in international interventions. Invited panelists shared their experiences and expertise on the question of WoG and the impact of fragile and failing states on national security concerns. The panelists engaged the audience in a discussion that included viewpoints from academia, the military, government agencies, nongovernmental organizations, and industry. Despite the broad range of viewpoints, a number of overarching themes and tentative agreements emerged. The reader will find them in the chapters of this edited volume.

The Strategic Studies Institute and the co-editors of this volume join in thanking the faculty, students, and staff of KSU for their extraordinary efforts in organizing and implementing the symposium, and in the preparation of this book. We also extend a very special thanks to KSU President Dr. Daniel S. Papp and Dean of the College of Humanities and Social Sciences Dr. Richard A. Vengroff for their energetic support of and commitment to the event and the publication of this book. In addition, we would like to thank Dr. Jack Moran, Associate Professor of Political Science, for skillfully moderating one of the panels; Mackenzie Duelge, INCM Ph.D. student who, as graduate assistant for the symposium, helped coordinate the conference logistics and co-authored the conference brief; and INCM Program Administrator Rose Procter, whose tireless efforts and great dedication ensured the successful organization and effective implementation of the symposium. Finally, our thanks go to the first cohort of INCM Ph.D. students, all of whom volunteered to serve as program liaison and campus guides to the panelists.

KSU and SSI are pleased to present this book, and we hope that readers will engage us further in the kinds of issues and debates that surfaced at the symposium and that are captured and extended in the pages that follow. For both national and international security, we must continue to develop effective tools and implement coordinated strategies of conflict management.

DOUGLAS C. LOVELACE, JR.
Director
Strategic Studies Institute

PREFACE

THE WHOLE OF GOVERNMENT APPROACH TO SECURITY, AND BEYOND

Daniel S. Papp

Throughout most of the 20th century, national security focused primarily, and sometimes exclusively, on military affairs. In the 21st century, this has changed as new and more comprehensive ways of thinking about, studying, and planning for national security and global security are being adopted in response to new security challenges and threats that go beyond the dangers posed by traditional causes of war and conflict. In addition to terrorism, these other threats to security are posed by, but not limited to, shortfalls of energy and nonfuel mineral resources, scarcity of food and fresh water, encroaching desertification, and cyber attacks. To some, these new challenges and threats present as much, and over time perhaps more, of a challenge and threat to security as do guns, bombs, and missiles.

The faculty of the Ph.D. Program in International Conflict Management (INCM) at Kennesaw State University (KSU) recognized this reality and, in conjunction with the Strategic Studies Institute (SSI) of the U.S. Army War College (USAWC), structured a series of meetings and conferences to discuss emerging security challenges and threats to debate and analyze the strengths and weaknesses of the Barack Obama administration's whole of government (WoG) approach to dealing with these challenges and threats. This volume contains papers delivered at the first KSU-SSI conference.

Why are such meetings and conferences valuable and why is this volume worth reading? According to many, including high officials in the previous George Bush and current Barack Obama administrations, the often interrelated and predominantly nontraditional nature of many of the emerging challenges and threats to national and global security require new ways of thinking and new plans of action. While traditional military capabilities are requisite to counter traditional military challenges and satisfy traditional military needs, new thinking about security is needed if the 21st century world is to become safer and more secure.

Steps were initiated to move in this direction during the Bush administration (2001-09) when at various times the President implied that the United States should unite defense, diplomacy, and development ("The Three Ds") to achieve a more peaceful and secure world. This so-called Three Ds conception sought to link ways in which both traditional and nontraditional challenges and threats to security could be countered. Conversely, critics of the Three Ds concept asserted that boundaries between the Three Ds prevented effective implementation of policies to counter traditional and nontraditional challenges and threats. Other critics avowed that defense, diplomacy, and development by themselves were not sufficient to cope with 21st century security challenges and threats, and that a more inclusive concept was needed.

These criticisms were undoubtedly key factors in influencing the Obama administration to adopt a new approach to traditional and nontraditional security challenges and threats in its May 2010 *National Security Strategy* (NSS), which declared that "a broad conception of what constitutes our national security" was needed, and that the international order that the

United States sought to create could only be reached by:

> . . . resolv[ing] the challenges of our times—countering violent extremism and insurgency; stopping the spread of nuclear weapons and securing nuclear materials; combating a changing climate and sustaining global growth; helping countries feed themselves and care for their sick; resolving and preventing conflict, while also healing its wounds.

But how to do this? Again according to the May 2010 NSS, the answer was to adopt a WoG approach to national and global security that viewed national and global security, as well as the challenges and threats to national and global security, in a comprehensive manner. Thus, the May 2010 NSS argued that a more holistic approach to national and global security must be developed and implemented.

That more holistic approach is what the conference from which this volume is derived examined. The conference itself was an eye-opening and mind-expanding exercise in thinking about 21st century challenges and threats to security, and what is needed to respond to these challenges and threats to make the world a more safe and secure place. Indeed, the KSU Ph.D. Program in INCM, and SSI of the USAWC, are both fully committed to educating students, conducting research, and participating in programs that will help achieve these laudable objectives as we move deeper into the 21st century. We trust that readers of this volume will appreciate, and in their own ways contribute to, these same objectives.

Finally, I would like to thank the Director of SSI, Professor Douglas Lovelace, and Dr. Robert H. (Robin) Dorff for helping to plan and execute the conference, as well as for chairing a panel and co-editing this volume; I would also like to thank Dr. James Pierce and Ms. Rita Rummel for their excellent work in publishing this monograph. Additionally, thanks also to Dean Richard Vengroff of the Kennesaw State College of Humanities and Social Sciences; Dr. Volker Franke, Director of the KSU Ph.D. Program in INCM; and the entire INCM staff, but especially Ms. Rose Proctor, for their invaluable work in planning and conducting the conference.

ENDNOTES - PREFACE

1. See for example, President Bush's July 17, 2001 address to the World Bank in which he said that the United States "must be guided by three great goals," the first "to keep peace with military forces in support of freedom and free states," the second "to ignite a new era of global economic growth through a world trading system that is dramatically more open and more free," and the third "to work in true partnership with developing countries to remove the huge obstacles to development, to help them fight illiteracy, disease, unsustainable debt." George W. Bush, "Speech to the World Bank," Washington, DC, July 17, 2001. Even after the September 11, 2001, attacks on the United States, Bush emphasized a non-explicit form of the Three Ds. For example, in his March 22, 2002, speech to the United Nations, "Financing for Development" Conference in Monterrey, Mexico, Bush declared his intention to increase U.S. development assistance by 50 percent and create a "Millennium Challenge Account" to help developing states. George W. Bush, "Speech to the United Nations 'Financing for Development' Conference," Monterrey, Mexico, March 22, 2002. Similarly, Bush in his introductory remarks to the September *2002 National Security Strategy of the United States of America* also obliquely referenced what later became the Three Ds:

> We will actively work to bring the hope of democracy, development, free markets, and free trade to every corner of the world . . .

> The United States will deliver greater development assistance through the New Millennium Challenge Account to nations that govern justly, invest in their people, and encourage economic freedom. We will also continue to lead the world in efforts to reduce the terrible toll of HIV/AIDS and other infectious diseases. . . .
>
> We are also guided by the conviction that no nation can build a safer, better world alone. Alliances and multilateral institutions can multiply the strength of freedom-loving nations.

2. "The Three D's: Defense, Diplomacy, and Development," Washington, DC: Center for American Progress, August 1, 2008, available from *www.americanprogress.org/issues/2008/08/three_ds.html.*

3. The White House, *National Security Strategy,* Washington, DC: U.S. Government Printing Office, May 2010, p. 51.

4. Barack Obama, "Introductory Remarks," in *Ibid.*

5. The White House, *2010 National Security Strategy,* pp. 14-16.

CHAPTER 1

INTRODUCTION

Volker C. Franke and Robert H. Dorff

When President Barack Obama unveiled his administration's *National Security Strategy* (NSS) in May 2010, he proclaimed:

> We live in a time of sweeping change. The success of free nations, open markets and social progress in recent decades has accelerated globalization on an unprecedented scale. This has opened the doors of opportunity around the globe, extended democracy to hundreds of millions of people, and made peace possible among major powers. Yet globalization has also intensified the dangers we face—from international terrorism and the spread of deadly technologies to economic upheaval and a changing climate.[1]

A decade into the new century, the security architecture established in the aftermath of World War II seems to be "buckling under the weight of new threats."[2] Today, America faces security challenges from violent extremist organizations, ongoing operations in Afghanistan, Iraq, and most recently Libya, the proliferation of weapons of mass destruction (WMD), the global financial crisis, the revolutionary wave of demonstrations and uprisings in the Arab world and, more generally, weak and failing states. These challenges are exceedingly dynamic and complex, in part because of the ever changing mix and number of actors involved and the pace with which the strategic and operational environments change. To meet these new security challenges more effectively, Secretary of State Hillary Rodham Clinton and then-Secretary of Defense Robert Gates advocated strengthening civilian instruments of national power and enhancing America's whole-of-government (WoG) capabilities. "Development," Secretary Clinton explained, is "one of the most powerful tools we have for advancing global progress, peace, and prosperity."[3]

Indeed, our experiences since the end of the Cold War have demonstrated that development and security are intrinsically linked, and that political stability, economic opportunity and lasting peace are predicated on the successful transformation of violent conflict and the creation of sustainable legitimate government. In the past, the international community, the U.S. Government included, responded to emerging security challenges largely in an ad hoc fashion by "recreating and refashioning the necessary tools, strategies, and relationships anew with each crisis."[4]

Today, however, responding quickly to global crises and emerging threats has become part of the *modus operandi* in the White House, the Pentagon, and at the State Department (State). As a result, conflict management in fragile, failing, and failed states has become the new face of U.S. national security. Active engagement in conflict or post-conflict environments draws heavily on military and civilian capabilities and resources alike, and more than ever before requires the close coordination and cooperation of a wide range of state and nonstate, international and domestic actors. In today's conflict contexts, the political, security, economic, social, and cultural spheres are so highly interdependent that failure in one sphere risks failure in all others. No single actor or agency and no single strategy suffice for developing and implementing enduring and sustainable solutions to these challenges.

Drawing lessons from the operational experiences in Iraq and Afghanistan showed the need for improved coordination between civilian organizations and the military and, as a result, in July 2004 Congress authorized the funds to create the Office of the Coordinator for Reconstruction and Stabilization (S/CRS) in State to lead, coordinate, and institutionalize U.S. Government civilian capacity to support stabilization and post-conflict reconstruction efforts. Recognizing existing inefficiencies in responding to international crises both in terms of time and resources, President George Bush signed National Security Presidential Directive (NSPD) 44 in December 2005, outlining the responsibilities of the new office for integrating more effectively the government's civilian and military capacities. NSPD-44 specifies that America "has a significant stake in enhancing the capacity to assist in stabilizing and reconstructing countries or regions, especially those at risk of, in, or in transition from conflict or civil strife, and to help them establish a sustainable path toward peaceful societies, democracies, and market economies."[5] Aimed at promoting the security of the United States "through improved coordination, planning, and implementation for reconstruction and stabilization assistance,"[6] NSPD-44 charges the State Department with coordinating and strengthening "U.S. reconstruction and stabilization assistance" and with harmonizing "such efforts with U.S. military plans and operations."[7]

Acknowledging the need for building and integrating joint civil-military capabilities for advancing American interests as well as interests shared with other countries and peoples, President Obama underscored in his foreword to the 2010 NSS that:

> our armed forces will always be a cornerstone of our security, but they must be complemented. Our security also depends on diplomats who can act in every corner of the world, from grand capitals to dangerous outposts; development experts who can strengthen governance and support human dignity; and intelligence and law enforcement that can unravel plots, strengthen justice systems and work seamlessly with other countries.[8]

Aimed at strengthening civilian conflict management capacity, the President requested more than $320 million in his fiscal year (FY) 2010 Budget for the Civilian Stabilization Initiative (CSI), in part to support the recruitment, development, training, and equipping of the Civilian Response Corps (CRC), authorized by Congress in 2008 "to help address the rise of new challenges to U.S. national security, including weak governance, political conflict, and internal violence in countries around the world."[9] The CRC consists of civilian federal employees who are specially trained and equipped for rapid deployment "to provide conflict prevention and stabilization assistance to countries in crisis or emerging from conflict."[10]

Effective conflict prevention and transformation, most experts agree, require greater coherence between security, governance and development policies, and enhanced coordination among governmental agencies and with local, regional, and international partners. With its increased emphasis on civil-military cooperation to more effectively meet the mission objectives in peace building and stability operations—including the CRC—the U.S. Government has recognized the benefits of employing what some observers have termed smart power: using the right tool, or combination of tools, for each operational context.[11]

Secretary Clinton explained:

> With the right tools, training, and leadership, our diplomats and development experts can defuse crises before they explode. Creating new opportunities for advancing democracy, promoting sustainable economic growth, and strengthening the rule of law in fragile states are all overlapping and mutually reinforcing endeavors. They cut across bureaus and offices and agencies. They demand not just the skills of our State Department diplomats and USAID [U.S. Agency for International Development] experts, but also the expertise of civilian specialists across the U.S. Government."[12]

The need for the comprehensive integration and coordination of civilian and military, governmental and nongovernmental, national and international capabilities to improve efficiency and effectiveness of conflict prevention/resolution and post-conflict stabilization and peace building efforts is widely recognized. While many academic and policy observers, military experts, and peace practitioners have lauded Washington's efforts for integrating civil-military relations and strengthening interagency cooperation, others have criticized contemporary attempts at creating WoG responses to international crises and conflicts for over commitment of resources, lack of sufficient funding and personnel, competition between agencies, ambiguous mission objectives, and undermining the military's primary purpose of defending the national interest. The "buzz" the WoG idea has generated merits a closer look at the advantages and disadvantages of the concept and calls for a more systematic analysis of its challenges and opportunities.

On February 25, 2011, a number of leading civilian and military experts came together at a symposium held at Kennesaw State University to evaluate the benefits and shortcomings of the WoG approach in response to the increasingly dynamic and complex global security environment. Intended to facilitate dialogue between academic experts, military leaders, policymakers, and civilian practitioners, the symposium provided an opportunity for a state of the art analysis of current WoG approaches and their effectiveness for coordinating stabilization and peace building efforts and, eventually, for shifting the burden of stability operations to civilian actors and enabling the timely scaling-down of military deployments.[13]

This volume presents the central arguments and key findings of the symposium, tracing the genesis of the conception of a WoG approach, critically examining current WoG practices, and drawing lessons from the operational contexts of Iraq and Afghanistan. The first part of the book describes the overall global security context within which peace building and stability operations are currently conducted, examines the merits of WoG approaches as effective conflict management strategies, and discusses their efficacy for responding to a range of emerging threats.

In Chapter 2, Robert Kennedy provides a framing analysis of the security environment of the early 21st century with specific focus on the role and position of the United States, and outlines the issues and challenges Washington confronts as it attempts to address emerging threats through an integrated interagency approach. While it is easy to declare that agencies ought to cooperate, Kennedy argues, such cooperation is neither easily embraced nor successfully implemented. Effective integration will require giving up agency fiefdoms and jointly addressing threats ranging from fragile and failing states to terrorism and totalitarianism.

Mary Habeck takes Kennedy's argument to task and examines the particular challenges underlying the planning and implementation of government-wide reforms in general, and of WoG efforts in particular. In Chapter 3, she looks specifically at ambiguities in the definition of planning, organizational and structural frictions, and coordination failures that undermined integration attempts during Operation IRAQI FREEDOM. Discussing a range of proposals for alleviating these problems, Habeck concludes that any sustainable solution is predicated on broad-based government consensus and enforcement from above at the presidential and/or congressional level. In her view, proponency, advocacy, and leadership are required.

Reversing the tables, in Chapter 4 Michael Ashkenazi discusses the unintended side-effects of Western, and particularly American, WoG efforts on the recipients of foreign assistance and developmental aid. Acknowledging the two-fold objectives of development—to alleviate misery from poverty and to reduce security threats posed by the "have-nots"—Ashkenazi argues that development, as conceived in the West, is premised on the systematic, intentional, and irreversible destruction of to-be-developed societies, with the risk of raising indigenous resentment and, as a result, further aggravating potential threats to the West. Therefore, Ashkenazi concludes, effective integrated development strategies must connect individuals and agencies in the donor and recipient communities. In terms of WoG efforts, they will remain largely irrelevant if the existing and perhaps inherent contradictions in development (what it is and what it does for donors and recipients) cannot be reconciled.

The second part of this volume addresses some of the practical challenges of implementing WoG approaches to international conflict management and specifically to U.S. intervention in fragile states. Echoing Ashkenazi's advocation of comprehensive integrated development strategies, Lisa Schirch conjectures that one of the key shortcomings of current WoG approaches is their lack of integration with organizations that help build and maintain the strong civil society structures imperative to sustainable peace and effective development. Following a discussion of existing tensions between strategies of national and human security, Schirch argues in Chapter 5 that successful stabilization and security require an even more comprehensive "whole of society" approach that must include the interests and perspectives of diverse sectors of civil society in the target countries.

Addressing WoG efforts from a macro perspective, Melanie Alamir reflects in Chapter 6 on the overall utility of WoG approaches for achieving desired political end states by examining systematic challenges at three levels: the donor country's political system, the recipient country's political system, and the system of international crisis response. When considering outcomes, Alamir shows that WoG approaches, despite their theoretical appeal, have only limited practical utility because the nature of international interventions depends on the types of parties involved. Effective interagency cooperation is particularly difficult to achieve in weak states that lack stable political structures. Cooperation in donor countries on the other hand is determined largely by domestic political considerations of efficiency and accountability, shifting focus away from the intervention's primary targets and desired outcomes.

Tracing the application of WoG to issues of U.S. national security, Charles Dunlap analyzes the merits and limitations of greater coordination across government agencies in light of the marked expansion of diplomatic and civilian development capabilities. Examining some of the unintended consequences of integrating response strategies to security threats, Dunlap contends in Chapter 7 that, despite the widely accepted WoG mantra, in some instances a unilateral approach that relies primarily on one particular agency is the preferred or only practical alternative. As a result, Dunlap advocates considering WoG as just one tool in the smart power toolbox that, when selectively employed, may be very effective, but that should not serve as a default in all circumstances.

Building on Dunlap's argument, James Stephenson warns in Chapter 8 that U.S. presence in recipient states has increased to unsustainable levels, in part as a consequence of the uncritical embracing of WoG approaches. As a result, Stephenson argues ambassadors have become chief executive officers (CEOs) of complex interagency missions, and the military has become ever more engaged in stability operations that have become largely indistinguishable from civilian stabilization and reconstruction efforts. A successful WoG approach, Stephenson conjectures, would streamline efforts and have the various agencies and their representatives team up to serve the overall mission objectives before they consider individual agency interests. Specifically, and to offset continued strain on military resources, Stephenson suggests an expansion of civilian capacity for taking on a widening set of responsibilities for diplomacy and development and, ultimately, the projection of smart power.

In Chapter 9, Jack LeCuyer argues that it is unreasonable to expect successful WoG efforts at the "tip of the spear" or on the ground, if there is a lack of integration and coordination at the hub of the national security system. LeCuyer specifically criticizes the fact that the role of the National Security Council (NSC), irrespective of the rapidly changing global security environment, has remained largely unchanged since its inception in 1947, and its staff continues to focus primarily on the urgent and crisis management instead of long-term strategic planning. In order to improve the performance, adaptability, and efficiency of the overall national security system for meeting new threats, LeCuyer recommends the proper resourcing of the NSC staff so that they can fulfill their role as strategic managers who actively contribute to the integration of the national security interagency system to achieve a WoG success at the strategic level.

The third part of the book examines WoG efforts in the field and attempts to draw lessons learned from operational experiences in Afghanistan and Iraq to potential future interventions. Looking in from "outside the box," Christopher Holshek explores the extent to which lessons drawn from Iraq and Afghanistan can be applied to other mission contexts. Although winning hearts and minds has been a cornerstone of American counterinsurgency strategy, Holshek argues in Chapter 10 that it has proven counterproductive in different cultural and operational environments and its techniques and tools—e.g., Provincial Reconstruction Teams—have only limited applicability in places like sub-Saharan Africa. Consequently, Holshek suggests, there is also much to be learned from operational experiences beyond Afghanistan and Iraq. These more general lessons, Holshek concludes, should not only have profound implications for U.S. WoG engagements around the world, but also should help re-shape the American approach to national security writ large back home, because "we can no longer afford any other way."[14]

Using a combination of historical and current case examples, William Flavin asks in Chapter 11 whether and to what extent civil-military teaming efforts may present an effective and efficient alternative to addressing the problems associated with current conflicts. Flavin identifies what constitutes a successful team and analyzes the effects of successful civil-military teaming on transitioning conflict. Flavin concludes that successful mission accomplishment is possible, as long as the focus of the civil-military teaming efforts is on the population, actively engaging local stakeholders and building legitimacy and local capacity to provide good governance.

Exploring lessons from the use of contractors in peace and stability operations, Doug Brooks and Mackenzie Duelge argue in Chapter 12 that by far, the biggest drain in Afghanistan and Iraq has been waste stemming from failures of planning, coordination, contract oversight and management, flexibility, and communication. Specifically, Brooks and Duelge examine the extent to which a generally negative attitude towards contractors has hindered their ability to perform and has interfered with the success of stability operations. Analyzing shortfalls in current practices framing government-private sector partnerships, Brooks and Duelge conclude that consolidating contracting government-wide as a hybrid approach, rather than a pure WoG approach, may be the most effective way to unify communications and record keeping, while keeping the work on the ground divided among those most qualified to do it. Ultimately, this kind of hybrid approach, the authors suggest, could not only help eliminate waste, but could also improve oversight, flexibility, and ethical behavior.

Focusing on the need for a qualitatively deeper command of cultural matters, Gregory Meyjes argues in the concluding chapter that U.S. interventions, whether based on a military or WoG approach, are only as viable as their conceptual framework permits; to be successful they require a three-tiered approach to ethnic, state, and global realities, based on a grasp of ethno-cultural dynamics. Instead of the prevailing two-dimensional approach whereby traditional national security efforts are complemented by local information in theater, Meyjes describes international conflict management strategies grounded in cultural self-awareness, intercultural competence, recognition of collective cultural rights, and the protection of sub-state ethno-nationalities. These insights, processes, and capabilities, Meyjes concludes, revolve around the inescapability of ethno-cultural justice as the key to peace and stability in multiethnic societies and, by extension, to international security. They are deemed critical for intervention and WoG more generally to meet the demands of a world greatly imperiled by ethnic conflict.

The chapters in this book reflect the perspectives of authors who have seen, worked with, and studied both the problems and the approaches to conflict management in a variety of different settings and contexts. Not all of them are enthusiastic proponents of the WoG concept for implementing conflict management; nor are they all strict skeptics of the concept. It is no surprise, then, that together the chapters in this edited volume do not offer the reader a collective answer to questions about the future of WoG. But together they do provide important and necessary insights into the challenges we face and the considerations we must include in our efforts to address the complexities of linking development and security in an integrated effort to manage conflict as part of an overall strategy. WoG is certainly one conceivable strategic *way* to achieve this linkage. Is it the best or the most appropriate way? What is success and what should we reasonably expect to accomplish? Is WoG a strategically useful concept for even thinking about the available tools in our conflict management efforts? These are only a few of the questions raised and addressed by the authors in the chapters that follow. We believe these chapters are well worth reading by those who wrestle with these problems as scholars, practitioners, or both.

ENDNOTES - INTRODUCTION

1. Foreword to the *National Security Strategy*, Washington, DC: The White House, May 2010, p. i, available from *www.whitehouse.gov/sites/default/files/rss_viewer/national_security_strategy.pdf.*

2. President Obama, in his remarks accepting the Nobel Peace Prize, available from *www.nytimes.com/2009/12/11/world/europe/11prexy.text.html?ref=europe.*

3. Available from *www.usaid.gov/press/frontlines/fl_aug09/p1_clinton080902.html.*

4. Coordinator for Reconstruction & Stabilization, *Smart Power in Action: 2009 Year in Review*, Washington, DC: U.S. Department of State, available from *www.state.gov/documents/organization/137690.pdf.*

5. *National Security Presidential Directive 44 (NSPD-44)*, Washington, DC: The White House, pp. 1-2, available from *www.fas.org/irp/offdocs/nspd/nspd-44.pdf.*

6. *Ibid.*, p. 1.

7. *Ibid.*, p. 2.

8. *National Security Strategy*, p. i.

9. Remarks by Robert Loftis, Acting Coordinator for Reconstruction and Stabilization, commemorating the third anniversary of the Civilian Response Corps (CRC), July 16, 2011, available from *www.civilianresponsecorps.gov/newsroom/168618.htm*.

10. See the CRC website, available from *www.civilianresponsecorps.gov/*.

11. See Richard L. Armitage and Joseph S. Nye, Jr., "A Smarter, More Secure America," Report of the CSIS Commission on Smart Power, Washington, DC: Center for Strategic and International Studies, November 2007, available from *www.csis.org/media/csis/pubs/071106_csissmartpowerreport.pdf*. For further information on the CSIS Commission on Smart Power, see *www.csis.org/smartpower/*.

12. Available from *www.civilianresponsecorps.gov/*.

13. For further detail on the KSU-SSI Symposium, see the symposium website available from *ksussi.hss.kennesaw.edu/*.

14. See the Human Security Report Project's *Human Security Report 2009/2010*, Simon Fraser University, available from *www.hsrgroup.org/human-security-reports/20092010/overview.aspx*.

PART I

CHAPTER 2

SECURITY SECTOR REFORM: 12 CENTRAL QUESTIONS FOR RESPONDING TO THE SECURITY CHALLENGES OF THE 21ST CENTURY

Robert Kennedy

At the end of the Cold War, John Mearsheimer penned an article, "Why We Will Soon Miss the Cold War,"[1] in which he suggested that one day we might wake up lamenting the loss of order afforded us during the Cold War. Though his concerns were focused on the potential rise of instabilities in Europe, they have nonetheless unfortunately proven true in the wider context of global instabilities that now give rise to activities that threaten the security of the United States as well as that of other nations. Indeed, the security challenges that now confront the United States are exceedingly complex. The reasons are many and varied. However, often they stem less from the prospect of war among nation-states than from threats that arise from intrastate instabilities that have emerged following the end of the Cold War. As a result, processes and structures designed to meet the demands of the Cold War and the threats to U.S. national security posed by the Soviet Union are no longer adequate. In recent years, to meet the challenges of the 21st century security environment, there have been calls for an integration of the instruments of national power, from across government collaborative planning to integrated responses organized on an interagency basis.

This chapter examines the security environment that has come to characterize the early 21st century and outlines the issues and challenges the United States confronts as it attempts to address the threats of tomorrow through an integrated interagency approach. The chapter concludes that the emerging environment does indeed demand a greater integration of effort than has thus far been emblematic of U.S. foreign and security policies, and to accomplish that will require, at a minimum, answers to a number of central questions, which are addressed below.

THE SECURITY ENVIRONMENT OF THE 21ST CENTURY

When the Cold War ended, so ended a conflict that spanned nearly half a century, consumed vast resources, and threatened the annihilation of much of humanity. For many, the horizons seemed bright. Visions of a more peaceful world order were entertained. However, relief from conflict was brief. Iraq's invasion of Kuwait and conflicts in such places as Bosnia, Somalia, Rwanda, Kosovo, and finally the attacks on September 11, 2001 (9/11), shattered illusions that the world had reached the "End of History," as Francis Fukuyama argued, when conflict is replaced by "economic calculations, the endless solving of technical problems, environmental concerns, and the satisfaction of sophisticated consumer demands."[2]

Indeed, history did not end. Conflict has not been replaced by other concerns. For the time being, the security environment of the early 21st century does not threaten human annihilation. Nevertheless the dangers are real and in many respects demand more articulated approaches than those used to hold the Soviet Union at bay during the Cold War. So how has the security environment changed, and what are the dangers that lie ahead?

Cold War Restraints Gone.

Gone are the Soviet Union and threats of nuclear annihilation. Also gone is the stability imposed by the bipolar nuclear standoff that in many respects resulted in the "Long Peace" as John Lewis Gaddis put it, and with it went the systemic discipline that rendered the rise of dissident groups difficult, if not impossible, in many parts of the world. With the demise of the Soviet Union, the cooker lid has been released and pressures within have emerged to wreck their havoc. Multi-national, multi-ethnic, multi-religious, and/or multi-tribal states, often created by the stroke of a pen on a map and once held together by dictators, supported by one side or the other during the Cold War, frequently have given way to weak and feckless governments in the post-Cold War period. The internal cohesion imposed by the restraints of the Cold War has disappeared, exposing historic tensions among differing groups and giving rise to instabilities, failing governments, and internal conflicts, as well as creating havens and new opportunities for violent and extremist groups.

Diminished Deterrence.

Furthermore, the deterrence equation that often held conflict in check has been undermined. Deterrence of conflict works best when the costs and risks are shared and stark. During the Cold War, the cost of acquiring the ability to deliver a devastating military attack on the United States or any of its client states by the Soviet Union or vice versa was immense, and the risk was the potential for mutual annihilation.

However, even during the Cold War, deterrence had its limits. Threats of massive retaliation broke down in lesser conflicts where direct attacks by one superpower on the homeland of the other superpower were not the issue. Nevertheless, where the superpowers abetted and served as mentors and suppliers of needed economic aid and military arms and equipment to competing factions in so-called Third World countries, the superpowers were usually able to keep conflict in check, modulating the behavior of their respective client states to ensure that superpower fundamental security interests were not directly threatened.

Today, the cost of attacks such as those on the World Trade Center or the Pentagon is a trifle in comparison to the devastation they could cause. Moreover, many of today's potential aggressors are not state actors. Nor do they require the assistance of a state to threaten the security of others. They hold no territory that can be easily threatened with a military counterattack. They do not mind sacrificing themselves, their families, or others to accomplish their objectives. Furthermore, precise knowledge of which of the many individuals or independent or semi-affiliated groups perpetrated an event may not be known. Yes, known terrorist training camps can be attacked, forces can sometimes be sent to foreign lands in an attempt to ferret out the perpetrators, alliances can sometimes be forged to bring the weight of the international community to bear. But successful outcomes are not assured. As a result, the risks to the aggressors of effective military reprisal are often low, and the threat of such a reprisal is largely ineffective. Hence, if the efforts of such groups are to be thwarted, other approaches for dealing with the threats they pose will need to be added to the arsenal of policy tools.

Globalization.

The globalization of technology, the media, and know-how also has played a major role in altering the contemporary security environment. The Internet, still in its infancy as the Cold War was coming to an end, now provides easy access to a breadth of information that in the past only the most dedicated, diligent, determined, and educated segments of society could acquire. Globalization of communications and the concomitant emergence of a wide range of communications technologies have made instant interchange with any place or person on the globe the standard rather than the exception. Money can be moved, people contacted, and plans instantly shared or changed. Such technologies have had a vast and often positive impact on societies. But they do have a darker side.

Today terrorists, criminals, extremist organizations, and others bent on doing harm can gain access, with the mere click of a mouse, to information widely available on the Internet on such things as how to combine commonly available materials to make bombs, the advantages and limitations of using certain chemical compounds or pathogens to cause harm, and how to construct nuclear weapons. They can obtain information often available through the Internet or the media or both on such activities as the movements of individuals they may wish to target, materials they may wish to acquire, and actions planned by governments or in progress to thwart their efforts. They can move funds instantly to support their activities and communicate with cohorts around the world in order to coordinate their efforts. They can also attack cyber networks and endanger national political, economic, and military infrastructures, with global implications for the safety and welfare of peoples.

Loose Nukes and the Proliferation of Weapons of Mass Destruction.

Since the breakup of the Union of Soviet Socialist Republics (USSR) concerns have been voiced over what has come to be known as the "loose nuclear weapons" problem. The term "loose nukes" originally referred to nuclear weapons that no longer could be accounted for following the collapse of the Soviet Union. It is estimated that during the Cold War, the USSR had more than 27,000 nuclear weapons and enough weapons-grade uranium and plutonium to triple that number.[3] Given the severe economic stress, rampant crime, and widespread corruption following the breakup of the Soviet Union, concerns were expressed that nuclear weapons, particularly so-called "suitcase bombs," may have fallen into the hands of terrorists or criminals.[4]

Today the term "loose nukes" has acquired a wider definition, referring not only to nuclear weapons, but also to nuclear know-how and fissile materials. The problem created by the breakup of the USSR is further exacerbated by the continued proliferation of nuclear weapon states and potential proliferation of fissile materials as additional nations are added to the number of states possessing nuclear weapons. Today, in addition to the five so-called "declared" nuclear weapon states under the terms of the Nuclear Non-Proliferation Treaty (NPT) (China, France, Russia, the United Kingdom, and the United States), three states not parties to the Treaty have tested nuclear weapons—India, Pakistan, and North Korea. Israel is believed to have nuclear weapons, and Iran (an NPT state) is believed to be seeking to develop nuclear weapons.

For all that has been said about the stability induced by the acquisition of nuclear weapons during the Cold War, the further proliferation of such weapons threatens to induce instabilities of grand proportion as opportunities for acquiring materials and know-how multiply. Arguably, it is the acquisition of the fissile materials—plutonium and highly enriched uranium (HEU)—that poses the most difficult problem for terrorists or criminals seeking to build a nuclear weapon or an improvised nuclear device. Creating a nuclear weapon from HEU is technically easier than building a plutonium weapon. HEU is the ingredient required to produce the simplest gun assembly weapon of the type dropped on Hiroshima, Japan. Such weapons need not be tested to assure an atomic explosion. In 2002, the U.S. National Research Council warned that such weapons could be fabricated without state assistance.[5]

Unfortunately, HEU is widely available today. A 2003 estimate noted that there were about 50 tons of HEU available in civilian power and research programs in over 50 nations[6] and perhaps as many as 2,000 tons in nuclear weapons programs globally.[7] It only takes as little as 40-60 kilograms (kg) of HEU to produce a crude nuclear device. There have been no confirmed reports of missing/unaccounted for nuclear weapons, but there is ample evidence of a black market in nuclear materials. In the 1990s, U.S. authorities discovered attempts by al-Qaeda to obtain nuclear materials. Then Central Intelligence Agency (CIA) Director George Tenet told Congress that Osama bin Laden had sought to acquire or develop a nuclear device. Russians report that they have broken up hundreds of nuclear-material smuggling deals. The International Atomic Energy Agency (IAEA) has reported more than 100 nuclear smuggling incidents since 1993.[8] In April 2010, Georgian president Saakashvilli reported that his country had seized a shipment of HEU, presumably smuggled through the Caucasus.[9]

Moreover, the problem may not be entirely one originating in foreign lands. Russia has accused the United States of lax protection standards at nuclear and biological facilities. They contend that secret information from the U.S. Los Alamos Laboratory ended up in the hands of drug gangs, that several U.S. institutions dealing in viruses failed to provide sufficient security to prevent an intruder from entering their facilities, and that some 1,500 sources of ionizing radiation (e.g. spent nuclear fuel rods) were lost by the United States between 1996 and 2001.[10]

President Barack Obama highlighted the issue on the eve of the Nuclear Security Summit held in Washington, DC, in April 2010, warning that the prospect of nuclear terrorism is "the single biggest threat to U.S. security, both short-term, medium-term and long-term. This is something that could change the security landscape of this country and around the world for years to come."[11]

Hyper-Ethnicism, Religious Extremism, and Tribalism.

Unlike the most devastating conflicts of the 20th century, which were frequently driven by fanatical nationalism or the Cold War that was driven largely by ideology, many of today's conflicts are fueled by hyper-ethnicism, religious extremism, and/or tribalism.[12] It is the very absence of nationalism (that state of mind, that collective group consciousness, that sense of being one with nation[13]) that often not only leads to conflict but also confounds efforts at conflict management and resolution. Seemingly irreconcilable differences, fueled by parochial interests and diverse ethnic, religious, and tribal groupings make it difficult to find common ground upon which to build a stable peace. Furthermore, in places like Afghanistan, where tribal cultures oftentimes eschew western ethics and the western sense of fair play, duplicity in diplomatic dealings and a willingness to sell one's community to the highest bidder, make any permanent settlement problematic. One has only to read Peter Hopkirk's works on Central Asia[14] to gain a historical appreciation of the complexities of achieving permanence to any deal done in such a tribal environment or to understand the concerns expressed by U.S. military leaders currently in Afghanistan as they try to piece together local coalitions to fight against al-Qaeda or the Taliban. A deal done today may be a deal undone tomorrow for any number of reasons that are unlikely to be well understood by western diplomats or military leaders.

Latent as Well as Manifest Frustrations.

In addition to the issues mentioned above, instabilities also can arise from latent frustrations over corrupt, incompetent, or authoritarian governments brought to the fore by natural or manmade disasters (earthquakes, floods, inability to protect against guerrilla or terrorist attacks, etc.); unforeseen political events such as assassinations of political figures; or economic downturns and corresponding rising unemployment. In the former category, for example, the earthquake that devastated Managua in 1972 and the blatant corruption that saw little relief money finding its way to those in need, flooded the ranks of the Sandinistas and helped create an unstable situation that ultimately led to the overthrow of the dictator Anastasio "Tachito" Somoza Debayle. Similarly, the December 2007 assassination of Benazir Bhutto exacerbated extant political turmoil in Pakistan and contributed to events that led to the August 2008 resignation of President Pervez Musharraf. Of course, recent events in Tunisia, Egypt, Yemen, Libya, and elsewhere in the Middle East bear testimony to the impact of the combined effects of economic downturn, unemployment, and popular discontent with authoritarian rule. Blatantly manifested frustrations, such as those arising from the inability of the Israelis and Palestinians to resolve issues arising from over a half century of tensions between these peoples, also remain a major source of global concern as irritants spill over and sometimes threaten the security and safety of peoples of other nations.

Today's Challenges.

Today the United States is faced with a multiplicity of threats and challenges, none of which is as perilous or as potentially deadly as the Cold War confrontation between the two superpowers. Nonetheless, some of the problems pose potentially dangerous consequences for the United States, its allies and friends, and indeed others. However, for the most part, the dangers that lie ahead flow not "from the strength of determined opponents," but often "from the weaknesses of other states."[15] To be sure, the United States must guard against the rise of potentially hostile military peer competitors, as well as be prepared to protect its security interests and those of its allies. Of course, these tasks do not, a priori, demand the expansion or use of military power. Rather, a commonality of interests among leading states in a less ideologically driven world might lead cooler heads to find win-win solutions to complex problems involving competing or conflicting interests.

The United States also must address the difficult security challenges that a nuclear North Korea or the further proliferation of nuclear weapons may pose, for example, in Iran. Nor can the United States ignore determined opponents who attempt to acquire capabilities disproportionate to their relative size through access to high-tech arms or through the use of the damaging and potentially crippling compounding effects of cyber and other technologies that are increasing available on a global scale.

However, the problem of fragile, fractured, and failing states that has largely arisen as a result of changes in the post-Cold War security environment is likely to remain among the more serious security challenges that confront the United States and the world community in the decades ahead. Such states can provide a breeding ground and safe haven for crime; drug and human trafficking; ethnic, religious, and tribal strife; and violent extremist groups. Here one has only to think, as President Obama has suggested, of al-Qaeda or some other terrorist group armed with weapons of mass destruction (WMD), especially nuclear weapons or devices. They also can destabilize entire regions, making wider conflicts more probable. Thus, precluding instabilities and mitigating and managing conflicts, particularly in fragile, fractured, or failing states, but also elsewhere, are among the major security challenges confronting the United States.

The operative question, then, is how should the U.S. Government address such challenges? The answer has become increasingly clear that the kind of relatively undifferentiated containment policies, which relied principally on military power during the Cold War, will not suffice. Rather, successfully addressing the security environment of the 21st century will require the skillful application of smart power[16] which integrates the instruments of America's soft and hard power.

INTEGRATING THE INSTRUMENTS OF NATIONAL POWER: ISSUES AND CHALLENGES

More than a decade ago, the Hart–Rudman Commission signaled the need for "*strategic fusion* of all appropriate instruments of national power," noting, "The nature of the future security environment appears to require advanced, integrated, collaborative planning and organized interagency responses beyond what is possible under the current interagency system.[17] In January 2009, the Department of Defense (DoD) *Quadrennial Roles and Missions Review Report* struck a similar note supporting efforts "to increase unity across the government for addressing common national security problems"—a so-called "whole-of-government" approach.[18] Likewise, Secretary of State Hillary Clinton has affirmed:

> One of our goals coming into the administration was . . . to begin to make the case that defense, diplomacy and development were not separate entities, either in substance or process, but that indeed they had to be viewed as part of an integrated whole and that the whole of government then had to be enlisted in their pursuit."[19]

It is, of course, facile to contend that U.S. efforts to preclude, limit, and terminate conflict and assist countries in their transformation to peace and stability require greater coherence between and among U.S. security, governance, and development policies, as well as enhanced coordination, and consolidation among U.S. governmental agencies and with local, regional, and international partners. If national or grand strategy can be defined as the integration of the instruments of national power (political, economic, psychological, military, etc.) to achieve national objectives, then it only makes sense that all agencies of government entrusted with such tasks be integrated in efforts to address threats and potential threats to U.S. security. Indeed, it is surprising that some 235 years since its founding, over 100 years since the United States emerged on the world scene following the Spanish-American War, more than 66 years since the end of World War II and the emergence of the United States as a superpower, and 20 years since the end of the Cold War, only in recent years has Washington begun to take seriously the notion that an integrated effort in foreign and security policy is required.[20] Nevertheless, integrating the efforts of the many U.S. departments and agencies that have foreign and security responsibilities in a whole of government (WoG) approach raises a number of important, indeed critical issues:

1. What Should Be the Objectives of America's Foreign Security Policy?

Beyond simply responding to crises as they arise around the world, does the United States have a vision of itself in the world? Has it defined the kind of world it hopes will emerge in the 21st century and the role the United States can play in encouraging the emergence of such a world?[21] Henry Kissinger noted over 30 years ago: "[W]e will never be able to contribute to building a stable and creative world order unless we first form some conception of it."[22] He further argued that there was "no focal point for long-range planning on an interagency basis." As a result, often "foreign policy turns into a series of unrelated decisions—crisis-oriented, ad hoc and after-the-fact in nature." Thus longer-term objectives are seldom considered.[23] Today, the need to frame short-term responses within the context of a broad vision of U.S. long-term objectives remains a continuing foreign policy challenge.

Perhaps, equally important, does the United States have a clear conception of the political, economic, psychological, and military challenges it is likely to confront in attempting to forge a dynamically stable (i.e., stable, yet creative) environment and has the United States defined a broad strategy, which includes other international actors,[24] that is designed to shape the strategic environment through a blending of the instruments of soft and hard power and a balancing of short-, medium-, and long-term objectives?

Washington bureaucrats may have found it exhilarating following the breakup of the Soviet Union to contend that the United States had won the Cold War and that Russia need not be consulted on major issues of the day. They also may have been inclined to roll their eyes dismissively when a Central Asian country was mentioned. They failed to see the future importance of Russia and the countries of Central Asia to any conception of a secure world. They soon found out that America needed Russia as a partner in addressing a number of important security considerations, and the assistance of some Central Asian countries in its war on terrorism. The ability to see forward, to think beyond conventional limits—outside of the box, if you will—is essential if U.S. policymakers are to address successfully current and future security challenges. Yet such a trait is not always welcomed nor rewarded in Washington.[25] Breaking with this pattern is requisite in the setting of foreign policy and national security objectives.

As has now become all too evident, acting alone the United States cannot address successfully many of the issues that now confront or will confront it in the future. Shaping the political environment so that the cooperation of others is forthcoming is likely to be one of America's most important tasks and difficult challenges. This will require the United States to be seen as working not just to advance its own interests but also those of the broader community of nations. No WoG approach will be successful if this is not understood. This will require leadership. But leadership[26] "does not come cheap." As Joseph Joffe noted a decade ago,

> [T]he price [of leadership] is measured in the currency of obligation. Leaders succeed not only because of their superior power, but also because they have a fine sense for the quirks and qualities of others—*because they act in the interest of all* [emphasis added]. Their labor is the source of their authority. And so a truly great power must not just prevent but pre-empt hostile coalitions—by providing essential services. Those who respect the needs of others engage in supply-side diplomacy: They create a demand for their services, and that translates into political profits, also known as "leadership."[27]

Thus the vision that must serve as guide to America's foreign and security policy objectives must transcend narrow and often short-term national self-interest. The model for action must reflect Breton Woods, Dumbarton Oaks, and Marshall Plan values rather than narrower national concerns. This is likely to entail a broadening of the scope of national security beyond traditional concepts. This also is where vision may play its greatest role, and ignorance cause the greatest distraction.

2. When Should the United States Become Involved?

With a vision to the future, where, when, and under what circumstances should the United States become involved in issues confronting other nations? Since the end of World War II, the United States has deployed its military forces far and wide and been otherwise involved in countless efforts around the globe in the name of preventing the spread of communism, preserving the peace, averting humanitarian disasters, and/or precluding or managing instabilities and conflicts. For example, following World War II, U.S. military forces occupied Germany, Japan, the southern half of Korea, and a part of Austria, and reoccupied the Philippines. The United States also went to the assistance of South Korea when it was attacked by North Korea; South Vietnam when it was threatened by the communist-led Viet Cong; Kuwait when it was attacked by Iraq; and Kosovo when it was under attack by Serb forces. Following the 9/11 attacks, U.S. forces were deployed to Afghanistan where they remain to this day, attempting to shore up Afghan security forces, assisting in the defeat al-Qaeda and their Taliban supporters, and assuring a more democratic, stable peace. U.S. forces also were deployed to Iraq for a variety of reasons, and as of this writing, a significant number remain there to help forge a stable environment and democratic peace. More recently U.S. forces have been deployed to the Mediterranean in support of a United Nations (UN) mandated "No Fly Zone" established to protect civilians from attacks by the Gadhafi regime and its supporters.

Furthermore, U.S. military forces have been involved in vast numbers of other security related efforts. This is not to mention the many covert activities involving U.S. military, paramilitary, and intelligence agencies in which the United States has engaged in order to advance American interests.[28] In addition, to direct and covert U.S. involvement in foreign countries, the United States often has provided security related and development assistance not just to assist poor countries, but also to address potential instabilities that might lead to conflict and more recently as a weapon against terrorism. Also, financial aid and technical assistance frequently have been provided to foreign governments to strengthen and professionalize their military and police forces, as well as economic and humanitarian assistance to stabilize their economies, encourage development, alleviate poverty, mitigate disasters, and the like. Such developmental assistance is often channeled through multinational organizations and nongovernmental organizations and/or provided directly through bilateral agreements with recipient countries.

Many of the above-mentioned efforts have been relatively low cost. However, some have been a heavy burden, costly in lives and national treasure, and sometimes resulting in great domestic dissent and division among the American polity, a weakening of America's reputation, a consequent weakening of support abroad, and have been counterproductive in terms of long-term policy objectives.

Thus, among the more important factors that must be considered as Washington addresses the challenges of the coming decades is: Under what circumstances and how should the United States get involved? Clearly the United States has had an expansive view of its appropriate global role since the end of World War II. The operative question is whether, in their entirety, the long-term benefits of each of those efforts have outweighed the costs. Did the U.S. Government have processes in place at the time to answer that question before engaging, for example, in Vietnam in the 1950s and 1960s or Iraq in 2003? Does the United States have such processes in place now to address the current crises in Libya and at other locations in the Middle East or those that may arise elsewhere? Should it?

These are not unreasonable questions, driven by a desire for retrenchment or pessimism about America's future. As Washington attempts, to put it in former Secretary of Defense Robert Gates' words, "to adapt and reform our 63-year old national security apparatus to be more effective, above all, at building the capacity of other countries to provide for their own security,"[29] it is reasonable to ask whether the United States needs to be as involved in the future in the security affairs of other countries to the same extent that it was during the Cold War. It is reasonable to ask in what countries America's security demands involvement today; precisely why, to what ends both in terms of immediate, local objectives, and in the broadest strategic context; and under what circumstances are those ends likely to be achievable. Involvement has costs. Over extension of a nation's resources can be just as threatening to its future as under involvement in meeting its challenges.

An important corollary to questions of when and where the United States should become involved is the question: *How* should it be involved? Senior administration officials including the President and Secretary of State have indicated that they regard economic development as a weapon against terrorism. President Obama, signaling his support for development assistance for poor countries, noted: "Extremely poor societies . . . provide optimal breeding grounds for disease, terrorism, and conflict."[30] The proposition clearly seems plausible. It is reasonable to assume that the poor, the uneducated, those with little and therefore little to lose, embittered by societal disparities of wealth, and with few if any prospects for improvement are more likely to be recruited into the ranks of the terrorists. The problem is that studies have shown that "There is no evidence that sympathy for terrorism is greater among deprived people."[31] According to Alan Krueger, former U.S. Assistant Secretary of the Treasury for Economic Policy and professor at Princeton University, studies have shown little evidence that a typical terrorist is usually poor or ill-educated. Indeed, Krueger examined 956 terrorist events from 1997 to 2003 and found that the poorest countries, those with low literacy, or those with relatively stagnant economies, did not produce more terrorists. Moreover, he found that when data were restricted to suicide attacks, there was a statistically significant pattern in the opposite direction, with people from poorer countries less likely to commit suicide attacks. Other studies have had similar results.[32] On the other hand, many of these same studies suggest that terrorist organizations prefer better educated, better skilled, more mature individuals, particularly for attacks on important targets, and that as economic conditions worsen, high unemployment among these groups enables terrorist organizations to recruit from the ranks of such individuals.

Hence one conclusion that can be drawn from this is that while promoting economic development in the poorest countries may well be a good idea, it is unlikely to be a fully effective tool in terms of reducing or eliminating terrorism, or for that matter, other dissident and potentially dangerous groups. Rather, more selective assistance aimed at reducing unemployment or underemployment among the better educated, better skilled, more mature individuals, may be of relatively greater value.

Moreover, an equally plausible proposition is that extremely poor nations provide optimal breeding grounds for terrorism and conflict because they are unable to develop and maintain effective governmental sovereignty. As a result, drug cartels, terrorist organizations, and other extremist elements are able to establish themselves within areas where the weak state is unable to maintain control. Such conditions may demand that relatively greater emphasis be placed on efforts to eliminate corruption, improve legal systems and law enforcement, assist in political integration, and the like.

So in deciding which implements in the foreign policy tool bag to choose in a given situation, the development tool needs to be carefully assessed along with other policy instruments in terms of their short-, medium-, and long-term implications for U.S. objectives.[33] Undifferentiated economic development is a worthy goal from a humanitarian perspective. However, in terms of advancing American security, the determination of how the United States should become involved should be the product of a fully integrated process among governmental agencies that envisions responses as an integrated and collaborative effort.

3. Who Should Decide When the United States Should Get Involved, the Extent of Involvement and Upon What Criteria Should Those Decisions Rest?

Of course, decisions on U.S. involvement ultimately rest with Congress and the President. Congress must authorize and appropriate funds for such efforts. The President, as head of the executive branch and commander in chief of the armed forces (and militia when called to federal service) is pledged to "preserve, protect and defend the Constitution of the United States." And, constitutionally, only Congress can declare war, though America's Founding Fathers would be appalled at the increasing usurpation of power by American presidents, with congressional acquiescence, in introducing American armed forces into hostilities or taking the nation to war.[34] However, this is another issue.

The present issue is: Does the United States have in place the human capital to make appropriate recommendations to the President, senior national security advisors, and the Congress? Is there a team of professionals armed with sufficient historic and cultural knowledge, a clear view of past and contemporary political, economic, psychological, and military realities, an understanding of the strengths and weaknesses of the various instruments of national power, a broad strategic prospective, and "patterns of thinking that best match resources and capabilities to achieving the desired policy ends"?[35] In other words, are there trained strategists capable of identifying and evaluating an array of political, diplomatic, economic, informational, and military options and making recommendations concerning whether, to what extent, and in what manner the United States should become involved in the security concerns of other nations?[36] If not, how can these strategists be acquired and under whose authority should they reside—the National Security Council (NSC), the Department of State (State), the DoD, the now moribund National Security Policy Planning Committee established in the last months of the George W. Bush administration, or perhaps some new agency?[37] Will such a body require an expanded interchange with experts in academia, with society at large, and with foreign experts? And, how would such a system be managed?

Perhaps equally important, upon what criteria should decisions for involvement be based? The aggregate of national priorities as set by Congress, the President, members of the President's Cabinet, or for that matter the U.S. *National Security Strategy* (NSS) can seem, and often are confusing, competing, and/or opaque and therefore seldom serve as guides to specific foreign or security policy related decisions. In theory, decisions concerning U.S. involvement in foreign nations should be grounded in an evaluation of unfolding foreign events in terms of U.S. national interests. Yet "national interests" is an amorphous term, with decreasing clarity as one moves from defense of the homeland against attack, to providing for the economic well-being of American citizens, to insuring a favorable world order, to advancing American values, including humanitarian; and as one tries to differentiate between and among those interests that can be tabbed as survival or vital (both of which are generally understood as justification for some level of military response if needed) and major, or peripheral.

In 1944 Walter Lippmann wrote: "Fate has brought it about that America is at the center, no longer the edges, of Western civilization. In this fact resides the American destiny."[38] As a result, during the Cold War a tendency emerged to equate a loss to communism anywhere in the world, to a loss everywhere. Such thinking was central to President Dwight Eisenhower's famous "falling domino" principle.[39] In his 1955 letter to British Prime Minister Churchill, Eisenhower wrote:

> We have come to the point where every additional backward step must be deemed a defeat for the Western world. In fact, it is a triple defeat. First, we lose a potential ally. Next, we give to an implacable enemy another recruit. Beyond this, every such retreat creates in the minds of neutrals the fear that we do not mean what we say when we pledge our support to people who want to remain free.[40]

Thus, the distinction between what was a vital and what was a peripheral interest became blurred. All interests seemed vital. All threats seemed to demand an American response.

Today, as in fact the history of the Cold War proved, all challenges to American interests are *not* vital. All challenges to American interests, all opportunities to protect or enhance those interests, do not demand a direct American response, and those that do, need to be carefully evaluated in terms of their immediate and long-term implications for U.S. national security and the cost, risks, and probabilities of success associated with policy responses that might be contemplated. Though this approach seems to be generally understood in Washington, it remains unclear whether U.S policymakers have in mind clear criteria for making such judgments.

Recent efforts to bring some clarity to this equation, as the United States carefully chose its response to events in Libya as rebels attempt to overthrow the long repressive government of Muammar Gadhafi, are somewhat encouraging, though not definitive. Then Secretary of Defense Gates and Secretary of State Clinton made it clear that the United States does have a number of interests associated with the conflict and a stake in the outcome. But as Gates put it, the events in Libya are "not a vital national interest to the United States," while making it clear that other interests may warrant American action,[41] including the limited use of American military forces.[42]

4. When/Under What Circumstances Should the United States Assume the Leading/Senior Partner Role and When Should it Play Primarily a Supporting Role?

One critique of American efforts in Vietnam was that it quickly transformed itself into the senior partner. It became America's war to win or lose. As a result, it is argued that the United States lost the leverage needed to force the South Vietnamese government to make changes in its manner of governance that might have had an effect on the outcome of the conflict. Has such become an issue as the United States attempts to encourage reforms in Afghanistan or elsewhere? Some, perhaps many, initiatives such as the ongoing effort to bring stability to Somalia may best be addressed by others (namely in this case, Uganda and Burundi under the command of the African Union), with the United States playing, as it has, a supporting role in efforts to defeat the al-Qaeda supported Shabab.

Likewise, U.S. reluctance to play the leading role in Libya was likely driven, at least in part, by concerns that such a role might be counterproductive to long-term American objectives in the region and elsewhere. When contemplating the deployment or employment of U.S. military forces abroad, the United States must not only consider the risks and costs of such action in terms of U.S. lives and national treasure, but also the risks, costs, and opportunities understood in terms of broader national interests. Such interests include, for example, garnering the cooperation of others in efforts to curb terrorism, limit the proliferation of weapons of mass destruction, forge new cooperative relationships in the post-Cold War environment, and build a more peaceful, dynamically stable world order. In such an environment, effective leadership demands the United States avoid, whenever possible, unilateral action. Moreover, when the United States does act, effective leadership does not always require being out in front. As President Obama has put it:

> American leadership is not simply a matter of going it alone and bearing all the burdens ourselves. Real leadership creates the conditions and coalitions for others to step up as well: to work with allies and partners so that they bear their share of the burden and pay their share of the costs; and to see that the principles of justice and human dignity are upheld by all.[43]

Perhaps equally important and inherent in the President's comments is the requirement to create among others a sense of ownership of the objectives, the processes, and the outcomes. Such ownership on the part of others reinforces notions of shared responsibility, often bears fruit in terms of cooperation on other issues, and can contribute to reducing perceptions of

American hegemony and beliefs that the United States is driven by a desire to create a world order solely in its interests and image.

5. Does the United States Have in Place Individuals Who Can Manage the Processes of a Whole-of-Government, Integrated Approach?

Does the United States have professionals who understand the bureaucratic processes across departmental lines, can work in the interagency environment, and together forge consensus for effective action? If so, are there enough of them to manage integrated WoG solutions to the many complex challenges that lie ahead? If not, it might be wise to examine carefully the 2010 study by the Project on National Security Reform (PNSR), *The Power of People.* In that study, the PNSR contends:

> . . . the strategic environment of the 21st century and the President's *National Security Strategy* demand that the United States establish an Integrated National Security Professional system [INSP system]. Complex problems require National Security Professionals [NSPs] who are trained and experienced to collaborate across interagency and intergovernmental boundaries in both day-to-day work and crisis response. Many of these individuals have been designated under the current program, which lacks centralized management, strong leadership, a formalized human capital program, and a common funding source. Without these system attributes, the United States will not be able to develop and sustain the well qualified workforce of NSPs it requires.[44]

This is not to say that some progress on this issue has not already been made. Building on the lessons of Hurricane Katrina, President George W. Bush's

2007 Executive Order 13434 mandated that departments and agencies establish programs for the "Development of Security Professionals." The executive order called for those programs to provide the U.S. Government with security professionals who by their training, education, and professional experience will emerge with enhanced mission knowledge, skills, and experience and consequently be better able to manage and direct integrated interagency responses and thus "enhance the national security of the United States, including *preventing* [italics added], protecting against, responding to, and recovering from natural and man-made disasters, such as acts of terrorism." [45]

In response, departments and agencies of the U.S. Government have established programs and created courses open not only to members of their organizations but also to those of other organizations involved in national security. Critical shared capabilities have been identified. Some rotational assignments have been established and memoranda of understanding have been signed, permitting reimbursement of individuals assigned to other agencies. Moreover, department and agency programs often include educational components that are to help individuals develop an understanding of the cultural, religious, political, and social norms of other peoples and a modicum of foreign language capability if the mission so requires, as well as the ability to think creatively and strategically.[46]

However, the PNSR study notes, among other things, "results have been agency-centric and therefore disparate and non-uniform. Programs also suffer from a lack of centralized leadership, ill-defined roles and responsibilities, lack of a common lexicon, poor communication among programs, no direct funding source, and a lack of clearly defined metrics for evaluation."[47] To address such deficiencies, the PNSR study calls for an Integrated Security Professional System and sets a pathway to achieve such a system.

Of course, the success of any program designed to produce security professionals will turn not just on developing people who understand the interagency system and can manage human and material resources. Successful management and direction will largely depend on their ability to understand the context in which decisions must be made. This will demand individuals who, in their areas of responsibility, have at least a modicum of understanding of the history, culture, traditions, politics, and the past and current conditions that might lead to a crisis, and who can put the dots together in such a fashion as to successfully manage efforts to prevent a crisis from emerging or wisely manage efforts to assist in stabilizing a situation once a crisis has occurred.

6. Does the United States Have the Ability to Assess Accurately What is Likely to be Necessary in Order to Restore Stability in Pre- or Post- Crisis or Conflict Situations?

In 2008 under the auspices of the Reconstruction and Stabilization Coordinating Committee,[48] an interagency working group was formed. The Working Group was co-chaired by the Department of State Office of the Coordinator for Reconstruction and Stabilization (S/CRS) and the U.S. Agency for International Development (USAID) Office of Conflict Management and Mitigation, and included representatives of the Office of the Secretary of Defense, Joint Forces Command, and the Army's Peacekeeping and Stability Operations Institute. The Working Group ran a successful trial of an Interagency Conflict Assessment Framework (ICAF) in a workshop on Tajikistan. The ICAF provides tools for agencies of the U.S. Government to develop a shared understanding of the dynamics of a particular crisis and prepare for interagency planning for conflict prevention, mitigation, and stabilization. It assists interagency teams in understanding why unstable conditions exist and how best to engage in order to transform the situation. Thus, an ICAF analysis is designed to "be part of the first step in any interagency planning process to inform the establishment of USG [U.S. Government] goals, design or reshaping of activities, implementation or revision of programs, or re/allocation of resources."[49]

As with so many other assessment tools, the value of this tool will depend strongly on the personnel chosen to employ it. Indeed, such a tool is likely to require personnel with foresight, who possess a significant level of understanding of the historical, cultural, political, economic, and other factors that are likely to affect a given situation and often will need to be drawn together quickly. Thus only time will tell whether such a tool will be effective.

7. Does the United States Have the Organization and Personnel to Help Stabilize Pre-and Post-Crises or Conflict Situations?

While the jury is still out, some substantial progress has been made. In 2004, the S/CRS—recently designated the Bureau of Conflict and Stabilization Operations—was created by congressional authorization. Its "mandate was to organize the civilian side of the U.S. government to run large stabilization operations such as Iraq and Afghanistan effectively and to create a pool of civilian experts with the right skills to deploy in such operations."[50] In December 2005, President G. W. Bush issued National Security Presidential Directive (NSPD)-44, directing the Secretary of State to take the lead in coordinating and integrating all U.S. stabilization and reconstruction efforts. The idea was that this office would not take on the functions performed by others in State or other agencies of government, but rather would plan, organize, and coordinate the activities of the different agencies under the policy guidance of the NSC and the Secretary of State. By early 2007, eight departments and agencies—Agriculture, Commerce, Health and Human Services, Homeland Security, Justice, State, Treasury, and USAID—agreed to build a Civilian Response Corps (CRC) drawn from employees of the eight agencies and to establish procedures, collectively called the Interagency Management System, for running future stability operations. The Department of Transportation joined in February 2011.

The concept called for 250 Active and 2,000 Standby members drawn from the eight designated agencies and a 2,000 member CRC composed of individuals from outside of the Federal government who would enlist for 4 years. The full-time job of Active members would be to deploy in foreign crises. Standby members would have full-time positions in one of the eight agencies, but be available for deployment in large crises, while CRC members would be available for deployments of up to 1 year. Congress began funding the Active and Standby components of the CRC in 2008. By the end of 2010, there were 131 Active and over 1,000 Standby members including agronomists, development specialists, diplomats, economists, engineers, law enforcement and corrections officers, lawyers, public administrators, health officials, and others with a range of skills needed in foreign crises to assist in restoring stability, promoting economic recovery and sustainable growth, and advancing the rule of law as quickly as possible in fragile or failing states.

Even as the CRC was in the process of being established, its members along with the S/CRS created a civilian-military planning group and produced an Afghanistan strategy approved by the American ambassador and the NSC. In 2010, the Corps participated in 292 deployments to 28 overseas posts. Major deployments included Afghanistan, Haiti, the Kyrgyz Republic, and Sudan.[51]

Nevertheless, budgets for reconstruction and stabilization among the collaborating agencies remain uneven. Lack of agreement on what constitutes reconstruction and stabilization hinders interagency collaboration. Guidance on roles and responsibilities is unclear and inconsistent.[52] Moreover, the CRC, which was to be composed of experts outside of government, was authorized but as of this writing has yet to be funded by Congress. State is now proposing that the Reserve be replaced by a more cost-effective "Expert Corps" consisting of an actively managed roster of technical experts, willing but not obligated to deploy to critical conflict zones.[53] However, there is no certainty that Congress will be any more willing to fund such an expert group than it was the CRC.

On the brighter side, development resources managed by State and USAID under the purview of the Secretary of State have grown from about $10 billion in Fiscal Year (FY) 2000 to $26 billion in FY 2010.[54] However, funding for State and USAID programs suffered a setback in FY 2011.[55] The DoD also has taken steps to create a body of personnel able to assist in, among other things, stability operations through the creation of a Civilian Expeditionary Workforce (CEW), the Afghanistan/Pakistan (AFPAK) Hands program, and the Ministry of Defense Advisors (MoDA) program. The programs work hand-in-hand. Created in January 2009, the CEW draws on DoD civilians from a variety of career fields, including civil engineering, contracting, financial administration, and transportation, as well as foreign affairs and language specialists and lawyers. Workforce members are trained and equipped to deploy overseas in support of worldwide DoD missions, including "combat, contingencies, emergency operations; humanitarian and civic assistance activities; disaster relief; restoration of order; drug interdiction; and stability operations . . ."[56]

The AFPAK Hands program was initiated in 2009 by then Chairman of the Joint Chiefs of Staff Admiral Mike Mullen. AFPAK Hands is a language (Pashto and Dari for Afghanistan, Urdu for Pakistan) and cultural immersion initiative for DoD military and civilian personnel aimed at creating a cadre of personnel who can assist the United States in building better long-term relationships with the Afghan and Pakistani people, governments, and militaries.[57] The program requires a 45-month commitment for those who join and two deployments to Afghanistan or Pakistan of 12 and 10 months, respectively. As of March 2011, 179 AFPAK Hands have been deployed and 160 were in training.[58]

The Ministry of Defense Advisors program was developed as a result of experiences in Afghanistan and Iraq that highlighted the need to supplement efforts to improve the tactical proficiency of security forces in those countries with improvements in the functioning of government ministries. Senior DoD civilians deploy as advisors for up to 2 years under the auspices of the CEW to share their expertise with their foreign country counterparts and forge long-term relationships while strengthening government security ministries. To date advisors have been deployed to support Afghan ministries of defense and interior.[59]

8. Which Agency Should be the Lead Agency?

Many of the issues involved in addressing the problems of fragile, fractured, or failing states and the all too often accompanying instability are political in nature—effective governance, official corruption, advancing democracy, developing and protecting civil society, professionalizing police forces, improving economic conditions, resolving humanitarian issues, providing food and shelter, disaster relief, etc. However, few, if any, of these issues fall under the sole purview of a single department of government. For example, while State has responsibility for the overall management of foreign policy, The Department of the Treasury is involved in such efforts as economic sanctions and embargoes and provides foreign technical assistance. The Department of Agriculture, among other things, provides international food assistance. The Department of Commerce advises on export controls. The Department of Justice is involved in drug enforcement. Actions by the Department of Homeland Security can have an impact on a wide range of issues affecting foreign governments. Furthermore, as the President and other administration officials have noted, frequently there is overlap and wasteful duplication of effort that could be addressed by a greater integration of effort. Of course in all of this, the DoD is the 800-pound gorilla with a lion's share of the resources and control over a large segment of America's intelligence capabilities. Moreover, military personnel by education, training, and experience are likely to be better organizers and managers of complex processes and somewhat better at developing strategies built upon an integration of the instruments of national power.[60] A process needs to be developed that will allow for a rapid determination of the lead agency and flexibility in the movement of sufficient resources to support lead agency efforts to coordinate and fund WoG efforts, particularly where time is of the essence.

Often State, acting in conjunction with USAID, serves as the lead agency in reconstruction and stabilization efforts. However, lack of personnel and funding hamper State/USAID's ability to respond to rapidly developing situations that demand a large deployment of resources. Some steps have already been taken to ameliorate the problem. In 2006 Congress authorized the Secretary of Defense to spend up to $100 million to:

> . . . provide services to, and transfer defense articles and funds to, the Secretary of State for purposes of facilitating the provision by the Secretary of State of reconstruction, security, or stabilization assistance to a foreign country.[61]

The flexibility provided in this bill, which included the authority to provide services and transfer articles and funds to the Secretary of State, was lost when the provisions of the bill expired in 2010. However, in 2009 Congress, in the FY 2010 Department of State Foreign Operations, and Related Programs Act, appropriated $50 million to a Complex Crisis Fund (CCF).[62] The CCF provides USAID, in consultation with the Secretary of State, with funds "to support programs and activities to prevent or respond to emerging or unforeseen crises overseas."[63] The funds, which could not be used to mitigate disasters, were to remain available until expended.

Though the appropriations fell far short of the Obama administration's requests for a range of reconstruction and stabilization programs,[64] the bill freed State from sole reliance on funds transferred from the DoD to support stabilization and reconstruction projects. Since the monies appropriated are unprogrammed, they provide State the needed flexibility to respond quickly to emerging or unforeseen events.

In its February 2010 defense budget request for FY 2011, the Obama administration sought $100 million for a CCF. However, Congress only funded $40 million. The President's FY 2012 budget request includes $125 million to advance cooperative efforts to address national security challenges. Monies requested include funding for a new Global Security Contingency Fund ($50 million) that integrates DoD and State resources to address security crises[65] and the existing CCF ($75 million).[66] The budget request also includes authority to reprogram an additional $450 million from the defense budget, if needed.

Though clearly greater efficiencies in expenditures can be achieved, given the nature of the security and stabilization problems that must be addressed, at current levels, appropriated monies are unlikely to be sufficient. Some combination of "pooled funds" for use by agencies involved in reconstruction, security, and stabilization and separate funding for State efforts clearly has merit. Thus, Congress should take seriously the President's request, including authority to reprogram funds to meet emerging security, reconstruction, and stabilization requirements. However,

in addition to an increase in overall funding for such programs, if a reduction in the militarization of stabilization and reconstruction is a desired end, the balance between pooled and separate funding may warrant a relook.

9. What Role for America's Armed Forces?

Since traditional treats may continue to emerge, how should the armed forces be structured and trained to meet traditional threats as well as the challenges of the changed security environment of the 21st century? Secretary Gates politely noted: "Our military was designed to defeat other armies, navies, and air forces, not to advise and equip them."[67] Yet increasingly U.S. military forces are asked to undertake such tasks as peacekeeping and stability operations, which often entail use of the instruments of soft power—community relations, humanitarian efforts, negotiations and bargaining, getting mothers and babies to hospitals, etc. Indeed, stability operations have become a core DoD mission.

Yet the question remains: Is there adequate time to train soldiers to be effective fighters, trainers, and general peacemakers? Is there adequate time to train officers, generals, and admirals to be effective combat leaders and political strategists? Clearly, the actions of soldiers in unstable or conflict situations can have an enormous political impact. Yet time devoted to educating soldiers on the historical and contemporary traditions, cultural sensitivities and the like of the countries to which they are to be deployed or perhaps are already deployed likely comes at the cost of training that could directly affect the success of their military mission. Furthermore, such efforts may well be resisted or resented by some who have preconceived notions about the role of the military and its relationship to the application of "soft power."

On the other hand, if the future of American security depends as much upon stability operations in fractured states as upon battlefield successes, then altering traditional career paths in order to create a new generation of officers and soldiers trained in stability operations is absolutely essential to success in meeting 21st century threats.

10. Are Current Intelligence Efforts Adequate?

Given the complex nature of the 21st century security environment, has the United States adequately assessed its intelligence needs? Are mechanisms for defining and communicating priorities from Cabinet departments and the NSC and translating those priorities into collection programs and analysis adequate? Are intelligence resources adequate to meet informational requirements for long-term planning as well as crises—e.g., people, languages, and technologies for collection, interintelligence agency coordination, and analysis? Do Cabinet departments and other agencies have quick access to information needed to make effective policy choices?

11. How Should the Efforts of Those Willing to Assist be Integrated?

How should America's efforts be calibrated with those of other governments, international government organizations (IGOs) and nongovernmental organizations (NGOs)? The effectiveness of integration will greatly depend on an understanding of the goals of such organizations, their organizational structure, the personalities and temperament of their leaderships, and how they actually operate. This may be a complex task. For example, in Afghanistan today there are approximately 16 IGOs, six NGO coordinating bodies, about 15 national local NGOs, and a vast number of foreign NGOs. There are additional NGOs that focus on women and on children. In Haiti, estimates of the number of NGOs are as high as 10,000. Furthermore, many NGOs eschew dealing with, let alone working in coordination with, the U.S. Government, or for that matter the agencies of any government.

There are no easy solutions to this problem. Nevertheless, well-integrated and coordinated efforts are likely to result in more effective solutions at less cost. The United States is not devoid of experience in such matters. Perhaps knowledge of past successes and failures should be put to work to improve future coordination and integration.

12. How Should the Entire Process be Funded?

Current practices allow departments and agencies to decide how best to arrange their budgets in order to address national security issues as they see them. According to Gene L. Dodaro, Director of the Government Accountability Office and acting Comptroller General, this arrangement has created "a patchwork of activities that waste scarce funds and limit the overall effectiveness of federal efforts." According to Dodaro, "Different organizational structures, planning processes and funding sources to plan for and conduct their national security activities . . . can hinder interagency collaboration," resulting in "budget requests and congressional appropriations that tend to reflect individual agency concerns."[68]

GAO director Dodaro was not the first to recommend changes to the national security budgeting processes. Among others, in a 2008 report, the Project on National Security Reform recommended "the creation of an integrated national security budget," arguing that the current budgeting system exhibits "gross inefficiencies" and further noting:

> Since we do not budget by mission, no clear link exists between strategy and resources for interagency activities. As things stand, departments and agencies have little incentive to include funding for interagency purposes; they are virtually never rewarded for doing so. As a consequence, mission-essential capabilities that fall outside the core mandates of our departments and agencies are virtually never planned or trained for—a veritable formula for being taken unawares and unprepared.[69]

Similarly, in November 2009 the Center for American Progress, a think tank led by President Obama's transition chief, concluded:

> The United States has the capability to confront these threats to global security and stability, but in order to do so most efficiently and effectively, we must also address the imbalance between key elements of our national power. A unified national security budget that enables policymakers to more readily make the trade-offs necessary between defense, economic development, and diplomacy is the best vehicle to prepare the U.S. government to confront the threats of the 21st century.[70]

Altering current budgeting processes will not be an easy task. At present, there is no office in the executive or congressional branches of government staffed with the expertise to undertake the task of developing a unified national security budget. Moreover, such an undertaking would likely encounter resistance from entrenched bureaucratic interests that would be loath to relinquished cherished budgetary prerogatives.

CONCLUSIONS

There is growing consensus that while the U.S. Government may have been structured adequately to address the problems of the Cold War, a major rethinking is necessary if it is to be able to address successfully the relatively more complex problems of the 21st century. During the Cold War, the United States confronted an adversary that could, in a matter of minutes, inflict unimaginable destruction on its peoples and territory. However, that adversary was geographically defined. Its leadership was relatively conservative, rational, methodical, and reasonably predictable. There were, of course, other threats to U.S. security. However, those threats paled in comparison to the dangers posed by the Soviet Union, and many were assumed to be and were, in fact, aided and abetted by the USSR.

Today the Cold War is gone, and with it are gone the relative stability and predictability of the security environment. Restraints that frequently held intrastate, and often interstate, conflict in check have been removed. Threats are more amorphous and diffuse. Historic multi-ethnic, multi-religious, multi-tribal, and/or multi-national tensions and latent frustrations over corrupt, incompetent, or authoritarian governments threaten the internal stability of states, fracturing some. Weak, fractured, failing, or failed states provide havens for violent and extremist groups. The proliferation of know-how and materials used in the construction of weapons of mass destruction and the globalization of communications provide new opportunities and increase exponentially the dangers posed by such groups.

Add to that mix a Russia that has yet to find its way to the West, the rise of China, a North Korea that has threatened to use its newly developed nuclear weapons, an Iran that may be seeking nuclear weapons, and the unresolved but highly volatile situation in the Middle East, and you have a much more complex global security environment than the one that existed during the Cold War. If the United States is to deal effectively with such an environment, it will require an extraordinary effort by the Intelligence Community. As James Woolsey, former Director of Central Intelligence, put it, today "...it is as if we were struggling with a large dragon for 45 years, killed it, and then found ourselves in a jungle full of poisonous snakes—and the snakes are much harder to keep track of than the dragon ever was."[71] It also will require a clear understanding of U.S. foreign and security policy objectives and the capabilities and limitations of American soft and hard power in advancing those objectives, as well as a coterie of knowledgeable individuals who can advise the President and senior policy makers if, when, and how the United States should become involved in the affairs of other states. Equally essential, efficient and effective foreign and security policies will demand highly integrated interagency planning by well-trained professionals, and closely coordinated and highly integrated interagency responses.

The security environment of the 21st century will no longer permit Cabinet departments and government agencies to operate as individual fiefdoms, closely guarding their prerogatives and turf. Rather, they will need to function as part of a WoG team capable of delivering well-coordinated and integrated efforts to shape the global environment and advance American and global interests. This will not be an easy task and will require answers to the many questions raised above.

ENDNOTES - CHAPTER 2

1. "Why We Will Soon Miss the Cold War," *The Atlantic*, August 1990, pp. 35-50.

2. Francis Fukuyama, "The End of History?" *The National Interest*, Summer 1989, p. 18.

3. See "Loose Nukes," *Council on Foreign Relations Backgrounder*, updated January 2006 available from *www.cfr.org/publication/9549/loose_nukes.html.*

4. Lieutenant General Alexander Lebed, former Russian Military Intelligence Directorate (GRU) defector Stanislav Lenev; and former science advisor to Russian President Boris Yeltsin Alexi Yablokov confirmed the existence of such weapons. Lebed contended during a *60 Minutes* interview: "[M]ore than a hundred weapons out of the supposed number of 250 are not under the control of the armed forces of Russia." Official Russian sources denied the allegations. See, for example, "'Security Issues Relating to Russia,' House Floor Speech by Congressman Curt Weldon," October 28, 1999 available from *www.fas.org/irp/congress/1999_cr/floor_102899.htm;* and Carey Sublette, "Alexander Lebed and Suitcase Nukes," May 18, 2002, available from *nuclearweaponarchive.org/News/Lebedbomb.html.*

5. Why Is Highly Enriched Uranium a Threat? *NTI*, updated September 2009, available from *www.nti.org/db/heu/index.html.*

6. *Ibid.*

7. Thomas B. Cochran, "Safeguarding Nuclear Weapon-Usable Materials in Russia," paper presented at the "International Forum, Illegal Nuclear Traffic: Risks, Safeguards and Counter-

measures," Washington, DC: Natural Resources Defense Council, Inc., June 12-13, 1997, available from *docs.nrdc.org/nuclear/files/nuc_06129701a_185.pdf.*

8. "Loose Nukes."

9. "Enriched uranium seized in Georgia," *Atlanta Journal Constitution*, April 22, 2010.

10. "Russia accuses US of loose weapons control," *The China Daily,* August 8, 2010, available from *www.chinadaily.com.cn/world/2010-08/08/content_11116561.htm.*

11. "Obama: Nuclear Terrorism is 'the single biggest threat' to U.S.," *USA Today* (The Oval), April 11, 2010, available from *content.usatoday.com/communities/theoval/post/2010/05/obama-kicks-off-nuclear-summit-with-five-leader-meetings/1.*

12. There are some who argue that "al-Qaeda-ism" is an ideology based on a radical Salafist interpretation of Islam. See for example, Hamid Reza Esmaeili, "Recognizing the Political thought of Al Qaeda," *Iran Review,* June 10, 2008, available from *www.iranreview.org/content/Documents/Recognizing_the_Political_Thought_of_Al_Qaeda.htm.*

13. See Hans Kohn, *The Idea of Nationalism,* New York: The Macmillan Company, 1961, pp. 10-11.

14. For example, see Peter Hopkirk, *Like Hidden Fire: The Plot to Bring Down the British Empire,* New York: Kodansah International, 1994; Peter Hopkirk, *The Great Game: The Struggle for Empire in Asia,* New York: Kodansah International, 1994.

15. See James R. Locher III, *"Forging a New Shield,"* Project on National Security Reform, November 2008, p. ii, available from *http://the-american-interest.com/article.cfm?piece=539.*

16. See for example, *CSIS Commission on Smart Power,* Washington, DC: Center for Strategic and International Studies, 2007.

17. U.S. Commission on National Security/21st Century (Hart-Rudman Commission), Washington, DC, April 15, 2001, Vol. 1, pp. xi, 4.

18. *Quadrennial Roles and Missions Review Report*, Washington, DC: U.S. Department of Defense, January 2009, p. 31.

19. Address by Secretary Hillary Clinton, Washington, DC: Brookings Institution, May 27, 2010.

20. Of course, there have been many calls for an integration of foreign and security policy efforts across agency lines. For example, one might point to the Foreign Assistance Act of 1961 and its subsequent amendments, or to various presidential executive orders, or, for that matter, to various presidential policy directives that charge the National Security Council (NSC) with advising and assisting the President in integrating all aspects of national security policy.

21. For example, see Robert Kennedy, *Of Knowledge and Power: The Complexities of National Intelligence*, Westport, CT: Praeger Security International, 2008, pp. 13-14.

22. Henry Kissinger, "Central Issues of American Foreign Policy," in Kermit Gordon, ed., *Agenda for the Nation*, Washington, DC: The Brookings Institution, 1968, p. 614, cited in Henry Kissinger, *White House Years*, Boston, MA: Little, Brown and Company, 1979, pp. 66. See also Henry Kissinger, *American Foreign Policy*, 3rd Ed., New York: Norton, 1977, p. 97.

23. See, for example, Kissinger, *American Foreign Policy*, pp. 29, 39.

24. In 1977, Kissinger wrote: "The best and most powerful expression of American purposes in the world have been those in which we acted in concert with others," *American Foreign Policy*, p. 97.

25. To be fair, agencies often have convened so-called "red teams" to challenge conventional wisdom. However, it is not always clear that such teams are chosen to think outside the box as much as to juxtapose one conventional wisdom against another, as was apparently the case in the Team A/Team B approach taken to estimate Soviet strategic capabilities in 1976. See Kennedy, *Of Knowledge and Power*, pp. 109-110.

26. I substitute "leadership" for the word "Primacy" used by Joseph Joffe in the quote that follows.

27. Joseph Joffe, "Who's Afraid of Mr. Big." *The National Interest,* Summer 2001, available from *findarticles.com/p/articles/mi_m2751/is_2001_Summer/ai_76560814/pg_10/?tag=content;col1.*

28. A partial list might include such efforts as the Berlin airlift; Lebanon in 1958 to protect against threatened insurrection and again in 1982-83 to facilitate the restoration or order and Lebanese sovereignty; Thailand and Laos to support anti-communist forces seeking to prevent communist elements from creating an unstable environment that might have resulted in the overthrow of the government in those countries; the Dominican Republic in 1965, ostensibly to protect American lives during a period of instability; El Salvador, to strengthen the government in its fight against guerrilla forces threatening an overthrow of the government; Grenada to help restore order and rescue American students following instabilities caused by an internal power struggle and the murder of the prime minister; Bolivia, Columbia, and Peru to combat drug production and trafficking; the Philippines to assist the government in preventing a coup; Panama on various occasions to preclude instabilities and protect American lives; Bosnia and Herzegovina to provide humanitarian relief; in support of the North Atlantic Treaty Organization (NATO) bombing of Serbian forces during the Yugoslav War of the 1990s; Somalia to provide humanitarian relief and restore order; Macedonia in the 1990s and Haiti in the 1990s and 2004 to maintain stability; and East Timor as a part of a UN-mandated International Force for East Timor to restore peace. Among the covert activities that might be mentioned are Iran, 1953; Guatemala, 1954; Cuba and the Democratic Republic of the Congo, 1960; Iraq, 1968; Chile, 1973; Afghanistan, 1978-80; Nicaragua and El Salvador, 1980s; Iraq, in the early 1990s; Serbia, 2000; Venezuela, 2002; and Somalia, 2006-07.

29. Robert Gates, *Remarks as Delivered by Secretary of Defense Robert M. Gates,* Washington, DC: The Nixon Center, February 24, 2010, available from *www.nixoncenter.org/index.cfm?action=showpage&page=2009-Robert-Gates-Transcript.*

30. "Exploding misconceptions," *The Economist,* December 18, 2010, p. 146.

31. *Ibid.*

32. For example, Claude Berrebi of the Rand Corporation, examining data on the characteristics of suicide bombers recruited by Hamas and the Islamic Jihad from the West Bank and Gaza, concluded that nearly 60 percent of the suicide bombers had more than a high school education, compared with less than 15 percent of the general population. The Pew Global Attitudes Project of 2004 concluded that more schooling equated to greater support for suicide bombing aimed at America and other Western targets. *Ibid.*

33. For example, in terms of the Middle East, surely resolving the Arab-Israeli conflict is likely to contribute to a reduction in incentives for terrorist attacks against Israel, as well as those countries perceived as its ally. One also can look elsewhere around the world for irritants that encourage terrorism and that beg for political solutions. Furthermore, greater long-term investments in international educational programs such as those that have been run by the DoD since the end of the Cold War offer some hope. Educational programs such as those at the George C. Marshall European Center for Security Studies in Garmisch-Partenkirchen, Germany; the Asia-Pacific Center for Security Studies in Hawaii; the Africa Center; the Center for Hemispheric Defense Studies; or the Near East-South Asia Center view security in its broadest context and in part have been aimed at altering value systems that see strict authoritarian rule as the only avenue to unity, and progress or restrictions on civil and political rights as the only means to stability, or which fail to see corruption as a pathology inhibiting political and economic progress and social improvement. Also to be considered is a widening of professional and personal links to the American military, not only those which focus on U.S. military programs of support in foreign countries, but also programs which include foreign officers in American military educational institutions, from U.S. military academies to war and defense colleges. Such programs seem to have had an impact on the so far relatively peaceful transition from the near 30-year rule of Hosni Mubarak in Egypt. Despite the inherent authoritarian nature of military life, the American military is an excellent transmitter of democratic values, and the inculcation of these values among indigenous leaders can play an important stabilizing role in failing or failed states.

34. See Robert Kennedy, *The Road to War: Congress' Historic Abdication of Responsibility*, Westport, CT: Praeger Security International, 2010.

35. Daniel W. Drezner, "The Challenging Future of Strategic Planning in Foreign Policy," in Daniel W. Drezner, ed., *Avoiding Trivia*, Washington, DC: Brookings Institution Press, 2009, p. 8.

36. See, for example, *Forging a New Shield*, pp. 344ff.

37. Several alternatives have been proposed. For example, see Michael Donely, "Rethinking the Interagency System," *Occasional Paper #05-01*, McLean, VA: Hicks & Associates, Inc., March 2005, pp. 6-9.

38. Walter Lippmann, *U.S. War Aims*, Boston, MA: Little, Brown, and Company, 1944, cited in Ted McAllister, "America's Vital Interests," *First Principles*, August 10, 2009 available from *www.firstprinciplesjournal.com/articles.aspx?article=1298&theme=amsec&loc=b*.

39. President Eisenhower's News Conference, April 7, 1954, *Public Papers of the Presidents*, 1954, p. 382, available from *http://www.presidency.ucsb.edu/ws#axzz1nKDHF1gl*.

40. Cited in John Lewis Gaddis, *Strategies of Containment*, Revised and Expanded Ed., New York: Oxford University Press, 2005, p. 129.

41. For example, there is an ongoing debate in the halls of the Pentagon over whether mass atrocity prevention is a DoD core mission.

42. See, for example, "Gates Says Libya Not Vital Interest," March 28, 2011, available from *www.military.com/news/article/gates-says-libya-not-vital-interest.html*.

43. President Barack Obama, "Remarks by the President in Address to the Nation on Libya," March 28, 2011, available from *http://www.whitehouse.gov/the-press-office/2011/03/28/remarks-president-address-nation-libya*.

44. *The Power of People: Building an Integrated National Security Professional System for the 21st Century*, Project on National Security Reform, November 2010, p. xiii. The *Quadrennial Defense Review* recognized this deficiency, calling for the full implementation of the National Security Professional program. See *The Quadrennial Defense Review*, Washington, DC: Department of Defense, February 2010, p. 71.

45. Executive Order 13434, May 17, 2007, sec 1.

46. For example, see Department of Defense Instruction Number 1430.16, November 19, 2009.

47. *The Power of People*, p. iii.

48. President George W. Bush's National Security Policy Directive (NSPD) 44 created the Reconstruction and Stabilization Policy Coordinating Committee. The committee is chaired by the Coordinator for Reconstruction and Stabilization and a designated member of the NSC staff and has broad interagency representation.

49. "Interagency Conflict Assessment Framework," Washington, DC: U.S. Department of State, Office of the Coordinator for Reconstruction and Stabilization, pp. 1-3, available from *http://pdf.usaid.gov/pdf_docs/PCAAB943.pdf.*

50. "A Look Back: Ambassador Herbst Retires, Reflects on Four Years as Coordinator for Reconstruction and Stabilization," Summer 2010, Civilian Response Newsletter, U.S. Department of State, September 22, 2010, available from *www.state.gov/documents/organization/148080.pdf.* Also see "2010 Year in Review: Conflict and Stabilization," Report, Washington, DC: U.S. Department of State, Office of the Coordinator for Reconstruction and Stabilization, February 9, 2011.

51. *Ibid*.

52. For example, see *The Power of People*, pp. 31, 208.

53. "Quadrennial Diplomacy and Development Review," Washington, DC: U.S. Department of State, 2010, p. 145.

54. "Leading Through Civilian Power: The First Quadrennial Diplomacy and Development Review," p. 116.

55. See Department of Defense and Full-year Continuing Appropriations Act, 2011, H.R. 1473, P.L. 112-10.

56. See Department of Defense Directive 1404.10, January 23, 2009.

57. Army Sgt. 1st Class Matthew Chlosta, "'Afpak Hands' Begin Immersion Training," American Forces Press Service, May 5, 2010, available from *www.defense.gov/news/newsarticle.aspx?id=59031.*

58. Karen Parish, "'AfPak Hands' Strive for Cultural Awareness," American Forces Press Service, March 3, 2011, available from *www.defense.gov/news/newsarticle.aspx?id=63019.*

59. For example, see "MoDA," U.S. Department of Defense, available from *www.defense.gov/home/features/2011/0211_moda/.*

60. In recent years, concern has been expressed that education available from American military educational institutes—staff and particularly war colleges—has become skewed toward operations, with less thought devoted to educating strategists. Nevertheless, in contrast, State provides its officials nothing comparable to the continuing education provided U.S. military officers other than sending a few Foreign Service offers to the National Defense University or the various service war colleges.

61. National Defense Authorization Act for Fiscal Year 2006, Public Law 163, 109th Cong., 1st sess., January 6, 2006, p. 3458.

62. See Division F of the Consolidated Appropriations Act, 2010, Public Law 111-117, 111th Cong., 2nd Sess., December 16, 2009, available from *www.gpo.gov/fdsys/pkg/PLAW-111publ117/pdf/PLAW-111publ117.pdf.*

63. *Ibid.*, p. 3327.

64. See, for example, Nina M. Serafino, "Department of Defense 'Section 1207' Security and Stabilization Assistance: Background and Congressional Concerns FY2006-FY2010," CRS Report for Congress, March 2, 2011, p. 4.

65. Global Security Contingency Funds are similar to Section 1207 funding. They are Defense and State pooled funds and the Secretary of State must consult with the Secretary of Defense before funds are expended.

66. See "Fact Sheet, State and USAID—FY 2012 Budget," available from *http://www.state.gov/r/pa/prs/ps/2012/02/183808.htm.* Also see "FY2012 Prevention Budget Priorities: Testimony Submitted to the House," Friends Committee on National Legislation, March 29, 2011, available from *fcnl.org/issues/ppdc/fy2012_budget_priorities_testimony_submitted_to_the_house/.*

67. *Ibid.*

68. Walter Pincus, "GAO urges changes in budgeting for national security," *Washington Post*, January 18, 2010.

69. *Forging a New Shield*, pp. v, vii, xi.

70. *Integrating Security: Preparing for National Security Threats of the 21st Century*, Washington, DC: Center for American Progress, November 2009, p. 4.

71. "Testimony of R. James Woolsey," U.S. House of Representatives, Committee on National Security, February 12, 1998.

CHAPTER 3

THE PUZZLE OF NATIONAL SECURITY PLANNING FOR THE WHOLE OF GOVERNMENT

Mary R. Habeck

INTRODUCTION

In the fall of 2005, the School of Advanced International Studies (SAIS) of Johns Hopkins University hosted a 1-day symposium to analyze and critique whole of government (WoG) planning for the invasion of Iraq. While Operation IRAQI FREEDOM (OIF) had been highly successful during Phases I through III, the war plan suffered from several strategic flaws during Phase IV (the post-conflict period), including a failure to predict or prepare for an insurgency. The symposium at SAIS brought together, for the first time since the invasion occurred, many of the planners for Phase IV to talk about their experiences and to discuss what might have gone wrong in the process that was supposed to prepare the U.S. Government for any contingency.

The conclusions reached by the participants shed a clarifying light on the challenges that the U.S. national security apparatus faces with WoG planning in general, as well as highlighting specific issues with planning presented by the new security environment after September 11, 2001 (9/11). In the run-up to the Iraq War, no government-wide standard procedure, organization, or leadership existed to guide planning across agency lines. There was no common definition for planning and little understanding of how planning processes differed within the various agencies, making it difficult to coordinate and integrate diverse plans into a general strategy that every agency would follow. The result was that Phases I, II and III, which were dominated by planners and operators from one agency (the Department of Defense [DoD]), flowed relatively smoothly, while Phase IV, which depended on close coordination between multiple agencies, experienced near-catastrophic failure.[1]

The George W. Bush administration took steps to rectify the situation after OIF, establishing offices to improve coordination between the DoD and the State Department (State), creating incentives for interagency staff assignments, and setting up processes for some joint operational planning. These efforts were, naturally enough, focused on post-conflict stability and reconstruction operations, and targeted the DoD, State, and the U.S. Agency for International Development (USAID), the main partners involved in OIF Phase IV. Other sorts of national security operations that might require interagency planning and other agencies beyond these three were relatively neglected, and a full reworking of WoG planning for national security issues has failed to materialize in the intervening years.

Any attempt to carry out government-wide reforms, even those confined just to national security matters, will run into difficulties, but there are particular issues associated with planning that have made this effort exceptionally challenging. This chapter will look at a series of general problems that became apparent during OIF, but have not yet been fully dealt with: the definition of planning, organizational and structural frictions, and coordination failures. The chapter then looks at how planning is further complicated—and yet made more urgent—by the current national security environment. The events of 9/11 and afterward demonstrate that the United States has serious gaps in its planning system that must be filled if the country is to confront and overcome the difficult challenges of the 21st century. A concluding section provides some proposals for alleviating these problems, while acknowledging that a real solution will only be implemented when a broad consensus emerges within the government that reform is necessary, or change is enforced from above through a presidential order and/or through action by Congress. Only then will the U.S. Government have one of the tools required to carry out its most basic function: providing for the common defense.

UNDERSTANDING THE PROBLEM: NATIONAL SECURITY PLANNING ACROSS THE INTERAGENCY

There are fundamental structural issues that impede an integrated planning process throughout the U.S. national security community, most importantly the vastly different ways that planning is understood and carried out across the interagency. Planning touches every facet of U.S. Government national security operations, beginning with the expression of policy by the President. This is given written form by the National Security Council (NSC) staff in the *National Security Strategy* (NSS), a document produced every 2 years that sets the objectives and priorities of the administration.[2] Each department then uses the NSS to create a document that describes, at times in detail, the agency's mission and objectives, how these will be achieved, and how the agency's objectives will, in turn, move national policy forward, thus aid-ing the government in achieving its objectives. Top-level documents are supplemented by more detailed implementation statements and, in some agencies, by contingency or longer-term planning papers.

Any attempt to implement and coordinate WoG planning would need to take into consideration issues such as differences in how this process is carried out within the national security community and the differing missions of the agencies, but it is the divergent views of what constitutes planning that are especially troublesome. Put most succinctly, the various agencies that make up the government often believe that they are having a communication about the same topic when, in fact, they are talking about quite different things. The word "planning," for instance, can mean everything from long-range or contingency to strategic or policy to operational planning, depending on the circumstances and the particular agency. The first category includes everything that is beyond the immediate, and may be very general in nature (i.e., a discussion of potential futures) or quite specific (such as a finely-grained strategy for how to build the force that the DoD believes will be necessary for the next 10 years). The second category is what agencies generally mean by the term "planning," but here again the opportunities for disagreement are vast. Strategic or policy planning means planning at its highest level, but it can range from a matching of overall means to ends with a detailing of pathways to achieve these ends, to a much more general document that gives the objectives and priorities for a department or even the entire government without detailing means, or ways. The final category was, before 9/11, the province of the military, which has personnel specifically trained for operational planning and which is one of the few government institutions that is regularly asked to engage in operations. Given these diverse ways that planning might be defined, if simply asked to begin "planning," it is unclear that any two agencies would have the same concept in mind.

A broad comparison of planning at State and the DoD shows how different the understanding of planning is within just two agencies. At the DoD, planning is an integral part of the functioning of the department, highly coordinated and sequenced, and describing in detail a matching of resources and ends over time. The planning cycle begins with the production of the *Quadrennial Defense Review* (QDR), the military's basic statement of strategy. The issuing of the QDR leads to the writing of a series of more detailed documents, some biennially and others annually produced, which take the guidance from the QDR and other high-level strategic statements and determine in great detail how particular offices, agencies, and the branches will do their part to fulfill the strategic objectives of the department. Planning for military operations (i.e., the creation of an operations plan [OPLAN]) is naturally well-developed within the DoD and is understood in a very precise and highly defined way, consisting of specific steps and agreed-upon categories, and leads directly to the issuing of orders to carry out the plan. Because of its importance to the core mission of the military, the methodologies used for operational planning tend to dominate the military's other forms of planning.

Before OIF, State also engaged in planning, but of a very different and more general sort than the DoD.[3] The office of the Secretary would produce for the department as a whole, a strategy statement which laid out the vision and specific objectives for the institution.

Each bureau and office produced its own paper that explained, in general terms, how it would implement the vision laid out by the Secretary. The department-wide office dedicated solely to long-term planning was (and is) the Policy Planning Staff, but its mission has always been to act as "a source of independent policy analysis and advice for the Secretary of State," rather than to provide detailed and comprehensive planning (in the military sense) for the Department as a whole.[4] Given the nature of State's missions, operational planning was not seen as necessary and, beyond a limited plan for evacuating embassies abroad, not widely practiced or even fully understood.

These differences in understanding of planning, and operational planning in particular, combined with problems in coordination, explain the problematic hand-off between the military and State officials at the start of OIF Phase IV.[5] The sort of detailed operational planning in which the military routinely engages was nearly unknown at State, and there were no professionals on its staff who could be dedicated to the task. The Office of Reconstruction and Humanitarian Assistance (ORHA), the civilian agency that was to take over planning and implementing Phase IV, thus became dominated by military planners rather than State officials as originally envisioned. When asked to provide inputs for the overall plan, State analysts used their extensive experience to produce documents that expressed serious concerns about the potential for sectarian violence and the possibility of an insurgency, but they did not generate a comprehensive plan that discussed ways and means to deal with these challenges. There was, as well, an inability within the highly-centralized military planning process to integrate this sort of nonspecific input, and thus no "branch" (i.e., contingency) plan to deal with an insurgency or sectarian violence was created by the DoD or the ORHA military planners. Some DoD planners even claimed that ORHA was positively discouraged from working with other agencies during the pre-war planning period.[6] The result was that every agency involved in OIF created its own plans for post-war Iraq, did not coordinate its plans with other agencies, and believed that the other agencies understood planning and the planning process in precisely the same way as their own.

In response to the near failure in Iraq, then Secretary of State Condoleezza Rice implemented a number of reforms at State and USAID: the addition of an office to oversee U.S. Government stabilization and reconstruction efforts (including planning for these missions), a new office in USAID for military affairs, and the creation of a "team" that "engages the Department of Defense . . . on global political-military policy issues and coordinates strategic planning between the Departments of State and Defense."[7] She created as well the so-called "F Process," which plans and coordinates State and USAID foreign assistance. Current Secretary of State Hillary Clinton built on these changes with the mandating of a *Quadrennial Diplomacy and Development Review* (QDDR), which provides longer-range planning and policy guidance, and synchronized State planning with that of the DoD. These substantial reforms brought, for the first time, resources together with planning at State and began to involve State in operational planning with the DoD as well.

The DoD carried out its own internal reforms after OIF, was a full participant in the process that led to the changes within State and USAID, and also proposed a strategy to reform planning throughout the interagency. The 2006 QDR called for "strengthening interagency operations," and discussed joint planning as a special focus for the military over the next 4 years. The QDR recommended in particular greater cooperation between the DoD and other agencies to leverage the military's comparative advantage in planning and the issuance of a new document called the *National Security Planning Guidance* to bridge the gap between the leadership's strategic or policy vision and implementation.[8]

Despite the deep reforms carried out by State, USAID, and the DoD, planning within other parts of the national security community was largely untouched. Before 9/11, planning across the interagency tended to follow the State rather than the DoD model, and this remained true after the near failures of OIF. The two exceptions to this general rule were, not coincidentally, new institutions created after 9/11: the National Counterterrorism Center (NCTC) and the Department of Homeland Security (DHS). NCTC adopted a WoG approach to operational planning, although narrowly directed at counterterror (CT) efforts and the new *Quadrennial Homeland Security Review* (QHSR), attempted to do for the DHS what the QDR does for the DoD (but without a full interagency process). Other departments such as Treasury, Justice, and the many agencies within the intelligence community, all of which have vital roles to play in the new security environment, have their own separate processes for planning, and see them as adequate for the missions that they are asked to perform. Even within State and USAID, the changes did not deal with operational planning beyond post-conflict phases of warfare. Thus despite the near catastrophe of OIF Phase IV, an approach to planning that will encompass the entire national security effort of the U.S. has not been realized as of this writing.

There are a series of meta-reasons for this failure: frictions between the agencies, no lead agency for reform, no mandated planning process or sponsor to impose one, and no comparable offices or officials dedicated to planning within each agency that could coordinate with each other. The frictions come from many sources, some of which are related to the need for a lead agency. As the 2006 QDR makes clear, the DoD sees itself as the obvious institution to shape a new planning process. The military's clear-cut rules for creating planning documents, its cadre of professionals who have been specifically trained for the task, as well as its experience in bridging the planning and implementation gap, seem to make it the obvious choice to take the lead on this problem. Yet the very confidence of the military creates anxieties and resentments among the other agencies, which have added to the delays over the realization of proposals for planning reforms. Other agencies are also not convinced that they need reform since, unlike State they have not yet suffered a failure comparable to the OIF Phase IV experience.[9]

Lack of a powerful sponsor for planning reform helps to explain why the changes that have occurred have been piecemeal and partial rather than systemic. It is here that the comparison to the Goldwater-Nichols Act is most helpful.[10] A series of near catastrophes in the 1970s and 1980s convinced both military and political leaders that greater jointness between the branches of the military was an absolute necessity. Yet despite this agreement, it took an act of Congress for reforms to move forward, and for the powerful Navy and Army, in particular, to cede some of their prerogatives for the greater good. In much the same way, agencies agree that greater coordination and cooperation is needed and that, in particular, a better process for WoG planning is vital. Despite this agreement , and the funding by Congress of a team to study and recommend such reforms (the Project for a National Security Reform [PNSR]), the entire process has stalled without the direct attention and support of the President or influential members of Congress.

A final challenge is posed by two related structural issues: a dearth of civilians trained in planning and a corresponding dearth of planning offices on an equal footing that could coordinate with each other. The creation within all the relevant agencies of a cadre of civilians who understand and are trained in strategic or operational planning is a necessary precondition for any reforms that will encompass the entire national security effort of the U.S. Government. While military planners might form the core of such a cadre, it is necessary to have civilians who understand the operations of their particular agency well and can provide the necessary nexus between the agency and the interagency planning process. In much the same way, the many existing planning offices lack the uniformity in how and what they plan that will allow close coordination between them. Offices can be created by fiat, but it will take time to train the cadres necessary to man these offices, a fact which again argues for reform to begin now.

THE CURRENT NATIONAL SECURITY ENVIRONMENT AND WHOLE OF GOVERNMENT PLANNING

If the complexities surrounding a WoG approach to planning create structural and organizational/cultural challenges that must be surmounted, the new security environment after 9/11 highlights why reform is so urgently required. Even before the events of 9/11, the need for better coordination and cooperation within the interagency was well-understood and commented upon by scholars and practitioners.[11] The terrorist attacks then and afterward, the growth of al-Qaeda and its affiliates, the rise of nonstate threats around the globe, and the inadequate capacity of traditional international mechanisms to deal with these problems argue more than ever for a transformation of how the United States is organized for national security, and the planning processes for national security in particular.

The most important shift in the security environment is the worldwide and irregular nature of the challenges confronting the United States. The evolution of al-Qaeda is but one illustration of how the threat from irregular forces is expanding. The group that attacked New York and Washington has aspirations both to carry out terrorist atrocities around the world and to provoke a global insurgency; and, since 9/11, it has begun to develop the capabilities to do so. In addition to branches in Iraq, Pakistan/Afghanistan, Yemen, North Africa, and Somalia, al-Qaeda has allies that align themselves with the group's objectives and ideology in Indonesia, India, Central Asia, Chechnya, and elsewhere. Al-Qaeda also has numerous individual supporters in many Western countries and within the United States itself. Planning for a regular war that turned irregular in a single country, Iraq stretched the capacities of the U.S. Government. Coordinating a global CT campaign since 9/11 has been difficult, but generally doable. But if the United States must carry out a global counterinsurgency, much more will need to be done to reshape the national security community to confront and overcome the challenge.

A significant implication of the ascendance of irregular threats around the globe is that the United States must coordinate the usual elements of American power (the military, State/USAID, and the intelligence community) with other agencies that have not traditionally been involved in national security on the international stage. To combat insurgencies in places like Iraq and Afghanistan, agencies like the Department of Justice, the Drug Enforcement Administration (DEA), and even the Department of Agriculture have been asked to take on new roles and responsibilities and to coordinate their actions with State and the DoD. Fighting the drug lord/criminal nexus that is spreading across the border from Mexico might require the DHS or the Department of Alcohol, Tobacco, and Firearms (ATF) to become involved in operational missions that would benefit from military experience with planning. Building capacity in threatened states so that they will be able to protect themselves has meant including local police and their expertise for training. Police and Federal Bureau of Investigation (FBI) agents are also the front line for combating radicalization within the United States itself, making it even more important for them to have access to information and planning that would otherwise be irrelevant for their daily work. In this new environment, a deep understanding of the human terrain (religious beliefs, general culture, languages, tribal relationships, and much more) becomes as important as knowing the physical terrain, which might require adding private sector resources, including U.S. academic and scholarly capacity, to the mix.

Coordinating U.S. agencies to fight a global war is daunting enough, but the nature of the new threats also requires much more coordination of both planning and action with other nations. The vast range of the challenges, and the capacities of potential partners to meet them, means that each agency would need careful time and attention to see how cooperation and coordination could be achieved. At one end of the spectrum is the planning necessary to work closely with allies such as Britain or Germany in an irregular war in Afghanistan. Working with capable partners like Mexico to deal with the drug cartels, or with Indonesia and the Philippines to prevent al-Qaeda affiliated groups from growing or spreading is less intense than a war, but made more difficult by the lesser capacity of the governments involved. Even more demanding is working with fragile countries such as Pakistan or Egypt to ensure that indigenous threats do not overwhelm the country or spread throughout their respective regions. Finally, there are the grave difficulties of working with failing states like Somalia or extremely weak states like Yemen and Chad, that have difficulty defending themselves, let alone stopping a group like al-Qaeda in the Arabian Peninsula. A serious discussion of internal U.S. planning reforms must take into consideration that any new offices, institutions, or processes created must work not only across the interagency, but with international partners and allies as well.

Finally, the events of 9/11 and afterward show that the U.S. Government is in dire need of planning that goes beyond the immediate. Almost all the strategic planning processes described above are predicated on cycles that run yearly, biennially, or, for a very few, every 4 years. Over the past 10 years, much has been written about the need for longer-term or contingency planning processes within the U.S. Government, since the planning that exists, even when called "long-term," often becomes focused on vital day-to-day matters and is ruled by the tyranny of the urgent. Perhaps more importantly, there are very few offices or people assigned to work on over-the-horizon planning, making it a challenge to find the right locus and trained personnel who would take on these tasks, since most planners have to be concerned with routine tasks or dealing with crises. As others have pointed out, a failure to plan beyond today has left the United States unprepared for future 9/11s and at the mercy of events, rather than being their master.[12]

There are two sorts of planning that would look beyond these limits: long-term and contingency. Long-term planning would provide analysis and context for trends or events beyond the near-term that might be threats to the United States. This sort of planning might also suggest general ways to prepare the country to meet these challenges. There are a few offices that provide certain types of long-term planning, including the National Intelligence Council, which prepares unclassified reports with a 20-year time frame, and the DoD's policy planning shop (now under the Deputy Assistant Secretary of Defense [DASD] for Strategy), which among other tasks provides long-range forecasting. Their analyses are not, however, well integrated into other interagency planning processes, nor does every agency have a relevant office that could coordinate with these entities. There is not, in other words, a systemic effort to provide well-coordinated planning for the long-term across the interagency.

Contingency planning is supposed to anticipate gaps in U.S. strategic planning, (i.e., Donald Rumsfeld's "unknowns unknowns"), and to prepare the country for high-impact/low-probability events.[13] When the United States does not pay attention to contingency planning, it can find itself dealing with crises and bolts out of the blue that leave the country without time to spend on a well-considered response. Once again there are several offices that are concerned with potential future threats (especially within the DoD), and that provide general concepts for dealing with them; but as with long-range planning, there is little interagency coordination and few other offices dedicated to this question. Even the DoD tends to do well with branch planning within an OPLAN, but less well with contingencies that are full of unknowns and therefore fall outside the range of detailed operational planning.

Any reforms to WoG planning would need to consider how to include, in an organic and systematic way, realistic and feasible planning for both contingencies and the long-term. For this particular sort of planning, each of these terms is vital: organic, since the planning would need to come from within each of the agencies and reflect their knowledge bases of future potential threats; systematic, since it would be across the interagency and as uniform and coordinated as possible; realistic, to avoid wild theorizing; and feasible, that is, creating plans that have some reasonable chance for application in the real world.

A PROPOSAL FOR REFORM

The relatively disorganized state of planning within the interagency, combined with the greater needs of the new security environment, mean that there has never been a larger gap between supply and demand for planning within the U.S. Government. Not long after OIF, a number of experts proposed that there be a new Goldwater-Nichols reform to reorganize the government's national security system and, among other things, implement the sort of planning that the new security challenges required.[14] As mentioned above, the ambitious PNSR was set up and funded by Congress to diagnose the fundamental problems that might exist and to propose a transformation in how the United States organizes to carry out the vital role of protecting itself. After months of work, the PNSR proposed a radical series of reforms—including wide-ranging changes to the strategy and planning processes within the government.[15]

Unfortunately, the Congress has thus far been unable to carry through the restructuring proposed by the PNSR and others. Despite this failure, it is worth discussing the minimum changes that should be put into place to create the necessary preconditions for planning reform. A first step, and one that would meet the most imperative needs, is the creation of comparable offices dedicated to carrying out planning within each relevant agency. Existing policy planning and strategy offices in the agencies would be the basis for the new organizations, but they would need to be standardized in composition, and the importance of their mission should elevate them administratively within each organization. Thus the heads of these offices should answer directly to the principal for the agency and coordinate their activity through the NSC interagency committee process.

Because strategic, long-term, and contingency planning is needed across the interagency, the offices would be dedicated to these tasks, rather than to operational planning. The main objective for the offices would then be to produce planning documents, consistent throughout the government and coordinated in time, sequencing, format, and process with each other. The papers would need to be more than just broad descriptions of department policy, but should instead be detailed plans to guide the operation of the agency and its coordination with other agencies, along with general guidance to prepare the department for extraordinary events or longer-term trends. The NSS, already mandated by Congress, would form the starting point for an agency's planning process, but even this seminal policy platform will need modification. Rather than simply listing the national security objectives of the Executive Branch, the NSS will need to be supplemented by a document that establishes priorities, ways, and means—including specific resourcing—for achieving these objectives, and include as well a strategic assessment of the risks of action and inaction. It follows that the Office of Management and Budget (OMB) will need a planning office as well, and must be included organically in the new national security planning process.

The simple writing of planning documents will not, however, ensure that particular policies are, in fact, carried out by either individual agencies or by the government as a whole. Thus the other main objective for these offices must be to follow up and report back to their principals on the implementation of their guidance. There are offices within some agencies that provide follow-up on specific issues, but there is far less assessment of progress on implementing the overall strategies of the agencies, and none that assesses progress across the interagency. The reports from the assessments would provide the basis for reworking strategic and contingency plans, providing the necessary flexibility for the planning process.

The obvious institution to coordinate planning across the interagency is a new directorate within the NSC staff, which would oversee, as well, implementation and work through frictions that are certain to appear. As others have suggested, this will require that the office be headed by at least a senior director and perhaps even a Deputy National Security Advisor, to increase the influence of the new directorate and to make clear that its mission is given priority.[16] The office would coordinate the writing of the NSS as well as the supplementary *National Security Planning Guidance* (NSPG) already recommended by the DoD and other observers. This seminal document would provide the detailed matching of means and ends necessary to implement the NSS, and thus be the backbone for the more finely grained documents produced by each of the agencies.

The new NSC directorate should also be charged with developing over-the-horizon strategies, including long-range policy forecasting and a series of strategic contingency plans. These documents, coordinated with the other planning offices, would provide the basis for guidance and implementation papers, similar to those created through the regular planning process, but somewhat less detailed and more flexible, given the longer time frames and conditional nature of the scenarios discussed.

The final purpose of the directorate is to provide periodic net assessments of national security policy implementation across the government. Conducted with the aid of the individual agency planning offices, the assessment would include a re-examination of assumptions and strategic objectives and recommendations for adjustments to the NSS, the NSPG, and other plans developed by the agencies. To allow fresh perspectives on policy, the process might include outsiders such as the Defense Policy Board, which already has the necessary clearances and access to provide well-informed advice. The military once again has experience with these sorts of assessments, which are generally carried out by commanders in the field every 6 months, and this might provide a guide for the timing of these regular assessments. The creation of a strong feedback loop will increase the flexibility of the planning and execution processes, and will introduce necessary fine-tuning of resourcing, emphases, and guidance from leadership. It will also, for the first time, provide the President with a detailed overview of how well his policy vision for U.S. national security is being executed.

The composition of the new planning offices is vital, given the multiple tasks that they will be asked to carry out. Strategy development (including contingency planning), strategic planning, and implementation oversight each require quite different skill sets and previous experience. The offices would thus need to include a mix of personnel: strategic thinkers, strategic planners, and practitioners working together as a close-knit unit. Strategic thinkers would be asked to match means and ends, weigh the risks of action and inaction, conceptualize long-term strategies, and envision scenarios for contingencies. Academics in universities or think tanks might be the best source for members of this group. Planners would take the concepts of the thinkers and generate detailed plans for implementation. They would need to be trained in strategic and perhaps operational planning, using as a model the U.S. experts in this field—the military—and would therefore most likely be drawn from that institution. The practitioners should have long experience in how the government works and would follow up with the other offices in their own agency on progress made in carrying out the strategies produced by the planning office.

CONCLUSION

Many of the proposals described above seem commonsensical and several (with variations) have been proposed by the PNSR and other keen observers of the U.S. national security system. The fact that there is an obvious need for reform, multiple proposals for how to carry it out, and yet little has been done to realize a WoG approach to planning suggest that two elements are still missing: the necessary desire for reform and sponsors who would be able to mandate it. With the exception of the DoD, State, USAID, and the new organizations created after 9/11, there has been little appetite for reform from the agencies that make up the national security system of the United States. This is unsurprising, since wide-ranging transformations of the government are rarely carried out without a serious failure in policy that pushes the system to seek change. Even then, there can be little movement without the support and constant pressure of powerful patrons—either the President himself or members of Congress—who would take on the project and see it through. Lacking a desire for reform and sponsors for change, the United States may have to again experience systemic failure before there is enough pressure to transform how the country carries out planning for its own survival.

ENDNOTES - CHAPTER 3

1. The Conference was titled "U.S. Military Operations in Iraq: Planning, Combat, and Occupation." Summaries of some of the papers presented and discussion is available from *www.sais-jhu.edu/merrillcenter-original/Iraq_Panel2_Summary.pdf*. For good analyses of Phase IV planning and its problems, see Olga Oliker, Nora Bensahel *et al.*, *After Saddam: Prewar Planning and the Occupation of Iraq*, Santa Monica, CA: RAND, 2008; Gregory Hooker, *Shaping the Plan for Operation Iraqi Freedom*, Washington, DC: WINEP, 2005; and Michael R. Gordon and General Bernard E. Trainor, *Cobra II: The Inside Story of the Invasion and Occupation of Iraq*, New York: Vintage Books, 2007, pp. 158-187.

2. The latest iteration of the NSS is available from *www.whitehouse.gov/sites/default/files/rss_viewer/national_security_strategy.pdf*.

3. This is not to be critical of State, since the way that planning occurred there fit the mission that the Department was designed to fulfill.

4. The official description of the Policy Planning Staff is available from *www.state.gov/s/p/*.

5. There were other issues internal to the military and its training and culture responsible for the failures of Phase IV planning. These have been pointed out by many observers and noted in one of the official histories of Operation IRAQI FREEDOM (OIF), Donald P. Wright and Timothy R. Reese, *On Point II: Transition to the New Campaign. The United States Army in Operation IRAQI FREEDOM, March 2003-January 2005,* Fort Leavenworth, KS: Combat Studies Institute Press, 2008, throughout, but especially pp. 66ff.

6. *Ibid.*, p. 71.

7. Available from *www.state.gov/t/pm/ppa/pmppt/* and *www.state.gov/s/crs/about/index.htm#mission*.

8. *Quadrennial Defense Review Report*, Washington, DC: Department of Defense, February 6, 2006, pp. 84ff.

9. This section is taken from personal experience of the author while in government.

10. For an in-depth look at the Goldwater-Nichols Act and the need for reform, see Gordon Nathaniel Lederman, *Reorganizing the Joint Chiefs of Staff: The Goldwater-Nichols Act of 1986*, Westport CT: Greenwood Press, 1999.

11. One result of this foment was the Hart-Rudman Commission, which issued a series of reports on how to reform the National Security interagency, including strategic planning, to meet the new challenges of the 21st century. See United States Commission on National Security/21st Century [Hart-Rudman Commission], "Road Map for National Security: Imperative for Change. The Phase III Report of the U.S. Commission on National Security/21st Century," Washington, DC, February 15, 2001.

12. Michèle A. Flournoy and Shawn W. Brimley, "Strategic Planning for U.S. National Security: A Project Solarium for the 21st Century," The Princeton Project on National Security, 2006.

13. Or "black swans:" see Nassim Taleb, *The Black Swan: The Impact of the Highly Improbable*, New York: Random House, 2007.

14. One of the purposes of the Princeton Project on National Security, available from *www.princeton.edu/~ppns/*; and also proposed by a similar project, "Beyond Goldwater-Nichols," run by the Center for Strategic and International Studies, available from *csis.org/program/beyond-goldwater-nichols*.

15. "Forging a New Shield," PNSR, December 2008, available from *pnsr.org/data/files/pnsr%20forging%20a%20new%20shield.pdf*; and "Turning New Ideas Into Action," Project on National Security Reform (PNSR), September 2009, available from *www.pnsr.org/data/files/pnsr_turning_ideas_into_action.pdf*.

16. For a wide-ranging discussion of how to organize for strategic planning, see Daniel Drezner, ed., *Avoiding Trivia: The Role of Strategic Planning in American Foreign Policy*, Washington, DC: The Brookings Institution Press, 2009. The essays by Will Inboden and Peter Feaver, "A Strategic Planning Cell on National Security at the White House"; and Aaron Friedberg, "Strengthening U.S. Strategic Planning," argue in particular for a location in the White House for the new institution.

CHAPTER 4

DEVELOPMENT IS DESTRUCTION, AND OTHER THINGS YOU WEREN'T TOLD AT SCHOOL

Michael Ashkenazi

INTRODUCTION: WHO, WHAT, AND WHY ARE WE "DEVELOPING"?

In virtually all seminal writing on development, development is viewed as a good thing.[1] Indeed, who could argue against better education, health care, employment, eradication of disease, and personal security? At the same time, some of the obvious targets for development—the leadership, and indeed the rank and file of underdeveloped societies—seem to be the most virulently opposed to development. A large (but unknown) proportion of Afghans, Sudanese, and other Africans seem to be at the forefront of the resistance to development. They resist—passively or actively—the package called "development" (though always happy to receive some of its material gifts) sometimes to the point of violence. The Muslim world in particular is seen as a hotbed of anti-development activity.[2] Afghanistan, where the U.S. Government and people are hugely involved, seems to move backward with every step forward. Clearly, we need to try to examine where the fault lines lie between what the subjects of development want (or do not want) to receive and what those acting in development want to give.

It is useful at the start to distinguish between development as a (cultural and political) *idea*, and development as a human *activity*. The former, as all ideological positions, is subject to interpretation and reinterpretation, and thus to argument and debate. The latter is a matter for organizational analysis.

Development as an activity is a multibillion dollar industry with two objectives: a humanitarian objective—to reduce misery from poverty and lack of modern practices, policies, and technology in those sectors of humanity which currently have not achieved some minimally accepted standard (such as the Millennium Development Goals); and a security objective—to reduce security threats by the have-nots against the haves. As such, development can be seen as one tool in military efforts at post-war stabilization, notably in asymmetric conflicts, e.g., Afghanistan and Iraq.

Analytically, I argue that development as it is conceived of in the West (the primary agent of development) starts with the *systematic, intentional,* and *irreversible* destruction of many features of the to-be-developed society and economy. As Michael Rosberg notes, this is driven by idealism—a poorly explored "social conscience theory"—which is based more on the moral view of the developer than on the identified needs and wants of the developing.[3] This kind of idealism-driven development, and the destruction it wreaks, can be a major cause, and is almost always a contributing cause, to resentment on the part of the to-be-developed when cardinal tenets of their culture are threatened. I demonstrate this argument by reference to both examples and analytical structures. In the last section of this chapter, I return to the issue of the whole of government (WoG): those in developing countries and those in the developed countries, to show how difficult the concept is to operationalize.

DEVELOPMENT AND THE "WHOLE OF GOVERNMENT"

While my major interest is in development, this interest relates to the issue of WoG as well. Starting as result of September 11, 2001 (9/11), American and other governments expressed an interest in, and the need for, a WoG approach to security and to development, in which programs will cross-cut agency and ministerial boundaries,[4] eliminating duplication, ensuring program continuity in the face of intradepartmental budget limitations, and bringing multiple viewpoints to bear. While the need for such coordination and interagency cooperation is palpable, I would argue that they are manifestly impossible: The functional vertical segmentation of governments is not arbitrary, but the result of some fundamental social rules.[5]

It is also worthwhile considering that where either development or government reform are concerned, WoG has two perspectives: the developing donor, and the development recipient; that is, as it may be, the governments of the United States and Afghanistan, or Germany and South Sudan, or Britain and Sierra Leone. Thus utilizing a WoG approach by the donor party needs to be matched by the recipient government as well.

It is with the recipient government(s) that I am concerned here. Since the major thrust of the WoG approach is somewhere within the semantic domains of change, development, and reform, it is on development that I focus most of my attention. In this chapter, I want to highlight and illustrate some of the problems of assuming that applying a WoG approach to development will be effective in the developing countries' governments. Much the same argument could be made about the donor country's government as well. Put bluntly, and somewhat more forcefully, the WoG approach is unlikely to work because there are some fundamental issues that need to be addressed first.

The Normative Paradigm of Development and Its Goals.

The normative paradigm of development (that is, the minimal set of elements that virtually *all* who have thought of as development would consider valid) operates at two distinct clusters of ideas. First, development is a process which has an effect on the wellbeing of individuals. Second, development is a process which has an effect on the wellbeing of the body politic. Ultimately, individual development will enhance political development, and/or political development will enhance individual development.

Beyond those points, development is a contested term. For the dyed-in-the-wool capitalist, development is about promoting and enhancing capitalism in states that have balance of payments deficits, lack industrial capacity, or have low gross national products (GNP). For liberals, development is about changing the entire range of social institutions in order to create social wellbeing at the individual or communal level.[6]

What is worth noting is the disconnect—sometimes by oversight—of the relationship, if any, between *political* development (using the term without prejudice) and *economic* development: The second is somehow supposed to follow once the first has been attained, but the mechanism is obscure.[7] I argue here that a further dimension is also missing: What to this chapter is critical, is the issue of the impact this social tinkering called development, has on essential social institutions. As I show here, this tinkering, however well-meant, has a major effect on often disregarded issues of any given culture. These may appear to be minor (to the onlooker), but of great import to the subject of this activity.

Simplifying the Concept of Development.

What does development actually *do*? I want here to simplify (perhaps over simplify) the development paradigm into a series of propositions:

- Underdevelopment is an economic condition where individuals/groups are unable to enjoy the benefits which individuals/groups in developed countries enjoy.
- These benefits fall into two classes: immediate levels of goods and services, and the ability to sustain that level of goods and services for the long term.
- In practice, development functions in three interrelated institutions: the political (including democratization and the right of choice), security (including adherence to the rule of national law and legally binding law enforcement), and the economic/material (including engaging in economically viable occupations, definite property ownership, and responsible fiscal behavior).
- *Sustaining* development, as well as *attaining* it, requires a level of popular education: political, so that people can identify their rights and work to ensure them those rights; security, so that people can ensure their own and others' security; and economic, so that people will know how to function as economic persons to their best (and thus the collective's) benefit.

- Development agents work to enhance and encourage abilities in those three domains, as well as to ensure that these practices/resources/abilities are sustainable.

Clearly as the causal arrow points, this argument requires some examination of context. As Myrdal notes, development is a total package: one cannot pick and choose, and certainly he feels that if implementation requires major modifications in existing institutions, then so be it.[8] Parenthetically, Marxist development theory would probably make the same argument.

Essentially, classic development therefore: (a) sees a society's institutions as a single whole; and (b) therefore acknowledges, even demands that that whole shift entirely into more developed modern institutional layouts. The results being obvious to the observer, the costs are negligible (to the observer). Here, I want to devote some time to these costs *as they appear to the subjects of development*.

SOME FUNDAMENTAL REALITIES OF HUMAN SOCIETY

The argument I provide here relies heavily on some of the fundamentals of how human societies are organized and, in order to ensure that we are speaking the same language, this section provides a very brief (and somewhat superficial) overview of a way to discuss these fundamentals. I also accept the fact that another social analyst might use different terms and dispute my view. However, the framework presented here remains a powerful means to examine human interactions, and, *inter-alia,* provide some predictive strength to the analysis. I rely heavily for some of this analysis on my predecessors, notably Barbara Myerhoff and Raymond Firth.[9] It is also useful to remember two things about social analysis: First, any kind of social analysis tends to focus on a particular *level of abstraction* for its analytical force. Thus an analysis at the level of very abstract social entities, e.g., ethnic groups and nations, cannot easily be compared to analyses at the level of interpersonal interaction. Second, often the level of analysis is a matter of where the analyst feels most comfortable, not necessarily an abstract or disinterested position. In this section I shall move from a very abstract level to a much more concrete one, endeavoring to state clearly the level dealt with.

Some Theory First: Structure and Organization, Determinacies and Indeterminacies.

For analytic convenience (and because we are unable to deal with the multiplex of meanings, and simultaneity of social activity) we group human activities into institutions: patterned ways that groups of humans have evolved to deal with some fundamental existence problems that all are faced with. This is, however, an analyst's tool: a presentation of reality, and sometimes not an effective one. Firth noted that we can see human institutions as structures (apparently static entities) or organizations (dynamic interactions) according to analytical choice, though it is difficult for mere humans to think of, let alone describe, the simultaneity of these views, somewhat like the difficulty of thinking of light as both particles and waves.[10]

Anthropologists, at least, tend to talk of institutions. Kinship and marriage (the regulation of reproduction and its consequences), politics (the contest for the right to regulate human activities), and economics (the organization of production, exchange, and consumption) among others are all "institutions"—basically, patterned ways of doing things. These have some freedom of play (how one actually goes about ensuring reproduction, for example) but are severely constrained by different societies in many ways (e.g., gay marriage). Institutions therefore have embedded within them processes that preserve the structure, and yet simultaneously have some other processes that create change. Virtually all institutions are dynamic: They change over time.

To examine the fundamental processes of *all* human societies, I want to follow Myerhoff who has argued for what she called the "porridge pot" theory of society.[11] Myerhoff's argument relies on two basic social processes she calls *determinacy* and *indeterminacy*. Determinacies are those processes which build up repertoires of regularity in any individual human or group's behaviors. In essence, these are the norms of which any institution is made up. Determinacies confer a social advantage: They allow individuals to *predict* what other social beings are doing. This is critical: If I extend a hand, I expect it to be shaken. If I drive at 55 mph, it is because I can predict others will do the same, and there will be penalties for those who do not. However, in every society there are processes of indeterminacy operating *simultaneously* with determinacies: You stick out your hand, expecting a similar response; I reach for your wallet. You drive at 55 mph; I drive at 70 and slip by the railway crossing while you wait impatiently. Cumulatively, indeterminacies break down the regularities that determinacies build up, thus bringing about change—somewhat like a pot of porridge that forms lumps (determinacies) until broken down by a spoon (indeterminacies), while other lumps are forming elsewhere.

These two processes happen simultaneously, sometimes in the same social institution, with individuals and groups dynamically working to shore up some parts of their social world, and to destroy other parts. This implies that like a light particle that is also a wave, all social structures are both dynamic and static *and,* constructive and deconstructive at the same time. This perspective allows the observer, at least abstractedly, to tie together the most abstract level of nations, cultures and communities, with the intermediate abstraction of social institutions, and the concrete activities of individuals and their personal networks of association.

In the final analysis, all this sociological verbiage boils down to the acts of individuals. Individuals act, and are acted upon simultaneously, not by institutions nor by social structures, but by other individuals, interacting with them and the material world through many channels simultaneously. Nevertheless, and even though many people will state and believe that they are unique and their activities are *sui generis,* one can clearly identify repetitive patterns in human behaviors. Here, too, one can see that in some instances individuals support the status quo (whatever that might be), in other words, support determinacy processes, and at other times try to destroy it, creating indeterminacy.

Production and Reproduction in the Development Paradigm.

Production (in the larger sense of ensuring the survival of individuals and their society) and *reproduction* (ensuring the survival of a society over time) are the two fundamental human activities upon which all others are based. Production and reproduction are always regulated, with agreed-upon (within the society) degrees of freedom, which may be great or little. For example, development is always associated with engaging and harnessing the whole of a population (not just the government) in development, which in turn implies much about gender equality in access to development benefits. However, as I shall show below, this can pose insurmountable barriers for both development and, ultimately, the whole of a government.

Reproduction is never haphazard, always regulated. As in all forms of reproduction practiced by humans, one can identify two fundamental social rules: (a) No marriage may take place within a socially defined group (otherwise known as the universal incest rule); (b) Men decide (otherwise known as the male domination rule).[12] It is useful to note at the outset that Fox's rules are *not* ideological statements, but *empirical* ones, identifiable in the overwhelming majority of societies we have information about; whether this is a good or bad thing is a different discussion. Each of these statements needs some amplification.

All societies have rules about who is excluded, who is preferred, and who is included in the pool of potential mates for marriage. Prescriptive rules—who is forbidden—tend to be stricter of course. Nevertheless, proscriptive rules can also play a major role, for instance in the Arab world, ensuring that resources are kept within the patrimonial group of brothers. This makes sense notably in a world in which *most* people one comes into contact with can become hostile (often legitimately so, by social rules) for what in other societies might be considered minor transgressions.

All societies also have bias towards the dominance of men. Even in societies such as modern Sweden that *claim* gender equality, a careful analytical scheme would disclose that this is not the case. Thus, in virtually all societies we know, the preferences of men dominate, and it is the male point of view that takes precedence in matters of reproduction.

Pashtun Family and Marriage and the Schooling of Women.

The relationships between men and women in Afghan society are complex, and worthy of study. Here I extract from what those more knowledgeable than I have written into a simple set of propositions:

1. Men control women's fertility absolutely, and treat it as a political (one can create alliances by transferring fertility rights) and economic (one can sell the fertility rights) resource.

2. Women create a risk for men and their reputation when this fertility is not under control.

3. Thus women need to be controlled by men to as great a degree as is feasible.

4. The value of a girl child lies therefore largely in the fertility potential she represents; threats to that potential can have very serious economic and political consequences.

Now, against these, let us consider the possibility of offering women/girls an education—part of essentially *non-negotiable development theory.*[13] Educate a girl child, and an Afghan *wali* (an Islamic term which essentially means the guardian of a minor, including a woman) is faced with a real problem: For a great deal of her time, a girl child *will not be under control*. Conceivably, the education the child receives will allow her to be able to offer additional economic benefits to her allied family and spouse, *but there is no fertility benefit whatsoever*, and it is the issue of fertility that is at stake. In other words, looking at the issue from the Afghan perspective—all risk, no gain. Note that what a *wali* offers is *not* his charge as a person: That plays a minor role in the marriage institution. What he offers is control of her *fertility*—an immutable quality that cannot be improved upon, but given human biology, can be easily threatened.

In theory, of course, one could change the institution. To give a fanciful example from other societies, if proven fertility (having had children) was more valued in Afghan society than total fertility control (including virginity and chastity), female education would be less problematic. But changing the reproduction institution, which is fundamental to Afghan society, would change the entire society radically to the point that it would be a different society.

From the Afghan cultural perspective, the introduction of the discussion about human rights, the defense of women, and the defense of little girls might strike *individual* resonance, but culturally, the efforts to ensure that a man does *not* have his full rights in marriage is an attack on the real fundamentals of cultural life. Not only that, but a quick scan through the development literature would appear, to an unbiased eye, let alone an Afghan one, as truly triumphalistic since fundamental change of a cherished institution (male dominance) is more or less an important sub theme.[14]

Unsurprisingly, as I argue here, the average Afghan individual is very easily able to identify with an anti-developmental perspective, since very early on he is exposed to the idea that this is out to destroy not some superficial cultural practice, but the very bases—political, economic, reproductive and social—of his life.

Cattle Raiding and Marriage in Southern Sudan.

Another example, from a rather different post-conflict development area, is that Southern Sudan is riven by linguistic (which also means cultural) distinctions, with some 400 local languages playing a part in the mosaic. One of the larger people groups within Southern Sudan are the Nuer (about 3/4 million people) divided into several smaller, occasionally competing, sub-groups. Given the natural surroundings (a scrub bush, with shallow soils that do not permit plough agriculture; annual flooding; and high temperatures), the Nuer economy is based largely on cattle (supplemented by some subsistence crops, and more recently, urban labor). The Nuer are polygamous, with wealthy older men having up to several tens of wives. Nuer social structure is a dynamic in which cattle and women play a dominant mutual role as exchange objects. Cattle are raised by men and used by them to purchase wives. The wives produce sons, who, in turn, must produce cattle to buy wives. Men to whom one is related by male descent are critical for survival because aggression is highly valued in Nuer society, and local quarrels and feuds are common, for which one needs as many allies as possible, one's brothers and sons being the best allies. Feuds and quarrels occur for two reasons: the theft of cows (remember, more cows allow for purchase of more wives, and thus for greater authority and power) and the theft of wives (if one is relatively poor in cattle, one can steal a woman; and of course, nonpayment of bride-price leads to quarrels and feuds and is viewed as a form of theft as well). It needs to be emphasized that for the Nuer as for their cultural relatives, the Dinka, the only cattle that can be used for bride-price are cattle that have been raised, or cattle that have been stolen. Bought cattle, from, for example, the proceeds of construction labor, are ineligible.[15]

This dynamic—cattle to wives to sons to more cattle—characterizes Nuer society to an extraordinary degree. The process, in fact, defines who is a "real" Nuer, for example, in contrast to their linguistic relatives the sedentary Shilluk, or to "fishing Nuer" who live mainly on Nile fish.[16] Ecologically speaking, the system is relatively well-balanced, and has allowed the Nuer historical opportunities for dominance throughout central Southern Sudan.

Now, let us consider this through the lens of development. In 2005, a mission from the U.S. 4F Club visited Southern Sudan, and, among their recommendations was the establishment of cattle ranches along the lines (presumably) of the visitors' central and western U.S. heritage. Presumably, monogamy played a part, as did suppression of cattle rustling. Unsurprisingly, this initiative never saw the light of day. We cannot lose track of the idea that *raiding, polygamy, and cattle are an essential part, in fact the defining characteristic, of the Nuer as a people*. So, the question is which elements of Nuer society is one going to "develop"? Because, and this needs to be kept in mind, *any* change in these three major factors will destroy Nuer society—for the better or the worse is irrelevant. From the perspective of the majority of Nuer, these are values worth fighting for.

The Tale of Rinderpest.

As an example of the social and material destructiveness of development, in the 1970s, after much effort, a Swiss charity managed to introduce and implement an inoculation program against rinderpest (a common and deadly cattle disease) into Southern Sudan. The program was largely a success by 1993, notwithstanding the civil war.[17] Rinderpest is an insect borne-disease, particularly prevalent in forested areas. The southern, forested part of Southern Sudan (current Central, Western, and Eastern Equatorial states) has been settled for millennia by farmers, who burn new fields out of the bush every few years. By 2005, however, and continuing to today, these farmers have been under constant pressure by development. In the first instance, swidden farming has a bad reputation among modern agricultural specialists, since it is seen as destructive and inefficient. No less important in the Sudanese context, the forested areas which were of no interest to the transhumant cattle herders—Dinka, Toposa, Nuer, Murle, and others—because of the rinderpest, are now open for exploitation. Development in one area, and the cultural prejudices of the development agencies, have meant that the Bari-speaking and other farmers are, effectively, losing their livelihoods and ways of life. Unsurprisingly, they are somewhat prejudiced against some aspects of development.

IS DEVELOPMENT GOOD FOR HUMAN SOCIETIES? A SUMMARY OF THE OBJECTIONS

I have noted above that for analytical purposes social scientists identify and characterize human societies in the form of regular patterns of activity, which we call institutions. The reality is, of course, that these institutions are merely analytical illusions (or aids, if we want to be charitable). In reality, all institutions intertwine, supporting one another, while at the same time offering individuals and groups within a society means and ways to manipulate the rules: processes of determinacy and indeterminacy.

Is Development Good?

So is development good? Well, that obviously depends on one's perspective (a trite conclusion), but it is worth examining further. Development is a slippery concept, not least because it originates in, and is a child of, Western perceptions. The closest we have ever gotten to a universal (or at least value neutral) definition of development are the Millennium Development Goals (MDG). This is not to say that they are either perfect or unimpeachable, but the MDG at least have the virtue of measurability: They are empirical rather than being ideological. The American idea that development implies "being like us because we are the most developed" and, of course, similar versions from other countries such as the United Kingdom (UK), the former Union of Soviet Socialist Republics (USSR), and the Nordic countries, are highly ideological and must be treated with caution. These ideas represent what Rosberg calls "morals based development."[18] Even the MDG, however, hide within them the seeds of destruction of complex, often finely balanced cultural institutions which we tamper with only to destroy. Provide the Nuer with more cattle than they need, and raiding *increases,* not declines, because bred cattle are plentiful, and lose their appeal. Remove the cattle entirely, and substitute some other productive activity, and, as the Nuer argue, they will no longer be Nuer *and the Nuer are as passionately attached to being Nuer as Americans are to being American.*

Given that: (a) institutions are all fundamentally and deeply intertwined; and that (b) the contest between determinacy and indeterminacy is a constant, development is *inherently* destructive. This would not pose a problem but for the *causes* of determinacy: the need to be able to predict. We all want the convenience of being able to predict the next social move of our social peers. That is our comfort zone, from which we venture only when we can perceive a definite personal advantage. These determinacies are expressed in what we call culture: basically, sets of determined patterns we are used to and feel comfortable with, which we feel will be retained "forever" and within which we can be free to see to our own comfort. We are passionately attached to these cultures, not because they are inherently of value: That is a superficial explanation. We are attached to them because they are so fundamental to our comfort. Development will *inevitably* destroy many aspects of any given developing culture. As such, it will *inevitably* be resisted, because it is *not* possible to pick and choose. Change the economic fundamentals, and the kinship and marital consequences will emerge as well: Change only arises from the ashes.

WHOLE OF GOVERNMENT, CONFLICT MANAGEMENT, AND CONFLICT MANAGERS

What does all of the destruction of development have to do with WoG, conflict, and conflict management? In this section, I will make reference mainly to the "receiving" government (that is, the "underdeveloped") with which I am more familiar, but the same principles can be applied to the donor government and its attempts to institute a WoG approach.

Governments in the Development Game: "Natives" and "Stabilizers."

Governments may not be the best development agents because they have multiple, sometimes conflicting objectives. Consider that a government policy is likely to differ in its priorities from the policies of an external peacekeeping or stabilizing force. In fact, even the *definition* of development may differ quite radically.

Well, what do governments want? Primarily a government wants two things: control over the domain of force, and a steady income to finance its goals. In the modern world, both of these depend highly on ensuring that the government and its state can keep up with the Joneses technologically: The monopoly of force superficially depends on a state's ability to possess armed forces that can outgun any competition, and subsistence economies are losers in the long-run economic sweepstakes. However, technological upkeep, in turn, depends highly on a pyramid of education, social "rationalization," and adaptability to change—all of these constituting ongoing threats to the current order, in other words, these are all processes that bring about *indeterminacy*. As indeterminate processes *whose outcome the average individual cannot foresee*, they are going to be strongly resisted by anyone (which means virtually everyone) who feels out of their comfort zone (that is, out of their ability to predict).

This is true even within government (including its instruments of force: the armed services). Yes, many individuals will feel comfortable with this or the other aspect of a new developmental process, because, at the individual level, *some* individuals are always entrepreneurial and able to find opportunities.[19] However, the vast mass of people exploit only those opportunities which *clearly* benefit them, thus allowing for only a very slow process of breakdown of the "traditional" system. Remember, from each individual's perspective, cheating (i.e., producing indeterminacies) works *only* if everyone else is playing by the rules (i.e., producing determinacy). Radical change causes most individuals to freeze, like rabbits in a headlight: "How can I exploit this opportunity?" becomes "How do I maintain at least my status quo?" Determinacies are adhered to.

It would be surprising not to find this occurring in the armed forces as well. Given, for example, the cases in Afghanistan and Sudan where being armed is a traditional form of activity with clear and known rewards. Armed men will be driven towards following well-known patterns that yield results that can be predicted, and are therefore desirable, rather than taking risks by following untried and untested new paths, such as engaging in peaceful pursuits.

To a lesser or greater degree, this is followed within the civil side of government as well. Government managers (that is, the key personnel for change) are as reluctant to face organizational change as any other managers.[20] Thus while they may subscribe to prevailing policies at least publicly, they are as likely as any other individual to resist them in private. We need therefore to reach, finally, the sinews of the WoG—its people.

Managers in the Development Game: "I'm Exempt, Of Course."

While studies of managers in developing countries often attribute to them a "western" existence,[21] this needs to be taken with caution. Alex Inkeles' very wide study of modernization focused on *attitudes* towards modernization.[22] He pointed out that the concept of modernization is a composite of many elements, in which modern attitudes clash with traditional ones in the same person. In this case, development should be seen as a form of modernization.

It must be kept in mind that government managers are not exempt from social rules. Those responsible for development in a given country are themselves subject to producing both determinacy and indeterminacy: They expect to be able to predict others, while allowing themselves tactical leeway to be unpredictable. However, indeterminacy at this analytical level can be seen to be largely egocentric: "How can *I* take advantage of the situation." *I* in this case do not want the *system* to change, and, in fact, I will resist such change overtly or covertly as the situation requires, since I am familiar with it and its rules. I merely want to exploit it insofar as I can. In other words, while for *some* aspects of development (or in the terms used here, in some institutional clusters) a government employee will be supportive of development, once the fact that development will affect *all* social institutions dawns, he may very well oppose the foreseen changes—violently.

Given this analytical picture, it is hardly surprising that there is resistance to development. It is built into the system. To make things worse, it is built in at both input and output ends. So let us consider output of change for a moment.

Rewards for Development.

What are the rewards for development for the individual government actor/official concerned? One of the major interesting features of both the American and the Chinese Communist systems is the emphasis on financial reward. To quote Deng Xiaoping, "Getting rich is glorious."[23] While there are similarities in the purposes to which riches are put in China and the United States, there are also many differences—something worth considering. So what are the rewards for development?

We have already noted that for governments (a collective illusion we can, nevertheless, view as a single body for a given level of analysis) the keys remain the monopoly of force, and the financial sinews to fulfill objectives, including the monopoly of force. But is this true of the elements that make up government—the "workers in the vineyard"? What rewards do they get?

Primarily, I would argue, the rewards for developing governments' employees—the people who actually do or do not carry out policies decided upon by their superiors—need to be examined very carefully. The first substrate is clearly money—cash, or in other words, a salary. This is far more complex than can be discussed here, since it involves relative rewards, payoffs, perceptions of equity, and other peripheral issues. Crucially, however, the cash itself constitutes only part of the reward. Once the cash is secured, what next? With the exception of a few eccentrics, money is not an inherent reward. It is what can be done with money that causes gratification. A case in point is Somali pirates. One way of identifying a Somali pirate, I have argued, is that they are able at a fairly young age to acquire additional wives: a critical marker for wealth and maturity in Somali society. Similar identifying markers could be found for male Sudanese bureaucrats (multiple wives, cattle herds, farming estates). I imagine one could identify similar features of Afghan bureaucrats who appear "successful" in their own cultures (a large *chaykhana*[24] would certainly be on the list).

It is useful to note that each of these examples is nondevelopmental: Part of the cultural baggage of development is gender equality, and thus monogamy and cattle should be replaced by corporate shares and stocks, and large areas devoted to the entertainment of male guests for political purposes would no doubt offend the idea of equality. The critical point here, however, is that many of the individuals in the countries concerned are *aware* that development may well threaten these coveted rewards. After all, rewards are coveted because they are *scarce*. So while a government agent may support development policies as lip service (one of the array of survival techniques everyone learns) he/she may well be, at the same time, implacably opposed to the implications that development brings, that he/she is aware of, but the outside developer is not. Education of women will threaten the monopoly on fertility (Afghan version) or the ability to participate in cattle exchange and growth (Sudan version). In both cases, for the external developer, the challenge will be to find some way to modify the rewards *which means destroying the old system of rewards, that is, the old cultural values.* Alternatively, as is the case in reality, the outside development agency assumes unthinkingly that higher economic rewards will be used in much the same way, and for the same purposes as he/she would use them, and thus that the reward is not a problem.

CONCLUSIONS AND RECOMMENDATIONS

Putting together what has been said here with the findings of others, notably Gilbert Rist and Rosberg, leads to conclusions at four levels.[25]

1. At the theoretical level of social conscience that motivates a WoG approach to development, there is going to be *fundamental* if unexpressed opposition to the fiat of getting everyone behind the approach.

2. At a slightly lower level of abstraction are Rist's two fundamental arguments: that economic success is bought by the coin of self-definition, and that there is an assumption of growth without limit.[26] Both because of demographics (birth rate) and because there is always a resource limitation, this is not going to happen. *Someone* will always have the short end of the stick.

3. At another, still lower level of abstraction and growing concreteness, is the issue of development as destruction as presented here and the consequent resistance that this causes.

4. Finally, is the power of greed: People in developing areas utilize strategies for survival which, on the whole, are egocentric. When they use cooperative strategies, they do succeed (e.g., Vietnam, China).

I am not a great believer in the unalloyed benefits of development for a number of reasons. Primarily my suspicion is pointed at governments. Notably, the motives for governments, and for the people who make them up, as well as their citizens or subjects, are very different. Nevertheless, development is worthwhile, because of moral and philosophical, as well as material reasons. Like fire, development makes a good servant, but a very bad master. As such, we need to address developing anyone with a great deal of caution. We need to understand first of all that development is not an unalloyed good. In fact, while there are overt individual and collective benefits, these *may well be perceived, by the subjects of development, to be outweighed by negative consequences.*

Second, when we examine the benefits and drawbacks of development, we need to be clear about the level of analysis. What benefits government does not necessarily benefit those in it, and may well be viewed as utterly destructive by Joe Bloggs in the street. This in turn implies that a careful teasing out of the different analytical levels is critical for development to occur with lessened resistance.

Third, and slightly more positively, parsing the perceived benefits and drawbacks allows us also to identify, to some degree, individuals who might support or oppose development. However, and this is a critical point, by-and-large such individuals are those who see some positive benefit to themselves—junior people seeing in change an opportunity to supersede their superiors, or senior officials who foresee economic opportunities in social upheavals, for example in the discontinuity from the previous social and cultural regime, in other words, from indeterminacy.

Such individuals are double-edged swords, as examples from Afghanistan's power structure show.[27]

Critically, therefore, whether one does or does not adopt a WoG approach is a secondary issue, in my opinion. Given that development *is likely to affect all areas of life,* the involvement of the entire governmental structure in development issues is in effect, a tautology. Governments and their structures are essentially at the same time institutions (in government's guise as an arena for political contestation) and an organizational expression of social institutions (economics, socialization, etc.). To take this a step further, insofar as security is linked to development (and we have seen that it is: Development creates resistance for reasons discussed above, and this resistance is often violent), the resistance to development is easily mobilized within government, where the conflict between determinacy and indeterminacy in both inputs and outputs can be at its sharpest, because government agents/functionaries are at a position to do something, not just resist passively.

What *is* crucial is to understand how *within* government structures and organizations inputs and outputs affect individual perceptions and reactions. One needs to assume the following axiom: "Every development activity has both negative and positive consequences." What this means, essentially, is that a clear and detailed mapping of development activities—what is known more-or-less systematically as a "do no harm" approach—needs to be carried out for all levels of a development activity. Note, for example, the provision of water sources for households in a settlement—a development activity par excellence.[28] However, what role does the traditional (highly polluted, distant, inconvenient) water system play? Are you affecting ownership? What about the time spent (by women, one might add) on getting water, or the social exchanges at the well side which might be crucial for social cohesion?

There is no cut and dried formula for assessing whether there will be support or opposition to development as a whole (notwithstanding attempts to implement a "no harm" strategy). What can be examined with a high degree of validity is the potential opposition to or support for specific projects. This requires:

1. Carefully examining the social dynamics of people who might be affected by the project for the short and the long term.

2. Assessing the benefits and disadvantages *in their terms*.

3. Negotiating strategies which will mitigate deleterious features to those who will suffer them.

Finally, only if the development agent is able to demonstrate clearly and in an unbiased fashion that: (a) The development activity, whatever it is, outweighs doing nothing; *and* (b) that there are sufficient resources (including that most difficult to estimate—long-term developer willpower); *and* (c) that there are clear indicators of when to stop—only then may it be necessary and wise to force development through.

Final Words.

I believe I have highlighted three major issues in this chapter: First, development is a complex activity that *can be* and *must be* analyzed in great detail and at many levels to ensure success rather than failure. To me, success means that the human condition—perhaps measured grossly by the MDG, perhaps using other measures—be improved *for individuals*. This is not wishy-washy liberalism, but a cold-blooded recognition that more complex human structures are emergent properties of smaller atoms representing individuals, who, as individuals as well as in the collective, can make or break development, and that greed trumps morality over time and space.

Second, governments are not where it is at. Assuming that the locus of success, in Afghanistan or anywhere else is at the governmental level is heading for failure. Governments are made up of people, who may be simultaneously enthused by one aspect of development and disgusted by another; be honest with personal monies and relationships and corrupt with public funds; and utilize and excuse violence while preaching peace and tolerance. And this may be just *one* person.

Third, development agencies repeatedly focus on *their own* problems, not the problems of the subjects of development. They *may* be aware of the problems of their colleagues in other departments or programs within their own government while viewing these simultaneously as working in the same direction and as competitors for funds, posts, and kudos. In a similar vein, the solutions to underdevelopment are, more often than not, lazy solutions. Rather than doing proper spadework, developers apply tried-and-tested solutions *from their own experience* to problems with superficial similarity in other contexts; and they screw up.

Whether one involves part of government or the whole of government to solve problems in, say, Afghanistan, would make, in my opinion, very little difference. Analytically-speaking, what has been done is merely to look for the issues and solutions *at the same level of analysis*. Whereas, the real problem, and the real solution (however lengthy, difficult, time and treasure-consuming it is) lies at a different analytical level entirely.

REFERENCES

Alatas, S. F. 1997. "Islam And Counter Modernism: Towards Alternative Development Paradigms," in Masudul Choudhury, ed. *Islamic political economy in capitalist-globalization: An agenda for change*. Kuala Lumpur, Malaysia: Utusan Publications & Distributors. International Project on Islamic Political Economy Universiti Sains Malaysia.

Ashkenazi, Michael. 2009. "Made in the Developed World: Piraterie, Fischfang und Giftmüll in Somalias Gewässern" [Made in the Developed World: Piracy, Fish Theft, Waste Disposal in Somali Waters], in P. Hippler *et al.* eds., *Friedensgutachten,* Berlin, Germany: Lit Verlag, 2009, pp. 149-160.

Bailey, R. G. 1989. "An appraisal of the fisheries of the Sudd wetlands, River Nile, southern Sudan." *Aquaculture Research*, Vol. 20, No. 1, pp. 79–89.

Bell, Gerald D. 1967. "Determinants of Span of Control." *American Journal of Sociology*, Vol. 73, No. 1, pp. 100-109.

Blaut, J. M. 1973. "The Theory of Development." *Antipode*, Vol. 2, No. 5, pp. 22-26.

Firth, Raymond. 2005. *Elements of social organization*. London, UK: Routledge.

Fox, R. 1983. *Kinship and marriage: an anthropological perspective*. Cambridge, UK: Cambridge University Press.

Giustozzi, Antonio. 2003. *Respectable Warlords? The Politics of State-Building in Post-Taleban Afghanistan*. Crisis States Programme Development Research Centre Working Paper Series 1, No. 33.

Gleitsmann, Brett A., Margaret M. Kroma, and Tammo Steenhuis. 2007. "Analysis of a rural water supply project in three communities in Mali: Participation and Sustainability." *Natural Resources Forum 31*, pp. 142-150.

Inkeles, Alex, and D. H. Smith. 1970. "The fate of personal adjustment in the process of modernization." *Journal of Comparative Sociology*, Vol. 11, No. 2, pp. 81-114.

Inkeles, Alex, and David H. Smith. 1983. *Exploring individual modernity*. New York: Columbia University.

Kay, G. B. 1975. *Development and underdevelopment: A Marxist analysis*. London, UK: Macmillan.

Keren, Michael, and David Levhari. 1979. "The Optimum Span of Control in a Pure Hierarchy." *Management Science*, Vol. 25, No. 11, pp. 1162-1172.

Korten, David, with Frances Korten. 1972. *Planned change in a traditional society: Psychological problems of modernization in Ethiopia*. New York: Praeger.

Kurtenbach, Sabine, and Matthias Seifert. 2010. "Development Cooperation after War and Violent Conflict—Debates and Challenges." INEF Reports 100/2010. Duisburg, Germany: University of Duisburg-Essen.

Makhoul, Jihad. 1999. "Development from Below: An Exploratory Study of the Concept and Process of Development From Lay People's Point of View." University of Wollongong Thesis Collection. Wollongong, New South Wales, Australia: University of Wollongong.

Moghadam, Valentine M. 1992. "Patriarchy and the Politics of Gender in Modernising Societies: Iran, Pakistan And Afghanistan." *International Sociology*, Vol. 7, No. 1, March 1, 1992, pp. 35 -53.

Myerhoff, Barbara. 1977. "Secular ritual: Forms and meaning." Pp. 3-25 in S. F. Moore and B. Myerhoff, *Secular ritual*. Assen, The Netherlands: Van Gorcum.

Normile, Dennis. 2008. "Rinderpest: Driven to Extinction." *Science*, Vol. 319, No. 5870, pp. 1601-1609.

Obeid, R. A. 1990. "Islamic Theory of Human Development." *The Encyclopedia of Human Development*. Chicago, IL: Pergamon.

Piderit, Sandy Kristin. 2000. "Rethinking Resistance and Recognizing Ambivalence: A Multidimensional View of Attitudes toward an Organizational Change." *The Academy of Management Review*, Vol. 25, No. 4, pp. 783-794.

Richards, Alan. 2003. "Modernity and Economic Development: The 'New' American Messianism." *Middle East Policy*, Vol. 10, No. 39, pp. 56-78.

Rist, Gilbert. 1997. *The History of Development*. Cape Town, South Africa/London, UK: University of Cape Town Press/Zed Books.

Rosberg, Michael. 2005. *The Power of Greed: Collective action in international development*. Edmonton, Alberta, Canada: University of Alberta Press.

Tavakolian, Bahram. 1984. "Women and Socioeconomic Change among Sheikhanzai Nomads of Western Afghanistan." *Middle East Journal*, Vol. 38, No. 3, pp. 433-453.

Torres, Carlos C. 1972. "The Managerial Entrepreneur: Necessary Catalyst for Development." *Philippine Sociological Review*, Vol. 20, No. 4, pp. 380-384.

UNGA 2000. Resolution adopted by the General Assembly 55/2. United Nations Millennium Declaration. New York: United Nations.

Williamson, Oliver E. 1967. "Hierarchical Control and Optimum Firm Size." *The Journal of Political Economy*, Vol. 75, No. 2, pp. 123-138.

ENDNOTES - CHAPTER 4

1. Gunnar Myrdal, "What is Development?" *Journal of Economic Issues*, Vol. 8, No. 4, 1973, pp. 729-736.

2. Alan Richards, "Modernity and Economic Development: The 'New' American Messianism," *Middle East Policy*, Vol. 10, No. 39, 2003, pp. 56-78.

3. Michael Rosberg, *The Power of Greed: Collective action in international development*, Edmonton, Alberta, Canada: University of Alberta Press, 2005.

4. Tom Christensen and Per Laegried, "The Whole of Government Approach to Public Sector Reform," *Public Administration Review*, November/December 2007, pp. 1059-1066.

5. To consider the span-of-control issue in hierarchical organizations, see Gerald D. Bell, "Determinants of Span of Control," *American Journal of Sociology*, Vol. 73, No. 1, 1967, pp. 100-109; Michael Keren and David Levhari, "The Optimum Span of Control in a Pure Hierarchy," *Management Science*, Vol. 25, No. 11, 1979, pp. 1162-1172; Oliver E. Williamson, "Hierarchical Control and Optimum Firm Size," *The Journal of Political Economy*, Vol. 75, No. 2, 1967, pp. 123-138.

6. There are, of course, other definitions. For an Islamic definition, see S. F. Alatas, *Islam And Counter Modernism: Towards Alternative Development Paradigms,* in Masudul Choudhury, ed., *Islamic political economy in capitalist-globalization: An agenda for change,* Kuala Lumpur, Malaysia: Utusan Publications & Distributors, 1997; International Project on Islamic Political Economy, Universiti Sains Malaysia; M. S. Salleh, in *ibid*. For a Marxist definition, see G. B. Kay, *Development and underdevelopment: A Marxist analysis*, London, UK: Macmillan, 1975; among others.

7. See Rosberg for a detailed discussion of this particular disconnect.

8. Myrdal.

9. Barbara Myerhoff, "Secular ritual: Forms and meaning," S. F. Moore and B. Myerhoff, eds., *Secular ritual*, Assen, The Netherlands: Van Gorcum, 1997, pp. 3-25; Raymond Firth, *Elements of social organization*, London, UK: Routledge, 2005.

10. Firth.

11. Myerhoff.

12. R. Fox, *Kinship and marriage: an anthropological perspective*, Cambridge, UK: Cambridge University Press, 1983.

13. See United Nations Security Council (UNSC) Resolution 1325, S/RES/1325 (2000); and United Nations General Assembly (UNGA) 2000 Resolution adopted by the General Assembly 55/2, "United Nations Millennium Declaration."

14. Lauryn Oates, *Taking Stock Update: Afghan Women and Girls Five Years On*, London, UK: Womankind Worldwide, 2006.

15. Sharon E. Hutchinson, *Nuer Dillemas: Coping with Money, War, and the State*, Berkeley, CA: University of California Press, 1998.

16. R. G. Bailey, "An appraisal of the fisheries of the Sudd wetlands, River Nile, southern Sudan," *Aquaculture Research*, Vol. 20, No. 1, 1989, pp. 79–89.

17. Dennis Normile, "Rinderpest: Driven to Extinction," *Science*, Vol. 319, No. 5870, 2008, pp. 1601-1609.

18. Rosberg.

19. Sidney M. Greenfield, Arnold Strickon, and Robert T. Aubey, *Entrepreneurs in Cultural Context*, Albuquerque: University of New Mexico Press, 1979.

20. Sandy Kristin Piderit, "Rethinking Resistance and Recognizing Ambivalence: A Multidimensional View of Attitudes Toward an Organizational Change," *The Academy of Management Review*, Vol. 25, No. 4, 2000, pp. 783-794.

21. Carlos C. Torres, "The Managerial Entrepreneur: Necessary Catalyst for Development," *Philippine Sociological Review*, Vol. 20, No. 4, 1972, pp. 380-384.

22. Alex Inkeles and D. H. Smith, "The fate of personal adjustment in the process of modernization," *Journal of Comparative Sociology*, Vol. 11, No. 2, 1970, pp. 81-114; Alex Inkeles and David H. Smith, *Exploring Individual Modernity*, New York: Columbia University, 1983.

23. Otto Schell, *To Get Rich is Glorious: China in the 80s*, New York: Pantheon Books, 1984. Though there is no direct evidence, the quote is attributed to Deng.

24. In gender-segregated Afghan society where women of a household are not allowed to come into contact with male guests, hospitality is conducted in a *chaykhana* (tea house) which every influential man (or group of brothers) builds to entertain male guests and as a demonstration of wealth and prestige. The larger and more elaborate the *chaykhana*, the more the owner is claiming social and political ascendancy.

25. Gilbert Rist, *The History of Development*, Cape Town, South Africa/London, UK: University of Cape Town Press/Zed Books, 1997; Rosberg.

26. Rist.

27. Antonio Giustozzi, *Respectable Warlords? The Politics of State-Building in Post-Taleban Afghanistan*, Crisis States Programme Development Research Centre Working Paper Series Vol. 1, No. 33, 2003.

28. Brett A. Gleitsmann, Margaret M. Kroma, and Tammo Steenhuis, "Analysis of a rural water supply project in three communities in Mali: Participation and Sustainability," *Natural Resources Forum 31*, 2007, pp. 142-150.

PART II

CHAPTER 5

WHERE DOES WHOLE OF GOVERNMENT MEET WHOLE OF SOCIETY?

Lisa Schirch

In response to the challenges in Afghanistan and Iraq, top U.S. military and political leaders elevated the importance of stabilization activities such as development, called for strengthened civilian capacities, and put more resources toward civil-military cooperation. The U.S. Government is ramping up efforts to create this whole of government (WoG) approach. This chapter argues that WoG is not enough. Stabilization and security require a "whole of society" or comprehensive approach including the interests and perspectives of diverse sectors of civil society.

Research for this paper included five focus group dialogues between 140 people, including equal numbers of military personnel from U.S. and International Security Assistance Forces in Afghanistan, staff of civil society organizations in the United States and Afghanistan, and university professors and nongovernmental organizations (NGOs) working on civil-military relations across Africa and Asia. The research took place between 2010 and 2011. The research project was led by the author of this chapter, the director of the university-based program called 3P Human Security, and a partnership exploring peace building policy at Eastern Mennonite University. Co-sponsors of the dialogues included the University of Notre Dame, U.S. Institute of Peace, National Defense University, Peacekeeping and Stability Operations Institute at the U.S. Army War College, and the International Security Assistance Forces in Afghanistan. The research dialogues explored perceptions of commonalities; differences; tensions; and potentials for collaboration, cooperation, and communication between military and civil society personnel.

A comprehensive approach, according to U.S. military stability operations doctrine,[1] integrates cooperative efforts of the departments and agencies of the U.S. Government, intergovernmental agencies and NGOs, multinational partners, and private sector entities such as civil society organizations (CSOs) to achieve unity of effort toward a shared goal. But in this comprehensive approach, civilian government, civilian contractors, CSOs, and the civilian public are very different kinds of civilians, each requiring a different form of relationship and communication with military forces. The intense challenges of coordinating government civilians with military personnel and the increasing use of civilian contractors confuses and overshadows the distinct nature of how an independent civil society relates to military forces and plays important roles in democratization, good governance, stability, and peace. The current WoG approach ignores a large part of the equation necessary for peace and security, how government and military forces will relate to local and international civil society efforts related to development and peace.

Based on a series of five dialogues between civil society and European and U.S. Government and military personnel, this chapter provides an orientation to the perceptions, tensions, and opportunities between civil society organizations and government and military personnel in conflict-affected regions.[2] Current tensions between government and military personnel on one hand and many civil society actors on the other, make it impossible to achieve a comprehensive approach. While many CSOs play important roles in peace and security, they are best able to play these roles when they are independent from government and military forces. A whole of society approach recognizes the key roles civil society plays in building security from the ground up and gives civil society space and independence to play these roles without being tightly coordinated with government or military forces. A comprehensive approach that respects the independent roles of civil society is most likely to enable their contributions to stability and security. This chapter makes the case for a more robust conception of civil society, a better understanding of historic civil society-military tensions, and a set of recommendations to address these tensions.

MILITARY STABILIZATION EFFORTS AND CIVIL SOCIETY

U.S. military personnel increasingly conduct humanitarian, development, and peace building activities to achieve stabilization effects under a new Department of Defense Directive[3] that puts stabilization on par with warfighting. In this new emphasis on stabilization activities, military forces use activities frequently referred to as "winning hearts and minds" (WHAM) or "quick impact projects" (QIPs)[4] to achieve a variety of impacts related to their stabilization mission. Military personnel listed the following goals for such activities.

- Functions of Military-Led Development for Stabilization:
  - Address Drivers of Instability: to address perceived root causes of violence. For exam-

ple, developing job creation programs such as rebuilding factories or large public works projects to address unemployment.

- Win Loyalty of Local Population for Local Government: to gain support of local populations for U.S. and Coalition efforts to support the local government.
- Win Loyalty of Local Elites/Host Nation Support: to supply local elites with public goods such as humanitarian aid, schools, or bridges so as to increase and extend the state's local legitimacy and authority.
- Gain Access/Information: to provide an opportunity to gain access to and information about local populations.
- Force Protection/Undermine Insurgent Recruitment: to convince local populations of U.S. military goodwill, and reduce their incentive to attack military forces.
- Humanitarian Access: to provide humanitarian assistance in insecure areas where the United Nations (UN) and NGOs are not able, as per Geneva Conventions.[5]

Historically, military strategy advised on how to "pacify" civil society. Today, in contrast, *building* civil society is a key element in reconstruction and stabilization strategies. Military leaders list "building civil society" and "local ownership" as important elements in their stabilization strategies and seek NGOs as implementing partners to carry out these projects with government or military funds. The North Atlantic Treaty Organization (NATO) civil-military cooperation (CIMIC) policy states: "The immediate purpose of CIMIC is to establish and maintain the full cooperation of the NATO commander and the civilian authorities, organizations, agencies, and population within a commander's area of operations in order to allow him to fulfill his mission."[6] Current U.S. counterinsurgency guidance identifies empowering local populations to interact effectively with their own government as key.[7]

But many CSOs do not want military or government representatives to call them or use them as "force multipliers" since they believe this approach makes them soft targets for armed opposition groups. Many CSOs conducting humanitarian aid, development, and peace building vehemently oppose military involvement in these activities, and some are withdrawing from all contact with military personnel. Many claim that military efforts in these activities more often undermine rather than complement efforts by civil society in places like Afghanistan.[8] Residual military references to more widespread "population control and pacification" as well as the metaphor of "human terrain" continue to raise suspicions, misunderstandings, or confusion of military objectives by CSOs.[9]

Furthermore, CSO research calls for examining the underlying assumptions about and effectiveness of QIP and WHAM efforts.[10] Civil society organizations claim some stabilization activities using humanitarian and development programs endanger their safety; undermine sustainable development; are not cost-effective; and lead to unintended, counterproductive effects.[11] While military personnel focus on short-term, quick-impact relief and development efforts to reduce immediate national security threats, CSOs generally take a long-term, relationship-based approach. Civilians do not yet have the capacity to coordinate massive humanitarian relief efforts and acknowledge there may be a temporary role for the military in extreme cases or in situations where military capacity to rebuild factories and roads is beyond the scope of any CSO. However, very little research or consultation mechanisms exist to help deconflict military stabilization from CSO peace and development work.

TOWARDS A BROADER CONCEPTION OF CIVIL SOCIETY ORGANIZATIONS

While there is growing interest in a comprehensive approach that includes partnerships with civil society, a lack of knowledge of and antagonism toward civil society pose challenges to this approach. In Iraq and Afghanistan, the U.S. WoG developed programs to rebuild the Iraqi and Afghan *states*, but largely neglected local society leaders working on development and peace in these countries. The overwhelming efforts to achieve some semblance of a WoG approach meant personnel focused more on internal coordination with other U.S. civilians or military personnel and devoted relatively less energy to listening closely to and working with local civil society.

This approach fundamentally misunderstood and devalued the importance of local civil society and the importance of having local consent and cooperation in efforts to build a stable and democratic country in Iraq and Afghanistan. An active local civil society is an indicator of a functioning and democratic state. CSOs work both in partnership with the state to complement and supplement its capacity and in oversight of the state to hold it accountable for its responsibilities and transparent governance.[12] Speculatively, without an active and strong civil society pushing for accountability in the United States, for example, there would likely be a much greater level of corruption. The same is true also for Iraq, Afghanistan, and beyond.

CSOs are groups of citizens not in government that organize themselves on behalf of some public interest. CSOs include religious and educational groups, media, community-based organizations (CBOs), business and trade associations, traditional and indigenous structures, sports associations, musicians, artists, and more. CSOs conduct a wide variety of activities including humanitarian aid, economic development, health, agriculture, human rights, conflict resolution, participatory governance, and security sector reform, as well as disarmament, demobilization, reintegration, and fostering moderation and coexistence. Some CSOs contribute to a comprehensive approach to countering extremism and terrorism by conducting conflict assessments, providing aid, development, and deradicalization to vulnerable groups, helping reconcile divided groups, and fostering participatory governance and security sector reform.

NGOs are a type of CSO. There are several types of NGOs: humanitarian, religious, developmental, human rights, research, environmental and peace building. There are both local NGOs (LNGOs) and international NGOs (INGOs). Many NGOs hold several mandates. NGOs must meet specific legal requirements for organizational oversight and accountability.

In the five dialogues that were researched for this chapter, military personnel shared their concerns and perceptions of civil society organizations, especially INGOs who many saw as naïve, lacking patriotism, self-righteous, illegitimate, or corrupt. CSO challenges mirror those found in the state itself; there are incapable and corrupt CSOs operating in the midst of legitimate CSOs. Some CSOs also exacerbate conflict and violence by failing to recognize complex local dynamics. CSOs also experience limitations in their ability to maintain consistent funding due to donors' shifting priorities, evaluate their work in complex settings with multiple variables, and deal with growing government repression restricting CSO activities. Those CSOs that work on peace building are currently threatened with imprisonment if members communicate with groups like the Taliban or insurgent groups in Iraq, even if the goal of the communication is to move the group away from violence.[13]

The dialogues illustrate that it is important for military and government personnel to build relationships with diverse civil society leaders from both the local society and INGOs operating in the country. Civil society has no single representative, and CSOs do not agree on all issues. For-profit entities and nonprofit NGOs conflict over the missions and motivation guiding their work. LNGOs and INGOs often differ in their long-term commitment to the local context. Local CSOs' strengths lie in their cultural, linguistic, and socio-political knowledge of and long-term commitment to the local context. International CSOs' strengths lie in their technical knowledge, capacity building, broader resources, experience across contexts, and ability to advocate to international policymakers. INGOs often hire talented local staff at salaries higher than local government or CSOs can afford. This can create parallel governmental structures that undermine local capacity. International CSOs and the military both increasingly articulate the goal of "local ownership," and both struggle to operationalize it by involving local people in the upfront assessment and design of programs.[14]

One of the primary tensions between government, military, and civil society members in the dialogues was the distinction between CSOs acting as government contractors or as independent partners. Most CSOs make a distinction between the nonprofit work they do, motivated by the humanitarian values and principles detailed in Figure 5-1, and for-profit contractors who exist to help the state carry out its mission. CSOs assert that they are independent, impartial, and even neutral in the way they interact with communities, addressing human needs and working with communities to achieve locally-driven development and peace efforts to improve their lives. Often, these are not in contradiction with government plans. But in the midst of a war, development projects become politicized, and it can be difficult for CSOs to work with military and government funds and projects. CSOs assert that their space to operate independently from government and the military is shrinking, with more armed actors targeting CSOs who collaborate with government and military counterinsurgency plans. CSOs find themselves as the "soft targets" of this soft power approach where CSOs are the "force multipliers" and "implementing partners" of government-designed projects. They lament the loss of "humanitarian space," as defined by International Humanitarian Law (IHL), which refers to the ability to pursue humanitarian missions without fear of attack and while maintaining independence, impartiality, and freedom of movement. The term does not refer to physical space but to the clarity of civilian roles.

Humanitarian Imperative: to save lives, alleviate suffering, and uphold dignity.

Independence: to make decisions, program plans, and strategies free from political goals.

Impartiality: to provide resources regardless of the identity of those suffering.

Partial to Human Rights: to work in support of the human rights of all people.

Neutrality: to not take sides in armed struggles.

Do no harm: to avoid harming others intentionally or unintentionally.

Accountability: to consult and be accountable to local people and long-term sustainability.

Figure 5-1. Principles of Civil Society Humanitarian, Development, and Peace Building.[15]

Many CSO efforts follow a set of principles aimed to reduce human suffering and increase the quality of life. Often termed "humanitarian principles," many also apply to CSOs involved in development and peace building. Not all CSOs follow these principles. Military personnel interviewed for this project expressed confusion over the definitions of independence, impartiality, and neutrality in the dialogues that informed this chapter. Many perceived CSO claims to neutrality as insincere since many CSOs accept government funds. But CSOs in the dialogues insisted they can both follow their principles and accept funds where a shared goal exists and that taking these funds does not mean that CSOs agree with all government policy or are government agents. CSOs make a distinction between broadly supporting good governance and development but remaining politically independent and not supporting a specific government or political party.

TENSIONS BETWEEN HUMAN SECURITY AND NATIONAL SECURITY

In conflict-affected regions, also known as "non-permissive settings," key tensions and differences between CSOs and the U.S. military and government center on how they define and pursue security. All actors see the need for stability and security. But when asked "stability for whom and for what purpose?" their perceptions diverge. A whole of society comprehensive approach requires first getting agreement on the goals of stability missions. This requires addressing the tensions between two different security paradigms.

A "human security" paradigm emphasizes the safety of individuals and communities. It recognizes the interdependence between shared security threats facing people around the world. Human security includes civilian protection, fostering stable, citizen-oriented legitimate governments with participatory democracy, human rights, human development, and peace building. It requires a locally led, bottom-up approach including civil society and local government that works, when necessary, with civilian-led, legitimate, multilateral actors.

"National security" paradigms, on the other hand, traditionally prioritize political and economic interests of the state deemed central to the nation's survival or way of life. The 2010 *National Security Strategy of the*

United States also names key U.S. values in freedom, human rights, and democracy.[16] For example, the narrative of national security interests harnessed both economic and humanitarian dimensions when the uprising in Libya threatened supply from Libyan oil fields at the same time as Gaddhafi's forces used brutal repression of Libyan citizens. But in other places, such as the early days of the uprising in Egypt, U.S. policymakers cited U.S. national interests in stability, even though Egyptian citizens were calling for the ousting of the current regime. This illustrated the tensions between U.S. national interests and the human security of those abroad.

Some military and CSO leaders think human security and national security need not contradict and, in fact, often overlap. These leaders want military services to focus on population-centric security.[17] Human security and national security often do overlap; transnational threats from natural disasters, diseases, trafficking of humans, weapons proliferation, extremist groups, and drug trafficking challenge both national security and human security. But it is not clear which takes precedence in situations like the people's movement for democracy in Egypt or Nigeria when U.S. values in democracy and freedom conflict with U.S. economic and geopolitical interests. With wider consultation, the two approaches could better complement each other.

But there are also other questions of legitimacy and consent. Both local and international CSOs question the legitimacy of security missions, national or international, when military forces act without the consent of local populations, and when no legally enforceable mechanism exists to hold forces accountable to legitimate local political decisionmaking bodies. CSOs cite a long legacy of military forces acting against the interest of local citizens to achieve access to resources or geo-political gains. Greater consultation with CSOs before and during military interventions could help achieve greater legitimacy, consent, and collaboration on human security goals.

Yet another tension is civilian casualties inflicted in enemy centric warfare. The U.S. Government gives military services the authority to use both kinetic (violent) and nonkinetic (nonviolent) means to detect, deter, and destroy an enemy. U.S. military actions are subject to international laws such as the Geneva Convention that include provisions to do the least amount of harm and reduce civilian casualties. Counterinsurgency emphasizes population-centric security, focusing on the safety of local citizens. Many CSOs focus exclusively on human security and make explicit commitments to do no harm. Civilian casualties and human rights violations increase CSO-military tensions and highlight the tensions between a human security and national security approach.

CIVIL SOCIETY AND THE COMPREHENSIVE APPROACH

Any comprehensive approach or unity of effort requires unity of understanding and unity of mission. Local CSOs often complain that international actors do not take the time to consult with local civil society to discuss local social, political, and economic factors. They balk at military human terrain teams and complain that the "we know best" attitude ignores democratic principles and the will and capacity of local CSOs to provide cultural advice. Military personnel on the other hand, may wish to consult CSOs, but have no way of identifying whom they should consult. Underfunded and understaffed U.S. Agency for International Development (USAID) offices are also often unaware of local NGO capacity. The comprehensive approach cannot have a unity of effort including CSOs until there is a shared understanding of the causes driving conflict and violence and a transparency of where national security interests and human security overlap and where they do not.

CSOs see communication, not integration, as necessary for a comprehensive approach. Many CSOs resist terms that name them as "force multipliers" or requests for them to "coordinate" with or "implement" a mission and strategy perceived as different from their own. However many CSOs *do* recognize the benefits of policy dialogue and communication with government and military personnel. Yet few consultation structures exist to engage with those CSOs willing to provide policy advice, share conflict assessments, or discuss overlapping human security goals (see Figure 5-2).

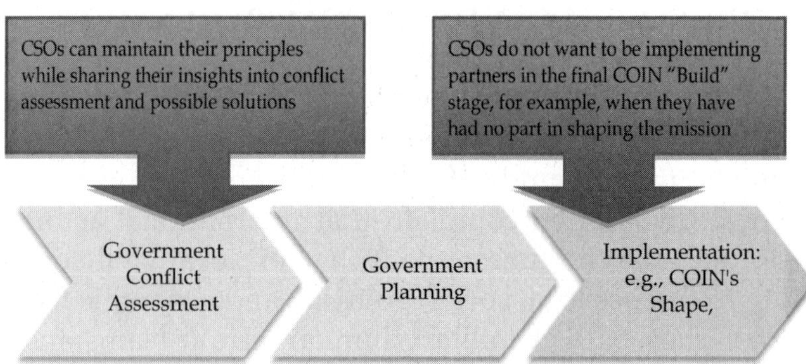

Figure 5-2. Consultation Structure.

MECHANISMS FOR CIVIL SOCIETY-MILITARY RELATIONS

Civil society-military relations differ according to the local context. In many countries, civilian governments control the military. In others, there is no democracy, and the military controls the government. Context, history, and each specific mission shape civil society-military relations.

Humanitarian CSOs identify a spectrum of civil-military relationships that exist at the operational level (see Figure 5-3). The type of CSO-military relationship depends on whether missions align, or there is sufficient humanitarian space for CSOs to maintain their principles.[18] The first category, "curtail presence" refers to situations (such as during the height of the Iraq war) when civil society-military relations disappear and it becomes impossible for CSOs to operate in the same space as armed personnel because of a lack of security and humanitarian space. The other categories, defined by the UN Office for the Coordination of Humanitarian Affairs (OCHA), represent a range of levels of contact or communication between representative CSOs and military personnel. Some nonhumanitarian CSOs also use these categories to decide on their level of interaction with military personnel.

Curtail Presence	Where it becomes impossible for CSOs to operate safely, international CSOs may pull out and local CSOs may go into hiding.
Coexistence/ Communication	Where CSOs, government and military operate in the same space but their missions do not align, only basic communication on logistical details takes place.
Coordination	Where CSOs, government and military missions partially align, there may be some basic coordination to promote CSO core values in human security.
Cooperation	Where CSOs, government and military missions partially or fully align, there may be collaboration on joint projects, particularly in disaster relief or demobilization, disarmament, and reintegration/reconciliation (DDR).

Figure 5-3. Operational Level Civil-Military Relationships.

CSO-military communication happens informally and formally. Where there is no coordinating body, groups coordinate informally when working in the same area, or groups coordinate via "Heineken diplomacy" as individual people build relationships over an informal drink in a public bar. **Coordination by command** refers to some type of government Civil Military Operations Center (CMOC) or international coordinating agency (e.g., UN OCHA) that has legitimacy through formal authority, through the rewards for being coordinated (e.g., funding) or the punishments for not following commands (e.g., denial of access to certain areas or refugee camps). Given CSO humanitarian principles of independence, coordination by command has not worked in places like Afghanistan, Haiti, or Rwanda. More often, there is a degree of **coordination by consensus** when a recognized coordination body builds consensus among diverse actors to work in ways that complement rather than conflict. (See Figure 5-4.)

In Rwanda, the United Nations Rwanda Emergency Office (UNREO) successfully led coordination by consensus. Co-leaders from UN and NGO backgrounds were able to facilitate participatory style of meetings in a neutral location separate from UN military offices.

In Ghana, CSOs, government, and security forces coordinated rapid response to potential violence via a "National Architecture for Peace." During the 2008 elections, civil society leaders mediated between political candidates to deescalate impending election-related violence.

In the Philippines, Filipino military leaders attended training at a civil society-led peace building institute on negotiation, mediation, and peace processes. Military leaders then asked for a peace building training program for thousands of military personnel.

In Thailand, civil society worked with the military to write the national security policy for the southern border provinces from 1999 to 2003. The process of developing this strategy together changed how top military leaders saw their role in supporting a human security agenda.

In Afghanistan, the U.S. State Department and International Security Assistance Forces (ISAF) in Afghanistan have a staff person with the title "NGO Liaison." The ISAF NGO Liaison helped build momentum around a successful CSO pilot police program to improve sector security reform (SSR) and police-community relations.

In the United States, the Department of Homeland Security (DHS) Office for Civil Rights and Civil Liberties consults with a group of approximately 20 Arab, Muslim, Sikh, South Asian, and Somali community leaders. DHS draws on this group for crisis rapid response phone consultations, for broad community consultations to identify concerns and brainstorm solutions, and to develop DHS cultural competency.

Figure 5-4. Examples of Coordination and Cooperation Models.

AN AGENDA FOR CIVIL SOCIETY-MILITARY DIALOGUE ON HUMAN SECURITY

As part of this research, a year-long set of five dialogues between local civil society, international NGOs, U.S. military forces, and U.S. Government personnel, identified an agenda for addressing the tensions preventing and opportunities for improving civil society-military/government partnerships in a comprehensive approach. These included developing a research agenda, discussing options for operational mechanisms, training, joint work on budget and legislative issues, and a look at a longer-term human security commission to continue to build a more effective whole of society approach that can help overcome some of the shortcomings of the more limited WoG approach identified in this chapter. This chapter closes with some concrete recommendations for addressing the obstacles to a comprehensive whole of society approach advocated here.

Research.

1. The Relationship Between "Security" and "Development." A wide array of research demonstrates an association between low levels of development and the likelihood of violent conflict. Yet the underlying assumption that development contributes to stabilization and security is not yet proven. CSO efforts in war zones over many decades have often had little impact on conflict dynamics. Research suggests that harnessing development programs for stabilization and counterinsurgency goals is often counterproductive, endangering and undermining long-term development and peace building, wasting development funds, and inadvertently fueling both corruption and insurgency.[19] Local CSOs ask: "Do they think we're stupid?" suggesting that local people tend to see through simplistic hearts and minds programs.[20] During interviews conducted for this project, military personnel, on the other hand, cite specific positive outcomes from their hearts and minds QIPs, though to date it is difficult to find research documenting these outcomes. Future research should examine specifically *the complex relationship between development and security and if and how development contributes to either short-term stabilization or longer-term human security.*

2. Integration vs. Civil Society Space. Many development actors argue that development best contributes to both national and human security goals when it is free from short-term political and security imperatives. In other words, they argue that development and defense goals should be separate. The comprehensive approach assumes stabilization requires integrating development with security efforts. Is it possible to design effective short-term stabilization programming that contributes toward long-term development goals and vice versa? Future research should examine *the perceived benefits of the integration model to security/stabilization, the costs of this model to humanitarian and civil society space, and the alternatives to the existing civil military integration model.*

3. The Relationship Between Stabilization Programs and NGO Insecurity. The number of NGO personnel targeted and killed each year is increasing. Many assume an increase in the use of development activities for stabilization, and confusion between military and CSO personnel, coupled with shrinking humanitarian and civil society space, are making NGOs the "soft targets" for armed opposition groups. Military personnel question this assumption, pointing to the increased attacks by insurgents against all kinds of civilians. Future research should document *the relationship between military hearts and minds QIPs and NGO insecurity.*

Operational Mechanisms.

1. Mechanisms for Multi-stakeholder Consultations. CSOs, civilian government, and military personnel do not have adequate forums for information exchange, monitoring of civil-military guidelines, or general discussion of issues related to conflict assessment, planning, and implementation. Future research should examine *which mechanisms could provide a forum for CSOs to share conflict assessments, advise on policy options, or address field-level issues with the U.S. Government and military.*

2. Mechanisms for Funding CSOs. The Department of Defense (DoD) administers up to 25 percent of U.S. development assistance. U.S. military commanders use the Commanders Emergency Response Fund and Provincial Reconstruction Teams to influence CSOs to implement hearts and minds QIPs with military funding. This places some CSOs in a dilemma of balancing their need for resources with principles of responding impartially to human need and being independent from government, which they perceive as essential to their security and access to local populations. Many CSOs will only accept funds from civilian donor agencies that allow the CSOs to independently identify program plans through impartial needs assessments. Future research should examine *what alternative funding mechanisms, such as channeling development dollars through Embassy development offices, national governments, or international donor pools, could best address this dilemma.*

3. Development of Shared Standards. CSOs, governments, and military personnel all share similar challenges of fostering local ownership and accountability, and monitoring what is working and what is not in their efforts. While CSOs oppose military-led development, they do argue that such development should at the very minimum be transparent. Any transfer of resources for humanitarian assistance or development programs into a community can foster corruption and unintentionally give legitimacy to unpopular local leaders and armed groups. Future research could examine whether developing *shared standards could help to build civil-military transparency on program effectiveness, cost, and sustainability.*

Training.

1. "Conflict Sensitive Development" Training for the Military. Despite decades of development expertise, even many CSO development projects still fail to address causes of poverty and do more to fuel local conflict than mitigate it. Development and peace building CSOs have undergone extensive training in a "Do No Harm" methodology to avoid negative impacts of their work.[21] The Australian and United Kingdom (UK) Departments for International Development co-train civilian and military personnel to understand the potential for harm in the development process and provide basic guidance for QIPs. *Given broad concerns on military-led hearts and minds QIPs, future training for the U.S. military could include principles for a conflict-sensitive approach to development, known to NGOs as "Do No Harm," to deconflict military approaches to short-term stabilization and long-term civil society development processes.*

2. Training on CSO-Military Relations: Missing Guidance. While a number of civil-military guidelines exist to clarify humanitarian NGO and military interaction, guidance on military involvement in development and peace building is missing. Despite high-level endorsement, there is still minimal wider understanding or monitoring of these existing guidelines. Civil society organizations are reluctant to establish guidelines for military involvement in areas they contest, such as development and peace building. Yet the increasing number of military personnel conducting development creates urgency for short-term pragmatic agreements. Moreover, in the broader field of peace building, Organization for Economic Cooperation and Development (OECD) guidelines on SSR, and DDR call for civilian oversight and participation working with military personnel when shared goals exist.[22]

Both CSOs and the military suffer from a lack of training and capacity for managing their interactions. Knowledge of existing humanitarian NGO guidelines and International Humanitarian Law is lacking. Quick field guides for U.S. military personnel that address issues with nonhumanitarian CSOs and the use of development and peace building activities for short-term stabilization goals are absent. Future research could examine *what curricula and training opportunities could assist CSOs and the military to advance their understanding of the issues outlined in this chapter.*

Legislation and Budget.

1. Legalizing Civil Society Humanitarian, Development, and Peace Building Efforts. Current War on Terror legislation makes it impossible for many CSOs to play positive roles in countering extremism, fostering democracy and providing civilian oversight of SSR and DDR. CSO contact with groups on terror lists is illegal, even when that work aims to end violence via negotiation training or DDR activities. Future research could examine *what the military and CSOs could do to help educate Congress about the roles of civil society in countering extremism and the need for more precise legislation that would permit the work of legitimate CSOs with groups on terror lists.*

2. Budgeting for Comparative Advantage. The 2010 UN CIMIC Policy calls for military personnel to support the creation of "an enabling environment . . . maximizing the comparative advantage of all actors operating in the mission area."[23] CSOs want military personnel to focus on population-centric security, not development. CSOs and military personnel generally agree that civilian agencies do not yet have the *size* capacity to address all the humanitarian, development and peace building needs in complex conflict settings and military organizations do not have the *skill* capacity for these tasks. CSOs believe there is no quick military fix to this problem, as these forms of assistance require extensive expertise to be effective and to avoid negative impacts. Future research could examine *what CSOs and military officials could do together with Congress* *to create an institutional plan and funding mechanisms to address the lack of civilian size capacity.*

Human Security Commission.

1. Broader Research and Dialogue on Human Security. Defense Secretary Robert Gates and Admiral Michael Mullen both called for "demilitarizing U.S. foreign policy." Addressing the tensions between CSOs and military personnel in the United States requires a dialogue including Congress, the administration and civilian agencies, the international community, and the many for-profit contractors who also work on security and development. How does the United States balance its own national interests when they conflict with broader global human security and without the distracting influence of those motivated by profit or power? Future projects could include setting up *a Human Security Commission, congressional hearings, or a whole of society dialogue process to examine national security and global human security.*

ENDNOTES - CHAPTER 5

1. See *US Army Field Manual* (FM) *3-07, Stability Operations,* Washington, DC: Department of the Army, October 2008.

2. See the following publications resulting from these dialogues: Lisa Schirch, "Civil Society-Military Roadmap on Human Security," Washington, DC: 3D Security Initiative, 2011; Lisa Schirch, *Civil Society and the U.S. Government in Conflict-Affected Regions: Building Better Relations for Peacebuilding,"* Washington, DC: Woodrow Wilson International Center for Scholars, 2010.

3. U.S. Department of Defense Directive 3000.05, *Military Support for Stability, Security, Transition, and Reconstruction (SSTR) Operations,* Washington, DC: U.S. Department of Defense, April 2007.

4. See UK Stabilization Unit, *Quick Impact Projects* (QIPs), New York: United Nations High Commissioner for Refugees, May 2004, p. 19; *QIPs Policy Directive*, New York: United Nations Department of Peacekeeping Operations, February 12, 2007.

5. The goals listed above were gleaned from the comments of various military personnel involved in the five focus groups which were the main basis for this chapter.

6. *Civil-Military Coordination in UN Integrated Peacekeeping Mission (UN-CIMIC)*, New York: United Nations Office of Military Affairs, Policy and Doctrine Team, October 2010.

7. *U.S. Government Interagency Counterinsurgency Guide*, Washington, DC: U.S. Department of State, January 2009.

8. See, for example, Matt Waldman, "Caught in the Conflict: Civilians and the International Security Strategy in Afghanistan," A briefing paper by 11 NGOs operating in Afghanistan for the NATO Heads of State and Government Summit, April 3-4, 2009, p. 14; Ashley Jackson, "Quick Impact, Quick Collapse: The Dangers of Militarized Aid in Afghanistan," Oxfam, Afghanistan, 2010.

9. Anthropologists' Statement on the Human Terrain System Program, Arlington, VA: American Anthropological Association, January 26, 2010.

10. Report on Wilton Park Conference 1022, "Winning 'Hearts and Minds' in Afghanistan: Assessing the Effectiveness of Development Aid in COIN Operations," March 2010.

11. "The US Military's Expanding Role in Foreign Assistance," Washington, DC: InterAction, January 2011.

12. High-Level Panel on UN-Civil Society, and Global Governance, Paper by Panel Chairman Fernando Henrique Cardoso, 2004.

13. See David Cortright with George A. Lopez, Alistair Millar, and Linda Gerber-Stellingwerf, "Friend not Foe: Civil Society and the Struggle Against Violent Extremism," South Bend, IN: Kroc Center for International Peace Studies at the University of Notre Dame, 2008.

14. Several of the civil society-military dialogues for the research for this chapter revealed these tensions.

15. These principles are drawn from a wide range of materials on NGOs. For a good example of the discussion, see Hugo Slim, "Relief agencies and moral standing in war: principles of humanity, neutrality, impartiality and solidarity," *Development in Practice*, Vol. 10, Nos. 3-4, August 1, 2000.

16. *National Security Strategy of the United States,* Washington, DC: The White House, May 2010.

17. Shannon D. Beebe and Mary Kaldor, *The Ultimate Weapon is No Weapon: Human Security and the New Rules of War and Peace,* New York: Public Affairs, 2010.

18. Edwina Thompson, "Principled Pragmatism: NGO Engagement with Armed Actors," Monrovia, CA: World Vision International, 2008.

19. See, for example, P. Fishtein, "Winning Hearts and Minds? Examining the Relationship between Aid and Security in Afghanistan's Balkh Province," Medford, MA, Feinstein International Center, Tufts University, November 2010. See also A. Wilder, "Losing Hearts and Minds in Afghanistan," in *Afghanistan, 1979-2009: In the Grip of Conflict,* Washington, DC: Middle East Institute, December 2009.

20. See, for example, M. Bradbury, "Do they think we're stupid? Local perceptions of 'hearts and minds' activities in Kenya," Humanitarian Practice Network, July 2010.

21. Mary Anderson, *Do No Harm: How Aid can Support Peace – or War,* Boulder, CO: Lynne Rienner, February 1999.

22. *Security Sector Reform and Governance,* Paris, France: Organisation for Economic Cooperation and Development, 2005.

23. *UN-CIMIC* Policy, Civil-Military Coordination in UN Integrated Peacekeeping Missions, New York: United Nations, October 2010.

CHAPTER 6

SECURITY SYSTEM REFORM IN WEAK OR FRAGILE STATES: A THREEFOLD CHALLENGE TO THE WHOLE OF GOVERNMENT APPROACH

Fouzieh Melanie Alamir

PROBLEM STATEMENT

The issue of whole of government (WoG) approaches has been high on the agenda of debates on international conflict management and crisis response in recent years. Interestingly, very similar debates have been taking place in several national arenas as well as international fora, including big international organizations such as the United Nations (UN), the North Atlantic Treaty Organization (NATO), and the European Union (EU). The international attention attributed to the topic leads to the question on the prospects, challenges, and limits of WoG. Beside this immanent perspective, this chapter will also reflect upon whether WoG approaches can help us to better achieve political end states.

In doing so, the WoG approach comprises three dimensions that require separate consideration as they touch upon three separate and completely different, though interacting policy arenas which are characterized by specific actors, procedural mechanisms and organizing principles:

1. The recipient country's political system.
2. The donor country's political system. And,
3. The system of international crisis response.

Weak or fragile states pose a particular challenge since they usually lack the institutional and political preconditions to apply a WoG approach. Even in Western donor countries, policy coherence between the different departments involved in international conflict management is more often than not wishful thinking rather than best practice. Finally, the system of international crisis response is primarily shaped by national and organizational interests that are not conducive to comprehensive policy approaches. Hence, the challenges of a WoG approach differ considerably in these three policy arenas and therefore require specific coping strategies.

In order to elicit the prospects and challenges of a WoG approach in practice, recent international security system reform (SSR)[1] efforts will serve as suitable examples. Programmatic papers of SSR, according to the Organization for Economic Cooperation and Development (OECD) Development Assistance Committee (DAC) guidelines,[2] explicitly recommend WoG as one of the primary implementing principles for SSR programs and activities. Moreover, SSR processes and projects in many parts of the world provide ample experiences and reference cases.

Following a definition of the WoG approach, a brief outline is given on the concept of SSR before scrutinization of the challenges of WoG by arenas and deriving recommendations on coping strategies. The following arguments will draw on practical case examples for illustrative purposes but, due to the given space limits of this chapter, will not go deeper into the cases and analyze details.

WHAT CHARACTERIZES A WHOLE OF GOVERNMENT APPROACH?

The term *whole of government* is, though widely used, not based on a commonly accepted definition. The least common denominator is an understanding of WoG as policies that have been conceptualized, decided, and implemented by legitimate state actors in a coordinated fashion. The Australian Management Advisory Committee defines it as:

> Whole of government denotes public service agencies working across portfolio boundaries to achieve a shared goal and an integrated government response to particular issues. Approaches can be formal and informal. They can focus on policy development, program management and service delivery.[3]

However, public services in advanced industrialized societies such as security, health care, social services, or critical infrastructures are, to a growing extent, delivered and/or operated by nongovernmental actors or different formats of public-private partnerships. Moreover, hardly any modern political decisionmaking process can be conceived of without civil society interests and perspectives being taken into account. It is therefore doubtful whether the strict exclusion of nonstate actors in a definition of a WoG approach is useful. In particular with regard to international conflict management and crisis response where nongovernmental actors play an essential role in achieving policy goals, it seems more adequate to develop a WoG definition by coming from the procedural side rather than from the actor's side. In this perspective and for the purposes of this chapter, WoG will be defined as:

> policies and/or public services as a result of a coordinated process of cross-departmental and cross-organizational decision making, program design, implementation, and evaluation. State actors are the lead and primary actors of a WoG approach, but nonstate actors can be included at all stages of the policy cycle as long as they share the overarching policy goals and contribute in the spirit of a unity of effort.
>
> According to this definition, the main features of an ideal WoG approach are:
>
> - a common understanding of a shared responsibility by all actors involved;
> - a common understanding of the political issue at stake;
> - a coordinated process of problem analysis, including all relevant perspectives;
> - a coordinated process of political decisionmaking based on shared political goals and a common stocktaking of resources, ways, and means;
> - a coordinated process of program design, providing for goal orientation, complementary integration of the single strands of activities, and efficiency of the overall effort;
> - a coordinated process of program implementation, avoiding duplication and unintended effects as well as unity of effort;
> - a coordinated process of permanent evaluation and adaptation, if necessary, assuring effectiveness of activities over time.

Apart from the definition, it may seem useful to add some remarks on the question of why and what for. Taking into account that international conflict management and crisis response is confronted with complex interdependencies between political, security, economic, and social factors, WoG approaches help to improve coherence and interface management among these overlapping dimensions. In addition, a confusing multitude of actors represent divergent interests and goals as they are acting on different levels in overlapping fields of action with varying mandates and roles. Moreover, the actors differ in terms of their pace of activities, levers and instruments, skills and capacities, as well as institutional cultures. Against this backdrop, improved coordination via WoG approaches is needed to reach common political objectives and intended end states, to ensure a goal-oriented and effective use and an even distribution of resources, to guarantee transparency and credibility, to avoid contradictions or collision of activities, and to prevent duplication of activities. In other words, the WoG approach is designed as a vehicle to improve *how* we are doing things.

WHAT IS SECURITY SYSTEM REFORM?

The origins of the concept of security system reform can be traced back to the late 1990s, when issues of conflict, peace, and security pushed on the international development policy agenda. Against the background of a growing awareness of the security-development nexus and the importance of good governance as a factor for successful and sustainable poverty reduction and development, the SSR concept was a practical answer to the immediate needs to improve human security and the more long-term needs to strengthen state capacities to provide security and rule of law.

In the commonly accepted understanding, the security system encompasses:

- the *legislative bodies* (adopt laws and exert parliamentary control);

- the *judiciary and penal system* (prosecute breach of law and execute court decisions);
- the *executive authorities* such as ministries and national security advisory bodies (provide policy guidelines and monitor core security actors);
- the *core security actors for domestic affairs* such as police, intelligence services, disaster response agencies, border guards, and customs authorities (enforce law and maintain public order);
- the *core security actors for external affairs* such as armed forces and gendarmerie (defend state sovereignty, territorial integrity, and population);
- *nonstatutory forces* such as militias, private security companies, etc. - not part of the state institutional setting, but part of the system; (pursue particular interests); and,
- last but not least, *civil society actors* such as unions, media, nongovernmental organizations (NGOs), etc. (represent and articulate societal security interests vis-à-vis the state).

Based on this understanding, security system reform is a concept aimed at four central objectives:

1. Improve democratic governance: The security system needs to operate on the basis of rule of law in a transparent and politically accountable fashion.

2. Improve delivery of security and justice services: The security system must strengthen capacities to ensure law enforcement and to safeguard basic safety and security needs of the population.

3. Create local leadership and ownership: SSR will not succeed unless it is driven by local people and organizations. And,

4. Ensure sustainability: Better delivery of security and justice services must not break down when foreign assistance ends.

If we were to sketch a model of a democratically controlled and effective security system as the normative reference of SSR, it could be outlined as follows:

- The security system in general:
  - operates in compliance with the given constitution and with international law;
  - receives a separate and adequate share of the state budget for the performance of its tasks; and,
  - is managed according to principles of transparency, proportionality, economy, effectiveness, and efficiency.

- The institutions and actors of the security system are:
  - functionally specialized and organizationally autonomous;
  - willing and able to think and act as a network despite a clear assignment of competencies and tasks; and,
  - adequately furnished with financial resources, infrastructure, material, technology, and staff.

- The actors/personnel of the security system:
  - are recruited through a transparent process, based on professional suitability criteria and open to all those who meet these criteria;
  - are adequately remunerated so that there is little vulnerability to corruption;

  - have a professional understanding of their role as service providers in the field of security and public order; and,
  - identify positively with the professional role assigned to their service and receive public recognition.

- Civil society is:
  - in a position to understand and critically evaluate the tasks and processes of the security system;
  - capable of articulating its own security needs and interests; and,
  - able and willing to assist and cooperate with the security system, where possible and necessary.

It is important to point out that the concept of SSR puts high emphasis on the systemic nature of the security system. Numerous linkages between and within the different sub-sectors of the security system with a complex mutual impact structure require that reforms take into account the interdependencies. Comprehensive approaches are therefore an inherent requirement of security system reform efforts.

CHALLENGES OF A WHOLE OF GOVERNMENT APPROACH IN THE POLITICAL SYSTEMS OF WEAK OR FRAGILE STATES

By weak or fragile states, we refer to countries which lack the capacity to meet citizens' basic needs and expectations such as the provision of public safety and security, maintenance of rule of law, and provision of basic services and economic opportunities for their citizens. For the purposes of this chapter, we do not need a more differentiated concept distinguishing types of fragility, but our definition includes post-conflict countries at the stage of state and nation-building, as well as states in decline.

The structure and policy processes of a national security system are shaped by the constitutional framework, the history, the regional security environment, and the constellation of political forces, as well as the political culture of a country. The security system constitutes one of the cornerstones of the identity of a country and builds the heart of the survivability of the state. This explains why most weak or fragile states display an imbalance between the defensive, respectively repressive functions of the security system (defense against internal and external threats, preservation of the political and economic system, law enforcement, safeguarding of national sovereignty, assertion of the state monopoly of force) and its protective functions (provision of political oversight, conflict prevention, protection of individuals and minorities) to the detriment of the latter. This implies in most cases a predominance of the executive branch, a judiciary that is politically dependent, and/or dysfunctional, marginalized parliaments, a weak or disorganized civil society, and a political culture characterized by fear, lack of pluralism, etc. The security system does not only mirror the (weak or fragile) governance system as a whole, but it shapes and perpetuates the governance system and its shortfalls to a large extent. This explains why SSR is crucial for long-term stabilization and sustainable development of conflict prone countries.

The demand for a WoG approach to SSR in a recipient country refers to four dimensions:

1. The local agents of reform (representative and willing to cooperate).

2. The goal of the SSR program (comprehensive and based on shared goals).

3. The program design (taking due account of cross-sectoral interdependencies). And,

4. The procedures of implementation (inclusive across relevant actors and institutions).

Regarding the agents of WoG, we have to ask not only who are the drivers of reform, who are supporters, and who are beneficiaries, but also who are opponents or possible spoilers, who will win and who will lose, who is included, and who is left aside? Liberia is a good example for SSR in a post-conflict environment after a protracted civil war which left state structures, civil society, and the economy in ruins. After signing the Comprehensive Peace Agreement[4] in 2003, initial SSR efforts in the transition period from 2003-05 suffered from the lack of a consensus within the political elite and a weak local ownership. Hence, the transitional government was able to provide neither for a discernible national security policy nor for a coherent and comprehensive national framework for SSR. The buildup of the military was practically completely donor-driven and implemented by a U.S. private company (DynCorps). Police reform was supported by the UN, but remained piecemeal and was conducted without corresponding efforts in reforming the judicial system. As a consequence, the overall pace of reforms was slow, and the SSR endeavor was imbalanced. It was only after the first post-conflict elections in October 2005, that newly elected President Ellen Sirleaf tasked the Governance Reform Commission in 2006 to take a lead role in SSR by providing professional and intellectual leadership, holding widespread consultations with all affected groups of the state and society, and by developing a *National Security Strategy* on this basis. Under the lead of this interagency body, the SSR process gained a more comprehensive domestic political base and some momentum. However, steering and coordination of the whole process have been widely left to external donors, and big challenges remain to be solved.[5]

Taking into account that political landscapes in weak or fragile states are often polarized and/or fragmented, it is highly unlikely to find political partners who are strong enough to launch and implement comprehensive SSR reforms while not driven by particular group or party interests. SSR approaches in weak or fragile states, where divergent group and institutional interests were reconciled on the basis of shared responsibilities and common political goals are hard to find. If so, they are rather the *result* of SSR attempts than its starting point, such as in Liberia. This dilemma can hardly be overcome by external donors so that the only option of coping is to undertake thorough analyses of the stakeholders in advance and to be well aware of the risks and possible consequences of the choice of political partners in the longer run.

With regard to the goal of an SSR program, we have to consider its breadth and depth, as well as the political process that led to goal formulation. Is the program courageous enough to address structural deficits of the security system or is it rather incremental in ambitions? Does it really tackle sensitive issues? Are the goals based on a broader political debate and also shared by those who will be negatively affected by the reforms? Indonesia provides a good example of an SSR process that was mainly driven by local elites. Since the downfall of the Suharto regime in 1997, SSR has been put on the agenda as an integral part of the

Indonesian democratization process. Driven mainly by the military, SSR initially focused on depoliticization of the military and the formal separation of the military and the police. The military has formally withdrawn from day-to-day politics and from parliament, while it has also addressed substantial structural and programmatic reforms such as the establishment of a civilian defense minister, the publication of a defense white paper, a defense doctrine and strategy, and new regulations for procurement. Moreover, it has taken a politically neutral stance in general elections, and efforts have been made to reduce the role of the military in the economy. Notwithstanding these remarkable achievements, the military still has a big role to play in Indonesian politics, especially at the local level, and its economic power is still prevalent. Apart from the successful formal separation of the police from the military, police reform has been slow due to lack of resources and political will, and there is still too much overlap between police and military activities. Judicial reform lags behind. Political oversight bodies lack expertise in security issues and civil society organizations still play a minor role in SSR. The overall SSR process has lost momentum in recent years. As the proponents for SSR have not extended their political base to include a broader range of civilian interest groups, the reforms remain military biased, lack a comprehensive framework, and tend to remain incremental pertaining to more thorough reforms.[6]

The Indonesian SSR process has taken place against the backdrop of peace and relative regional stability, drawing on established state and governance structures. Despite these beneficial preconditions, the initial military sponsorship has not yet been transformed into a more inclusive ownership structure. So is it realistic then to demand a comprehensive and inclusive process of political goal formulation in a weak or fragile state? The structural deficits of political systems in weak or fragile states are even less conducive to inclusive processes of political goal formulation and to comprehensive approaches of reform. Therefore it is highly unrealistic to assume a WoG approach by weak or fragile countries' governments in formulating goals. From the perspective of international assistance to SSR processes, one faces a dilemma as political consensus and a culture of inclusion and compromise cannot be imposed by external actors. On the one hand, there is a high demand and need for local ownership; on the other, this implies that reform processes will be driven by particular interests and thereby remain to a high degree contingent in their goals and approaches. Even if programs are highly donor-driven, local agents will have to take over some time sooner or later. Efforts to raise awareness and facilitate change may have some impact, but at the end of the day there is not much that can be done by external actors to stimulate more inclusive processes of goal formulation in partnering governments of recipient states.

A WoG approach in SSR program designs should be measured by the degree of interconnection of the different strands of activity, and the embeddedness of the program in a broader reform context. If a program aims, for example, at strengthening the operational capacities of core security actors, does it take into account aspects of political accountability, professionalization, and responsiveness to people's needs? If a program focuses on one sector only, e.g., on police reform, does it consider the interdependencies between the police, the justice and penal system? The examples of Liberia and Indonesia, although the former has been highly donor-driven, and the latter driven by domestic actors, have displayed a considerable degree of compartmentalization of the SSR process and imbalances between the different strands of reform. Taking into account what has been said with regard to the local agents and political goals of many SSR processes, it is consequently not very likely to find efforts of comprehensive programming by local elites of weak or fragile states. Partly due to a lack of concepts and knowledge, but primarily due to the dominance of particular interests and as a result of the deficient governance system and its consequences, SSR programs under conditions of a fragile political and security situation, tend to be focused on strengthening operational capacities of the military and/or police, and tend to neglect judicial reform, political oversight agencies, and human security aspects. International donors can try to raise awareness of their partners or might even be tempted to condition their support, but as long as there is a lack of domestic actors able and willing to promote the security governance and human security aspects of SSR, external pressure will come to nothing.

Finally, procedures of implementation are a reflection and function of the local agent structure, goals, and program designs. If there is no broad base of local stakeholders following a common vision, SSR programs will consequently rather reflect particular interests and be a result of internal power plays. Hence, procedures of implementation reflect this and usually suffer from the deficiencies of the political system of the weak or fragile recipient country. Donor countries can, to a certain extent, influence procedures of implementation by facilitating or demanding cross-sectoral approaches or the inclusion of civil society groups. Therefore they should have both a thorough understanding of all relevant and affected actors as well as independent communication channels with these actors.

The consequences of a lack of functioning governance structures and procedures are evident. In order to be sustainable and successful, SSR requires a minimum of functioning institutions. This is the dilemma in weak or fragile states. Moreover, SSR often takes place in situations of insecurity, no peace, no war, or ongoing conflicts at least in some areas of the country. In coping with this dilemma, SSR programs should put particular emphasis on trying to create and/or strengthen local ownership. This implies very careful stakeholder analyses and also explicit consideration of how to deal with reluctance or resistance to reform. For post-conflict contexts, stabilization is crucial, although it is important to consider institution and capacity building aspects right from the start and to embed them in a long-term strategy. Any one-sided focus on military reform or on the strengthening of operational capacities of the security forces without ensuring political oversight and control should be very carefully weighed against the possible unintended negative effects. International donors might take the role of facilitators of cross-departmental and interagency debates. In weak or fragile states, where governance structures are declining and/or ruling elites corrupt and clinging to power, it is important to rely more on nongovernmental actors and to build on already existing local initiatives focusing in human security aspects. Facing the dilemmas of SSR in weak or fragile states, careful analysis and weighing of pros and cons might lead donors to not engage directly in SSR projects, but rather in programs that aim to strengthen civil society and civilian governance capacities in general.

CHALLENGES OF A WHOLE OF GOVERNMENT APPROACH IN THE DONOR COUNTRIES' POLITICAL SYSTEMS

The demand for WoG in implementing SSR programs does not only apply to recipient countries, but also to the approach of donor countries in their process of decisionmaking, allocating resources, programming, and implementing SSR programs. In this perspective, WoG refers to the level of domestic policy coherence, i.e., interdepartmental and interagency consultation, coordination, and cooperation among the national agencies and actors involved; and in all phases of the project cycle.

As the national political systems of major Western donor states are too different to be generalized, this chapter will concentrate on the example of Germany as a donor country. Four departments are usually involved when it comes to German contributions to international SSR efforts: The political lead agency for all civilian and military activities abroad is the Ministry of Foreign Affairs (MoFA). Military contributions to international SSR programs such as training of military personnel, military counseling or other supporting roles, is led by the Ministry of Defense (MoD). Contributions to international police reforms such as training, counseling, or mentoring, are conducted under the auspices of the Federal Ministry of Interior (MoI). All other capacity-building measures are led by the Ministry for Economic Cooperation and Development (MoECD). The latter relies on both governmental and nongovernmental agencies to implement programs and activities. Although the division of roles and responsibilities seems to be theoretically clear, there have been numerous shortfalls of interdepartmental and interagency policy coherence in actual practice.

This will be demonstrated by looking at the German engagement in the Afghan SSR endeavor since 2002. At the outset, German military contributions to the International Security Assistance Force (ISAF) and the German lead role for police reform in Afghanistan, as well as German humanitarian contributions, were generally decided under the auspices of the MoFA, but implemented independently by the respective line ministries. The sole unit with an overall picture of German governmental contributions to reconstruction in Afghanistan was the Task Force Afghanistan in the MoFA. When the debate on the Provincial Reconstruction Teams (PRT) gained momentum in 2003 and Germany decided to get involved, the issue of improved interagency coordination came on the agenda, coinciding with a general rise of development activities in Afghanistan. Although the German PRT concept combined the diplomatic, the military, the police, and the development strand of activities under a common umbrella, in fact civilian development representatives physically stayed outside the barracks, while the other three representatives shared shelter in military compounds. Lines of reporting remained stove-piped via the respective line ministries. Areas and issues of activities were neither coordinated nor complementary. It took several years until the departments involved developed genuine interagency coordinated activities such as common funds and complementary projects in the context of the PRT framework. Only with the takeover of the ISAF Regional Command North by the Germans in 2006 did German civil and military contributions begin to concentrate in that region and be successively streamlined.

The reasons for the slow progress in interagency coordination and cooperation were complex. First of all, the departments have a strong say in shaping German policies, and there is no tradition of systematically tackling strategic issues in a concerted, cross-departmental approach.[7] Secondly, West German sovereignty in foreign and security policy matters had been restricted by the provisions of the General Treaty between the four Allies and the Federal Republic of Germany (1955), until the Two Plus Four Settlements in late 1990 resulted in the unified Germany gaining her full sovereignty. Accordingly, West Germany maintained a comparatively low foreign and security policy profile during the Cold War period, concentrating on economic integration into Western Europe and relations with the former German Democratic Republic. Hence, there was no need and no precedence for systematic cross-departmental coordination in the field of foreign and security policy due to the historic restrictions of German sovereignty for many years. Thus, knowledge of each other, viable working relations, and cross-cutting networks were weak or lacking. In addition, there was a lack of institutionalized interagency consultation or coordination bodies at all levels. Finally, as the line ministries have their own pace and principles of project implementation, the criteria, rhythm, and focus areas had to be successively readjusted. This was particularly challenging for the MoECD which usually pursues long-term projects with a long-term presence on site, relying on local partners, used to keeping distance from the military, working in flat hierarchies, and building on the trust of the local population. In contrast, the police and the military are used to rather short-term presence in barracks, separated from the population, self-reliant in logistics, and used to working in strong hierarchies. Moreover, the logic of military stabilization and civilian reconstruction did not easily harmonize, particularly in the wake of a steady deterioration of the security situation on the ground. Altogether and taking into account the given constitutional and institutional preconditions of German foreign and security policy, the German departments reacted slowly, but did well in adjusting to the challenges of improved coherence in delivering SSR contributions in Afghanistan. As indicated above, common situational awareness and cross-departmental information sharing and decisionmaking have been considerably improved. Coordinating bodies have been installed at the State Secretary level and below, and a denser network of exchange or liaison officers between the four ministries involved has facilitated day-to-day coordination. In addition, common training and exercises as well as common pre-deployment preparations enable a better understanding of the common effort in advance. These achievements were partly due to growing pressure on the ground; partly a consequence of a growing awareness, intensive political debates, and demands on the domestic front; and partly they were simply the result of a normal learning process.

One might argue that a lack of coherence within the political systems of donor countries is not so important, since SSR usually takes place in highly complex settings with numerous international governmental and nongovernmental agencies involved. And in fact, seen from the perspective of goal attainment in the recipient state, WoG at the level of domestic donor state procedures does not make too big a difference. But seen from a national donor perspective, civil and military contributions to international SSR processes are part of the overall foreign and security policy of a country and require proof of effectiveness in outcome as well efficiency in the use of scarce national resources vis-à-vis the national legislature and the constituencies. Besides, improved interagency coherence at the national level helps strengthen the stance and credibility, particularly vis-à-vis the different partners in the recipient country, but also within the international donor community.

As the German example has shown, WoG approaches in the domestic political system of a donor country can be improved within the given constitutional constraints and in the longer run, when the domestic and external pressure are high enough. One lever for improving coherence has been the systematic facilitation and institutionalization of interagency consultation and information flow at the earliest possible stage of the project cycle. Another measure has been the conduct of cross-departmental trainings and exercises. The OECD DAC additionally recommends developing an overall policy for fragile states, conducting joint interagency analyses and assessments, developing joint country-specific operational strategies, clearly defining political leadership (respectively the lead and coordinating roles), and creating incentives for cooperation.[8] In general, all procedural measures should be accompanied by deliberate efforts to create a new mindset of common interests and cross-departmental responsibility. This might even induce positive spillover effects for other policy arenas.

CHALLENGES OF A COMPREHENSIVE APPROACH IN THE SYSTEM OF INTERNATIONAL CRISIS RESPONSE

The demand for a WoG approach at the international level seems to be a contradiction in itself, since the international community is not a unified actor with a common legal, institutional, and cultural point of departure, comparable to a nation-state. Therefore, it would be more precise to speak of a comprehensive rather than a WoG approach in this respect. Characteristics of an ideal comprehensive international approach to crisis response are:

- common political goals and strategies in order to ensure unity of effort;
- a division of roles and responsibilities between civil and military actors with regard to tasks and fields of action in order to ensure best use of expertise and resources; and,
- a coordinated implementation of activities regarding the pace and the focus areas of the activities in order to avoid duplication or overlap of efforts as well as blind spots.

The system of international crisis response mirrors the characteristics of the international system in general. Policies and activities are driven by nation-states; their perceptions, interests, and political or financial capacities; and their willingness to engage, while the system lacks a binding framework specifying who engages where, why, with what, how, and for how long. This applies to the overall setting of the international engagement as well as to the development strand of international aid. With regard to the overall setting, there are no clear rules and regulations as to which organization should be the lead or whether a task lies in the responsibility of civilian or military actors. Military operations might be conducted under the aegis of the UN, NATO, the EU, the African Union, or temporary coalitions of willing states; and it is rather political and situational factors than a systematic division of tasks that drive the decision for one format or the other. Concerning SSR processes, particularly in unstable security contexts, it is not easy to define whether and to what extent SSR tasks are a military or a civilian responsibility. This often leads to a blurring of civilian and military activities with a tendency of military stabilization operations to take over policing and even development tasks. With regard to the development strand of activities, coordination is only a little better. Although the UN, the EU, and the OECD DAC have been quite successful in creating international standards, mainstreaming certain topics, and harmonizing donor activities, their recommendations are not binding and there is no reasonable division of labor between the UN, the EU, and major national donor states. In many cases, organizational competition, duplication of efforts, or simple uncoordinated parallelism of activities prevail. Besides, there is an unmanageable scope of governmental and nongovernmental agencies, the latter often working on behalf of national governments or international organizations. Moreover, as far as nongovernmental agencies are concerned, competition for resources sometimes impedes their willingness to coordinate or cooperate.

SSR in Afghanistan is a clear example of the flaws of the international system of crisis management. It had started as a highly ambitious undertaking built on five parallel pillars with different lead nations: buildup of the Afghan National Army under U.S.-lead; buildup of the Afghan National Police under German lead; judicial reform under Italian lead; disarmament, demobilization, and reintegration (DD&R) under Japanese lead; and counternarcotics under British lead. Lacking an overarching vision of the future security system and in the absence of a steering body, the lead nation concept resulted in an uneven pace of reform with heterogeneous dynamics evolving in each pillar. Furthermore, important linkages among the SSR pillars as well as between SSR and the overall reconstruction process were neglected. As the Afghan stakeholders have never come close to developing a shared vision of the political end state of reconstruction nor of the priority SSR needs, the whole process was primarily donor driven despite the declared principle of Afghan ownership.[9]

As a consequence, the emerging security system in Afghanistan is marked by many imbalances and deficiencies. While the buildup of the armed forces is generally considered to have been successful in terms of operational capabilities, the oversight and control mechanisms have been neglected. The buildup of the police lags behind in many respects—numbers, capabilities, countrywide presence, professionalism, and most of all with a view to trust in the population. Originally a police task, police reform has become to a large part a military business due to the lack of international police capacities. The pace of judicial reform has been very slow and suffering from lack of resources, skilled personnel, and the challenges of the duality of traditional and modern forms of justice. Moreover, the important linkages between police, justice, and penal reform have long been almost completely left aside. The DD&R process, and the subsequent Disarmament of Illegally Armed Groups program, have, in sum, been unsuccessful as the black market still provides arms and weapons in abundance, and armed groups have had no shortage in supplies. Besides, the labor market can hardly absorb ex-combatants and offer alternative livelihoods. Counternarcotics efforts could not stop the establishment of a viable transnational network of masterminds, traders, producers, and more and more also consumers of poppy or related products. Despite the reduction of the number of poppy cultivating provinces, the overall cultivation output could not be cut back. At large, the whole SSR process has not sufficiently been coordinated with other major areas of the Afghan reconstruction process such as governance reform, education, improving livelihoods, rebuilding infrastructure, etc. Inherently, the focus of the SSR endeavor has been on strengthening military capacities while the whole reconstruction process, against the backdrop of a growing insurgency threat, has been security biased to the detriment of improving governance capacities and livelihoods.[10]

These shortcomings were well-recognized, and the donor community undertook remarkable efforts to improve overall coherence and coordination on the basis of the Afghanistan Compact.[11] Numerous coordinating bodies evolved bottom up at Kabul, provincial, and district level, encompassing overall reconstruction and SSR issues as well as SSR sector specific coordination needs. However, coordination efforts on site were constrained by diverging political interests in the donor capitals. Above all, the move towards improved international coherence and more inclusion of the Afghan Government came at a time when dynamics on the ground had already shifted towards the worse. Given the political setting of interests and perceptions in 2001, it was unrealistic to expect a comprehensive donor strategy based on common political goals and a common vision on the future of Afghanistan. Taking into account the development of the international approach to Afghanistan,[12] it cannot take us by surprise that coordination mechanisms evolved only successively and bottom up.

Therefore, coping strategies to improve international donor coherence require first and foremost more coordinated comprehensive analyses, more consideration of long-term possible effects and risks, more long-term strategic approaches, and more integration of in-depth expertise at the political-strategic level during the decisionmaking and planning phase. But as we know, this is highly unlikely to be realized. More pragmatic recommendations would focus rather on the establishment of international interagency fora for consultation and coordination at strategic, operational, and on-site tactical levels at the earliest possible stage. Coordination mechanisms and steering bodies should, ideally, be part of UN mandates. Institutionalization of interagency consultation and coordination via standardization (handbooks, guidelines, check-lists, establishment of consultation mechanisms, provision of obligatory procedures, etc.) can at least partly overcome the high personnel turnover and the associated loss of knowledge. Bilateral agreements at political headquarter level between the major agencies involved (memoranda of understanding, letters of intent, or other provisions) can facilitate and channel cooperation at field level. In order to improve mutual knowledge and understanding among organizations and agencies and to strengthen the will for cooperation, common interagency preparatory training and exercises have proven to be of high value.

SUMMARY AND CONCLUSIONS

For assessing the prospects and challenges of a WoG approach in the context of international conflict management strategies, in particular with view towards weak or fragile states, we have broken the concept down to three separate, but interacting policy arenas: the recipient state's political systems, the domestic political system of the donor states, and the system of international crisis response. In order to further operationalize the WoG concept, we have chosen recent security system reform efforts in different parts of the world as examples to demonstrate the particular challenges of practically applying WoG in the different policy arenas.

Regarding the political system of recipient states, we face a fundamental challenge when demanding a WoG approach: The structural governance deficits of weak or fragile states make any WoG approach to security system reforms from within the recipient partners in general highly unlikely. Bearing in mind that local ownership and sensitivity to local political dynamics and culture are crucial to launching successful and sustainable SSR processes, these deficits can neither be circumvented nor overcome by choosing a donor-driven approach. This is so first, because donor engagement is always limited in scope and time, and the initiative will have to pass to local agents of reform sooner or later. Secondly, donors always depend on local actors to implement their projects and thus cannot escape the given institutional setting, power constellation, and political culture in the recipient state. Finally, any donor-driven approach will be restricted by the structural conditions of the international system of crisis response as the international donor community is itself struggling hard to achieve greater coherence. A donor-driven approach to SSR therefore provides no guarantee for more comprehensive SSR programs, for higher inclusiveness, or for better coordination of activities. External influence on reform processes, particularly in weak and fragile states, will always remain limited. Therefore, the coping strategies that were recommended above may help to minimize the risks for international donors or may broaden the range of possible positive options, but there is no definite strategy to successfully tackle or overcome the governance deficits in weak or fragile states. SSR under such circumstances is and can only be like building the ship at sea. After all, in the face of the numerous institutional, political, infrastructural, economic, and cultural impediments to reform in the political systems of weak or fragile recipient countries, the lack of a WoG approach seems to be of rather secondary importance.

The challenges of WoG in the political system of donor countries are of a completely different nature. As shown above, there are levers for practically improving interagency coherence in the overall approach to international crisis response of a donor country within certain limits. However, we should be realistic about the possible effects of improved coherence in this arena. Seen from the perspective of a donor country, interagency coordination and cooperation are of high importance in terms of political accountability regarding effectiveness and efficiency of engagement vis-à-vis the domestic audiences. Besides, domestic policy coherence is a means to strengthen the assertiveness of a state in international contexts. But seen from the perspective of goal achievement in international SSR programs, it is doubtful whether the application of WoG approaches in domestic processes of positioning and decisionmaking of donor countries really make a remarkable difference. Even if national approaches of donors strictly adhered to WoG principles, they could hardly shape the overall international approach to crisis response since the latter follows its own mechanisms and rules. Hence, the above recommended coping strategies are helpful with regard to the policy processes and interests of donor countries, but will have only very limited impact on the outcome of SSR programs in recipient countries.

The system of international crisis response is, as depicted, highly contingent on situational factors and power constellations of the major national donors involved. In the first instance, international crisis response policies do not follow the needs articulated by recipient countries, but the interests and capacities of donor countries in the light of their perceptions of the needs. In addition, when taking into consideration the limited external possibilities for exerting influence especially in weak or fragile states, one has to be realistic about the possible impact of international assistance and crisis response. Under this caveat, however, pragmatic efforts to improve international interagency coherence in program designs and implementation could make a difference. The recommendations above for improving coherence will not guarantee better outcomes of SSR processes, but will considerably improve international delivery of assistance and thus help to enhance the chances for better outcomes.

In sum, we can state that the notion of WoG as a practical guideline for international crisis response policies is appealing in theory, but elusive and very difficult to apply in actual practice. The findings of this chapter may seem somewhat disillusioning as they lead to the conclusion that possibilities to improve

WoG approaches in the three interacting policy arenas of international conflict management are highly limited, particularly with regard to the most important one, namely the domestic arena of recipient states. The target audience of the WoG debate is primarily located in the capitals of donor states and strategic headquarters of international organizations, while its impact on practical outcomes in reform processes in recipient states is confined. Limitations, however, do not mean that efforts to improve coherence according to the given recommendations are pointless. To the contrary, identifying the limitations of practical applicability of the WoG concept helps to avoid wrong expectations and to localize its value and relevance as a primarily normative concept, targeted to policy processes in and among donor countries.

So far, WoG can be regarded as a set of principles and procedural measures in international conflict management that, within the depicted limits, may help us implement strategies, programs, and activities in a better way. However, it seems very doubtful whether it can also help us do the right thing. Particularly when we take the international engagement in Afghanistan since 2001, which largely triggered the recent debate on WoG approaches, it may seem that the WoG debate has somewhat replaced a more thorough reflection of the strategic goals and their feasibility in Afghanistan. The international donor community should therefore not forget to critically reflect on *what* we do rather than to delve too deeply into *how* we do it.

ENDNOTES - CHAPTER 6

1. Some relevant players speak of security *sector* rather than security *system* reform. The Organization for Economic Cooperation and Development-Development and Assistance Committee (OECD-DAC), which has issued major programmatic papers on security system reform (SSR) and can thus be regarded as a reference institution in terms of conceptualizing SSR, uses the term "security system reform." For the purpose of this chapter and with regard to the assumed development perspective of international conflict and crisis management, we also adhere to the term "security system reform." It stresses the systemic nature of the security system, i.e., the complex interdependencies between the different elements of the security system and points to the fact that reform efforts of the security system can only be successful if they take these interdependencies into account.

2. Organization for Economic Cooperation and Development (OECD) *Guidelines and Reference Series: Security System Reform and Governance*, Paris, France: OECD Development Cooperation Directorate (DAC), 2005.

3. "Connecting Government. Whole of Government Responses to Australia´s Priority Challenges," Management Advisory Committee, Commonwealth of Australia 2004, p.1.

4. "Comprehensive Peace Agreement Between the Government of Liberia and the Liberians United for Reconciliation and Democracy (LURD) and the Movement for Democracy in Liberia (MODEL) and Political Parties," Accra, August 18, 2003, United States Institute for Peace, Peace Agreements Digital Collection, available from *www.usip.org/files/file/resources/collections/peace_agreements/liberia_08182003.pdf.*

5. See, for example, Adedeji Ebo, "The Challenges and Opportunities of Security Sector Reform in Post-Conflict Liberia," Occasional Papers No. 9, Geneva, Switzerland: Geneva Centre for the Democratic Control of Armed Forces, December 2005, available from *www.dcaf.ch/Publications/;* Thomas Jaye, "An Assessment Report on Security Sector Reform in Liberia," Report to the Governance Reform Commission (GRC) of Liberia, September 23, 2006; Mark Malan, *Security Sector Reform in Liberia. Mixed Re-*

sults from Humble Beginnings, Carlisle, PA: Strategic Studies Institute, U.S. Army War College, March 2008, available from *www.strategicstudiesinstitute.army.mil/pdffiles/pub855.pdf*; International Crisis Group, "Liberia: Uneven Progress in Security Sector Reform," Africa Report No. 148, January 13, 2009, available from *www.observatori.org/paises/pais_67/documentos/148_liberia___uneven_progress_in_security_sector_reform.pdf*.

6. See, for example, Riskal Sukma and Edy Prasetyono, "Security Sector Reform in Indonesia. The Military and the Police," Clingendael Institute, Working Paper No. 9, February 2003, available from *www.clingendael.nl/publications/2003/20030200_cru_working_paper_9.PDF*; Muhammad Najib Azca: Security Sector Reform, Democratic Transition, and Social Violence: The Case of Ambon, Indonesia, Berghof Center for Constructive Conflict Resolution, August 2004, available from *www.berghof-handbook.net/documents/publications/dialogue2_azca.pdf*; Riefqi Muna, "Local Ownership and the Experience of SSR in Indonesia," Timothy Donais, ed., *Local Ownership and Security Sector Reform*, Geneva, Switzerland: Geneva Centre for the Democratic Control of Armed Forces, LIT, 2008, pp. 233-251; *Country Profile Indonesia*, Waterloo, Ontario, Canada: Centre for International Governance Innovation (CIGI), Security Sector Reform Resource Centre, 2010.

7. The German political decisionmaking process is governed by three principles: the chancellor principle, stipulating that the chancellor defines the political guidelines of the government; the Cabinet principle, according to which political decisions are taken by all members of the Cabinet; and the departmental principle. According to the latter, the German Constitution endows the heads of departments with considerable power as independent and responsible actors for their area of competency within the framework of general guidance by the chancellor. In terms of hierarchy, the chancellor principle tops the departmental principle, which remains embedded in the Cabinet principle. In fact, however, the balance between the chancellor, the Cabinet, and the ministers is highly influenced by contingent factors such as the constellation between the coalition parties, the personality and standing of the major actors, etc.

8. See "Whole of Government Approaches to Fragile States," DAC Guidelines and Reference Series, OECD DAC 2006.

9. See, for example, Mark Sedra, "Security Sector Transformation in Afghanistan," Geneva Centre for the Democratic Control of Armed Forces, Working Paper 143, Geneva, Switzerland, 2004; Antonio Giustozzi, "Shadow Ownership and SSR in Afghanistan," Donais, ed., *Local Ownership and Security Sector Reform*, pp. 215-231.

10. For overall assessments of the SSR process in Afghanistan, see, for example, *Fortschrittsbericht Afghanistan zur Unterrichtung des deutschen Bundestages* (*Progress Report on Afghanistan to the German Parliament*), December 2010, available from *www.auswaertiges-amt.de/cae/servlet/contentblob/583368/publicationFile/155891/110704-Zwischenbericht.pdf; jsessionid=06279A6CkFFFAA94EF53D0701168 46C2D; Report on Progress Toward Security and Stability in Afghanistan and United States Plan for Sustaining the Afghanistan National Security Forces*, Washington, DC: U.S. Department of Defense, April 2011.

11. "The Afghanistan Compact," the London Conference on Afghanistan, January 31 to February 1, 2006, available from *www.nato.int/isaf/docu/epub/pdf/afghanistan_compact.pdf.*

12. For more details, see Fouzieh Melanie Alamir, "The International Approach to Afghanistan—Could We Have Done Better?" Gerhard Justenhoven, ed., *Afghanistan in der Sackgasse?* (*Afghanistan in the Dead End?*), Hamburg, Germany: Institut für Theologie und Frieden, 2011.

CHAPTER 7

A WHOLE LOT OF SUBSTANCE OR A WHOLE LOT OF RHETORIC?

A PERSPECTIVE ON A WHOLE OF GOVERNMENT APPROACH TO SECURITY CHALLENGES

Charles J. Dunlap, Jr.

> The Department [of Defense] supports institutionalizing whole-of-government approaches to addressing national security challenges. The desired end state is for U.S. Government national security partners to develop plans and conduct operations from a shared perspective.
>
> *Quadrennial Defense Roles and Missions Review Report*, 2009[1]

INTRODUCTION

In the U.S. Government, the "whole of government" mantra is firmly embedded in official rhetoric as the idea-*du-jour*. Moreover, as the quote above indicates, in the national security realm particularly, it is officially considered a bedrock principle.

Indeed, the Obama administration—building on themes developed previously by the Bush and Clinton administrations[2]—explicitly incorporates a whole of government (WoG) approach in the *National Security Strategy* issued in May of 2010.[3] In the administration's conceptualization, a WoG approach in the national security sphere essentially involves, among other things, greater coordination across government agencies, and a marked expansion of diplomatic and civilian development capabilities. Military and civilian institutions are, the strategy insists, to "complement each other and operate seamlessly."[4]

The purpose of this chapter is to briefly trace the application of the WoG approach to security issues, highlight a few of its strengths and weaknesses, and examine the potential unintended consequences. It will argue that while a WoG approach certainly has its merits, it is not—and never will be—a panacea. Moreover, this chapter contends that in some instances a unilateral approach, that is, one that wholly or primarily relies upon a particular agency, is the preferred or only practical alternative. The chapter will also suggest that when extended to the domestic context, a WoG approach strategy may be unsettling, and even counterproductive, to the Nation's long-term strategic and political interests.

Finally, this chapter advocates considering a WoG approach as just one tool in the smart power toolbox. It argues that as such, a WoG approach is most effective when selectively employed, and not as a default in all circumstances.

IRREGULAR WAR AND THE RISE OF THE WoG APPROACH

As the Congressional Research Service (CRS) recently observed, for "well over a decade, there has been widespread concern that the U.S. government lacks appropriate civilian 'tools' to carry out state-building tasks in post conflict situations."[5] Operations in Haiti, Somalia, Bosnia, and elsewhere were cited as examples of situations where it fell to America's armed forces to perform a variety of state-building tasks "such as creating justice systems, assisting police, and promoting governance."[6]

The February 2011 report points out:

> The military was called upon to perform such missions not only for its extensive resources but also because no other U.S. government agency could match the military's superior planning and organizational capabilities. In addition, because of its manpower, the military carried out most of the U.S. humanitarian and nation-building contribution, *even though some believed that civilians might be better suited to carry out such tasks,* especially those tasks involving cooperation with humanitarian NGOs [nongovernmental organizations].[7]

Still, the current impetus for a WoG approach is much traceable to reconstruction and stability issues arising out of the irregular wars in Iraq and Afghanistan. Defined by the Pentagon as a "violent struggle among state and nonstate actors for legitimacy and influence over the relevant population(s),"[8] irregular war was exactly what the Department of Defense (DoD) found itself fighting after toppling the Baathist government of Iraq, and the Taliban regime in Afghanistan.

The DoD may have anticipated security issues, but it seems clear that it nevertheless expected that once the conventional fight ended, the task of physically reconstructing the country and rebuilding its economic societal institutions—essential elements of strategic victory in irregular war—would be the responsibility of other government agencies and the international community.

Things, however, did not work out that way. According to analyst Gordon Adams, although "whole of government" was among the "buzz words" that arose in direct response to the post-major combat operations stage in Iraq and Afghanistan, the DoD found itself:

> frustrated by the absence of a significant, flexible, well-funded civilian capacity at the State Department and USAID [U.S. Agency for International Development], able to take responsibility for post-conflict reconstruction and stabilization after U.S. combat operations concluded.[9]

That, it seems, was enough for the DoD to take matters into its own hands.

DoD authorities responded by attempting a rather significant re-orientation of the armed forces to fill the perceived post-conflict reconstruction and stabilization capability gap. In late-2005, the DoD issued a directive entitled *Military Support for Stability, Security, Transition, and Reconstruction (SSTR).*[10] Designed to support President Bush's National Security Presidential Directive (NSPD)-44,[11] this watershed policy document (designated Department of Defense Directive [DoDD] 3000.05) declared that stability operations are a "core U.S. military mission" and one that, according to the directive, was to be "given a priority comparable to combat operations."[12]

That document was followed in 2008 by the Army's own *Stability Operations* manual which implemented the DoD policy.[13] The Army's manual contained an explicit definition of the WoG approach, describing it rather amorphously as an "approach that integrates the collaborative efforts of the departments and agencies of the U.S. government to achieve unity of effort toward a shared goal."[14]

In accord with DoDD 3000.05, the 2006 *Quadrennial Defense Review* (QDR) did not use WoG approach terminology, but said as much in declaring that:

> The Department of Defense cannot meet today's complex challenges alone. Success requires unified statecraft: the ability of the U.S. Government to bring to bear all elements of national power at home and to work in close cooperation with allies and partners abroad.[15]

These sentiments were echoed in the 2009 *Quadrennial Defense Roles and Missions Review Report*[16] wherein the DoD affirms its support for the "maturation of whole-of-government approaches to national security problems," adding that any solution such an approach produces will "be based on employing integrated flexible, mutually-supporting interagency capabilities."[17] For its part, the 2010 QDR is replete with specific references to the WoG approach.[18]

In the meantime, however, the Army and the Marine Corps also issued their counterinsurgency (COIN) doctrine, *Field Manual* (FM) *3-24*, which became the "bible" for operations in Iraq and later Afghanistan.[19] A multifaceted document subject to a myriad of interpretations, it was popularly imagined as a kinder, gentler way of achieving success in COIN situations by eschewing violence against insurgents in favor of a population-centric strategy aimed at winning "hearts and minds," much through nation-building and reconstruction efforts. Journalist Steve Coll described it thusly in the *New Yorker*:

> [Popular] among sections of the country's liberal-minded intelligentsia. This was warfare for northeastern graduate students—complex, blended with politics, designed to build countries rather than destroy them, and fashioned to minimize violence. It was a doctrine with particular appeal to people who would never own a gun.[20]

It is also a doctrine that, on the face of it, is perfectly suited to a WoG approach. In fact, it devotes an entire chapter to integrating civilian and military efforts.[21] Nevertheless, the doctrine makes it clear that nation-building tasks are essential for COIN success and, if necessary, the military must endeavor to accomplish them even in the absence of civilian partners. That circumstance occurred. For example, commanders were obliged to turn to their "in-house counsel" (uniformed military lawyers called Judge Advocates or "JAGs") for even such activities as rule of law reconstitution—a task that would appear to be better conducted by civilian personnel.[22]

Unsurprisingly, therefore, when DoDD 3000.05 was re-issued in 2009, the DoD acknowledged the importance of civilian partners, but reiterated that the DoD must be prepared to take the "lead" in such activities as establishing civil security and civil control, restoring essential services, repairing, and protecting critical infrastructure, and delivering humanitarian assistance until it is feasible for another agency to take over.[23]

THE MERITS OF A WoG APPROACH

Taken at face value, the notion of exploiting all the government's potential in the service of national security is eminently reasonable and wise. Plainly, national defense is the most basic rationale for government. Our own Constitution cites "provide for the common defence" as one of the key responsibilities of government.[24] Accordingly, the judicious bringing to bear of government's full range of capabilities is consistent with the fundamentals of good government and wise defense policy.

Perhaps most important—but not often discussed—are the merits of the military *not* doing many of the nation-building and reconstruction tasks. Among other things, if not engaged in nation-building, the military could concentrate on its institutional responsibility for national defense, particularly with respect to existential threats which nation-building and reconstruction do not address.[25]

After all, the role of the armed forces is, as the Supreme Court put it, "to fight or be ready to fight wars should the occasion arise."[26] Moreover, the Court points out that "[t]o the extent that those responsible for performance of this primary function are diverted from it . . . the basic fighting purpose of armies is not served."[27] Therefore, when the armed forces divert resources and—of even greater concern—*focus,* to the conduct of operations not intrinsic to warfighting, their ability to conduct bona fide combat operations inevitably degrades.

There are, however, other important factors favoring a WoG approach. As talented as military personnel are, it seems obvious that the more facets of the U.S. Government that can be brought to bear, the more likely there will be an injection of an authentic expertise when the task is not a traditionally military one. On the other hand, while the armed forces may have manpower and resources to address many nation-building tasks, that does not necessarily mean that they possess the range and depth of experience required to solve the convoluted problems arising in civil society.

As just one example, consider that the military is instinctively authoritarian and, as the Supreme Court has drily observed,"the army is not a deliberative body," rather "it is, by necessity, a specialized society separate from civilian society." How could such an organization have the experience and mindset to establish courts and legislatures where the essence of their function is deliberation?

In addition, there is another important consideration, which is the psychological impact on the host nation of a foreign military leading these efforts. Many in America's military seem blissfully unaware of the image they may unintentionally present when they serve as the "face" of the United States in nation-building endeavors. One can only imagine what the residents of a failed nation think when they see people in uniforms—not civilian officials—as the ones who are the main representatives of the United States in the reestablishment of their society's institutions, to include those expected to exercise civilian control of the armed forces.[28] Regrettably, the population may assume, for example, that it is military direction (as opposed to civilian leadership) that leads to success in the modern world. This could have unwanted political consequences over time if the electorate comes to perceive the armed forces as preferable to civilian leadership.

Closer to home, there are other benefits to removing the armed forces from the conduct of nation-building activities not directly involving physical security or military operations against insurgents. Specifically, the long-term involvement in such activities in Iraq and Afghanistan may be causing a subtle but troubling change in the perspective of members of America's armed forces. In 2006, historian Douglas Porch—citing the work of British historian Hew Strachan—made this melancholy observation:

> Politicians who engage in nation building endeavors, especially those with a counterinsurgency dimen-

sion must be prepared to deal with the political and military professional fallout. This includes the evolution of a stab-in-the-back as a guiding principle of civil-military relations and its leaching into domestic politics—that is, the belief that, in modern counterinsurgency warfare, win or lose, the military ends up feeling betrayed by the civilians.[29]

We may be beginning to see this phenomenon, much because of the way operations have been conducted in current wars. As this writer has observed elsewhere:

> Given responsibility not only for security, but also for governance, education, and economic development in wide swaths of territory in Iraq and Afghanistan, a generation of US officers has become accustomed to being 'warrior kings'.[30]

As such, there is a real risk that even after their nation-building duties in contingency areas end, military officers may want to arrogate to themselves decision-making that democracies leave to civilians.

A disturbing manifestation of what might be an emerging mindset is found in an October 2010 article written by Marine Corps Lieutenant Colonel Andrew Milburn that was published in the prestigious military journal, *Joint Force Quarterly*.[31] Milburn made the unprecedented argument that military officers have the obligation to disobey even *lawful* orders if they subjectively decide that such orders are "likely to harm the *institution writ large*—the Nation, military, and subordinates—in a manner not clearly outweighed by its likely benefits."[32] While the notion of disobedience of lawful orders is an anathema to most officers, it is nevertheless true, as journalist David Wood observes, that many uniformed officers today are chafing for a "bigger role in [the] policy decisions" that historically have been the province of civilian decisionmakers.[33]

Importantly for a WoG approach analysis, Wood maintains that the "current unrest among midcareer officers is new" and reasons that:

> today's majors, lieutenant colonels, and colonels grew up in counterinsurgency warfare, leading men into combat as young platoon leaders and having to create new ways of operating in dangerously complex political and social environments never imagined by their elders.[34]

As such, it may be that traditional—and *critical*—concepts of appropriate civil-military relations are under stress at least to some degree because of the nation-building tasks which military officers have had to perform in the absence of civilian capability that a WoG approach might otherwise provide.

In short, a WoG approach that displaces reliance upon the armed forces as the principle agent of nation-building and post-conflict reconstitution may well serve the interests of the targeted nation by better portraying the role of civilians in a democracy, serve the interests of the U.S. armed forces by allowing greater focus on its quintessential warfighting responsibilities, and also serve American society itself by ameliorating burgeoning civil-military tensions. Nevertheless, implementing a WoG approach effectively involves substantial challenges.

WoG APPROACH CHALLENGES

Although Congress has grappled with the idea of building civilian capability for nation-building for most of the decade, numerous difficulties still exist to implementing a WoG approach—not the least of which are inadequate resourcing and authority.[35] In 2004 the Office of the Coordinator for Reconstruction and Stabilization (S/CRS) was created within the State Department with a mission statement that would seem ideally suited to relieving the military of much of its current responsibility. S/CRS is supposed to:

> lead, coordinate, and institutionalize U.S. Government civilian capacity to prevent or prepare for post-conflict situations, and to help stabilize and reconstruct societies in transition from conflict or civil strife, so they can reach a sustainable path toward peace, democracy, and a market economy.[36]

The centerpiece of the S/CRS effort is the Civilian Response Corps (CRC). Drawing experts from eight Federal departments or agencies, the CRC is a "group of civilian federal employees who are specially trained and equipped to deploy rapidly to provide reconstruction and stabilization assistance to countries in crisis or emerging from conflict."[37] Although Secretary of State Hillary Clinton applauds the fact that in just 2 years the ranks have grown to over 1,000 civilian responders, the reality is that only 250-300 can deploy at any given time.[38]

It is difficult to understand how such a relatively small group—not much larger than a couple of companies of soldiers—could possibly obviate the need for substantial military involvement to accomplish the same tasks. After all, Iraq[39] and Afghanistan[40] are both nations of more than 29,000,000 people. Even with reserves—which Congress has not funded—the whole CRC was never contemplated to number more than a few thousand persons.

According to the S/CRS, "many analysts have expressed doubt about S/CRS ability and capacity to carry out its mission."[41] Some of that doubt is blamed on a "perceived lack of funding by Congress," but there are also misgivings about an "anti-operational social culture in the State Department."[42] There seems to be real difficulty with a program that depends upon large numbers of highly-expert civilians *voluntarily* agreeing to serve in austere and dangerous circumstances. This appears to be an impediment, with troubling and perhaps intractable implications for future operations.

As evidence of this issue, consider a 2007 *New York Times* article reporting that many diplomats and Foreign Service employees of the State Department refused assignments to Iraq.[43] Steve Kashkett, vice president of the American Foreign Service Association, insisted that "there remain legitimate questions about the ability of unarmed civilian diplomats to carry out a reconstruction and democracy-building mission in the middle of an active war zone."[44]

As a result, the *Times* says that those employees who did agree to deploy "tended to be younger, more entry-level types, and not experienced, seasoned diplomats."[45] The former head of S/CRS recognizes the problem and admitted in a March 2010 interview that "the State Department must shed the 'risk-averse culture' it adopted in the mid-1980s."[46] He added, "Obviously, you cannot ignore risk, but we need to be willing to manage risk rather than simply avoid it."[47]

Other government employees seem to carry a rather robustly different sense of entitlement when serving in war zones, and this can complicate a WoG approach. For example, a 2008 audit found that Federal Bureau of Investigation (FBI) agents were improperly paid millions of dollars in overtime while on 90 days of temporary duty in Iraq.[48] This investigation found that the agents billed the government on average $45,000 overtime pay, often for simply watching movies, exercising, or even attending parties.[49]

Civilians clearly want to be well paid if they work in dangerous areas. Journalist Nathan Hodge writes that when anthropologists, hired to conduct analysis of the "human terrain" in Iraq and Afghanistan, were converted from "well-compensated contractor status" to government employee status, "around a third of the program's deployed workforce quit."[50]

Besides manning issues, recent reports from Afghanistan about program execution are not encouraging.[51] Critics insist that S/CRS remains poorly funded and is often ignored.[52] Consequently, reporter Spencer Ackerman says that in Afghanistan "American diplomacy and development work in conflict areas remains largely a military job."[53] He says that U.S. soldiers—not American civilians—"politic with local potentates on reconstruction projects."[54] Thinking beyond the specific difficulties with S/CRS, the issue may become this: Can a WoG approach work at all in the U.S. Government?

Analyst Todd Moss has his doubts. The former State Department official acknowledges that a WoG approach may work in other nations, but has reservations about its prospects in the United States. Moss says:

> in the United States—with its sprawling federal structure and huge agency staffs and budget—just getting everyone around one table is perhaps too much to ask. The interagency process in any country is a strain. [Managing those tensions is actually what policymaking is all about.] Yet the process can become convolut-

> ed and bogged down when the scale is out of whack. Simply put: when you have too many people at the table, nothing gets done.[55]

It may be that a WoG approach can suffer from a form of the same malady as that which debilitated American corporations late in the last century, that is, over-diversification. Many companies acquired widely-diverse businesses and put them under the umbrella of a single conglomerate, apparently thinking that the mutual support of the whole would be stronger and more profitable than the individual parts. One can readily see how such thinking would resonate with WoG approach goals. Unfortunately, it often does not work.

Notwithstanding what might be called a "whole of business" approach, the *Economist* observes that the idea "went out of fashion in the 1980s and 1990s . . . when companies began to see again the virtues of 'sticking to their knitting'."[56] Sometimes, it seems, a single-focused entity is better at a specific task than an assemblage of actors with assorted backgrounds. Conglomerates that did succeed were ones that expanded but did not stray far from their core competencies. The chief executive of Bombardier, a Canadian manufacturing firm that acquired new businesses, did so by ensuring that "each new sector we entered shares certain fundamental similarities."[57]

This may mean that a WoG approach may need modification, or at least clarification. Not every security issue needs—or profits from—the application of all the tools in the proverbial toolbox. In some circumstances, a WoG approach may be exactly the wrong strategy; not every agency has the requisite core competencies to add value to the resolution of a particular national security issue. If it is necessary to have a bumper sticker for such a more nuanced approach, then smart power may be it.

THE BETTER CONCEPTUALIZATION FOR THE WAY AHEAD?

Secretary Clinton's articulation of smart power shows it is related to, but not exactly coterminous with, a WoG approach. Although she does not claim to have invented the smart power term, in her 2009 confirmation testimony she defined it as using the "range of tools at our disposal—diplomatic, economic, military, political, legal, and cultural" to address international issues.[58] It does not seek to bring every tool to bear in every instance; rather, smart power is about "picking the right tool, or combination of tools, for each situation."[59] Importantly, Clinton says that under a smart power approach, "diplomacy will be the vanguard of foreign policy."[60]

To be sure, Clinton is not foreswearing a WoG approach; however, she does seem to conceive it differently than has previously been the case. Writing in the November/December 2010 issue of *Foreign Affairs,* Secretary Clinton elaborated on her smart power concept and its distinct emphasis on *civilian* power:[61]

> By drawing on the pool of talent that already exists in U.S. federal agencies and at overseas posts, the United States can build a global civilian service of the same caliber and flexibility as the U.S. military.[62]

In addition to its civilian focus, there is much about the particulars of smart power worth noting carefully. As already observed, it recognizes that sometimes "picking the right tool" suffices. If the number of participants can be minimized, the hazards of navigating the interagency coordination process that concerned Mr. Moss might diminish.[63] Moreover, it suggests that there can be affirmative benefits of discrete approaches by separate government agencies. Consider the U.S. Africa Command (AFRICOM) experience.

AFRICOM might be considered one of the most aggressive models of at least a modified form of a WoG approach. Established in 2007, it represents an innovative effort by the DoD to address the varied needs of a multifaceted continent.[64] It sees itself as a "different kind of command" because it is fashioned with a:

> much more integrated staff structure . . . that includes significant management and staff representation by the Department of State, U.S. Agency for International Development (USAID), and other U.S. government agencies involved in Africa.[65]

One of the most unique aspects of AFRICOM is its leadership arrangements. Unlike any other military organization, it designates a State Department ambassador as its "co-equal" deputy.[66] Notwithstanding the language of co-equality, AFRICOM makes it clear that the ambassador's military counterpart—a Navy admiral—exercises command authority in the AFRICOM commander's absence only because "U.S. law does not allow a State Department official to hold military command authority."[67] Despite the absence of legal authority to command, AFRICOM says the "co-equal" State Department official nevertheless "directs" a variety of military activities, including disaster relief and, somewhat mysteriously, "security sector reform."[68]

The precise distinction between a civilian with authority to "direct" and a military officer empowered to "command" is unexplained and puzzling. While no one questions the value of close working relationships with the Department of State, there is a point at which the intermingling in pursuit of an undifferentiated WoG approach becomes an unproductive infatuation that could dangerously confuse the military chain of command in a crisis. Even more importantly, it may send the wrong message about our diplomats around the globe whose legal status and safety depends upon the perception and reality that they are noncombatant civilians apart from our military forces.

According to a 2009 U.S. Government Accountability Office (GAO) report, various stakeholders raised similar issues. They were concerned that AFRICOM "could blur traditional boundaries between diplomacy, development, and defense." [69] Likewise, the S/CRS reports "mixed feelings" among many about AFRICOM:

> While many at the State Department and USAID welcome the ability of DOD to leverage resources and to organize complex operations, there also is concern that the military may overestimate its capabilities as well as its diplomatic role, or pursue activities that are not a core part of its mandate.[70]

Both the GAO and the S/CRS also report concerns that the size of the DoD "could dominate U.S. activities and relationships in Africa" to the detriment of foreign policy.[71] Essentially, the apprehension was that the command might unproductively "militarize diplomacy and development" on the continent.[72] In response, AFRICOM emphasized a WoG approach—with some success.[73] A subsequent GAO report showed AFRICOM made progress, but effective collaboration remains a daunting issue despite the remarkable integration of representatives of some 27 agencies.[74]

The best intentions can, nevertheless, create issues. For example, apparently AFRICOM originally saw as part of its mission the task to "improve accountable governance" of African states.[75] Exactly what that was supposed to mean remains unclear, but when the most fearsome military in the world starts talking about "improving" what it may decide is a sovereign nation's accountability, it is no wonder that the command has yet to find a home in any country on the continent. The notion of Americans "improving" governments via a military command is an understandably alarming concept to many nations, especially in the shadow of U.S. "regime change" operations in Iraq and Afghanistan.

No doubt it is a worthy aim of the United States to assist nations with bettering their governments, but this is a classic example of an area where America's armed forces ought to steer clear, and a WoG approach is affirmatively counterproductive. Africa has an unfortunate history of militaries "improving" governments by crushing the existing ones in the name of reform. AFRICOM certainly would not do so, but the juxtaposition of an intent to "improve accountable governance" with a military command invites untoward perceptions. Such a task may be appropriate for diplomats and civilian agencies to facilitate, in concert with other nations, international bodies, and NGOs, but not our military.

Clearly, the case for a U.S. military command focused on Africa is a good one, but trying to mix the armed forces and all it implies with activities better carried out via a distinctly diplomatic or civilian entity is obviously problematic. In this instance it appears that smart power must suggest a disaggregation of the respective functions that might better serve U.S. interests than the present WoG approach formulation. Mating a military entity with a diplomatic function could too readily serve to create unnecessary suspicions about U.S. intentions.

AFRICOM is not, however, the only example of questionable utilization of WoG approach-style thinking (if not precise application of WoG approach terminology). Specifically, recent domestic counterterrorism efforts have employed a WoG approach. Despite what Harvard Law professor Jack Goldsmith calls "strong sub-constitutional norms against military involvement in homeland security,"[76] the powerful technical surveillance capabilities of the DoD National Security Agency (NSA) have increasingly been brought to bear domestically to ferret out terrorism threats, as well as to address growing risks to cyber security.

Unfortunately, to the extent a WoG approach involves the military in domestic security activities, history does not provide much encouragement. In the 1960s, for example, military intelligence officers, in the name of national security, were enlisted to collect personal information on tens of thousands of Americans who, in reality, "posed no real threat to national security."[77] The military deployed—domestically—"more than 1,500 plainclothes agents to watch demonstrators, infiltrate organizations, and circulate blacklists."[78] As a result of the ensuing furor, congressional oversight increased,[79] and legislation such as the Foreign Intelligence Surveillance Act (FISA) was enacted.[80]

Nevertheless, in the aftermath of September 11, 2001 (9/11), NSA capabilities were used for domestic surveillance in contravention to FISA requirements. When this illegal activity was revealed, the NSA was sued successfully, and on December 2010 was ordered to pay $2.5 million in attorney fees and damages.[81] Despite this experience, the NSA recently signed a first-of-its kind WoG approach-style agreement with the Department of Homeland Security to collaborate in protecting civilian infrastructure from cyber attacks.[82] Although steps are being taken to protect privacy, civil liberty advocates remain skeptical.[83]

All this is important because if such domestic WoG approaches to security strategies involving the military go awry, they could put in jeopardy vital government interests. The U.S. armed forces are an all-volunteer force (AVF) depending upon the affection and respect of the American people to ensure that sufficient high-quality recruits choose uniformed service. Currently, the military enjoys extremely high levels of public confidence[84] and respect,[85] and that contributes immeasurably to the military's ability to sustain itself.[86]

If that confidence and respect is compromised by perceptions about illegal military involvement in activities that implicate civil liberties, the consequences for the AVF may be serious. Too many potential recruits may not want to involve themselves in a military organization that may appear to be improperly infringing upon the rights of citizens. Thus, as efficient as a WoG approach may be in this arena, on balance it may nevertheless be prudent as a matter of policy to develop the necessary capabilities fully independent of the armed forces.

CONCLUDING OBSERVATIONS

To be sure, a WoG approach should certainly be considered in devising solutions to the complex security challenges of the 21st century. Yet it is those very complexities that counsel against the undifferentiated application of the concept. Clearly, the WoG approach should not devolve into an insistence—or assumption—that every entity of government has some role to play in every national security issue. As discussed, there are real merits in keeping certain activities separate and, in any event, some activities are inappropriate assignments for the armed forces. Hence, in smart power terms, a WoG approach is just an option among several, and one that may—or may not—be appropriate for a given situation.

Although it is largely beyond the scope of this chapter, some mention should be made as to the effectiveness of a WoG approach in its most common and controversial application in the national security arena: post-conflict reconstruction and stabilization. It is an article of faith among purveyors of contemporary COIN theory that such WoG approach-oriented activities are indispensible to a population-centric strategy.[87] That strategy, encompassed in FM *3-24*,[88] aims to win the loyalty of the populace to the central government the counterinsurgents are supporting by facilitating that government's nation-building programs.

Bernard Finel, a Senior Fellow and Director of Research at the American Security Project, points out that critics argue that a:

> population-centric COIN [strategy] requires building responsive governmental structures, promoting economic growth, and eliminating endemic corruption—objectives that have almost never been successfully accomplished in the long, doleful history of international development.[89]

Increasingly, experts like Finel argue that an *enemy-centric* approach is more effective and better suited to American interests. It unapologetically aims to neutralize the insurgents directly as a means to force "a negotiated solution" – a result Finel argues is "consistent with the vast majority of conflicts in history."[90]

In an interview coinciding with the release of his new book, *The Wrong War: Grit, Strategy, and the Way Out of Afghanistan*, former DoD official-turned-embedded-writer Bing West offers an unvarnished assessment. Asked about the effectiveness of billions spent on reconstruction, West says:

> From [Afghan President] Karzai to the villagers, the response has been rational: take or steal every dollar the Americans are foolish enough to give away. In the US, the Great Society and the War on Poverty created a culture of entitlement and undercut individual responsibility. We exported that failed social philosophy to Afghanistan.[91]

Indeed, West is harshly dismissive of nation-building and the military's role in it:

> For 10 years, in Afghanistan, our new COIN doctrine has focused upon building a nation, and has not been successful. The COIN doctrine says our troops are expected to be nation-builders as well as warriors. I believe that is deeply flawed. Our military, despite the exhortations of the Chairman of the Joint Chiefs, should not be a Peace Corps.[92]

West's view, albeit undiplomatically stated, seems to be consistent with the majority of Americans who now consider the war in Afghanistan as something the United States should "not be involved in."[93] This writer has long believed that the armed forces should focus on the all-important task of warfighting, and avoid a variety of deleterious effects that can arise when the military becomes enmeshed in nation-building and related tasks, as part of a WoG approach or otherwise.[94]

Still, none of this is to say that a WoG approach is, per se, flawed. It ought to always be considered when addressing the multifaceted security issues of the 21st century. Again, filtering its utility through the smart power lens will likely find many opportunities where it can be profitably employed. It is the overly-mechanistic application of the concept of a WoG approach that can be the source of mischief and misdirection.

In the end, there is no substitute for wise contemplation of which situations can profit from a WoG approach, and which are most optimally addressed by another, single-entity tool. Such measured analysis of specific situations will ensure that the WoG approach methodology maintains substantive vitality and does not devolve into another exercise of empty pseudo-strategy. In that way, it can be a whole lot of substance, and not simply a whole lot of rhetoric.

ENDNOTES - CHAPTER 7

1. *Quadrennial Roles and Missions Review Report (QRM)*, Washington, DC: U.S. Department of Defense, January 2009, available from *http://www.defense.gov/news/Jan2009/QRMFinalReport_v26Jan.pdf.*

2. See Nina M. Serafino, *Peacekeeping/Stabilization and Conflict Transitions: Background and Congressional Action on the Civilian Response/Reserve Corps and other Civilian Stabilization and Reconstruction Capabilities*, Washington, DC: Congressional Research Service, February 2, 2011, available from *opencrs.com/document/RL32862/.*

3. *National Security Strategy*, Washington, DC: The White House, May 2010, pp. 14-16, available from *www.whitehouse.gov/sites/default/files/rss_viewer/national_security_strategy.pdf*.

4. *Ibid*.

5. Serafino, p. 1.

6. *Ibid*.

7. Serafino, p. 4 (italics added).

8. *Joint Publication (JP) 1-02, DoD Dictionary of Military and Associated Terms*, Washington, DC: U.S. Department of Defense, November 8, 2010, as amended through December 31, 2010, p. 189, available from *www.dtic.mil/doctrine/dod_dictionary/*.

9. Dr. Gordon Adams, *Interagency and National Security Reform: The Road Ahead*, Testimony before the Subcommittee on Oversight and Investigations, House Armed Services Committee, June 9, 2010, p. 52.

10. *U.S. Department of Defense Directive 3000.05, Military Support for Stability, Security, Transition, and Reconstruction (SSTR) Operations*, Washington, DC: U.S. Department of Defense, November 28, 2005, available from *www.usaid.gov/policy/cdie/sss06/sss_1_080106_dod.pdf* (hereinafter DoDD 3000.05, 2005).

11. President George W. Bush, National Security Presidential Directive (NSPD)-44, *Management of Interagency Efforts Concerning Reconstruction and Stabilization*, Washington, DC: White House, December 7, 2005, available from *http://crc.usaidallnet.gov/document/national-security-presidential-directive-44-nspd-44*.

12. DoDD 3000.05, 2005, para. 4.1.

13. *Ibid*., para. 1-17. When the DoDD was reissued, the phrasing was recalibrated to say "the Department of Defense shall be prepared to conduct stability operations with proficiency equivalent to combat operations." See note 23, para. 4a.

14. *Field Manual (FM) 3-07, Stability Operations*, Washington, DC: U.S. Department of the Army, October 2008, para. 1-17, available from *usacac.army.mil/cac2/repository/FM307/FM3-07.pdf.*

15. *Quadrennial Defense Review*, Washington, DC: U.S. Department of Defense, February 6, 2006, p. 83, available from *www.defense.gov/qdr/report/report20060203.pdf.*

16. QDRM, p. 31.

17. *Ibid.*

18. *Quadrennial Defense Review*, Washington, DC: U.S. Department of Defense, February 2010, available from *http://www.defense.gov/qdr/images/QDR_as_of_12Feb10_1000.pdf.*

19. *Field Manual (FM) 3-24, Counterinsurgency*, Washington, DC: U.S. Department of the Army, December 15, 2006; also designated as *Marine Corps Warfighting Publication 3-33.5, 1, Counterinsurgency*, December 15, 2006, available from *www.scribd.com/doc/9137276/US-Army-Field-Manual-FM-324-Counterinsurgency.*

20. Steve Coll, "The General's Dilemma," *The New Yorker*, September 8, 2008, available from *www.newyorker.com/reporting/2008/09/08/080908fa_fact_coll?currentPage=all.*

21. FM 3-24, Chap. 2.

22. See, for example, *The JAG Corp and the Rule of Law Reform: Q & A with Brigadier General Thomas Ayres L'91*, Philadelphia, PA: University of Pennsylvania Law School, September 21, 2010, available from *www.law.upenn.edu/blogs/news/archives/2010/09/qa_with_brigadier_general_thomas_ayres_l91.html.*

23. U.S. Department of Defense Directive (DoDD) 3000.05 *Stability Operations*, Washington, DC: U.S. Department of Defense, September 16, 2009, para. 4a (3), available from *www.dtic.mil/whs/directives/corres/pdf/300005p.pdf.*

24. U.S. Constituion, Preamble, Washington, DC.

25. *Parker v. Levy*, 417 U.S. 733, 743 (1974), available from *supreme.justia.com/us/417/733/case.html.*

26. *U.S. ex rel. Toth v. Quarles*, 350 U. S. 11,17 (1955) available from *supreme.justia.com/us/350/11/case.html*.

27. *Ibid*.

28. See for instance, Volker Franke, "The Peacebuilding Dilemma: Civil-Military Cooperation in Stability Operations," *International Journal of Peace Studies*, Vol. 11, No. 2, Autumn/Winter 2006, pp. 5-25.

29. Douglas Porch, "Writing History in the 'End of History' Era—Reflections on Historians and the GWOT," *Journal of Military History*, October 2006, p. 1078.

30. Anna Mulrine, "Can Troops Get Too Much Love? Military Struggles with a Dark Side on Veterans Day," *Christian Science Monitor*, November 10, 2010, available from *www.csmonitor.com/USA/Military/2010/1110/Can-troops-get-too-much-love-Military-struggles-with-a-dark-side-on-Veterans-Day*.

31. Lieutenant Colonel Andrew R. Milburn, U.S. Marine Corps, "Breaking Ranks: Dissent and the Military Professional," *Joint Force Quarterly*, Issue 59, 4th Quarter, October 2010, p. 101, available from *www.ndu.edu/press/lib/images/jfq-59/JFQ59_101-107_Milburn.pdf*.

32. *Ibid*. (Italics in original).

33. David Wood, "Military Officers Chafe for Bigger Role in Policy Decisions," *Politics Daily*, October 4, 2010, available from *www.politicsdaily.com/2010/10/04/military-officers-chafe-for-bigger-role-in-policy-decisions/*.

34. *Ibid*.

35. See Serafino.

36. U.S. Department of State Office of the Coordinator for Reconstruction and Stabilization, *About Us*, available from *www.state.gov/s/crs/about/index.htm#mission*.

37. *Ibid.*, at Civilian Response Corps, available from *www.state.gov/s/crs/civilianresponsecorps/index.htm*.

38. This is according to John E. Herbst, Coordinator for Reconstruction and Stabilization, U.S. Department of State. See Greg Bruno, *Waiting on a Civilian Surge in Afghanistan*, Washington, DC: Council on Foreign Relations, March 31, 2010, available from *www.cfr.org/afghanistan/waiting-civilian-surge-afghanistan/p21785* (interview with the Hon. John E. Herbst).

39. U.S. Central Intelligence Agency, *World Factbook - Iraq*, February 14, 2011, available from *https://www.cia.gov/library/publications/the-world-factbook/geos/iz.html*.

40. U.S. Central Intelligence Agency, *World Factbook - Afghanistan*, February 11, 2010, available from *https://www.cia.gov/library/publications/the-world-factbook/geos/af.html*.

41. Serafino, p. 21.

42. *Ibid.*

43. Helene Cooper, "Many U.S. diplomats refuse to work in Iraq - Africa & Middle East," *New York Times*, February 7, 2007, available from *www.nytimes.com/2007/02/08/world/africa/08iht-web.0208diplo.4516120.html*.

44. *Ibid.*

45. *Ibid.*

46. Bruno.

47. *Ibid.*

48. "FBI Agents Billed $45K Apiece for Iraq OT," Associated Press, December 18, 2008, available from *www.msnbc.msn.com/id/28299590/ns/world_news-mideast/n_africa/*.

49. *Ibid.*

50. Nathan Hodge, *Armed Humanitarians: The Rise of the Nation Builders*, New York: Bloomsbury, 2011, p. 255.

51. See notes 89 and 90 and accompanying text.

52. Spencer Ackerman, "Reconstruction Chief Quits, Putting 'Civilian Surge' in Doubt," *Danger Room*, September 28, 2010, available from *www.wired.com/dangerroom/2010/09/reconstruction-chief-quits-putting-civilian-surge-in-doubt/#*.

53. *Ibid.*

54. *Ibid.*

55. Todd Moss, *Too Big to Succeed? (W)Hole-of-Government Cannot Work for US Development Policy*, Washington, DC: Center for Global Development, October 5, 2010, available from *blogs.cgdev.org/globaldevelopment/2010/10/too-big-to-succeed-why-whole-of-government-cannot-work-for-u-s-development-policy.php*.

56. "Idea: Diversification," *The Economist*, October 7, 2009, available from *www.economist.com/node/14298922*.

57. *Ibid.*

58. Secretary of the Department of State Hillary Rodham Clinton, Statement before the Senate Foreign Relations Committee, January 13, 2009, available from *www.state.gov/secretary/rm/2009a/01/115196.htm*.

59. *Ibid.*

60. *Ibid.*

61. Hillary Rodham Clinton, "Leading Through Civilian Power: Redefining American Diplomacy and Development," *Foreign Affairs*, p. 13, available from *http://www.devex.com/en/news/leading-through-civilian-power-redefining-american/70521*.

62. *Ibid.*, p. 16.

63. See Moss, and accompanying text.

64. See generally, Lauren Ploch, *Africa Command: U.S. Strategic Interests and the Role of the U.S. Military in Africa*, Washington, DC: Congressional Research Service, November 10, 2010, available from *www.fas.org/sgp/crs/natsec/RL34003.pdf*.

65. *About U.S. Africa Command*, Washington, DC: U.S. Department of Defense, available from *www.africom.mil/AboutAFRICOM.asp*.

66. See Biography, *Ambassador J. Anthony Holmes, Deputy to the Commander for Civil-Military Activities*, Washington, DC: U.S. Department of Defense, U.S. Africa Command, available from *www.africom.mil/holmes.asp*.

67. See Biography, *Vice Admiral Robert T. Moeller, Deputy to the Commander for Military Operations*, Washington, DC: U.S. Department of Defense, U.S. Africa Command, available from *www.africom.mil/moeller.asp*.

68. *Ibid.*

69. *Actions Needed to Address Stakeholder Concerns, Improve Interagency Collaboration, and Determine Full Costs Associated with the U.S. Africa Command*, GAO-09-181, Washington, DC: U.S. Government Accountability Office, February 2009, p. 3, available from *www.gao.gov/new.items/d09181.pdf*.

70. Ploch, p. 6.

71. *Ibid.*

72. *Ibid.*

73. *Ibid.*, p. 4.

74. *Improved Planning, Training, and Interagency Collaboration Could Strengthen DoD's Efforts in Africa*, GAO-10-794, Washington, DC: U.S. Government Accountability Office, July 2010, *www.gao.gov/new.items/d10794.pdf*.

75. *U.S. Africa Command (AFRICOM): Questions and Answers*, Press Release, Embassy of the United States (Cameroon), U.S. Department of State, October 2, 2007, available from *yaounde.usembassy.gov/u.s._africa_command_africom_questions_and_answers.html.*

76. Jack Goldsmith, *The Cyberthreat, Government Network Operations, and the Fourth Amendment*, Washington, DC: Governance Studies at Brookings, December 8, 2010, p. 10, available from *www.brookings.edu/~/media/Files/rc/papers/2010/1208_4th_amendment_goldsmith/1208_4th_amendment_goldsmith.pdf.*

77. Stephan Dycus *et al*., "The Military's Role in Homeland Security and Disaster Relief," *National Security Law*, 4th Ed., 2007, p. 960.

78. *Ibid.*

79. See Brit Snider, *Congressional Oversight of Intelligence: Some Reflections on the Last 25 Years*, Durham, NC: Duke University, Center on Law, Ethics and National Security, 2003, available from *www.law.duke.edu/lens/downloads/snider.pdf.*

80. 50 U.S.C. §1801-1862, 2008.

81. Paul Elias, "Judge Orders Feds to Pay $2.5 million in Wiretapping Case," *Washington Post*, December 21, 2010, available from *www.washingtonpost.com/wp-dyn/content/article/2010/12/21/AR2010122105307.html.*

82. *Joint Statement by Secretary Gates and Secretary Napolitano on Enhancing Coordination to Secure America's Cyber Networks*, Washington, DC: U.S. Department of Defense, October 13, 2010, available from *www.defense.gov/releases/release.aspx?releaseid=13965.*

83. William Matthews, "DoD to Protect Some Civilian Infrastructure," *Defense News*, October 18, 2010, p. 6.

84. Lydia Saad, "Congress Ranks Last in Confidence in Institutions," Gallup, Inc., July 22, 2010, available from *www.gallup.com/poll/141512/Congress-Ranks-Last-Confidence-Institutions.aspx.*

85. "Honesty/Ethics in Professions," November 19-21, 2010, Gallup, Inc., available from *www.gallup.com/poll/1654/honesty-ethics-professions.aspx.*

86. *Cf.* Dan Blottenberger, "All Branches Meet Military Recruiting Goals," *Stars & Stripes,* January 14, 2011, available from *www.stripes.com/news/all-branches-meet-military-recruiting-goals-1.131869#.*

87. See, for example, Octavian Manea, "Counterinsurgency as a Whole of Government Approach: Notes on the British Army Field Manual Weltanschauung," *Small Wars Journal,* January 24, 2011, available from *http://smallwarsjournal.com/jrnl/art/counterinsurgency-as-a-whole-of-government-approach.*

88. See FM 3-24, and accompanying text.

89. Bernard Finel, "A Substitute for Victory: Adopting a New Counterinsurgency Strategy in Afghanistan," *Foreign Affairs,* April 8, 2010, available from *www.foreignaffairs.com/articles/66189/bernard-finel/a-substitute-for-victory.*

90. *Ibid.*

91. Michael Few, "The Wrong War: An Interview with Bing West," *Small Wars Journal,* February 21, 2011, available from *smallwarsjournal.com/blog/journal/docs-temp/679-few3.pdf.*

92. *Ibid.*

93. CBS News Poll, February 11-14, 2011, reporting that 54 percent of Americans believe the United States should not be involved in the war in Afghanistan, *PollingReport.com,* available from *www.pollingreport.com/afghan.htm.*

94. Charles J. Dunlap, Jr., "The Origins of the American Military Coup of 2012," *Parameters,* Winter, 1992-93, p. 2, available from *www.uwec.edu/sfpj/Origins.pdf.*

CHAPTER 8

WHOLE OF GOVERNMENT IN DIPLOMACY AND DEVELOPMENT: WHOLE OR HOLE?

James Stephenson

On December 15, 2010, Secretary of State Hillary Clinton released the first *Quadrennial Diplomacy and Development Report* (QDDR).[1] While much of the attention of the international development community was focused on what role the QDDR would articulate for the U.S. Agency for International Development (USAID), its embrace of the whole of government (WoG) approach to diplomacy and development seemed to pass almost unnoticed. Arguably, this is because in the implementation of U.S. foreign assistance WoG has grown like a fungus for over a decade. Since Operation IRAQI FREEDOM (OIF), it has become the *modus operandi*—WoG on steroids—for U.S. efforts to bring stability in conflict, post-conflict, and fragile states that may fall victim to conflict. As the QDDR states, ambassadors are now chief executive officers (CEOs) of complex interagency missions.[2] Where USAID once had almost sole responsibility for foreign assistance, more than a dozen agencies and government organizations now have their own mini-foreign aid offices, all ostensibly under chief of mission authority or at least a "unified effort," the term used where the military is present and not under chief of mission authority. Further, the military has become ever more deeply engaged in stability operations that are indistinguishable from civilian stabilization and reconstruction efforts, even in theaters where there is no obvious need for a uniformed presence, such as the Horn of Africa. Embassies are larger, with disparate agencies competing for foreign aid dollars, often working at cross-purposes. (In one West African country, the U.S. Africa Command [AFRICOM] funded a host country agency the country team was trying to abolish.) The proponents of WoG embrace the logic that the application of more human and bureaucratic resources *ipso facto* results in the efficient production of a better product—that competition engenders rigor. But does it? Is there any empirical evidence that the vast bureaucracies we created in Iraq, Afghanistan, and Pakistan are any more effective than the far smaller, flatter country teams we used in the past? Are domestic agencies really very good at foreign assistance and in foreign operating environments? Are ambassadors, by training and experience, prepared to be CEOs of "complex interagency missions?" Finally, with the imperative to cut deficits and the federal work force, does the QDDR, which calls for staff increases at the Department of State (State) and USAID, offer a sustainable business model?

These questions are particularly relevant, given President Barack Obama's promise in the State of the Union address on January 25, 2011, to overhaul the federal bureaucracy and consolidate its functions; while the Republican opposition promises to trim the federal workforce and specifically the size and resources of State and USAID, reversing the recent trend to increase the size and resources of both. The President spoke of the "fur ball"—my words—of overlapping federal rules, responsibilities, and jurisdictions. There are currently some 17 federal departments and agencies engaged in some form of foreign assistance—e.g., the Overseas Private Investment Corporation, the

Millennium Challenge Corporation, the Peace Corps, the Trade and Development Agency, the departments of Agriculture, Treasury, Justice, Health and Human Services, Commerce, Homeland Security (DHS), the Drug Enforcement Administration (DEA), the Centers for Disease Control (CDC), and—the largest of all—the Department of Defense (DoD)—to name a few. Foreign assistance has become the poster child for WoG, even though the Foreign Assistance Act of 1961 established USAID to consolidate all foreign assistance activities under a single federal agency to eliminate the polyglot of competing federal departments and agencies that foreign assistance had by then become.[3] What was seen as a vice in 1961, some now celebrate as a virtue—WoG—and posit that the world of diplomacy and development has become so complex that no single department or agency can meet its challenges. (Great Britain came to precisely the opposite conclusion over a decade ago in creating the Cabinet Department For International Development, separate from the Foreign Office.)

The intellectual debate over where responsibility for international development should reside in the federal government will continue, unabated by the release of the QDDR. However, our burgeoning deficits and national debt concerns are likely to eclipse that debate, pushing us toward the model most effective and cost efficient. The proponents of smaller government might argue that the outsourcing of State and USAID responsibilities to other federal agencies is cost effective; that WoG eliminates duplication and redundancy. (Why does USAID need agriculture experts when the Department of Agriculture already has them?) Or, they could argue that USAID and the mini-foreign aid offices in other departments and agencies be merged into the State Department. Or, as the development purists argue, the clock could be turned back to 1961 and USAID could be re-empowered as an autonomous agency with near sole responsibility for foreign assistance.[4] There may be other options, including the status quo, with fewer resources.[5] Unfortunately, many of the "experts" who will weigh in are academics or politicians who never served in the State Department, USAID, an American embassy, or even abroad. You may ask, "So what?" In answer, I point you to the military.

Last year, I had the privilege to contribute to the Capstone Concept for Joint Operations (CCJO), under the direction of Joint Forces Command (JFCOM). The CCJO looks 10-20 years into the future and tries to conceptualize what will characterize the demands and components of the wars we may have to fight. From the concept follows doctrine. From doctrine follows force structure, planning, procurement of equipment and systems, logistics, etc. Defining and articulating the concept is the work of scores of both uniformed and civilian personnel from varied backgrounds, who have experienced our current and past wars first hand. Even so, defining the components of the concept is exceedingly difficult, frustrating, and conducive to heated debate. There are four components to the CCJO: Combat, Security, Engagement, and Relief and Reconstruction. It seems simple, but what do the terms mean? How do they overlap? Does relief support combat? Is not engagement part and parcel of reconstruction? Participants came to the table with different constructs, prejudices, and opinions, but *all had field experience and expertise* relevant to one or more components. The process of give-and-take defined and articulated the concept. Finally, the production of the CCJO was not a political process whose outcome was predetermined by bureaucratic turf wars or power struggles, as was the case with State's QDDR and the competing vision of the National Security Staff's Presidential Study Directive. It was a sober, multidisciplinary attempt to prepare the joint services and country for future conflict.

Whether policies and practices that emanate from Washington evolve fairly rapidly, e.g., the repeal of "Don't ask—Don't tell" or the QDDR, the manner of their evolution matters far less than their impact and effect in the field—downrange for the military, at the country team level for civilians. As most of my experience in foreign assistance has been gained overseas, I confine my observations about WoG to its effects in the field, and begin with an observation of how country teams used to operate—until OIF.

"BEFORE, WE KNEW EACH OTHER AND HAD VAST EXPERIENCE"

The generic country team used to consist of the Ambassador, a handful of State Department Foreign Service Officers, the Defense attaché(s), USAID (where there was an assistance program), the Central Intelligence Agency (CIA), and perhaps representatives from the Departments of Commerce, Justice, and Treasury.[6] Either military or civilian experts, such as military cooperation or anti-narcotics, sometimes augmented this core team, as needed. In conflict and post-conflict countries, country teams were generally even smaller, usually to restrict the number of personnel put in harm's way. Further, because most civilians preferred not to serve in dangerous conflict/post-conflict posts, there existed a small cadre of personnel who, by choice, spent their careers serving in conflict environments. It was a tight, proficient fraternity, but often called on other agencies or the private sector to augment it with specific professional skills. It worked very well—from Central America to Eastern Europe, the Middle East, the Balkans, and Africa.

In preparation for this chapter, I interviewed a well-respected, career ambassador, without attribution, because I wanted candor. When asked if ambassadors were prepared to be "CEOs of complex interagency missions," the Ambassador replied that chiefs of mission had always been CEOs and sometimes were susceptible to empire building. However, embassies now have more agencies, represented by individuals who have no concept of what it means to be under chief of mission authority and whose loyalty is to their agency. That and the current push for whole of government give them license to operate independently. Domestic agencies have different, less precise reporting standards and requirements, and their unapproved reports often get into the decision process in Washington. With more agencies, ambassadors have to exercise more control, requiring, for example, that defense attachés obtain chief of mission clearance on all cables. When asked if WoG sometimes means that no one is in charge, the Ambassador responded that too often the wrong person is in charge, and that there has been a proliferation of responsibility and leadership to inexperienced agency personnel who have no commitment to the Mission, are not team players, and do not understand that country teams are enablers. This problem is compounded by powerful Combat Commands, such as Central Command (CENTCOM) and AFRICOM, that often attempt to operate independently in direct conflict with Mission policies and programs, and have to be reined in. The Ambassador closed with the lament, "Before, we knew each other and had vast experience—we were a team."

These observations tracked very closely with my own experiences in Grenada, El Salvador, Lebanon, and Serbia/Montenegro, where we had small missions of highly experienced individuals that operated as a team—a sometimes fractious team, but one that understood the conventions of being part of an embassy country team. That dynamic changed with OIF and the creation of the Coalition Provisional Authority (CPA).[7] Although the CPA was headed by a former career diplomat and benefited from the services of a handful of talented senior Foreign Service officers, it answered to and was staffed by the DoD. The CPA was a hybrid precursor to WoG that reluctantly utilized a few government agencies, such as USAID and the Department of the Treasury, but mainly relied on individuals—thousands of them—who were temporarily hired under U.S. Code Title 5 Section 3161, which gives temporary federal organizations hiring authority.[8] Most came from the private sector, and a very large proportion had never been overseas, much less worked in the most difficult venue of foreign assistance—conflict. So many inexperienced actors with so many individual agendas led to chaotic program design and implementation. There are critics and defenders of the CPA, but all might agree that the CPA was a completely new model, more an occupier and surrogate for governance than an enabler of Iraqi governance and development. It only lasted 14 months, but when State succeeded the CPA, it inherited most of its structure, many of its 4,000 personnel, and its philosophy that more is better. Months before the CPA ended, State Department plans were already far advanced to build and staff the largest embassy in the world. Seven years later, it still is the largest—but Afghanistan is catching up.

It is conventional wisdom that the Bush administration under-resourced both the kinetic and reconstruction efforts in Afghanistan to support its efforts in Iraq, effectively enabling the resurgence of the Taliban insurgency. The failings of the coalition and the Afghan government are far too complex to attribute simply to inadequate resources. In fact, the resurgence of the Taliban did not take hold until late 2005, 4 years after it was driven from power. One could argue that had early and sustained stabilization and reconstruction efforts focused more at the village level, rather than on building a strong central government from the top down, conditions for the return of the Taliban may not have ripened. Afghanistan has never had a strong central government, and indeed its rural population generally views central authority as an intrusive foreign presence. Nevertheless, the response of the Obama administration was a massive increase in troop levels and a concurrent five-fold increase in U.S. Government civilians to carry out stabilization and reconstruction. The late Richard Holbrooke, Special Representative for Afghanistan and Pakistan (AF-PAK), was the architect of the civilian expansion, effectively creating a new bureaucracy within the State Department in Washington, Kabul, and Islamabad. To meet the demand for personnel, both State and USAID were forced to deplete personnel resources at other missions and resort to temporary hires, often people with little relevant experience. Other agencies, such as the Department of Agriculture, also contributed to the buildup, but a very large number of personnel were temporary State hires, due to a shortfall from State,

USAID, and other agencies. It is too soon to tell if 1,250 civilians, distributed between the embassy fortress in Kabul, four regional centers, forward operating bases, and provincial reconstruction teams, will have enough impact on the lives of rural Afghan villagers to turn them away from the Taliban; but the evidence so far seems to the contrary. There is growing evidence that the large foreign presence and sheer volume of U.S. assistance is actually *fueling* corruption and instability, creating conditions favorable to the Taliban.[9] In culturally complex operating environments, doing less—smarter—and enabling an indigenous process of change is usually more effective than the blunt instrument of dollars and more bodies, particularly when their presence is unaccompanied by a viable strategy and plan of implementation.

SUSTAINABILITY OF WHOLE OF GOVERNMENT ABROAD

Since the bombings of the American embassies in Lebanon, Nairobi, and Dar Es Salaam, mandatory standards for construction of embassies worldwide have made them very expensive, fortress-like compounds, with a fixed amount of office space. In dangerous places like Iraq, compounds often include both offices and living quarters, further increasing the cost. (The new embassy in Baghdad cost over $700 million to build, reportedly over $1 billion a year to run, and does not have sufficient space for all agencies.)[10] In recent testimony before Congress, Ambassador James Jeffrey testified that State currently has a staff of 8,000 in Iraq, but in 2012 will expand to 17,000, comprised mostly of contractors, and will require operating costs of $3 billion a year.[11] In Islamabad, the U.S. Embassy is undergoing a $1 billion expansion to accommodate the increase in staff mandated by the late Mr. Holbrooke. The increased official American presence in Pakistan—3,555 visas issued to U.S. diplomats, military officials and employees of "allied agencies" in 2010—fueled a backlash of Pakistani popular opinion that the country is being overrun by American agent provocateurs. This perception was compounded by the recent killing of two Pakistani nationals by U.S. diplomat Raymond Davis, who, it turned out, is a CIA contractor.

Embassy compounds are designed at a point in time based upon the needed facilities to support current and planned increases in staff. Once constructed, they are rarely conducive to easy or inexpensive additions. When USAID began hiring new employees under its Development Leadership Initiative (DLI), which aims to at least double the size of its Foreign Service corps, it planned to place the new hires overseas following training in Washington. Unfortunately, those plans immediately ran up against the space limitations endemic to almost all American embassies. Ambassadors at numerous posts refused to accept the DLIs, as they are known, because they literally had no place to put them. USAID's personnel expansion is undoubtedly necessary, but it was begun before the current fiscal crisis. The new House Republican majority has already signaled that it will push for reductions in foreign aid, and that will undoubtedly include scaling back USAID's expansion plans. USAID is an integral part of U.S. diplomacy and development. It is much harder to make that case for the myriad other agencies with mini-foreign aid offices and spigots that WoG embraces. Carrying $14 trillion in debt and annual budget deficits in excess of $1 trillion, the U.S.

Government cannot afford WoG abroad, and it cannot afford the resource-intensive approaches used in Iraq, Afghanistan, and Pakistan. Moreover, Congress will no longer support those approaches when a leaner, more streamlined approach to diplomacy and development will not only work, but work more effectively.

A BETTER MODEL FOR THE 21ST CENTURY

In 1981, President Ronald Reagan was determined to thwart the expansion of communism in El Salvador, in spite of a deeply skeptical Congress over which hung the unpleasant memory of the war in Vietnam. To garner funding from Congress, Reagan was forced to agree that military advisors to the El Salvador Armed Forces (ESAF) would be limited to no more than 55 personnel in country at any time. This Milgroup, as it was called, could train and advise, but was strictly forbidden from engaging in combat or accompanying trainees in field operations. USAID was informally limited to 36 Foreign Service Officers and approximately an equal number of expatriate personal service contractors. The Embassy staff was even smaller. Initially, the military viewed the Milgroup limitation as a severe challenge, bordering on mission impossible. Most of the 55 advisors were highly trained special operations forces, fluent in Spanish, culturally adapted, and vastly experienced. The Milgroup did not have the numbers to win the war for the Salvadorans, so was forced to *enable* the ESAF by slowly turning it into a professional army that could, in time, defeat the Farabund Marti National Liberation Front (FMLN) insurgency.[12] On the civilian side, the State Department and USAID made the time consuming investments to *enable* the Salvadorans themselves to bring about the social, economic and political reforms needed to convert an almost feudal system into a viable democracy. Again, State and USAID officers were highly experienced, culturally adapted professionals. For most, it was not their "first rodeo," and they were there for the long haul. To be sure, military training outside of El Salvador augmented the Milgroup effort in El Salvador, and U.S. intelligence gathering and sharing aided the ESAF; but the Milgroup and civilian personnel restrictions turned out to be a serendipitous driver that forced the United States to enable the Salvadorans themselves to save their country. It took 12 years and cost the United States $4 billion and approximately 20 American lives; but it resulted in a negotiated peace agreement, the conversion of the FMLN into a loyal democratic opposition, and a vibrant economy supported by good governance and the rule of law. It was the projection of smart power 30 years before that term came into use.

Since 2002, the United States has invested over $130 billion in security, economic, and governance assistance to Iraq, Afghanistan, and Pakistan. This amount does not include military operations but does include security assistance and training performed by the military. For fiscal year (FY) 2012, the administration has requested $3.2 billion in operating expenses just for the State Department and USAID in Iraq. Since 2002, the United States has provided more than $55 billion for Afghan security, governance, and development, and over $18 billion to assist Pakistan, according to the U.S. Government Accounting Office (GAO)—and there is no end in sight.[13]

There is no question that State Department and USAID personnel need to be augmented if they are to meet their responsibilities for diplomacy and development and the projection of smart power. Unfortunately, the vision embraced by the QDDR and WoG is neither smart nor fiscally sustainable. Neither every problem nor every solution is an El Salvador, but if we start with the premise that diplomacy and development should be practiced by a highly trained and experienced cadre of enablers, the methodologies and costs will be fiscally sustainable, and WoG will be relegated to the diminished role it should have in overseas operations.

ENDNOTES - CHAPTER 8

1. *The First Quadrennial Diplomacy and Development Review (QDDR): Leading Through Civilian Power*, Washington, DC: Department of State, available from *www.state.gov/s/dmr/qddr/*.

2. *Ibid.*, Executive Summary.

3. The Foreign Assistance Act of 1961, as amended, Washington, DC: U.S. Agency for International Development, available from *www.usaid.gov/policy/ads/faa.pdf*.

4. Raymond Malley, "U.S. Foreign Economic Assistance in Perspective," *Foreign Service Journal*, December 2010, p. 15.

5. Noam Unger and Margaret L. Taylor, *Capacity for Change, Reforming U.S. Assistance Efforts in Poor and Fragile Countries*, Washington, DC: Brookings and Center for Strategic and International Studies (CSIS), April 2010.

6. *Department of State*, Washington, DC: Department of State, available from *www.usdiplomacy.org/state/abroad/countryteam.php*.

7. Department of State, *The Coalition Provisional Authority (CPA): Origin, Characteristics, and Institutional Authorities*, Wash-

ington, DC: Department of State, available from *fpc.state.gov/documents/organization/48620.pdf*.

8. U.S. Code, Title 5, available from from *http://www.law.cornell.edu/uscode/text/5*.

9. Afghanistan Forum, available from *afghanistanforum.wordpress.com/2010/04/04/andrew-wilder-winning-hearts-and-minds/*.

10. Alexandra Valiente, available from *https://alexandravaliente.wordpress.com/2011/06/24/permanent-u-s-iraq-and-afghanistan-occupations-planned/*.

11. *The United States in Iraq: Options for 2012*, Washington, DC: United States Institute for Peace, May 16, 2011, available from *www.usip.org/files/resources/The_United_States_in_Iraq.pdf*.

12. Major Paul P. Cale, "The United States Military Advisory Group In El Salvador, 1979-1992," *Small Wars Journal*, Vol. 13, available from *smallwarsjournal.com/documents/cale.pdf*.

13. Testimony Before the Subcommittee on State, Foreign Operations, and Related Programs, Committee on Appropriations, House of Representatives, *Foreign Operations*, Key Issues for Congressional Oversight, Washington, DC: U.S. Government Accountability Office, March 3, 2011, p. 4, available from *http://www.gao.gov/products/GAO-11-419T*.

CHAPTER 9

THE NATIONAL SECURITY STAFF: WHAT'S MISSING IN WHOLE OF GOVERNMENT APPROACHES TO NATIONAL SECURITY

Jack A. LeCuyer

> The United States must navigate an environment in which traditional organizations and means of response to global challenges may be inadequate or deficient. Indeed, the ability of the Nation to successfully compete in global issues is being tested in ways that were unimaginable until recently. To succeed, the United States must integrate its ability to employ all elements of national power in a cohesive manner. In order to deal with the world as it is, rather than how we wish it were, the National Security Council must be transformed to meet the realities of the new century.[1]
>
> Memorandum from the Assistant to the President for National Security Affairs

OVERVIEW

A whole of government (WoG) approach to national security at every level must begin at the top of the U.S. national security system, where the National Security Council (NSC) and the National Security Staff serve as the de facto hub of the national security system. Although the national security environment has changed dramatically since the NSC was created in 1947, the United States has not changed the fundamental way it manages our national security system or the role of the NSC staff/National Security Staff as strategic managers of the national security system to meet the challenges and opportunities of the new global environment. The National Security Staff remains focused on the urgent and crisis management rather than the long-term strategic view. A deliberate National Security Staff design based on strategic management functions, processes, and best practices will improve the balance between departmental and the necessary WoG practices required for the global security environment of the 21st century and ensure that the NSC is the *strategic manager* for improving the performance, adaptability, and efficiency of the overall national security system in achieving those national security goals and missions that contribute to our long-term prosperity and security. This chapter will answer three questions: Why have we not been able to achieve effective WoG national security efforts at the strategic level? What do we need to achieve them? How likely is it that we will be able to get what we need? The repeated failures of the current system over the last 20 years are compelling reasons to explicitly recognize this strategic management function as the crucial lynchpin of our national security system. A National Security Staff culture focused on policy development, and the urgent (crisis management) at the expense of the important, and reinforced by significant under-resourcing contributes to this lack of management at the strategic level. Initial steps by the Barack Obama administration offer hope for change but require a determined effort to imbue the NSC with strategic management functions and then resource it to accomplish them. Progress in resourcing the National Security Staff to accomplish the strategic management of WoG efforts to achieve desired national security outcomes will be increasingly important in our efforts to achieve success in stabilization and peace-building efforts.

THE CHANGING GLOBAL SECURITY ENVIRONMENT

The fall of the Berlin Wall in 1989 and the end of the Cold War in 1991 created a strategic vacuum that is characterized by what Erik Peterson has defined as the seven revolutions in population, resource management, technology, information and knowledge, economic integration, conflict, and governance as issues that embody both opportunity and risk for the United States.[2] With containment of the Soviet Union no longer the *raison d'être* of our national security system, and the rise of competing major economic powers, achievement of America's strategic goals of prosperity and security would now have to be achieved in a global context in which U.S. hegemony in the western world was replaced with competition and cooperation in many nontraditional sectors now truly linked globally in real-time because of advances in technology, and in which true power often lies beyond the hands of traditional federal government entities.[3]

Today's modern global security environment of the post-September 11, 2001 (9/11) world and the financial meltdowns of 2008 is characterized by complexity, uncertainty, speed, and real-time interconnectivity in domains that require WoG responses. No longer can we afford to view national security through the narrow lenses of military security and diplomacy against a background of state-to-state relations as we did during the Cold War. The dimensions of national security now include the global issues of economic security, environmental security, homeland security, pandemics, transnational terrorism, failing and failed states, rising states such as South Sudan, regional instability, cyber-terrorism, and the potential use of weapons of mass destruction (WMD). The United States depends on a networked global information grid and supply chain that is increasingly vulnerable to catastrophic attack. The global economy means that actions of a single actor, governmental or nongovernmental—e.g., Standard & Poor's or Moody's—can have significant and immediate global impact. Transnational nonstate criminal and ideological organizations, leveraged by technology and exploiting ungoverned spaces, have found new and increasingly sophisticated means of attack. Global climate change, demographics, and rising global demands for finite resources raise serious concerns over the availability of food, water, and other resources that threaten economic and political stability around the world and require new strategically agile and integrated WoG institutional responses to preserve our national security and prosperity.

However, these massive changes in the global national security environment have not resulted in a corresponding change in the fundamental way that the United States manages its national security interests at the strategic level from the way that they were managed during the Cold War. As one national security practitioner recently remarked,

> In many ways, Washington today is a lagging indicator of how we should address national problems. Our national security system is vintage 1947—a basic linear industrial age system. It is much like the Sears and Roebuck Catalog sales of the 1950's trying to compete with today's Amazon's online "one-click shopping." Our enemies are franchises while we operate our government and national security system as a regulated steel mill of the last century.[4]

DEFINING WHOLE OF GOVERNMENT STRATEGIC MANAGEMENT OF OUR NATIONAL SECURITY SYSTEM IN THE 21ST CENTURY

Barriers to interagency collaboration and WoG approaches are inherent throughout the current national security system. In a 2005 report, the U.S. Government Accountability Office (GAO) found that:

> The federal government faces a series of challenges in the 21st century that will be difficult, if not impossible, for any single agency to address alone. Many issues cut across more than one agency and their actions are not well coordinated. Moreover, agencies face a range of barriers when they attempt to work collaboratively.[5]

A more recent GAO assessment in June, 2010, noted that while some progress has been made:

> The federal agencies involved in national security will need to make concerted efforts to forge strong, collective partnerships, and seek coordinated solutions that leverage the expertise and capabilities across the community. Sustained and inspired attention is needed to overcome the many barriers to working across agency boundaries. Strengthening interagency collaboration—with leadership as the foundation—can help transform our U.S. government agencies and create a more unified, comprehensive approach to national security issues at home and abroad.[6]

It is useful to have an analytical framework to guide the discussion on the dimensions and minimum degrees of integration required for a WoG approach by organizations and individuals at each level—the strategic, the operational, and the tactical—in the future national security system.[7] In 2007, the National Security Professional Development Integration Office (NSPD-IO) was established to help coordinate NSPD activities related to President George W. Bush's Executive Order 13434[8] (*National Security Professional Development*) to develop a corps of national security professionals. It developed one such framework to display the dimensions and degrees of integration in WoG approaches as the following hierarchy:[9]

- **Collaboration**: Execute departmental and agency tasks jointly;
- **Cooperation**: Execute departmental and agency tasks in pursuit of common goals;
- **Coordination**: Solicit and respond to input from other departments and agencies;
- **Consultation**: Inform others who may need to know; and,
- **Communication**: Disclose information, plans, opinions/perceptions.

This hierarchy of progressive steps toward achieving integration—or WoG approaches—is important because it establishes precision in terms and expectations and who is accountable in departmental and agency actions at every level. It also points to problems when several of these terms are used interchangeably to define the responsibilities of the NSC in the National Security Act of 1947 (as amended).[10]

In the fast-paced and complex global security environment of the 21st century, it is axiomatic that at the strategic level, virtually all national security challenges require an integrated WoG approach across a variety of interagency and, in some cases, intergovernmental and private sector actors and equities. *At the strategic level – in the interagency space between the President/Ex-*

ecutive Office of the President (EOP) and the departments and agencies – integration or WoG efforts must be at the level of collaboration – the execution of national security tasks and missions jointly – between the multiple stakeholders to ensure that activities are defined by presidential policy and the President's national security strategy and planned, resourced, implemented, overseen, and assessed in a holistic manner. Strategic WoG collaboration requires all-source intelligence, national security and interagency staff ownership and review, decisionmaking, and accountability freed from the interests of specific departments or *lowest common denominator, short-term perspectives that can be passed off as cooperation or coordination.*

At the operational level—the departments and agencies—many 21st century national security challenges require *cooperation*—execution of separate tasks in pursuit of a common goal—and, in some cases, interagency and intra-agency *collaboration among various bureaus and offices* will be necessary as well. For cases in which cooperation is required, *strategic collaboration in Washington should ensure that separate operational activities are designed and executed to complement and reinforce one another.*[11]

Similarly, in the field at the "pointy end of the spear," or tactical level of stabilization and peacebuilding efforts, *coordination*—the solicitation and response to input from others—and *cooperation* must combine to achieve the *collaboration* required for the minimum requirements of field WoG interoperability. This means the ability of people, organizations, and equipment from separate departments and agencies to work together at all levels, and of leaders to exercise initiative in mutual support, including the ability to draw upon each other's information and expertise.[12]

A CONTINUING PATTERN OF FLAWED WHOLE OF GOVERNMENT ACTIONS

Unsurprisingly, our national experience since the fall of the Berlin Wall confirms that the lack of a true WoG approach to national security at the strategic level cascades to the operational and tactical levels, particularly in the domains of stability and reconstruction efforts in pre- and post conflict situations. Is there reason for optimism that this situation might change for the better? The answer to this overarching question lies in the answers to these questions: Why have we not been able to achieve effective WoG efforts at the strategic level? What do we need to achieve collaboration at the strategic level? How likely is it that we will be able to get what we need?

One way to assess the performance of the national security system since the end of the Cold War is to review specific cases of its operation. As part of its 2008 landmark study, *Forging a New Shield,* the Project on National Security Reform (PNSR) conducted a total of 107 case studies that represent one of the most extensive collections of U.S. national security decisionmaking and policy implementation assessments ever compiled. More than half of the events studied took place since the end of the Cold War in a national security system that remains basically unchanged. Of the cases occurring in and after 1990, 71 percent ended up with negative evaluations, reflecting both relatively high levels of interagency competitiveness, as opposed to collaboration and WoG approaches, and high cost (financial and political) to low benefit ratios.[13] In many of these cases, there is little evidence of any serious effort at end-to-end strategic management and serious assessment or attempts by senior national security officials to capture lessons learned for the future either during or following the events. Three examples suffice to demonstrate this pernicious and enduring pattern in stability and reconstruction operations.

Panama.

The first WoG challenge to be faced in President George H. W. Bush's much celebrated "New World Order" in 1989 was that of Panama, an abiding security concern for the United States for nearly a decade.

> The importance of a structured, cooperative process [and the cascading effect] to levels below the NSC principals became evident early on, when the high-level national security decision-making process clearly broke down over Panama.[14]

> The State Department responded by negotiating with Noriega over his departure from Panama, while Justice Department prosecutors investigated his involvement in drug-trafficking. The Central Intelligence Agency [CIA] reportedly, was also in contact with him. The Defense Department [DoD] pursued another security priority, maintaining bases and training in Panama. None of this activity was coordinated. *All of it together merely helped persuade Noriega that he could outlast a confused United States.* Ultimately, all of these U.S. government efforts failed . . . . Finally, the United States invaded Panama to remove Noriega at a cost of 23 American lives, at least several hundred Panamanian lives, and great damage to the Panamanian economy.[15] (emphasis added)

This pattern of lack of WoG or interagency cooperation prior to the Panama military operation (Operation JUST CAUSE) was replicated in the aftermath when integration of U.S. efforts on the ground were complicated by a dysfunctional U.S. embassy and complete lack of pre-invasion interagency planning for how to "win the peace."

The Balkans.

Emblematic of the performance of the U.S. national security system since the end of the Cold War is the observation of European Union Special Envoy Carl Bildt, who noted the dysfunction of the U.S. national security system during the Balkans crises of the mid and late 1990s. He stated that "the so-called interagency process in Washington often took on all of the characteristics of a civil war, *the chief casualty of which was often the prospect of coherence and consistency in the policies to be pursued.*"[16] (emphasis added) In the Bosnia crisis, Deputies Committee disagreements were supposed to be elevated to President Bill Clinton. However,

> . . . if a clear consensus was not reached at these meetings, the decision-making process would often come to a temporary halt, which was followed by a slow, laborious process of telephoning and private deal-making, since consensus views, rather than clarity, [were] often the highest goal of the process . . . the result was often inaction or half-measures instead of a clear strategy.[17]

Recognizing these difficulties, President Clinton issued Presidential Decision Directive (PDD)-56 (*Managing Complex Contingency Operations*) in May 1997. While notable in its intended improvements over previous interagency WoG planning efforts, departments and agencies resisted this interagency WoG approach. Departments complained that the planning templates and process were too laborious, too much like the military, and too detailed to keep pace with the fast-breaking events on the ground, both in the Bosnia peacekeeping operations and in Haiti. Lack of support by the departments and agencies ensured that PDD-56 never matured into a standard interagency WoG approach for planning and executing complex contingencies.[18] A follow-on study evaluating PDD-56 concluded that in peace-keeping efforts in Somalia, Haiti, East Timor, and Bosnia, and air-operations in Iraq, Bosnia, Sudan, Afghanistan and Serbia,

> The White House has failed to carry out its own written directive to train government personnel to manage complex peace-keeping operations. . . . [We have] the ironic situation of the NSC, which had the lead in carrying out PDD-56, not following a directive sent out by the president it advises . . . and [PDD-56] was largely ignored by an administration that has sent American troops on a record number of so-called "contingencies" on foreign soil.[19]

Iraq and Afghanistan.

This lack of WoG approaches at the strategic level in complex contingencies has persisted to the present, and even has been exacerbated as the United States found itself involved in wars in Iraq and Afghanistan:

> [At the strategic level in Washington, DC] Defense Department officials . . . repeatedly undermined the formal NSC process. Defense officials would refuse to provide advance copies of decision papers or status reports ahead of scheduled meetings or leave copies of reports for further examination. And finally, [D]efense officials repeatedly failed to attend scheduled meetings. According to one official, "I have never seen more high-level insubordination in almost 30 years than I have seen in this administration."[20]

In the field, the *cascading effect of this lack of collaboration at the strategic level* was most recently vividly demonstrated in the use of "high value target teams" in Iraq that were patiently nurtured and developed by Generals Stanley McChrystal and David Petraeus over an extended period of establishing personal relationships with a diverse group of agency players in the field. While these interagency teams were a major catalyst for success at the tactical ground-level during the "military surge" operations in 2007, the team members' parent bureaucracies in Washington were not much interested in supporting them. Middle management at the home headquarters and the agencies of team members proved to be a significant impediment to information sharing on the ground. According to one senior intelligence service source, if young CIA analysts in the field with the teams began using the pronoun "we" or explaining what the team leader wanted when making requests for support, CIA headquarters would conclude they had "gone native" and forgotten their longer-term perspective and the CIA mission; the headquarters would then restrict them from the more sensitive intelligence.[21] The safer the area in which an interagency team was based, the more pronounced bureaucratic differences became, with the Green Zone in Baghdad being the obvious example of a bad environment in which the sense of a common purpose was undermined. Sadly, once the crisis had passed, Washington bureaucracies began to lose interest in supporting the teams and to reassert their own priorities. By 2008, departments and agencies began pulling back people and cooperation, believing that information sharing and collaboration in the intelligence domain had gone too far (a problem that often confronts Ambassadors and Chiefs of Mission with their Country Teams on a routine basis in the steady state environment).

Equally serious and depressing, to date, once again, there has been no effort to attempt to institutionalize the lessons learned from these teams as interagency doctrine to be applied to future stability operations.[22]

Throughout the surge in Iraq, the Bush administration "War Czar," Lieutenant General Douglas Lute, cajoled recalcitrant departments and agencies into lending adequate support to the repeated demands of Ambassador Chester Crocker for the interagency effort. Both General Petraeus and Ambassador Crocker noted *that this was a first – that there was finally someone on the NSS [National Security Staff] who could force interagency support to the field from the strategic level.*[23] To the extent that the interagency teams were effective, it was because of a broader national security system support for the teams.

Departments and agencies could hamstring team performance by withholding their support. Teams whose members lacked organizational "reachback" were not very effective either. Consequently the cooperation of parent organizations could not be taken for granted but instead had to be actively and doggedly pursued by senior leaders in Iraq. . .and by senior leaders in Washington. Cajoling support from those parent organizations was a major preoccupation of senior leaders in Iraq.[24]

WHY HAVE WE NOT BEEN ABLE TO ACHIEVE EFFECTIVE WHOLE OF GOVERNMENT EFFORTS IN OUR NATIONAL SECURITY POLICY?

An Enduring Lack of Whole of Government Perspectives.

U.S. Government organizations *routinely communicate, consult, coordinate and cooperate, but they rarely collaborate* in a true WoG approach in the sense of sub-optimizing individual agency interests for the benefit of the larger enterprise.[25] Today's enduring Cold War legacy of a national security system is a continuing imbalance between departmental and agency stovepipes of enduring strong national security instruments such as intelligence and defense and a weak mechanism for integrating and implementing national security policies that involve other departments and agencies. *Statutory changes to the national security system (to include the landmark 1986 Goldwater-Nichols legislation) over the years have focused on improving the traditional individual instruments of power and their linkages to congressional oversight committees rather than their integration (collaboration) in a WoG effort at the strategic level.*[26] Even though there has been belated and wide-spread recognition that the dimensions and attributes of our national security had long been changing in ways that we did not anticipate when the national security system was established, WoG integration across departments and disciplines is still left almost entirely to an overburdened President.

Moreover, the national security interagency system's current hierarchy of committees developed by President George H. W. Bush and Lieutenant General

Brent Scowcroft in 1989 has traditionally focused almost exclusively on policy formulation to the exclusion of other issues[27]—especially the development of an actionable national security strategy, the alignment of resources with national security missions, policy implementation, and assessment of and accountability for the interagency or WoG performance. A former official in the administration of President George H. W. Bush, explains why WoG outcomes at the strategic level are so elusive:

> When it came time for decision, most representatives . . . came armed with a mandate to defend at all costs their particular bureaucratic sacred cows. But otherwise they were unwilling to support any policy decision, in which they took no interest and voiced no opinion. . . . The absence of a crisis or action-forcing event could be paralyzing even at Cabinet level.[28]

Finally, several contemporary experiments in interagency WoG planning at the strategic level have been only marginally effective because of significant barriers within the national security interagency system. For the last 3 years, the NSC has used the standalone National Counterterrorism Center's Directorate of Strategic Operational Planning (NCTC/DSOP) for planning and assessments of interagency counterterrorism activities. Importantly, the State Department and the CIA initially declined to participate despite statutory language, and there has been resistance in the White House to implementing reform in this area.[29] Both NCTC/DSOP and the Interagency Management System (IMS) developed by the Department of State Coordinator for Reconstruction and Stabilization (S/CRS)[30] for the interagency community are, at best, "coalitions of the barely willing" that are seldom used as departments and agencies have resisted (à la PDD-56) and continue to resist these integrative (collaborative) WoG efforts to link resources to plans on a multiyear basis and provide appropriate personnel incentives for individuals working in interagency planning positions. All too often, interagency planning for national security missions remains a short-term response to a crisis situation that results in ad hoc or inappropriate and reactive, after-the-fact resource alignment through discovery learning.

Designing and implementing effective standing national interagency planning systems that take into account all instruments of national power that report to the President through the National Security Staff and NSC is critical to achieving WoG perspectives and solutions at the strategic level that then cascade to the operational and tactical levels. However, the reality is quite different. As one former NSC staff member observed,

> [T]he easiest outcome to produce in the interagency process is to prevent policy from being made. The range of issues, the different policy perspectives of the various departments over which the department has the lead, and the clash of personalities and egos all place a premium on ensuring that the equities of all involved agencies are considered, and on building an informal policy consensus among the players.[31]

Panama, the Balkans, military operations in Iraq and Afghanistan, and efforts to establish WoG long-term planning and interagency management systems confirm that collaboration is a difficult force to harness and institutionalize. In each case, senior leaders have had to go around the national security system to achieve results. However, "It is not just a function of good leadership as is often assumed. On the contrary . . . organizations that want a reliable record of success do not rely on personalities to generate unity of effort. Neither should the national security system."[32]

WHAT MUST WE DO IN ORDER TO ACHIEVE WHOLE OF GOVERNMENT EFFORTS IN POLICY DEVELOPMENT AND IMPLEMENTATION?

President Obama, in his 2011 State of the Union speech, focused on our nation's future security and prosperity when he asked, "How do we win the future?" He then went on to note, "We can't win the future with a government of the past."[33] And regrettably, that government of the past, at least as regards the national security system, is, as former Secretary of Defense Robert Gates noted, the current "hodgepodge of jerry-rigged arrangements constrained by our outdated and complex patchwork of authorities . . . and unwieldy processes."[34] President Obama's *National Security Strategy* (NSS) appears to address Secretary Gates' complaint head-on:

> To succeed, we must update, balance, and integrate all of the tools of American power. . . .This requires close *cooperation* with Congress and a deliberate and inclusive interagency process so that we achieve integration of our efforts to implement and monitor operations, policies and strategies. . . . However, work remains to foster *coordination across departments and agencies.* Key steps include more effectively ensuring alignment of resources with our national security strategy, adapting the education and training of national security professionals to equip them to meet modern challenges, renewing authorities and mechanisms to implement and *coordinate* assistance programs, and other policies and

programs that strengthen *coordination.*[35] (emphasis added)

The President has identified the goals and outcomes of a transformed national security system that must be accomplished. A fundamental question is whether the NSC and National Security Staff create the strategic management framework for the WoG actions that are required for "winning the future"—and achieving our national security and prosperity?

STRATEGIC MANAGEMENT OF THE NATIONAL SECURITY COUNCIL AND STAFF PROCESSES

Transformation to a truly collaborative WoG national security system must begin at the top, or strategic level, of the system. *Strategic management* is the high-level management of the national security system and associated processes in the interagency space between the President/EOP and the departments and agencies, as well as the nonfederal stakeholders. Strategic management, properly employed, leverages and integrates all elements of national power in a WoG effort at every level to achieve our national security goals and objectives. The National Security Advisor (NSA) and the National Security Staff constitute the de facto hub of the national security system, and as such, they must overcome the current problems at the staff level and become the active managers of the interagency space within that system.

However, there is a persistent and excessive focus on urgent matters and policy formulation on the front end of the strategic management process by a small, under-resourced and overwhelmed National Security

Staff. More than one NSA has set out to rectify this situation, only to express frustration at being held hostage to the current national security system. Lieutenant General Scowcroft, architect of the current NSC system, was frustrated in his efforts to imbue his NSC Staff with a strategic management perspective.

> I always thought that the NSC, as the agent of the President, ought to have a long-range planning function. I tried it both times, and it never worked satisfactorily. Either nobody had time to pay attention to it, or you had to grab them when a fire broke out.[36]

More recently, former NSA Stephen Hadley attempted to achieve strategic management of the national security system in the waning days of the George W. Bush administration with "Record 2008." However, in this effort at oversight, as simple as it was, assessment and accountability for WoG implementation were firmly resisted by members of the NSC staff who viewed it as a personal assessment on their job performance rather than an assessment of the interagency performance in national security mission areas. Hadley recently commented, "I give us a B-minus for policy development . . . and a D-minus for policy execution."[37]

STRATEGIC MANAGEMENT FUNCTIONS OF THE NATIONAL SECURITY STAFF

The NSA and the National Security Staff must be able to carry out six core management functions to successfully manage the integration of the national security interagency system to achieve a WoG effort at the strategic level:

1. ***Policy formulation***: Develop and harmonize national security policies *for presidential approval;*

2. ***Strategy development***: Assess capabilities, risks, and opportunities and develop a broad national security strategy and national security goals and objectives *for presidential approval;*

3. ***Planning and resource guidance for policy implementation***: In partnership with the Office of Management and Budget (OMB), prepare interagency planning and resource guidance to the departments and agencies to achieve the President's policies and national security strategy *for presidential approval;*

4. ***Aligning resources with strategy***: In partnership with the OMB, ensure that department and agency budgets and other resources align with long-term strategic objectives for national security missions as well as unanticipated nearer-term contingencies rather than narrowly defined and often over-lapping departmental competencies. Integrated national security mission budget displays should be presented to Congress for consideration;

5. ***Oversight of policy implementation***: Ensure *implementation of presidential decisions to achieve a WoG effort* across all instruments of national power and the accomplishment of national security objectives; and,

6. ***Assessment of and accountability for interagency and intergovernmental performance***: Assess the interagency and intergovernmental accomplishment of national security objectives and policy outcomes and the implications for policy, strategy, resources, and implementation mechanisms.

Today's relatively stable national security system consists of a vast hierarchical network of interagency committees and groups that support the President as chair of the NSC. The Principals Committee consists of NSC members (statutory as well as those identified by executive order) absent the President, and is the senior interagency forum for consideration of policy issues affecting national security. A Deputies Committee supports the Principals Committee by preparing policy materials for more senior review, overseeing subordinate interagency groups, and managing day-to-day crises. Functional and geographic Interagency Policy Committees (IPCs) at the assistant secretary level and sub-IPCs coordinate the details of development and implementation of particular policy areas (or national security missions) in preparation for senior review.[38]

Since 1953, each President has begun his term of office by issuing a document that outlines the national security system for his administration. Without exception, these foundational documents have been anchored on the National Security Act of 1947 (as amended) and begin with the language *"to advise the President as to the integration of domestic, foreign, and military policies relating to national security."* President George W. Bush went on to further state:

> The NSC shall advise and assist me in integrating all aspects of national security policy as it affects the United States—domestic, foreign, military, intelligence, and economics (in conjunction with the National Economic Council [NEC]). The National Security Council system is a process to coordinate executive departments and agencies in the effective development and implementation of those national security policies.[39]

What the previous principal organizing documents for the National Security Council have not done since

President Eisenhower's Solarium Project and design of the NSC Staff in 1953 is to *define the national security system in terms of the areas of strategic management competencies or functions* that should underwrite the NSC's (and by extension, the Homeland Security Council's) work to support and advise the President in the role of integrator of a WoG national security system. Early on, the Obama administration moved to begin to define the strategic management function in stages and to establish the NSA and the National Security Staff as the strategic managers of the national security system.

Presidential Policy Directive-1 (PPD-1) (*Organization of the National Security System)* identifies the NSC as "the principal means for coordinating executive departments and agencies," firmly situates authority over the interagency at lower level, and effectively establishes the NSA and National Security Staff as the key WoG integrators at every level of the four-tiered NSC system.[40] General James Jones' memorandum on "The 21st Century Interagency Process" was directed at setting the stage for an active role for the NSC and its staff to manage the national security system and reflected his expectations of how the national security process should be structured and run based on his earlier discussions with the President-elect.[41] The memo defined the role of the NSC and, by extension, the NSC staff as managing a "process that is strategic, agile, transparent, and predictable—all in order to advance the national security interests of the United States."[42]

Finally, Presidential Study Directive-1 (PSD-1) (*Organizing for Homeland Security and Counterterrorism Findings and Recommendations*) further empowered the strategic management role of the NSC and its staff previously promulgated in PPD-1 by a major structural realignment that combined the separate Homeland Security Council (HSC) and NSC staffs into a unified National Security Staff that would strengthen the U.S. government's ability to develop and implement policies that comprehensively address the full range of transnational security challenges threatening the security of our country and the safety of our citizens in the 21st century.[43] The PSD-1 decision memo focused on policy implementation and creating a WoG culture within the National Security Staff in its roles of:

- Serving as honest brokers and arbiters among the departments and agencies;
- Ensuring proper management of and response to crises while ensuring that the National Security Staff will not "go operational" [a recommendation of the Tower Committee Report in 1987];
- Inculcating a culture of inclusion and integration into the [National Security] Staff; and,
- Institutionalizing a *culture of collaboration* across the interagency and the intergovernmental cast of players to ensure a team approach to solving multidisciplinary security challenges (emphasis added).[44]

These changes to the National Security Staff organizational design were presented as requiring no additional resources. In practice, the newly constituted National Security Staff remains focused almost exclusively on policy—that which is fun and exciting—and can be spun into a constant crisis mode through the systemic Staff cultural lens that focuses on the urgent rather than the important. Although there is a nod to the concept of oversight of policy implementation through the Deputies Committee and the IPCs, the National Security Staff organization promulgated by PSD-1 is an extremely flat one comprised of very thinly resourced directorates that currently have little, if any, capacity to go beyond policy formulation, response to an incessant torrent of national security crises, and staffing of the President.

THE NATIONAL SECURITY COUNCIL AND NATIONAL SECURITY STAFF AS STRATEGIC MANAGERS OF THE NATIONAL SECURITY SYSTEM: THE NEXT STEPS

Taken together, PPD-1, General Jones' memorandum, and PSD-1 confirm the conceptual role of the National Security Staff as the President's manager of the interagency national security system. In varying degrees, the major departments in the national security system are beginning to take steps through their quadrennial reviews to establish a more functional, performance-oriented management with regard to their core functions. The independent panel chartered by Congress to review the DoD *Quadrennial Defense Review* (QDR) and the PNSR have recommended reform measures that would require the National Security Staff to formally accept and acknowledge what is already a de facto reality—strategic management of the national security system as the basis for its advisory role to the President.

It is reasonable to extrapolate to a series of organizing principles to guide the National Security Staff in its role of strategic management of the national security system in fulfillment of the advisory functions for the NSC outlined in the National Security Act of 1947 (as amended). These principles include:[45]

- The National Security Staff drives the national security interagency system to meet 21st century national security opportunities and challenges.
- The National Security Staff maintains both focus on long-range strategic management (the important) and day-to-day activities (the urgent) to support the President and crisis management.
- The National Security Staff operates from a WoG and presidential perspective rather than a department or agency-specific perspective.
- The National Security Staff leverages and integrates all instruments of national power across the full spectrum of national security management functions. Those functions include policy formulation, strategy development, alignment of resources with strategy, oversight of policy implementation, and interagency performance assessment and accountability.
- The National Security Staff *collaborates* with transparency vis-à-vis the departments and agencies and, as appropriate, state, local, tribal, private sector, and nonprofit entities.
- The National Security Staff, through its role as chairs of the IPCs, leverages a robust structure of interagency mechanisms outside the EOP to develop strategic WoG options and plans for senior national security decisionmakers.

A deliberate National Security Staff organizational and process design based on the strategic management functions described earlier in this chapter, will improve the balance between departmental and the necessary WoG practices required for the global security environment of the 21st century. Strategic management of the national security system to achieve a WoG effort at the top of the system involves management of the end-to-end processes of policy formulation (the political guidance from the President), the strategy to achieve those policy goals, planning and resource guidance to the departments and agencies, alignment of departmental resources with national security missions, oversight of implementation, and assessment of and accountability for interagency outcomes.

HOW LIKELY IS IT THAT WE WILL BE ABLE TO TRANSFORM THE NATIONAL SECURITY STAFF TO PERFORM THE STRATEGIC MANAGEMENT FUNCTION OF OUR NATIONAL SECURITY SYSTEM?

The lack of a tradition of management of the national security system and WoG perspectives described earlier is gradually being replaced with a growing sense of awareness of the need for active WoG management at the strategic level. This is tempered by the enduring concern and recognition in PSD-1 that the National Security Staff should not conduct operations that would distract the Staff from its strategic focus and system management responsibilities. *Agreement on the assessment and assignment of the strategic management role and functions we expect from the National Security Staff* is the first critical step in defining the staff organization, the personnel requirements for the staff, and the staff processes to assist the President in integrating the interagency and intergovernmental efforts on a WoG basis at the strategic level in our national security system. This analysis does not intend to suggest that the strategic management functions in the interagency space outlined in this chapter require a super-department that would preempt the statutory authorities and prerogatives of Cabinet officers. It does confirm that meeting the statutory requirements of the National Security Act of 1947 (as amended) to advise the President in the complex environment of the 21st century through strategic management of the national security system requires that the National Security Staff (and by extension the OMB) be sufficiently and effectively resourced to perform these management functions.

Resourcing the National Security Staff (and the OMB).

The National Security Staff historically has remained very small relative to its system management functions. Since 1989, Presidents have begun their terms by down-sizing the National Security Staff, only to increase staff levels later on, if only to deal with the demands of crisis response and staffing for the President. However, the size of the National Security Staff—or at least the allocation to the strategic WoG management tasks since 1991—has not been and is not now adequate to the needs of the national security system. In terms that sound very much like President Franklin Roosevelt's 1939 Brownlow Commission[46] in its report on the increasing burdens of presidential management of government affairs, the 9/11 Commission noted with regard to the NSC staff:

> Even as it crowds into every square inch of available office space, the NSC staff is still not sized or funded to be an executive agency. . . . Yet a subtler and more serious danger is that as the NSC staff is consumed by these day-to-day tasks, it has less capacity to find the

time and detachment needed to advise a president on larger policy issues.[47]

Reasons for small staff size have included an imputed presidential desire not to be increasing the bureaucracy as well as the Cabinet departments' interest in limiting the President's capacity to manage them—but most especially an attempt by Congress to limit the President's power by limiting direct staff support and especially staff that is exempt from congressional oversight and confirmation.[48]

The result of insufficient resourcing is that the National Security Staff has very limited capacity to deal with a wide range of long-term or strategic WoG issues, and, by default, is focused almost exclusively on policy formulation while jumping from crisis to crisis and the daily inbox driven by the 24-hour news cycle.[49] This rapid pace continues to burn out staff, resulting in rapid turnover, thus reducing the capacity for institutional memory. As one NSC staffer described, "We stay late every night, work weekends—basically on 24/7."[50] Moreover, *this limited staff capacity has often resulted in the failure to anticipate and prevent issues from turning into crises or conflicts that could have been prevented or ameliorated.*

This traditional approach and concerns continue in today's newly constituted National Security Staff. Although White House officials say that they have explicitly planned for the stress that a major and extended crisis abroad will place on their policymaking structure, some acknowledge that it is impossible to know whether they are truly prepared. Says one senior White House aide, "At some point, maybe sooner rather than later, we're going to screw up mightily on something, and then we'll see how everyone reacts."[51]

Recent events on the Korean Peninsula and in Tunisia, Egypt, Libya, and the Middle East, as well as the U.S. response to the Japanese earthquake and tsunami only reinforce this concern. In an interview with experts on the National Security Staff, when asked whether the U.S. Government had contingency plans in case the Hosni Mubarak regime were to collapse in Egypt, NSC officials had to admit they did not.[52] Strategic surprise followed by "re-discovery learning" during crisis management continues to dominate the national security system at the strategic level.

Small staff size only tends to reinforce the traditional policy-based culture of the National Security Staff and undermine the broader intent of PDD-1, the Jones Memo, and PSD-1. Consequently, policy formulation and crisis management remain "sexy," intellectually addictive, and convey access to the President. Strategy, long-term thinking, and forward engagement to identify threats, risks and opportunities, and assessments of current policies are "boring" and have little traction within a policy-dominated culture that is focused on the urgent, and is increasingly, staffing the President. Former NSA General James Jones makes the point more directly: "The White House National Security Council is ill-organized to prepare for the future. The National Security Staff is geared to respond to the crisis of the day. You wind up becoming more tactical instead of strategic."[53]

A significant indicator of the need for and the expectation by the departments for this strategic management of the interagency space by the National Security Staff comes from the recent Department of State/U.S. Agency for International Development (USAID) Quadrennial Diplomacy and Development Review (QDDR) and its focus on defining State/USAID core competencies, instituting performance-based management, and frequent references to "in conjunction with or under the guidance from the National Security Staff."[54] Absent institutional reform and a laser-like focus on WoG approaches at the top of the national security system—strategic management by the NSA and the National Security Staff—that cascades to the departments, the hopeful and long-awaited QDDR reforms are doomed to failure in the same sense that the independent panel noted for the DoD QDR.

Design and sizing of the National Security Staff to support the NSC's statutory requirement to advise the President on the integration, or WoG, aspects of national security require that the staff be resourced and designed so that it can accomplish core strategic management functions effectively and efficiently. Key system management functions or WoG perspectives cannot be permitted to languish due to the lack of a properly resourced and designed National Security Staff.[55] Even in a time of budget austerity, the President deserves a fully resourced staff of national security professionals commensurate with his national security responsibilities. With a true WoG approach at the strategic level, the beneficiaries will be both the nation and those whom we ask to implement our national security strategy at the tactical level and in the field.

A STRATEGIC IMPERATIVE FOR "WINNING THE FUTURE"

The track record since the end of the Cold War in stability and reconstruction efforts is one of continued inability to achieve a WoG management at the strategic level. A significantly under-resourced National Security Staff, and a staff culture focused on policy development and the urgent at the expense of the important contributes to this lack of strategic management. Initial steps by the Obama administration offer hope for change but require a determined effort to imbue the National Security Staff with strategic management functions and then resource it to accomplish them.

An objective assessment of additional staff required for the National Security Staff and the OMB to perform the WoG strategy development, resource alignment, implementation oversight, and interagency assessment functions to support and sustain the QDDR as well as the other quadrennial reviews and after-action reviews of Iraq, Afghanistan, and the "Arab Spring" should be conducted with the help of outside management experts as soon as possible.[56] The White House should work with Congress to provide for transparency and the additional funding and manpower to ensure effective strategic management of the national security system in the interagency space by the NSA and the National Security Staff. Even a doubling of the size of the new combined National Security Staff, given the nature of the work expected at that level, is a very reasonable price for the WoG coherency and consistency of our national security system at the strategic level.

Absent a WoG coherency at the strategic level, we cannot expect it at the operational and tactical levels in stability and peacebuilding operations as a matter of routine. The repeated failures of the current system over the last 20 years are compelling reasons to explicitly recognize this strategic management function as the crucial lynchpin of our national security system. President Obama has clearly identified the NSC/National Security Staff strategic system management function in the two organizational documents—PDD-1 and PSD-1—he has issued thus far. This strategic system management can be done within the intent of the language of the National Security Act of 1947 (as amended) as described earlier. Formalizing the role of the NSA and proper resourcing of the National Security Staff as advisors to the President and the strategic system managers of the national security system through executive order and budgetary processes are strategic imperatives whose time has come if we as a country are to "win the future."

ENDNOTES - CHAPTER 9

1. Memorandum from the Assistant to the President for National Security Affairs General James L. Jones, "The 21st Century Interagency Process," March 18, 2009, available from *foreignpolicy.com/files/nsc_memo_21.pdf* (hereinafter "Jones Memo"). General Jones was a member of the Guiding Coalition for the Project on National Security Reform prior to becoming the National Security Advisor in December 2009.

2. Erik Peterson, *Seven Revolutions Initiative*, Washington, DC: The Global Strategy Institute, Center for Strategic and International Studies (CSIS), 2007.

3. See Joseph S. Nye, "The Future of American Power," *Foreign Affairs*, Vol. 89, No. 6, November/December 2010; *Soft Power: The Means to Success in World Politics*, New York: Public Affairs, a member of the Perseus Books Group, 2004; and Richard L. Armitage and Joseph S. Nye, Co-Chairs, *CSIS Commission on Smart Power: A Smarter, More Secure America*, Washington, DC: CSIS, 2007.

4. Major General William A. Navas, Jr., former Director of the National Security Professional Development Integration Office (NSPD-IO) during remarks at the roll-out of the Project for National Security Reform's (PNSR) *The Power of People: Building an Integrated National Security Professional System for the 21st Century*, a report completed in compliance with Section 1054 of the National Security Authorization Act of 2010.

5. *Results-Oriented Government: Practices That Can Help Enhance and Sustain Collaboration among Federal Agencies*, GAO-06-15, Washington, DC: U.S. Government Accountability Office, October 21, 2005, available from *www.gao.gov/new.items/d0615.pdf*.

6. John H. Pendleton, Director, Defense Capabilities and Management, Government Accountability Office (GAO), in testimony Before the Subcommittee on Oversight and Investigations, Committee on Armed Services, House of Representatives, June 9, 2010, GAO-10-822T, p. 3.

7. See also Project on National Security Reform, *Forging a New Shield*, Washington, DC: Project on National Security, November 2008, glossary (hereafter cited as *FANS*); and *Results-Oriented Government*.

8. In 2007, President George W. Bush issued Executive Order 13434 in recognition of the need for increased focus on identifying, training, and educating National Security Professionals (NSPs) who can work effectively and efficiently in interagency settings. To date, efforts to implement the executive order have been largely uncoordinated and shaped by individual agencies that have suggested a lack of administration guidance in the "strategic pause" between administrations and which lack a more systemic approach to this important national security endeavor.

9. Project on National Security Reform, *The Power of People: Building an Integrated National Security Professional System for the 21st Century*, Washington, DC: Project on National Security, November 2010, pp. 76-77.

10. Section 402 of the National Security Act of 1947 reads:

> National Security Council: The function of the Council shall be to advise the President with respect to the *integration* of domestic, foreign and military policies relating to the national security so as to enable the military services and the other departments and agencies of the Government to *cooperate* more effectively in matters involving the national security. . . . In addition to performing such other functions as the President may direct, for the purpose of more effectively *coordinating* the policies and functions of the Government relating to the the national security, it shall, subject to the direction of the President. . . . (emphasis added)

11. In the case of post-combat Iraq, the military's security-focused effort had to, at a minimum, be done in cooperation with other agencies' efforts to promote good governance, economic development, and the like. Military operations and civilian surge operations enable each other's success. The synergistic effect of both became greater than the sum of their separate efforts.

12. Successful field interoperability involves a wide variety of activities including equipment and protocols for communications, a culture of sharing that is encouraged by senior leadership, the ability to provide or exchange resources without legal or other inhibitions, common understanding of intents and capabilities, and clear standards for accountability that are also agile enough to embrace and expect cross-functional and interagency mutual support. In other cases, such as with Provincial Reconstruction Teams (PRTs) and Field Advanced Civilian Teams, *collaboration* may be required in field settings as well.

13. *FANS*, pp. 91-101.

14. *Ibid.*, pp. 183-184.

15. *Ibid.*, pp. 87-88.

16. Carl Bildt, *Peace Journey: The Struggle for Peace in Bosnia,* London, UK: Weidenfeld and Nicholson, 1988, p. 387.

17. Richard Holbrooke, *To End a War*, New York: The Modern Library, 1999, p. 81.

18. *FANS*, p. 78.

19. Rowan Scarborough, "Study hits White House on peacekeeping missions," *The Washington Times*, December 6, 1999, p. A-1.

20. David Auerswald, Chap. 2, "The Evolution of the NSC Process," in Roger L. George and Harvey Rishikof, eds., *Navigating the Labyrinth of the National Security Enterprise*, Washington, DC: Georgetown University Press, 2011, p. 46.

21. See Christopher Lamb and Evan Munsing, *Secret Weapon: High-value Target Teams as an Organizational Innovation*, Washington, DC: National University Press, 2011, p. 46; Interview with intelligence community official, October 29, 2009.

22. *Ibid.*; and Thomas E. Ricks, "The surge's 'secret weapon': Lessons of interagency high-value targeting teams," Foreign Policy, January 28, 2012, available from *ricks foreignpolicy.com/posts/2011/03/25/the_surges_secret_weapon_lessons_of_interagency_high_value_targeting_teams*.

23. Lamb and Munsing.

24. *Ibid.*

25. See "Organizing for National Security," Inquiry of the Subcommittee on National Policy Machinery, Senator Henry M. Jackson, Chairman for the Committee on Government Operations, United States Senate, 1961, p. 17; Arnold Kanter, quoted in Ivo Daalder and I. M. (Mac) Destler, "Arms Control Policy and the National Security Council," Oral History Roundtables, March 23, 2000; Robert L. Hutchings, *American Diplomacy and the End of the Cold War: An Insider's Account of U.S. Policy in Europe,1989-1992*, Washington, DC: The Woodrow Wilson Center Press, 1997, pp. 22–23; Vincent A. Auger, "The National Security System After the Cold War," in *U.S. Foreign Policy After the Cold War*, Pittsburgh, PA: University of Pittsburgh Press, 1997, p. 60; *FANS*, pp. 121-128.

26. This basic imbalance has only been exacerbated in the decades following the 1947 act. Since then, there have been numerous statutory modifications to the national security system, all of which reflect the basic pattern of consolidating, disaggregating, or creating new national security organizations dedicated to one area of expertise or another. From The Mutual Security Act of 1951, which created the Mutual Security Agency, to the Goldwater-Nichols Act of 1986 that completed the military unification originally embodied in the National Security Act of 1947 (as amended) to the creation of the Department of Homeland Security in 2002, to the Intelligence Reform and Prevention Act of 2004, which created the Office of the Director of National Intelligence—these are the most obvious examples of this effort to reinforce "stovepipes" in the executive branch and their relationships with congressional oversight committees.

27. The current national security system at the strategic level, created by President George H. W. Bush and Lieutenant General Brent Scowcroft, remains largely unchanged, with four levels of organizational bodies composed of Secretary, Deputy Secretary, Assistant Secretary, and working-level officials. The policy formulation process continues to be dominated by clashes of department-specific perspectives and frequently (a) fails to move issues to conclusion, (b) results in least-common-denominator truces among departments without the President being informed of disagreements, (c) produces weak policy recommendations being forwarded to the President, or (d) forces principals to operate around the national security system altogether.

28. Hutchings, pp. 22–23.

29. See Project on National Security Reform, *Toward Integrating Complex National Missions: Lessons from the National Counterterrorism Center's Directorate of Strategic Operational Planning*, Washington, DC: Project on National Security, February 2010.

30. For a description of the Department of State Office of the Coordinator for Reconstruction and Stabilization (S/CRS) Interagency Management System, see *https://crs.state.gov/Pages/Home.aspx*. See Cody M. Brown, *Roundtable Report: Role of the National Security Council, ABA Legal Affairs Roundtable Series on National Security Transformation*, Washington, DC, January 2011, p. 22, for

remarks of a former Coordinator for Reconstruction and Stabilization who noted during his comments at the ABA Legal Roundtable that:

> . . . [I]ntegration was achieved through interagency negotiations across the different agencies. At the resource level, the Office "didn't quite solve it". . . . because of pressure applied on the appropriators by USAID, the Office continues to be funded through two separate accounts in USAID and the State Department. Nevertheless, the Office was able to create a unified budget, but operations were not as smooth as they would otherwise be with a single funding stream. . . .

At the crisis response-level, i.e., execution, "the results aren't so good," he noted. To solve the "perpetual inefficiency of our government in responding to crises," the Office created the Interagency Management System which was approved by all of the relevant departments, " but of course it has never been used." In explaining why the system has never been used, he remarked:

> we operate in an inefficient way because it is politically convenient. When a crisis erupts, anyone who has a plausible stake in that crisis and enough political clout will grab a piece of it. And as a consequence, you have multiple working groups and multiple senior groups, multiple chains of information and chains of command all doing duplicative work that cuts against each other.

31. Alan G. Whittaker, Frederick C. Smith, and Ambassador Elizabeth McKune, *The National Security Policy Process: The National Security Council and Interagency System* (Research Report, October 8, 2010 Annual Update), Washington, DC: Industrial College of the Armed Forces, National Defense University, p. 39.

32. Lamb and Munsing.

33. Barack Obama, *State of the Union Speech*, January 25, 2011, available from *www.whitehouse.gov/the-press-office/2011/01/25/remarks-president-state-union-address*.

34. Robert M. Gates, remarks at The Nixon Center, Washington, DC, February 24, 2010, available from *www.defense.gov/speeches/speech.aspx?speechid=1425*.

35. *National Security Strategy of the United States*, Washington, DC: White House, May 2010, p.14, available from *www.whitehouse.gov/sites/default/files/rss_viewer/national_security_strategy.pdf*.

36. Brent Scowcroft, quoted in Ivo Daalder and I. M. (Mac) Destler, "The Role of the National Security Advisor," Oral History Roundtables, October 25, 1999, available from *www.cissm.umd.edu/papers/display.php?id=265*.

37. Bob Woodward, "Secret Reports Dispute White House Optimism," *Washington Post*, October 1, 2006, available from *www.washingtonpost.com/wp-dyn/content/article/2006/09/30/AR2006093000293.html*.

38. Brown, *Legal Roundtable*, pp. 5-7.

39. National Security Presidential Decision-1: Organization of the National Security System, Washington, DC, available from *www.fas.org/irp/offdocs/nspd/nspd-1.htm*.

40. Presidential Policy Directive-1, Organization of the National Security Council System, Washington, DC, February 13, 2009, available from *www.fas.org/irp/offdocs/ppd/ppd-1.pdf*.

41. Bob Woodward, *Obama's Wars*, New York: Simon & Schuster, 2010, p. 39.

> Jones said he had seen the Bush NSC up close. It was understaffed [and] under-resourced . . . . The national security adviser had little clout and failed to think strategically by plotting out the detailed steps and plans of a policy for a year or two. This was the biggest missing piece in the Bush operation. The national security adviser had to develop measurements to ensure reasonable progress was being made toward the goals. If not, the plans had to be revised—radically if necessary. Too much policy was on automatic pilot. Second, Jones said, the national security adviser had to find a way to get results

> without "micromanaging"' what the departments and agencies should do. . . . What sealed the deal for Jones was a promise Obama made. If he accepted, Obama said that on national security issues, "I will always ask your opinion or judgment before I do anything." It was a personal pledge. To the former commandant of the Marines, whose motto is "*Semper Fidelis*" ("Always Faithful"), it meant everything.

42. Jones memo.

43. Decision Memo, "Approval of PSD-1 (Organizing for Homeland Security and Counterterrorism) Findings and Recommendations," May 8, 2009, p. 2; Project on National Security Reform, unpublished White Paper, *Designing the National Security Staff for the New Global Reality*, Washington, DC, November 2010, p. 6.

44. Presidential Study Directive-1 (PSD-1), Organizing for Homeland Security and Counterterrorism, May 8, 2009, available from *www.fas.org/irp/offdocs/psd/psd-1.pdf*.

45. Jack A. LeCuyer and Nancy Bearg, *Designing the National Security Staff for the New Global Reality*, un-published paper for the Project on National Security Reform, Washington, DC, November 2009, p. 9.

46. See Samuel I. Rosenman, "Summary of the Report of the Committee on Administrative Management, January 12, 1937," *Public Papers and Addresses of Franklin D. Roosevelt*, Vol. 5, New York: Random House, 1941, p. 674.

> The New Deal had led to an extraordinary expansion of the functions of the federal government, and with this expansion, the management burdens of the President. Faced with these expanded responsibilities, FDR created the President's Committee on Administrative Management (the Brownlow Committee) to study ways to improve the management of executive affairs. The committee noted that "[T]he formal march of history depends more upon effective management than upon any other single factor" and that "the President of the United States, managing

the biggest business in the world, now has less assistance...than many State Governors, city managers and mayors, and executives of even small private concerns."

47. "The National Commission on Terrorist Attacks Upon the United States," *9/11 Commission Report*, New York: W. W. Norton & Company, Inc., 2004, p. 32.

48. LeCuyer and Bearg, p. 6.

49. David Rothkopf, *Running the World: The Inside Story of the National Security Council and the Architects of American Power*, New York: Public Affairs, 2005, p. 459.

50. Michael D. Shear, "In West Wing: Grueling Schedules, Bleary Eyes," *Washington Post*, July 13, 2009, available from *www.washingtonpost.com/wp-dyn/content/article/2009/07/12/AR2009071202081.html*.

51. Michael Crowley, "The Decider," *The New Republic*, August 12, 2009, available from *www.tnr.com/article/the-decider*.

52. Charles Levinson, Margaret Coker, and Jay Solomon, "How Cairo, U.S. Were Blinded by Revolution," *The Wall Street Journal*, February 2, 2011, available from *online.wsj.com/article/SB10001424052748703445904576118502819408990.html*.

53. Sandra Erwyn, "U.S. Still in Denial About 21st Century Threats, Says Former Obama National Security Adviser," *National Defense Blog Post*, April 18, 2011, available from *www.nationaldefensemagazine.org/blog/Lists/Posts/Post.aspx?ID=383*.

54. See U.S. Department of State and U.S. Agency for International Development, *Leading Through Civilian Power, the First Quadrennial Diplomacy and Development Review*, Washington, DC: Department of State and USAID, December 2010.

55. "I thought that President Clinton made a terrible mistake in proclaiming that he was going to cut the size of the staff. . . . I include cutting the NSC staff as a mistake because people work so hard there that you fry them after a while if you don't have a staff of sufficient size." Anthony Lake, quoted in Ivo Daalder and I. M. (Mac) Destler, "The Role of the National Security Adviser."

56. General Jones, in informal conversations in January 2010, estimated that 75-90 additional National Security Staff professionals, as well as plus-ups for the Office of Management and Budget (OMB) to focus on the management side of the house, would be needed to resource the effort to institutionalize the role of the National Security Advisor (NSA) and the National Security Staff as the strategic managers of the national security system for the President. In a session at the Stimson Center on June 15, 2011, General Jones was even more explicit and suggested that a National Security Staff level of 300-350 was required to move the Staff from its narrow tactical focus to a strategic one. This discussion mirrors the thoughts expressed in Bob Woodward's *Obama's Wars*, cited in endnote 41, indicating that the National Security Staff was overworked and undermanned.

PART III

CHAPTER 10

LESSONS FROM IRAQ AND AFGHANISTAN – LOOKING FROM OUTSIDE THE BOX

Christopher Holshek

The American-led interventions in Iraq and Afghanistan have generated many lessons. Among these is the need for superior civil-military and whole of government (WoG) approaches. However, many international interventions outside of Iraq and Afghanistan—with which Washington, but not much of the rest of the world, has been obsessed—already entail aspired levels of comprehensiveness and collaboration in whole of society settings. They are contextualized in radically different "security" paradigms. This is a paramount insight for American policymakers and practitioners looking to apply "lessons" from Iraq and Afghanistan. "Winning hearts and minds," central to American counterinsurgency, has often proven more counterproductive than effective, and techniques and tools like provincial reconstruction teams (PRTs) have more limited application in places like sub-Saharan Africa, home to the greatest concentration and frequency of both intrastate and nonstate conflict for at least the past decade. There may in fact be as much, if not more, to learn from the current transition-to-peace effort in Liberia with respect to the upcoming drawdown in Afghanistan as the other way around. All of this is best understood by looking from outside the box.

IRAQ AND AFGHANISTAN—OPERATING ON FAULTY STRATEGIC SOFTWARE

First and foremost, the strategic culture which the U.S. Government in general and the military in particular has operated with has been largely out of synch with the changed global security "ecosystem." The adjustment process has been slow and not always smooth. As far back as the peacekeeping operations of the 1990s, military interventions have been bedeviled by the nettlesome problem of finding balance in the working relationship between military and civilian actors and the "hard" (or coercive) and "soft" (or persuasive) inflections and instruments of power that they largely represent, though not necessarily monopolize. In response to the demands of the "asymmetric" and more hostile and complex operations environments following September 11, 2001 (9/11), the U.S. military in particular has looked to incorporate more of the latter as a combat multiplier. The realization, especially with respect to the early debacles in Iraq, was that: "Winning the peace is harder than winning a war, and soft power is essential to winning the peace. . . . Winning hearts and minds has always been important, but is even more so in a global information age."[1] Subsequent characteristically American national security approaches to foreign engagements have been heavily rooted in the Cold War, and U.S. engagements in Iraq and Afghanistan have been threats-based, post-conflict, and counterinsurgency-centric.

While the American military in particular has done a remarkable job of adapting to the challenges presented in asymmetric operational environments, it has been slowly realizing it has not so much had to think outside the box than to understand the box it has already been operating in. Beyond the difficulties in relearning counterinsurgency operations and the now-familiar tensions between military and civilian actors, particularly humanitarian relief organizations, there is mounting evidence, for example, that hearts and minds campaigns and the application of humanitarian assistance and development aid within a (national) security context have not only exacerbated these tensions, but are turning out to be counterproductive as a whole. In U.S. doctrine, "hearts" means persuading people that their best interests are served by (counterinsurgency) success, while "minds" means convincing them that the counterinsurgency force can protect them and that resisting is pointless.[2] Yet, the problem with applied counterinsurgency in Iraq and Afghanistan is that it has tended to view protection of the civilian population and as a means to an end (defeating insurgents), a tactic versus a strategy that risks calling into the question the legitimacy of the whole operation.

In Afghanistan, this national security psychology culminated in a huge distortion of aid—quantitatively, as the Commander's Emergency Response Program (CERP) funds nearly doubled to $1.2 billion in fiscal year 2010, far exceeding the U.S. Agency for International Development's (USAID) global education budget of approximately $800 million; and qualitatively, as CERP has been conducted under the rubric of the 2009 U.S. Army handbook, *Commander's Guide to Money as a Weapons System*.

Beyond military operations, the U.S. national security paradigm permeates development and makes it subservient to security interests. This is not new: "National security interests have always had a major influence over development assistance priorities, most notably during the Cold War," a hallmark article in *Foreign Policy*'s December 2009 issue observed:

> But never has aid so explicitly been viewed as a weapons system—a fact that is having a major impact on the development assistance policies and priorities of the United States and indeed of many other Western donors.[3]

Yet despite counterinsurgency and stability operations doctrine's heavy reliance on the assumption that aid wins hearts and minds, not to mention the billions of dollars spent on it, there is remarkably limited evidence from Iraq or Afghanistan supporting a link between aid and stability. The faith in this assumption is eroding in the face of considerable comparative research and historical evidence reaching the opposite conclusion—the social forces that development and modernization often unleash can be destabilizing, if not accomplished in proper cultural context. The major factors perceived to be fueling insecurity have little to do with a lack of tangible and measurable social services or infrastructure (from a Western perspective). Instead, one of the main reasons given by both Iraqis and Afghans for the insurgency was a disconnected, corrupt, and unjust government.

This is not to say that the problems with the hearts and minds approach to aid and security have not been encountered outside of Iraq and Afghanistan. For example, in reference to Kenya, Mark Bradbury and Michael Kleinman state the following:

> The idea that, by delivering aid, the U.S. military can change people's perceptions about the United States is premised on very simplistic assumptions. It is naive to assume that a project or series of small projects are

> sufficient to change people's perceptions, convictions, and values, regardless of the historical and contemporary local, regional, and global sociopolitical and economic context. As we found in this study, attitudes are influenced by a multitude of factors beyond the scope of aid projects, such as the relationship between the target population and the Kenyan state, their self-perception as Muslims, local leadership, the media, and, more importantly, their perception of the impact of U.S. foreign policy, both globally and in Somalia. Acceptance of aid does not automatically translate into acceptance of the policies or beliefs of the entity providing the assistance. . . . One of the most widely-voiced criticisms by people of the hearts and minds activities is their limited scale. Many are so small that they can have no discernible impact on poverty by themselves and, to many people, appear as little more than a public relations exercise. As a public relations exercise, their impact is undermined because people view the limited level of assistance provided as indicative of a lack of serious intent to improve their welfare and develop their communities. People in northern Kenya perceive the U.S. to be an economic superpower and believe they could do more.[4]

Accordingly, the instruments reflecting the militarization of foreign policy through the securitization of aid such as PRTs have likewise drawn mixed results, primarily because they have been tactical or operational fixes to essentially strategic problems but also because they reflect a security psychology incongruent to the problem. Despite the proclaimed efforts to civilianize PRT operations, for example, there is scant evidence that civilianization is a priority or that changes on the ground are keeping pace with the policy level. In Afghanistan, military engagement with civilian agencies through forums for civil-military relations dialogue continues to be pro forma, with disappointing outcomes and inadequate follow-up based on concerns raised by nongovernmental organizations (NGOs) and Afghan stakeholders.[5] Other somewhat more successful tactical and operational tools, such as the Tactical Conflict Assessment Framework developed by USAID and the Department of Defense (DoD), have limited application outside of Iraq and Afghanistan—they may be able to be used, but with great care. In another example:

> The civil-military guidelines developed by the Kabul-based Agency Coordinating Body on Afghan Relief (ACBAR) outline humanitarian principles as well as a protocol for NGO-military interactions in Afghanistan. These principles are fully consistent with the USIP [United States Institute for Peace]-facilitated "Guidelines for Relations between U.S. Armed Forces and Nongovernmental Humanitarian Organizations in Hostile or Potentially Hostile Environments." These guidelines provide some clarity to humanitarian assistance. They are less clear on the protocol for broader civil-military relations on peacebuilding, development, and security sector reform activities.[6]

Fortunately, there has been a learning curve of sorts. Shortly after taking over as Commander of the North Atlantic Treaty Organization (NATO) International Security Assistance Force in Afghanistan, General David Petraeus noted: "At the end of the day, it's not about their embrace of us, it's not about us winning hearts and minds; it's about the Afghan government winning hearts and minds."[7] With that remark, he may have signaled a subtle but significant change in the civil-military nexus in counterinsurgency, "stability operations," and "irregular warfare." (A curious term—what is "regular" warfare, and is every application of military power a form of "warfare?") In other words: it is not about "us"; it's about "them." Similarly:

> Anne-Marie Slaughter, [former] director of policy planning at the State Department, [said that] Afghanistan is 'the petri dish' for the administration's strategy on weak and failing states. And by that she means the Obama team's embrace of a nation-building plan that puts development in a place equal to security. Development must be understood less as providing aid than as building government capacity. 'That's the shift,' she says. 'There's a big emphasis not just on delivering services, which happens through contractors and NGOs, but enabling the government to provide the services.'[8]

Indeed, many of the lessons being learned by the U.S. in Iraq and Afghanistan are also being learned in other theaters and regions, such as in the Horn of Africa and by the U.S. African Command (AFRICOM). There are two main reasons for this. One is because many of the people serving in those places also served in Iraq and Afghanistan, drawing upon their experiences there; and the vast wellspring of collected data and knowledge from those operations (but hardly any others). More importantly, it is because the strategic culture that has nurtured them, and U.S. approaches to reducing threats to stability in Africa, is the same culture that has been applied to operations that have preoccupied the U.S. national security and military establishments over the past 10 years. Herein lies the fundamental issue to transferring lessons or best practices from, say, Kabul, Afghanistan, to Kinshasha, Democratic Republic of the Congo—they are essentially borne out of a *Weltanschuung* predicated on a view of security now very much in the minority in most of the rest of the world. Put another way, the:

> wars in Iraq and Afghanistan were conceived (in 2003 and 2001 respectively) as conventional military conflicts, and they remain substantially affected by that initial conception. . . . It is very difficult, halfway through an as yet incomplete war, to shift direction if for the previous several years you have been shooting at people you are now offering to protect. It lacks credibility."[9]

Even in the Obama era, at a time of increasing difficulty to justify foreign aid in the face of fiscal pressures, the threat-based, U.S.-centric national security paradigm continues to contextualize American foreign engagement:

> Obama has persistently argued that addressing the poverty and misery of people in remote places is a U.S. national interest. But the case he has made is, like Bush's, limited to the threat of terrorism and does not have much to say about, for example, the threat that collapsing states pose to more stable neighbors.[10]

Unlike for the United States, terrorism is not the most feared result of collapsing states. For many in P.M. Barnett's gap area, especially outside of Afghanistan and Iraq, "the threat of terrorism is a low priority relative to their other security concerns."[11] A running joke in Africa is that, if you want the United States to get involved in your country (i.e., spend money there), just say that al-Qaeda is there—much like many African strongmen during the Cold War would draw the United States in with the specter of Soviet or Chinese involvement, and to some extent still do with respect to the People's Republic of China (PRC). In the United States, of course, this is also the way to obtain congressional appropriation of security assistance or foreign aid funding—a main driver, no doubt, of the militarization of foreign policy and securitization of aid.

While some lessons may be transferrable, Iraq or Afghanistan cannot be a petri dish for dealing with fragile and failing states elsewhere in the world, because the learning process is the result of moving toward a paradigm with a priori cognitive assumptions about security long existent in much of the rest of the world. In places like Africa, which represent the bulk of security and development challenges, "human security" and civil society challenges such as poverty and food security, rule-of-law and justice, governance, economic development and job creation, and public health contextualize the security problem there, calling for more conflict prevention, peace (versus stability) operations, and comprehensive, whole of society approaches (versus whole of government [WoG]). Development, appropriately done, is therefore not just equal to security, it *is* security.

The human security paradigm focuses on the referent for security as the individual or community rather than the state (e.g., "It is about the security of *Angolans,* not the security of Angola"[12]). It is inherently people-centric, emerging from a post-Cold War, multidisciplinary understanding of security involving a number of research fields, among them, development studies and humanitarian intervention. The United Nations Development Program's *Human Development Report 1994* is considered a cornerstone publication, citing economic security, food security, health security, environmental security, personal security, community security, and political security as its main components—precisely how most underdeveloped nations, particularly in Africa, define security for them writ large.[13] Intrastate security, provided largely by the rule-of-law system, involving police, justice, corrections, and legal representation, is far more important than a military to protect from external threats. Yet, the overwhelming concentration of U.S. security sector assistance is on defense sector reform and foreign military assistance in terms of operational training and hardware.

To further understand why the national security paradigm has little efficacy in much of the 21st century ecosystem and places where most of the lessons from Iraq and Afghanistan may not directly apply, it is worth noting two things. First, the national security approach is essentially state-centric, designed to deal with threats emerging from peer competitors and other state-related risks. Yet, the majority of conflicts since the end of World War II have been increasingly intrastate, as Figure 10-1 shows.[14]

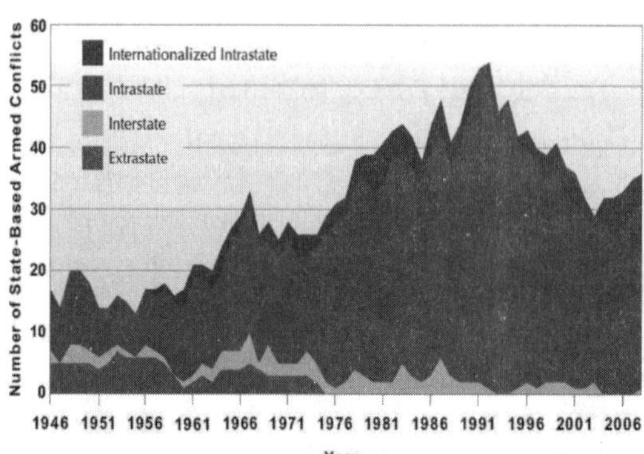

Extrastate conflicts (anti-colonial struggles) were over by the mid-1970s. Interstate conflicts, never very numerous, have become even rarer in the past two decades, while intrastate conflicts declined dramatically from 1992, but have increased modestly since 2003.

Data Source: UCDP/PRIO.

Note: Figure 10.1 is a 'stacked graph', meaning that the number of conflicts in each category is indicated by the depth of the band of colour. The top line shows the total number of conflicts of all types in each year.

Figure 10-1. Trends in State-Based Armed Conflicts by Type, 1946-2006.

The recent people-powered intrastate movements in North Africa and the Arab world stand in further contrast to Iraq and Afghanistan, with the demonstration of a bottom-up generated, soft-power-driven change, and the clear implications for the role that outside powers like the United States may (or may not) be able to play.

> As we have seen, freedom is better promoted through *SharePoint* than at gunpoint, and the relationships between peoples are more important than between governments. Bush may have broken the eggs in the Middle East, but Obama has the opportunity to help make the omelet.[15]

The second phenomenon is that, while nonstate conflicts are on the rise, the majority of these are in Africa—where the nation-state is hardly the established operating organizing principle of governance (and in some places may never be) and where the majority of conflicts, fragile, and failing states are concentrated globally—as Figure 10-2 depicts.[16] Although nation-states retain the unique advantage of being able to coordinate and apply the full range of power elements, growing seams and actors between nation-states present increasing vulnerabilities and threats. Within these nonstate seams, however, are not only the greatest threats to national security in the 21st century, but also the greatest opportunities, among them international governmental, nongovernmental and private sector civil society organizations, which have proliferated in number, variety, and capability.

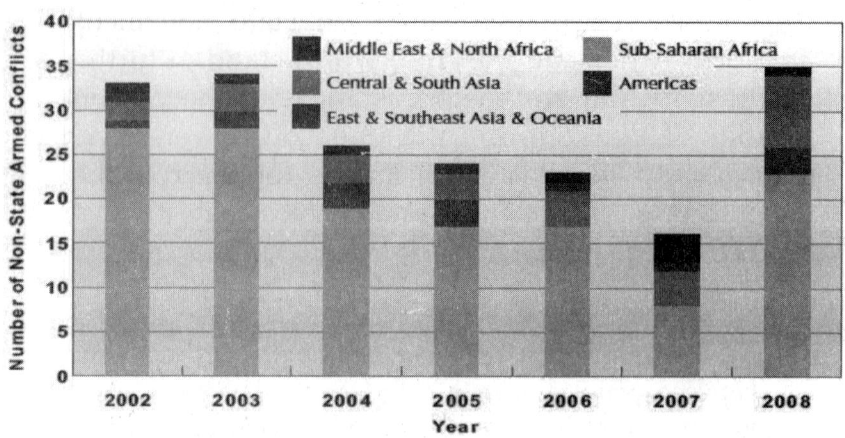

Data Source: Uppsala Conflict Data Program (UCDP)/ Human Security Report Project (HSR) Dataset.

Sub-Saharan Africa has experienced more non-state armed conflicts than all other regions combined. Europe was free non-state conflict between 2002 and 2008

Figure 10-2. Trends in Nonstate Armed Conflicts by Region, 2002-08.

Still, national security approaches may not be entirely inappropriate to tackling transnational armed threats such as the Lord's Resistance Army, astride at least four African nations or international criminal organizations—some of which may be linked to extremist groups and involved in the trafficking of humans, weapons, rare commodities such as diamonds, and drugs—constitute both national security and human security challenges. In any case, this calls for wider and deeper consultation and more collaborative, regional approaches than previously—and with hard power clearly ancillary to soft power, not vice-versa, as has been seen in Iraq and Afghanistan. It could therefore mean, as AFRICOM is instituting, a role for the military that is more supporting than supported (meaning civilian leaders are in greater charge), and adopting nonmilitary methods:

> Military planners can avoid negative outcomes by relying on the humanitarian 'do no harm' principle. In the context of the CJTF-HOA, and other similar missions, the do no harm principle suggests the following four guidelines. First, military projects should complement the work of civilian organizations, rather than duplicating or ignoring it. Second, focusing on the long-term sustainability of projects will ensure that any goodwill generated does not quickly evaporate. Third, military forces should also target their efforts to areas in which they hold a comparative advantage, such as disaster relief, logistics, and operating in insecure environments. Fourth and finally, hearts and minds operations should attempt to project an appearance of relative neutrality and humanitarian services separate from overt counterinsurgency activity. While one cannot expect a military operation to adhere to the NGOs' values of neutrality, impartiality, and independence, the 'do no harm' philosophy can provide a helpful metric for evaluating outcomes from both a humanitarian and political standpoint.[17]

There is, indeed, much to be learned about comprehensive and collaborative approaches in multilateral, human security situations from the approach of what has become known as civil society organizations which:

> . . . generally take a long-term, relationship-building based approach to development. Because of security, political and economic pressures, U.S. government and military officials often attempt shorter-term, quick-impact development. The challenge is to design short-term programming that contributes toward long-term

goals and to design long-term programming that supports short-term objectives."[18]

In other words: thinking globally while acting locally (or thinking strategically while acting tactically).

IT IS A MULTINATIONAL WORLD OUT THERE

The second major consideration in determining whether and how lessons from Iraq and Afghanistan may apply to other places has to do with the far greater imperative for collaborative as well as comprehensive approaches to fragile states. In Africa, the United States is never in the lead and rarely the dominant player. Very often, the United Nations (UN) (which maintains six of its 15 peacekeeping missions in Africa) and regional organizations, such as the African Union (AU) and the Economic Community of West African States (ECOWAS), are seen as mediating or arbitrating entities with respect to conflict resolution and conflict prevention. In addition to these dominant players there is an array of bilateral and nonstate actors that also help to shape the outcome in Africa—the United States among one of many. Security engagements are more multinational then lead-nation, guided by corresponding policy rule-sets and operational models.

Thus, U.S.-centric WoG formulations, such as defense, diplomacy, and development (The Three Ds), do not constitute the model for which most of the donor community for security, humanitarian, or development assesses and implements its programs and projects. "Peacebuilding," a word still seeking a consensus definition in the U.S. foreign and national security policy establishments, is the predominant term, as is "comprehensive approaches." Meanwhile, at the Pentagon, "peacekeeping" and other "peace support operations,"—terms not very widely used to begin with—have been supplanted by "stability operations," an expression very much posited on a national security model of security.

There is another important distinction between American and other approaches to security. Unilateral regime take-down and wholesale counterinsurgency operations in post-conflict environments are not the norm outside the Iraq-Afghanistan box—nor will they be. And both the United States and other international actors are learning that peacebuilding is most effective when done preemptively, i.e., in conflict prevention. In collaborative, human security environments, influence is more important than power, engagement more than response, and sustainability more than stamina.

Fortunately, Washington's view of the world, at least from a policy standpoint, appears to be adapting to these realities, especially in the oft-overlooked role of (strategic) communications:

> . . . if the Obama administration continues to embrace its role as a global convener, it should be careful not to repeat the past mistake of appearing to put the United States at the center of every global challenge, focusing too much on "us" and not enough on "them.". . . The goal is not simply to be liked. *It is to be more influential and therefore more effective at lower cost.* In a world where foreign public opinion has ever greater impact on the success or failure of vital American national interests, it should be weighed in making policy decisions and should shape *how* the United States pursues its policies and how U.S. leaders talk about American policies. Listening, understanding and engaging makes for better policy, helps to avoid unnecessary conflicts, and should ideally allow policymakers to foresee and

pre-empt objections to policies that sound worse in the field than they do in Washington.[19]

Specifically with respect to engaging the world's premier multinational organization, the 2010 *National Security Strategy*, under the rubric of "Pursuing Comprehensive Engagement," notes:

> In recent years America's frustration with international institutions has led us at times to engage the UN system on an ad hoc basis. But in a world of transnational challenges, the United States will need to invest in strengthening the international system, working from inside international institutions and frameworks to face their imperfections head on and to mobilize transnational cooperation.[20]

The *National Security Strategy* additionally affirms Secretary of Defense Robert Gates's anticipation of the need for greater military collaborative engagement capabilities, recognizing the growing mission to build partnership capacities as a strategic economy-of-force measure. In the 2010 *Quadrennial Defense Review* (QDR), he points out in numerous places that:

> America's interests are inextricably linked to the integrity and resilience of the international system. . . . America's power and influence are enhanced by sustaining a vibrant network of defense alliances and new partnerships, building cooperative approaches with key states, and maintaining interactions with important international institutions such as the United Nations. . . . Moreover, military forces must be capable of working effectively with a range of civilian and international partners. . . . Strong regional allies and partners are fundamental to meeting 21st century challenges successfully. Helping to build their capacity can help prevent conflict from beginning or

escalating, reducing the possibility that large and enduring deployments of U.S. or allied forces would be required."[21]

U.S. collaboration on a multinational level is not only more appropriate to the transformed security environment of the 21st century, generating greater strategic and operational capital, particularly in terms of soft power which has far greater currency in human security settings. In an era of burgeoning resource restraints, it is also more cost-effective. Echoing the theme of building partner capacities and multinational engagement as a strategic economy-of-force measure, U.S. Ambassador to the UN Susan Rice more pragmatically explained that:

> . . . UN peace operations are a crucial tool for managing international crises in which the only alternatives might otherwise be doing nothing at all or direct U.S. military intervention. . . . UN peacekeeping is also cost-effective for the United States: instead of paying 100 percent of the costs for a unilateral deployment, the United States pays about one-fourth of the costs for UN peacekeeping, with other UN members collectively sharing the burden for the rest.[22]

(It should also be taken into consideration that UN peacekeeping forces work at operational costs far below that of U.S. and many NATO forces. The reimbursement rate for UN peacekeepers set by the Department of Peacekeeping Operations (DPKO) is at around $1,200 per line soldier per month—much less than the pay and benefits for a U.S. soldier.) In fact, the most effective, low-cost, high-reward (and most underutilized) U.S. multinational military engagement program is the 30 or so U.S. military observers serving in UN missions.[23]

LEARNING TO DO MORE WITH LESS

This leads to the third major consideration. Resources for creating sustainable peace have been more limited outside the Iraq-Afghanistan box, which has received more money in security assistance and development aid from the United States and other donor nations than the rest of the world together. In 2010, the United States provided $1.7 billion and $3.3 billion in foreign aid to the Near East and South and Central Asia, respectively; it provided $648 million to Africa, $448 million to the Western Hemisphere, $631 million to Europe and Eurasia, and $158 million to East Asia and the Pacific.[24] This does not even include the nearly one trillion dollars of military-related costs for the wars in Iraq and Afghanistan. Meanwhile, as the United States has poured money into the Iraq-Afghanistan box, China in particular has seized the opportunity cost to gain greater influence in Africa and Latin America—China's foreign assistance and economic projects in Africa, Latin America, and Southeast Asia grew from less than $1 billion in 2002 to $27.5 billion in 2006 and $25 billion in 2007, with the largest increase in Africa.[25] In the meantime, ". . . direct U.S. [military or police] involvement in UN field missions has dwindled while involvement of other '21st century centers of influence', among them China, has grown. . . ."[26]

Donor entities working in such regions as Africa have never had the luxury of the scale of these kinds of financial resources. As the U.S. fiscal crisis grows, the more creative and collaborative approaches borne out of such restraints, such as microfinancing, are more commonplace than the typically American reflex to "throw money at the problem." And money is turning out not to be everything:

> Our research suggests that the failure to win Afghan hearts and minds is not because too little money has been spent. In fact, money has been part of the problem. Spending too much money with too little oversight in insecure environments is a recipe for fueling corruption, delegitimizing the Afghan government, and undermining the credibility of international actors. But policymakers also ignore the most obvious, effective, and quickest way to reduce corruption: reduce funding, especially in the most insecure areas, to levels more in line with what Afghanistan can absorb.[27]

In addition to throwing money at the problem, another U.S. tendency, whether in the military or foreign aid communities, has been to place a disproportionate amount of faith in physical or:

> . . . technical solutions to complex social and economic development problems and of the appropriateness and transferability of U.S. values and experience. This over confidence meant that too little attention was paid to local circumstances and values in the preparation and execution of aid activities.[28]

Aid workers in Africa and other regions where a human security paradigm has long been at work are much more familiar with constraints like the primacy of cultural context and absorptive capacity issues that their counterparts in Iraq or Afghanistan have more recently discovered.

Moreover, the United States is entering a new era of relative strategic scarcity, where more traditional resources to shape and influence events more to its liking are less at its disposal. By a number of measures, it is a country of deepening public and private debt and declining competitiveness. Beyond reducing America's throw-weight diplomatically, culturally, and (of course) economically this loss of relative financial and commercial power is also translating into an end of unilateral freedom of action. Asymmetric threats seen in Iraq and Afghanistan have already mitigated much of the longstanding U.S. advantage in hard power, while peer and near-peer competitors are better able to bankroll their own agendas. Perhaps most importantly, as information technologies and the lessons of low-tech, low-cost socio-cultural and information enterprises, such as those that brought on the uprisings in North Africa and the Middle East, present equalizers to traditional, industrial-era forms of power.

As the wars in Iraq and Afghanistan have demonstrated, traditional American bias toward coercive or hard power in general, albeit more expedient and more measurable, has also shown counterproductive costs and risks. Hard power is more resource-intensive, zero-sum, reactive, and short-term (i.e., tactical). Soft power, more appropriate to collaborative, human security settings, is more economical, renewable, engaging, synergistic, and long-term (i.e., strategic). It ultimately generates more peaceful, stable, and profitable outcomes, has further-reaching effects, is less costly and risk-intensive, and introduces more feasible, acceptable, and sustainable strategic options—as long as they are approached strategically. Indeed, the more collaborative, comprehensive, softer, and human security approaches, borne in part out of forced frugality, found in Africa and other places may now come more naturally to U.S. policymakers and practitioners, under far greater budgetary limits, as they look to transfer their own experiences with the balance of soft and hard power in Iraq and Afghanistan elsewhere. In this regard, there may be much to learn from those who have already worked much longer in that paradigm.

U.S. involvement, for example, in low-level counterinsurgency operations in the Philippines, has long taken the approach of following local lead in civil action programs. "Filipino doctors, dentists, and veterinarians come in to provide free care. Of utmost importance . . . is putting a Filipino face on all these operations."[29] Perhaps even more illustrative of the shifting paradigm is the U.S. response to Haiti, where the military clearly played a supporting role and the U.S. Government sought to work within multilateral frameworks rather than expend the resources to create a parallel structure:

> Early on, the United States decided not to create a combined Joint task force. With the UN already on the ground, a robust multinational force was in place. In addition, MINUSTAH countries contributing additional resources and personnel already had links to their local UN representatives. Creating a *combined* Joint task force would have conflicted with those efforts. Instead, Joint Task Force-Haiti deployed to conduct humanitarian assistance and disaster response operations. The purpose of Joint Task Force-Haiti was to support U.S. efforts in Haiti to mitigate near-term human suffering and accelerate relief efforts to facilitate transition to the Government of Haiti, the UN, and USAID. The military possesses significant capabilities that are useful in emergencies, but long-term plans for relief and reconstruction are best left to nonmilitary government agencies.[30]

LEARNING FROM LIBERIA

Perhaps U.S. policymakers and practitioners can learn the greatest lessons from truly multinational settings where the United States is one among many players. As the U.S. transitions from a "military mission to a civilian-led effort"—as the Senate Foreign Relations Committee terms it—in Iraq and prepares to undergo a similar conversion in Afghanistan, it may be instructive to examine a similar case study where there is a transition from military-intensive post-conflict peacekeeping to civilian-led peacebuilding with the aim of preventing a return to conflict in the major multinational intervention in Africa led by the United Nations Mission in Liberia (UNMIL), which is regarded as the most integrative of UN field missions.

In January 2008, UNMIL commenced its drawdown of forces parallel to the Government of Liberia's implementation of the Poverty Reduction Strategy (PRS), using the UN Development Assistance Framework (UNDAF) and other collaborative plans and tools designed to help build the capacity of the Liberian government, particularly at the county level, to deliver essential public services, among them security, governance, the rule-of-law, and economic and social development. The intent was to reach these conditions, articulated in a series of benchmarks, by the general election of October 2011, thus marking the end of drawdown and beginning the third and final UNMIL phase of withdrawal, characterized by local, civilian directed peacebuilding focused on self-sustainable development to supplant security-intensive, military-based peacekeeping operations.[31] The United States, in comparison, is facing same sort of transition management challenge in Iraq and Afghanistan.

In recognition of its role in underwriting this transition process, the UNMIL peacekeeping force's approach to civil-military coordination (CIMIC), for instance, changed substantially, based on the constant concern regarding "the increasing dependence of the Government of Liberia on the assets of the Force. . ."[32] The greatest risk for security and stability during the drawdown in Liberia has been that the dependency on the international presence in general and the UN military in particular persists as force capability diminishes. This dependence creates potentially destabilizing effects that risk the investment and sacrifices that many made in an attempt to bring lasting peace to Liberia—this is similar to the situations in Iraq and Afghanistan.

In fairness, however, opportunities in Liberia to facilitate transition to self-sustained peacebuilding have been better than in Iraq or Afghanistan. This is so for a variety of reasons: the relatively peaceful and stable situation enduring from earlier phases; the substantial development assistance presence still residing in Liberia; a central Liberian government with a strong leadership and a well-developed, home-grown, and locally developed transition plan; well-developed collaborative relationships and coordination mechanisms emphasizing integrated mission coordination under the "delivery as one" concept and viewing CIMIC as one among a number of mission coordination management tools; as well as a government and population that thinks positively of the international presence, due in no small part to an effective public information campaign.

Still, the UNMIL approach to CIMIC, which has become the model for the new UN-CIMIC policy for UN peacekeeping forces, is particularly interesting.

Recognizing that peace support operations involve an operational environment that is largely psychological rather than kinetic, UNMIL CIMIC emphasizes building both capacity and confidence in numerous ways beyond merely public relations. It directs that Liberians will be visibly in the lead of capacity-building efforts or events such as medical outreaches, even if most of the effort is resourced by the UN military force. In clear support of governance and security sector reform, when feasible, it also involves local military and police in CIMIC projects in order to build their capacity and, more importantly, promote public confidence in the government by transitioning the psychological capital of public trust in UNMIL to maintain security to Liberian government institutions. As General Petraeus would say, it's up to the Liberians to win hearts and minds.

Albeit going through its own learning processes, the CIMIC approach in Liberia takes into account the central issue of the two essential functions of any civil-military concept regardless of its name, place, or type of operation: how to manage the interaction between civil and military players; and most importantly, how to transition the process, as described above, in human security terms. The clear connectivity between security and development is consistent with the complex and interconnected environment and the integrated mission approach. Moreover, it establishes the role of the military as the enabler to the peace process, duplicating the civil-military relationship desired in democratic societies, and marking an unambiguous path to the end state of all peace operations—self-sustained peace and appropriately effective civil society.

Another outstanding feature of the Liberian example is the role of bilateral players, especially the

U.S. Country Team, which has often worked collaboratively with the Government of Liberia and UNMIL to enhance their goals common to U.S. national interests, especially security sector reform, but also with those of international partners, to include China, in fostering civil society and economic development. With regard to security sector reform, for which in accordance with UN Security Council Resolution 1506 the United States has responsibility for defense sector reform, the Country Team has applied Secretary of Defense Gates's admonition that, beyond the traditional national security centric tendency to focus almost exclusively on operational development of the armed forces:

> . . . there has not been enough attention paid to building the institutional capacity (such as defense ministries) or the human capital (including leadership skills and attitudes) needed to sustain security over the long term.[33]

In Liberia, the Office of Security Cooperation is synchronizing AFRICOM's Operation ONWARD LIBERTY program designed to enhance military institutional leadership and the DoD's Defense Institution Reform Initiative (similar to the Ministry of Defense Advisory program in Afghanistan) to build institutional capacity among the staff of the Ministry of Defense by providing civilian oversight. Perhaps most importantly, the synchronization of these programs will help improve civil-military linkages and foster the civil-military relationship often missing in fragile civil societies. The U.S. Embassy would also be wise to capitalize on UNMIL's best practices and stature in order to enhance the civilian staff components of their counterpart ministry through mentoring and advising in order to build capacity as well as confidence—multilateralism with a human face.

BUILDING PEACE IS BUILDING RELATIONSHIPS

In the human security environments of places like Liberia, perhaps the most important lesson being learned, with profound implications for everything including programming and budgeting to deployment and stationing policies, is that the work in such settings is fundamentally centered around building relationships on a human and not just institutional level, requiring sustainability more than stamina.

> Fundamentally, in peace or war we need to trust one another. We learn to trust each other through building a strong relationship, personal and professional. That is the key to building an effective team that works toward a common purpose. In Haiti, this proved to be the case within our own military and with our interagency partners, nongovernmental organizations, and foreign partners. When tough issues were encountered, their strong relationships broke down the barriers.[34]

When looking at the lessons of Iraq and Afghanistan, there is indeed much to be valued—not so much for what actually is applicable to other places and situations, but more for what should not be done. In the larger box of global human security, Iraq and Afghanistan are cases apart from Liberia. This is more so because of context and not content, partnership more than predominance, strategy more than operations and tactics, and human interaction more than organizational enterprises.

Finally, how Americans understand the contextualization of security interventions in the larger, more collaborative and complex world beyond Iraq and Afghanistan should not only have profound and far-reaching implications for U.S. WoG engagements around the world. It could also help reshape the American approach to national security writ large back at home, not just because the world outside our previous boxes is forcing us to, but because we can no longer afford any other way:

> 'We have always been able to win ugly by throwing money at a problem, but that is no longer the case,' Locher said. 'We have lost our margin for error and we are headed for a decade of austerity, when even great programs are being killed. The times call for a national security system that is effective, efficient, participatory and agile. Unfortunately, we don't have it—we have the opposite of that, a system that is archaic, designed 63 years ago, that still clings to Cold War concepts. At PNSR we have a saying, 'How can we secure our children's future with our grandparents' government?' We are not going to win the future with that government.'[35]

This should be seen as an opportunity more than a threat, for which a dynamic, multicultural country like America whose national ethos is *e pluribus unum* is most ideally suited. What one refuses to experience positively, one will most certainly experience negatively.

ENDNOTES - CHAPTER 10

1. Joseph S. Nye, Jr., *Soft Power: The Means to Success in World Politics*, New York: BBS Public Affairs, 2004, pp. x, xii, 1.

2. *U.S. Army Field Manual* (FM) *3-24, Counterinsurgency,* Washington, DC: Headquarters, U.S. Army, December 2006, Appendix A, p. A-26.

3. Andrew Wilder and Stuart Gordon, "Money Can't Buy America Love," *Foreign Policy,* Vol. 1, December 2009, available from *www.foreignpolicy.com/articles/2009/12/01/money_cant_buy_america_love.*

4. Mark Bradbury and Michael Kleinman, *Winning Hearts and Minds? Examining the Relationship between Aid and Security in Kenya,* Medford, MA: Feinstein International Center, Tufts University, April 2010, Executive Summary, pp. 5, 70.

5. Sippi Azarbaijani-Moghaddam, Mirwais Wardak, Idrees Zaman, and Annabel Taylor, *Afghan Hearts, Afghan Minds: Exploring Afghan Perceptions of Civil-Military Relations,* London, UK: British and Irish Afghanistan Agencies Group (BAAG) and European Network of NGOs in Afghanistan (ENNA), 2008, p. 77.

6. Lisa Schirch, "The Civil Society-Military Relationship in Afghanistan," *Peacebrief 58,* Washington, DC: United States Institute of Peace, September 24, 2010, pp. 3-4.

7. General David Petraeus, transcript of interview with David Gregory on NBC's "Meet the Press," August 15, 2010, available from *www.msnbc.msn.com/id/38686033/ns/meet_the_press-transcripts/.*

8. James Traub, "In the Beginning, There Was Somalia," *Foreign Policy,* July-August 2010, available from *www.foreignpolicy.com/articles/2010/06/21/in_the_beginning_there_was_somalia?page=full.*

9. Shannon Beebe and Mary Kaldor, "The Ultimate Weapon Is No Weapon," New York, BBS Public Affairs, 2010, p. 9.

10. Traub.

11. Bradbury and Kleinman, p. 212. The reference to Barnett is with respect to his description in *The Pentagon's New Map* of the non-developed world as the "gap," versus the "core."

12. Beebe and Kaldor, p. 5.

13. Mahbub ul Haq *et al., Human Development Report 1994*, United Nations Development Programme, Oxford, UK: Oxford University Press, 1994.

14. See the Human Security Report (HSR) Project's *Human Security Report 2009/2010*, Simon Fraser University, available from *www.hsrgroup.org/human-security-reports/20092010/overview.aspx*. Figure 10-1 is from the report available from *http://www.hsrgroup.org/*.

15. Christopher Holshek, "The 21st Century's 1989?" *The Huffington Post*, February 14, 2011, available from *www.huffingtonpost.com/christopher-holshek/the-21st-centurys-1989_b_822613.html*.

16. *Human Security Report 2009/2010*, Figure 10-2, is from the report available from *www.hsrgroup.org/docs/Publications/HSR20092010/Figures/20092010Report_Fig11_1_TrendsNonStateArmedConflictsRegion.jpg*.

17. Sarah Kenyon Lischer, "Winning Hearts and Minds in the Horn of Africa," *Harvard International Review*, May 2008.

18. Schirch, "The Civil Society-Military Relationship in Afghanistan," p. 4.

19. Kristin M. Lord and Marc Lynch, *America's Extended Hand—Assessing the Obama Administration's Global Engagement Strategy*, Washington, DC: Center for a New American Security, June 2010, pp. 10-12, 16.

20. *National Security Strategy*, Washington, DC: The White House, May 2010, p. 13.

21. Robert M. Gates, *Quadrennial Defense Review Report*, Washington DC: Department of Defense, February 2010, pp. iv, xiv, 7, 10.

22. Susan Rice, "Progress Report by the United States Mission to the United Nations, A New Era of Engagement, Advancing America's Interests in the World," New York: U.S. Mission to the United Nations, April 29, 2010, available from *www.usun.state.gov/briefing/statements/2009/april/126495.htm*.

23. Reimbursement rates for peacekeepers are not openly published by the UN; however, in addition to the author's personal knowledge, there are numerous sources that quote figures of just over $1,000 plus specialty pay and other allowances for the lowest-ranking soldiers. See also "Peacekeeping," *Wikipedia*, available from *en.wikipedia.org/wiki/Peacekeeping*.

24. See *Summary and Highlights, International Affairs Function 150, Fiscal Year 2010 Budget Request*, Washington, DC: U.S. Department of State, 2009, available from *www.state.gov/documents/organization/122513.pdf*.

25. Thomas Lum, *China's Foreign Aid Activities in Africa, Latin America, and Southeast Asia*, Washington, DC: Congressional Research Service, 7-5700, February 25, 2009, Summary.

26. Christopher Holshek, "U.S. Military Observers and Comprehensive Engagement," *Small Wars Journal*, Vol. 10, February 2011, available from *http://smallwarsjournal.com/jrnl/art/us-military-observers-and-comprehensive-engagement*.

27. Andrew Wilder and Stuart Gordon, "Money Can't Buy America Love," *Foreign Policy*, Vol. 1, December 2009.

28. Andrew Wilder, "Losing Hearts and Minds in Afghanistan," *Middle East Institute Viewpoints: Afghanistan, 1979-2009: In the Grip of Conflict*, December 2009, p. 143.

29. Stew Magnuson, "U.S. Special Forces Target Hearts and Minds," *National Defense*, February 2008, available from *www.nationaldefensemagazine.org/archive/2008/February/Pages/U2357.S2357.Special2357.aspx*.

30. Lieutenant General P. K. Keen, Major General Floriano Peixoto Vieira Neto, Lieutenant Colonel Charles W. Nolan, Lieutenant Colonel Jennifer L. Kimmey, and Commander Joseph Alt-

house, "Relationships Matter—Humanitarian Assistance and Disaster Relief in Haiti," *Military Review*, May-June 2010, p. 8.

31. For an excellent discussion and critique of UNMIL's approach to peacekeeping-peacebuilding, see Wilfred Gray-Johnson, "Assessing the United Nations Approach to Post-Conflict Peacebuilding in Africa: The Mission in Liberia," *Conflict Trends*, Issue 3, 2009, pp. 11-18.

32. UNMIL Force HQ Concept of Operations for the Conduct of Operations by the UNMIL Force for the Period January 1-December 31, 2008, p. 3.

33. Robert M. Gates, "Helping Others Defend Themselves: The Future of U.S. Security Assistance, *Foreign Affairs*, Vol. 89, No. 3, May-June 2010.

34. Keen *et al.*, p. 10.

35. James R. Locher III, President and CEO of the Project on National Security Reform, quoted in Kathryn Boughton, "National Security Expert Who Spoke in Kent Says bin Laden Outcome the Exception; National Security System Flawed," *Litchfield County Times*, May 2, 2011, available from *www.countytimes.com/articles/2011/05/02/news/doc4dbf1e831ef1e702049372.txt*.

CHAPTER 11

CIVIL-MILITARY TEAMING: A SOLUTION?

William J. Flavin

> Leading through civilian power saves lives and money. With the right tools, training, and leadership, our diplomats and development experts can defuse crises before they explode and create new opportunities for economic growth. We can find new partners to share burdens and new solutions to problems that might otherwise require military action. And where we must work side by side with our military partners in places like Afghanistan and Iraq and in other fragile states around the world, we can be the partner that our military needs and deserves.
>
> Secretary of State Hillary Clinton[1]

Can successful civil-military teaming solve many of the problems associated with current conflicts: state fragility, crisis in governance, insurgent attacks, and threats to public order from criminals and spoilers? This chapter considers several past and current examples of civil-military teaming, it identifies what constituted a successfully team, and it demonstrates what effect that team had on solving the conflict. This chapter reviews several case studies, the first, the 1946-57 time frame in Malaya, considered by many as the best example of successful civil-military teaming; the second, the 1967-73 period in Vietnam, particularly the Civil Operations and Revolutionary Development Support (CORDS) initiative; and, finally, the Provincial Reconstruction Team (PRT) initiative in Afghanistan from 2002 to the present. Each of these case studies describe some common elements of success and identify the pitfalls and shortcomings inherent in the civil-military teaming approach.

CIVIL-MILITARY TEAMING: CONTEXT AND PROBLEMS

The *U.S. National Security Strategy* (NSS), the Department of State *Quadrennial Diplomacy and Development Review* (QDDR) and the Department of Defense (DoD) *Quadrennial Defense Review* (QDR) all agree that a whole of government (WoG) approach is necessary to achieve national objectives. The QDR panel identified the need for a WoG approach in support of a comprehensive approach to address the most pressing national security problems.

> The need for enhanced—whole of government capabilities will be driven by the complex operating conditions, strong potential for civilian interaction, and the need in many cases to work closely with the agencies of a foreign government. It is in the interest of the Department of Defense to work closely with the National Security Council, the State Department, State/AID [Agency for International Development], and DHS [the Department of Homeland Security] to develop support for more enhanced civilian capability and for putting into operation—Whole-of-Government and Comprehensive Approach solutions to security challenges. . . .Before any type of contingency arises, U.S. governmental efforts typically rely on the U.S. State Department and other interagency interactions with the host nation on a day-to-day basis, including the military through the ongoing and routine activities of the Combatant Commands. This persistent engagement is required up to and through the end state of a contingency or crisis, and thereafter. A crisis or conflict will require the addition and integration of—

> whole-of-government and Comprehensive Approach capabilities. Although civilian agencies have historically held the lead role in maintaining and developing international relationships, the need to deploy civilian and international personnel in settings of—security insecurity (e.g., post-conflict states, failed states) requires a more integrated approach in terms of partnership with the military forces.[2]

The value of civil-military teaming to achieve a comprehensive approach has been validated by all of the observers of international crises for the last 60 years. Virtually all of the studies, guidelines, policy, and doctrinal manuals have identified WoG leading to a comprehensive approach as the basic foundation for success in addressing weak and fragile states, transnational criminal enterprises, and global financial or global biological threats. The 2006 U.S. Army *Field Manual* (FM) *3-24 , Counterinsurgency,* devotes an entire chapter to the integration of civilian and military activities. The recent U.S. Army FM *3-07, Stability Operations,* identifies two levels of effort, WoG and comprehensive.

> A whole-of-government approach is an approach that integrates the collaborative efforts of the departments and agencies of the United States Government to achieve unity of effort toward a shared goal. A comprehensive approach is an approach that integrates the cooperative efforts of the departments and agencies of the United States Government, intergovernmental and nongovernmental organizations, multinational partners, and private sector entities to achieve unity of effort toward a shared goal.[3]

The United Nations (UN), North Atlantic Treaty Organization (NATO), and the European Union (EU) have set as a goal the achievement of a comprehensive approach (Integrated Mission for the UN) to develop a shared vision among all of the relevant stakeholders. All of these organizations have attempted to achieve this goal over the last 10 years with varying degrees of success. They all agree that the problems of the world cannot be solved by military means alone. At times, a military effort may be necessary but is never sufficient to achieve sustainable peace and stability. Yet, as a result of the events that unfolded since World War II, the U.S. Government has ended up with a large and well-resourced military instrument of power that is out of proportion to the other instruments of power of the U.S. Government. It is an instrument that can generate a great deal of capability and capacity and therefore has assumed many civil tasks over time. Yet in all this, the military itself recognizes that the civil sector needs to be the final arbiter. The challenge is to operationalize the concept and engage with other agencies to achieve the best outcome.

William Olson has written extensively on this topic. Based on experience and study in this area, he provides the following cautions about a WoG approach. This first and primary is that the U.S. Government was designed to ensure that power should not be consolidated in the hands of the few to protect the liberty and freedom of the many. There are obstacles embedded in the U.S. Governmental system that work against the very coordination that is needed, however, to attempt to overcome these obstacles may require a significant political price; one that most are unwilling to pay. This presents a challenge because institutions are organized as stovepipes and are provided requisite authorities and funding that reinforce separation. Over time, the U.S. bureaucracy has grown into a maze of overlapping, redundant, and conflicting structures that has compounded the challenge.[4]

> Coordination occurs in a context that is different for each agency or involved player. Different agencies have different missions, decision making cycles, organizational structures, cultures, habits and practices, incentive structures, and legal constraints and imperatives. This institutional environment limits what agencies can do, but those limits are different for different agencies and can come into play in unpredictable ways.[5]

But the process is not the goal; it is the outcome. There is a limit to coordination. In attempting to coordinate the various stakeholders within a complex system you run the risk of exacerbating the problem and degrading the effectiveness of some of those stakeholders. At times the outcome may not require that all stakeholders be involved, and indeed the involvement of those stakeholders from every level, strategic to tactical, may be detrimental. Organizations are optimized to deliver much needed services, such as in the areas of governance, conflict resolution, and generating private enterprise. They can lose some of their efficiency by close cooperation and coordination. But while this is so for the civilian agencies, nongovernmental organizations (NGOs), and international organizations, the military needs coordination with these agencies to accomplish its mission. The missions today, as described above, require a civilian component, but all do not require a military component. This leads to the interesting situation where the DoD pushes for coordination with other agencies who at times do not see the same need to coordinate. This can lead to fears that the DoD is attempting to dominate the situation and force other agencies to adopt their management procedures—the militarization of foreign affairs.

Money turns planning into action. Money flows into each of the separate institutions with their individual authorities to spend. Cross-governmental teams have rarely been given separate fiscal authorities. There have been some concepts that pool the monies of several agencies. The United Kingdom (UK) has done so by pooling the monies of Defense, the Department for International Development (DIFID), and the Foreign and Commonwealth departments into a Security Sector/Conflict Prevention concept; consequently, U.S. Secretary of Defense Robert Gates and Secretary of State Hilary Clinton have recommended the idea for new, permanent, shared DoD-State resources and authorities for conflict prevention, post-conflict reconstruction, and security assistance.

However, the Executive Branch does not have the sole authority for the obligation of Federal funds. Congress is a key player in that they appropriate and authorize funds in ways that are different from the Executive Branch. Programs and timing of congressional funding can directly impact any attempt to gain a WoG let alone a comprehensive, response. Congress must be considered to be part of the solution. Consequently, coordination and cooperation are essential, and if programs are not executed with adequate resources, the results will lead to frustration or, worse, the idea that something has happened when it has not.

CASES

Malaya.

Dear Lyttelton

Malaya
We must have a plan.
Secondly we must have a man.
When we have a plan and have a man we shall succeed: not otherwise

Yours Sincerely

Montgomery (F.M.)[6]

In 1946, after World War II, the British returned to Malaya and attempted to re-impose rule with the creation of the Malayan Union.[7] But, they found a Malaya shaped by Japanese occupation that opposed a return to prewar ways. The British had lost their previous influence and authority, and the occupation had fueled ethnic tensions and nationalistic inclinations. Chinese and Indian minorities refused to be ruled by the Malay, and the Malay opposed giving the Chinese and Indians the vote and equal rights as the Malayan Union required. Capitalizing on these tensions, the Malayan Communist Party, founded in 1930 from primarily Chinese groups, organized resistance to British Colonial rule using Maoist protracted insurgent war. The Communists' objective was to defeat the will of the British to maintain the colony by undermining its legitimacy and economic investments.

The British initial response was neither comprehensive nor coordinated. European inhabitants of Malaya demanded immediate action and protection as they were driven off their plantations and mines by insurgent violence. In response to demands, the British military reacted with force, seeing the solution as a purely military one with little need to bother with political, informational, or economic factors. The search and destroy approach, in the eyes of the British military, was sufficient; therefore, it negated the need to develop a civil-military team or to develop a comprehensive strategy.

> The Malayan Emergency, officially declared in June 1948, was at first waged by the British as a conventional war, with soldiers seeking to hunt down and contain the Chinese Malayan guerillas, now reconstituted as the Malayan People's Anti-British Army (MPABA). The Malayan police force was not considered to have an operational role and the civil administration was left ignorant of military affairs. This was a campaign led by and carried out by the British Army, with limited support from the Royal Air Force and no input whatsoever from the various layers of civilian governance. By 1950, however, these methods seemed to be failing.[8]

The idea of a coordinated interagency command in Malaya was first proposed on February 23, 1950, when Sir Henry Gurney, the British high commissioner in Malaya, sent a telegram to Arthur Creech Jones, the Colonial Secretary. Based on his experiences elsewhere, he advocated a linked up WoG approach. Lieutenant-General Sir Harold Briggs was appointed as the chief of operations and developed what would be known as the Briggs Plan that was to be followed at all levels of government. Briggs stressed throughout that any operations undertaken by the army or police had to be under civil control, had to be within the law, and the purpose for which they were being conducted had to be clearly articulated to the local population. The framework had been described, but organization and leadership were still needed.

The plan did not go far enough. No one person was placed in charge of all the civil and military efforts. The police and the military could still operate separately with no overarching authority. After the murder of Sir Henry Gurney, General Briggs recommended that the Director of Operations have full and undivided control of all emergency policy, strategy, and tactics in Malaya. This was approved by London and the office of British High Commissioner, Secretary, and Director of Operations were merged. But Briggs became sick, and eventually General Sir Gerard Templer was appointed to the new office.

Templer stuck to the Briggs Plan as much as he could, but he developed and got approval for a structure that could execute the framework that Briggs had developed. For example, he consolidated all intelligence around one individual who would be responsible for coordinating the activities of police intelligence, naval intelligence, army intelligence, air force intelligence, and political intelligence. His role would include giving advice to each of these organizations, as well as being "completely responsible for collation and evaluation of all the intelligence available and for its presentation to those concerned in the proper form."[9] He also changed the organizations of the Police Force, Special Branch, Information Services, the Home Guard, and created a Combined Emergency Planning Staff.

With emphasis on the Special Branch of the Police as the primary intelligence gathering arm, security of the people, and focus on civil action, the institutional military was uneasy with the arrangement until results supported the concept. Templer was a military man, he understood the culture of the military, and was able to fight against it if necessary. It helped that the Home Secretary as well as the new Prime Minister, Winston Churchill, and Field Marshal Bernard Montgomery supported him.[10]

The UK successfully conducted a COIN campaign by creating a WoG plan and then developing the structure and procedures for executing that plan. The key to success was appointing the right individuals to lead and support efforts with political will and resources while having the wisdom from London to allow the field to execute the program successfully. All of the agencies involved had to sacrifice some of their sovereignty and accept institutional risk. Malaya was indeed a special case given the time, location, social, demographic, and political situation, but the outcome could have been quite different had the WoG approach not been used.

Malaya was what we call today a comprehensive approach that emphasized civil-military teaming coordinated at all levels in the country. The focus was on the population, building legitimacy and local capacity to provide the population good governance. It succeeded because there was a workable plan that established a framework, structures that were able to execute that plan, a platform for all stakeholders—including the local nationals—to be a part of the solution, a leader with the appropriate understanding and personality, resources, and a National Government in London that provided the requisite authorities but not direct interference.

Vietnam – CORDS

> In strong contrast to the sheer conventionality of most aspects of the GVN/US response, it (CORDS) did eventually prove possible to set up and carry out a major US/GVN wartime program specifically designed to meet many of the atypical problems of the people's war in South Viet Nam.
>
> Robert Komer[11]

As the British realized in Malaya in 1950, Washington, and especially the President, realized by 1967 that things were not going well in Vietnam, and something dramatic had to be done. Ambassador Henry Cabot Lodge, in his opening remarks at the 1966 Honolulu Conference before the Presidents of the United States and South Vietnam stated:

> We can beat up North Vietnamese regiments in the high plateau for the next twenty years and it will not end the war – unless we and the Vietnamese are able to build simple but solid political institutions under which proper police can function and a climate be created in which economic and social revolution, in freedom, are possible.[12]

Several studies completed in 1965 and 1966, most notably the "Program for the Pacification and Long-Term Development of Vietnam" (PROVN), written by the U.S. Army, all concluded that no two U.S. Government agencies shared a common vision or common approach on how to solve the problem of the conflict. All of the studies noted that pacification, as Ambassador Lodge outlined in his Honolulu talk, should be a major focus, and to that end the U.S. Government needed to rationalize the missions, roles, and priorities of all the U.S. agencies. Naturally, each agency, as well as the U.S. Embassy in Saigon, objected to those parts of the studies that impinged on institutional interests. President Lyndon Johnson was frustrated with the lack of action and appointed Robert J. Komer as a special assistant, giving him a strong mandate to tighten and strengthen the pacification program and deal with institutional resistance.

As in Malaya, having the right person in the lead at the right time was essential. Komer, who was running the Middle East shop in the National Security Council (NSC) along with William Colby, the Central Intelligence Agency (CIA) Far East Division Chief, ensured that key reports outlining the shortcomings of the conflict in Vietnam made it to key decisionmakers in Washington, DC, despite the censors in the Military Assistance Command Vietnam (MACV). These reports, along with the advice from Ed Lansdale and Ambassador Lodge, outlined the need for an effective pacification program and provided the catalyst for Komer, with the direct support of the President, to propose forming the Civil Operations and Revolutionary Development Support (CORDS) as a combined civil-military team under the direction of the military.

Again, success was based on a supportive policy, a workable structure, well-developed procedures, dedicated resources, and the right leadership. In CORDS, the U.S. military would be in charge of both civilian and military operations. Historically for the United States, it was rare to have civilians operating in a military chain of command. Komer was the first ambassador to serve directly under a military commander and have command responsibility for military and civilian personnel and resources. One of the innovations of the CORDS program was that all agencies agreed to have their performance evaluation reports written by the leadership of CORDS. Civil and military personnel wrote each other's efficiency reports and shared resources, leading to the type of unity of purpose that provided positive results. This, coupled with support from the highest levels, integrated the programs of the military, the CIA, the U.S. Agency for International Development (USAID), the United States Information Agency (USIA), and the Department of State. Additionally, CORDS was built as an organization that could directly lobby for and receive resources. The subordinate agencies were assigned, not attached, so that the funds used by CORDS were pooled and not located in each agency's individual stovepipes.[13]

The agencies agreed to sacrifice some of their sovereignty and resources to CORDS in support of pacification, because they were successful in having pacification defined so that some of their key programs remained outside of that definition, thus beyond CORDS control. For example, Komer insisted that land reform should be a major part of pacification under CORDS, but USAID succeeded in retaining control of that program. Komer finally gave up trying. The CORDS program, as a successful civil-military team, was effective in rationalizing country-wide pacification in its own operational stovepipe, from the tactical through the operational levels. Unlike Malaya, no individual or organization coordinated all governmental activities in Vietnam. The prerogatives of parent institutions, their cultures, and approaches remained factors that prevented a truly comprehensive approach. Each of the separate agencies of the U.S. Government continued to have separate programs running in Vietnam so there was no way around this at the operational level. CORDS constituted only one staff directorate out of five within MACV. Additionally, the MACV commanders in Vietnam, both General William Westmorland and his successor, General Creighton Abrams, ensured that there would be no linking of the pacification program with military combat operations.[14]

The existing military advisors for the Vietnamese Army, and special units like Special Forces and Rangers, remained outside of the control of CORDS. The best CORDS could offer was a bureaucratic overlay that facilitated better communication. The rift between regular military forces and the civilians and irregulars whose primary focus was on counterinsurgency and pacification, in particular, remained a problem. Ken Quinn, a Foreign Service officer with no military training who served four tours with CORDS in the Mekong Delta, posed the dilemma this way:

> There was always a little cultural difference between civilian and military [agencies], but one of the great lessons of CORDS was that it was not just the different colors of your clothes but where you sat that made a difference in your attitudes. The Army guys who were in the MACV team, and I generally saw eye to eye, but it was a different view than Army guys in the same town who were advisors to the ARVN 9th Division. The two groups saw different wars from different perspectives with different counterparts.[15]

Bruce Kinsey, a Foreign Service officer working for CORDS in Long An, recalled similar problems. Despite generally good relations between personnel working for CORDS, he remembered miscommunications with the regular military that had very real and tragic consequences:

> There was a village that I worked with like crazy. I had a cadre team in there. We strung up barbed wire and threw down tin cans on the perimeter so if the guerrillas came in you could hear them more easily. And we set up a school and the VC blew it up. It was fighting tooth and nail. The Third Brigade of the Ninth Division came in and set up at the end of the road that went through this hamlet. They ran these huge deuce-and-a-half trucks through there, full of garbage, and ammunition, and god knows what else. They were scared to death, so they ran them at fifty miles an hour. They killed like eleven Vietnamese kids. I talked to those people until I was blue in the face. And I put up signs saying, "U.S. Drivers—Friendly Hamlet—Slow Down" and they wouldn't.[16]

No civil-military teaming effort can be successful without host nation buy-in. Ensuring continual linking with the host nation as part of the effort can mean the difference between success and failure. In Vietnam, after Tet 1968, the Vietnamese Government under Nguyen Van Thieu was not interested in partnering in the countryside in civil programs in support of the CORDS efforts. Six months after Tet, he finally accepted a CORDS pacification campaign to push the government out to the countryside. But the implementation of this program by the Vietnamese government was more designed to secure their political future. What was learned in Vietnam, as in Malaya, is that even with successful civil-military teaming, unless it encompasses the comprehensive approach countrywide, including the host nation, success will be elusive.

Unlike the UK in Malaya, the U.S. governmental solution to Vietnam never embraced a comprehensive approach that emphasized civil-military teaming coordinated at all levels throughout the country.

Instead, all of the separate agencies of the U.S. Government continued to protect their own institutions, fearful of each other and especially concerned of being overcome by the much larger DoD. CORDS, operating in its own "lane," was the exception. It focused on the population, built legitimacy and local capacity to provide the population good governance, security, and economic opportunity. The CORDS program succeeded in its own lane because it developed a workable plan and a bureaucratic structure that was able to execute that plan, it had a leader with the appropriate understanding and personality, it had resources, and it had a President in Washington that provided the requisite authorities but did not directly interfere once the program was launched. However, in 1968 when Komer left, the Military Assistance Command used that opportunity to ensure that Ambassador William Colby, his replacement, stuck closely within the boundaries of the programs and reduced CORDS former independence. British Field Marshall Bernard Montgomery was correct in that you have to have the "man" to succeed at civil military teaming.[17]

Provincial Reconstruction Teams.

Afghanistan's experiment with civil-military teaming more closely resembles Vietnam than Malaya. But as in the other two cases, the United States came to realize that no progress was going to be made in Afghanistan until all of the agencies of the U.S. Government could work together. As General David Petraeus wrote to all of the U.S. Government agencies upon assuming command, there would be no pure military solution for the Afghanistan conflict. The solution, he wrote, lies in contributing to a "team of teams" to achieve unity of effort with diplomatic, international civilian, and Afghan partners to conduct a comprehensive civil-military counterinsurgency campaign.[18]

The initial focus of the U.S. national guidance for Afghanistan was on destroying the al-Qaeda terrorist organization, infrastructure, and other terrorist groups; convincing or compelling states and nonstate organizations to cease supporting terrorism; and providing military support to humanitarian operations. The focus was not on conducting a comprehensive approach toward addressing the drivers of conflict and building local Afghan capacity to transform conflict to obtain a viable peace. Instead, the U.S. national planning guidance focused on combat operations and was clear that the U.S. military would not participate in nation-building. In June 2002, following the deployment of the Commander Joint Task Force (CJTF) 180 (centered on the XVIII Airborne Corps), it became clear that success in Afghanistan was tied to the support of a viable state and the operational concept slowly shifted toward stability operations. One of the key organizations to carry out this new direction was the PRT.[19]

The civil-military teaming concept that was launched in Afghanistan in December 2002 consisted of U.S. interagency personnel based around an Army Civil Affairs lead that would also include representation from the Afghan government. The PRT's mission was: to facilitate information sharing among various agencies; to strengthen and extend Afghanistan governmental influence; to provide advice and assistance; and, to provide a safer environment by assisting with the regional development of the Afghan Nation Army (ANA) and local Afghan law enforcement authorities. The mission encompassed three major objectives: extend the authority of the Afghan central government; improve security; and, promote reconstruction. The PRT's role is to ensure that international efforts are in line with the host nation's development intentions and, in doing so, assess and, if possible, mitigate the constraints to development. As the security environment improves, the PRT is intended to be phased out as stabilization and reconstruction programs shift to longer-term development programs. The PRT will cease to exist when normal development operations can be carried out without its assistance.[20]

There are structural differences between the PRTs in Iraq and Afghanistan. PRTs in Afghanistan typically consist of 50 to 100 members, with only three or four representatives from civilian government agencies. Though an Air Force Lieutenant Colonel or Navy Commander leads the PRT, he does not have authority over non-DoD personnel. In Iraq, PRTs are similar in size but have a slightly smaller percentage of military personnel, and a Department of State officer directs the PRT. However, many DoD officers are still obligated to fill slots normally considered within the purview of civilian agencies. Additionally, there are multiple PRTs from different nations, each with their own procedures and objectives, working in their own sectors further compounding the problem.[21]

All of the studies of the PRTs conclude that they are not effective civil-military teams, and that there is no comprehensive approach at the operational level that even comes close to the level of coordination and cooperation in either Malaya or Vietnam. There is neither the structure nor the management procedures in theater to achieve the comprehensive approach that is required for success. Each country and the separate national and international funds, agencies, and organizations continue their own programs in parallel with the PRTs whose activities may be coordinated with kinetic military operations. Both in Afghanistan and Iraq, the shortcomings of Vietnam have not only been replicated but magnified.

Unlike CORDS, there is no unifying structure at all levels to coordinate the civil military approach of the PRTs. This has translated into a lack of clear operational guidance and the ad hoc nature of most of the programs and approaches. Unlike CORDS, where the efficiency reports of the members were written by CORDS members, each agency retains its own control in the PRTs. Civilian members sometimes have dual or triple loyalties. Civilian agency personnel answer to the PRT commander or team leader, to a line of operations (such as rule-of-law) director or agency mission director housed at the Embassy, and/or to their home agency in Washington. It is sometimes unclear whether a civilian agency representative is a member of the PRT or an agency liaison to the PRT. Neither the Department of State nor the DoD commander has been given authority over the members of the PRT who are from other agencies, so progress is made by consensus, if possible. The lack of central command for the PRT mirrors the larger problem in all of Afghanistan where multiple chains of command (embassy, U.S. Forces-Afghanistan [USFOR-A], Special Representative for Afghanistan and Pakistan, International Security Assistance Forces [ISAF], and allies) often lead to confusion and disagreement over mission goals.[22]

There are no Standard Operating Procedures (SOP) that all of the agencies have agreed to, therefore each agency uses its own set of procedures and approaches. Often, because the military runs the operational cell and has available funds, they call the shots thus giving the PRT a decidedly military bent. Because there is no official doctrine or tactics, techniques, or procedures for PRTs either in the United States or NATO, each theater and PRT rotation has to work out its own approaches based on previous handbooks, lessons learned, and desk-side guides. There is no doctrinal guidance on how PRTs are to conduct a collaborative planning and management process. The ISAF Handbook is the most frequently cited source for a PRT mission statement, and the Center for Army Lessons Learned (CALL) has issued a more detailed PRT Playbook containing tactics, techniques, and procedures (which they are in the process of revising), while the U.S. Joint Forces Command (JFCOM) produced a Pre-Doctrinal Research White Paper on PRTs. However, there does not appear to be one U.S. Government-sanctioned mission statement that is universally accepted. In Iraq, the only objectives provided to PRTs were in a set of metrics known as the Maturity Model, which measures provinces' performance in five areas: rule-of-law, governance, reconciliation, political developments, and economics. Though a useful tool in theory, its application is varied throughout the field and is subjective per the individual perspectives of team leaders. The result is that there is little continuity among PRT and within PRTs, particularly as the personnel rotate in and out on a frequent basis.[23]

Unlike CORDS, there are multiple sources of funding for the PRT, each with its own constraints and restraints, reflecting the agendas of the parent agencies. The situation has been termed by the Center for Complex Operations (CCO) report, "convoluted." The bulk of PRT funding is provided by USAID and by military units (primarily through the Commanders Emergency Response Program [CERP]). These two organizations exert direct control or provide substantial influence over the majority of U.S. PRT civil sector development projects and programs. From the CERP, the DoD elements can draw funds originally designed for a quick impact to stabilize an area and provide a bridge to long-term development, with relative ease. USAID personnel have access to the Local Governance and Community Development Program Fund (LGCD). Securing these resources, however, tends to be difficult and time-consuming. The Department of State recently established a Quick Reaction Fund (QRF) for its officers in Iraq. However, these funds are programmed according to each agency's priority, and there is no standard process for the collaborative resourcing, coordinating, and prioritization of funding for PRT projects. The result has been those with the most ready access to the money calls the shots—most often the military. Ultimately, PRTs often choose projects based on the convenience of funds and the vision of providing agencies rather than addressing either the drivers of conflict or the structural grievances. This creates tensions between DoD whose original focus for the expenditure of funds was to "win the hearts and minds" by funding quick impact programs that would provide the most visibility for the money in an information campaign and USAID whose focus is long-term development with little interest in short-term "hearts and minds" projects. Both organizations are under much pressure from their respective institutions to demonstrate progress, especially the military, because of a greater push to show immediate success. This fact, coupled with the strict statutory and regulatory guidelines that constrain the money flow, makes agencies disinclined to concede control without the achievement of an immediate tangible benefit to the parent institution.[24]

As in CORDS and Malaya, the involvement of the host nation is critical, as such, the PRTs have a spotty record. Often the local nations are not involved in PRT planning, because of the transitory nature of the personnel in the PRTs and its lack of a coherent approach among all of the ISAF PRTs, establishing the close working network with the host nation that is critical in these situations is extremely difficult. During interviews with key personnel in Iraq in 2008, many Iraqis at the provincial level were not aware of what the PRTs were trying to accomplish. Many saw them as part of the military force or just a place to leverage to get resources when they could not get them from their own government. The extent to which the PRTs were included in provincial processes varies widely. This is unlike the processes set up in Malaya where there was vertical and horizontal uniformity among all of the management and coordinating mechanisms. At times, the funding itself can get in the way of host nation development.[25]

> Many civilian members of PRTs see CERP-funded programs as no longer necessary, and that the types of projects funded by CERP and the process by which CERP is spent undermines the capacity-building mission they see as paramount: In the meeting with the commanding general, we said, This is a little counterproductive, because we've been telling the Iraqis that the money's running out and we've been using it as an opportunity to promote good governance, that they can't expect windfalls, they need to plan rationally and now you want us to turn around and say, Oh, each one of the PRTs has $50-60 million, and we have to spend it fast! That completely blows our good governance message out of the water.[26]

However, the PRTs are only part of what should be a comprehensive operational level approach, but the approach at the operational level is also flawed. Much of the success depends on personal relationships among individuals, and not the authorities, policy, processes, and mechanisms. There are disconnects among the U.S. military, allies, PRTs, U.S. Embassy, UN, other national embassies, other NGOs, and private contractors—all attempting to deal with the host nation. No overarching comprehensive approach exists. No formalized process has ever existed regarding the lines of communication and hierarchy between the PRT office at the embassy and the PRTs and their personnel in the field. Like so many other aspects of PRT planning and activities, American personnel working at the PRTs around Afghanistan have never known what to expect from their Embassy counterparts—leading to a great deal of confusion and frustration as each side strives to carry out its duties. Given the general ability of UN missions to maintain longer-term operations in host countries, PRT members should consistently try to search for and encourage areas of overlap between their own activities and those of UN bodies in Iraq and Afghanistan in an effort to increase the sustainability of potentially shared projects.

The PRTs in Afghanistan and Iraq have no doctrine that establishes a conceptual framework, no established structures that are able to execute activities within that framework and provide a platform for all stakeholders, including helping the local nationals to be a part of the solution. There is no single leader at either the operational or strategic level, with the appropriate access to higher authority and resources that is able to pull all of the various separate agencies together in a holistic manner. There is insufficient human capital to fill the teams with the correct capability. The concept of some structure, like a PRT, nested within an overall comprehensive approach at the operational level appears to be valid but the devil lies in the details, particularly in the execution.

Case Conclusions.

When civil-military teaming works from the strategic through the tactical level, it enhances a comprehensive approach that can enable the host nation to deal with the sources of conflict, improve local capacity, and build the foundation for a viable peace. But there are few examples of such success. A long practice in both the UK and the United States of subordinating military action to civil authority proved to be insufficient to create effective civil-military teaming. In the cases described above, certain best practices have been identified that have improved such teaming. These practices have been codified in the last few years, notably, in the *Guiding Principles for Stabilization and Reconstruction* by the United States Institute of Peace (USIP) and the U.S. Army Peacekeeping and Stability Operations Institute (PKSOI), and in *The Interagency Teaming to Counter Irregular Threats Handbook* developed by the Applied Physics Lab at Johns Hopkins in support of U.S. Special Operations Command. These practices are identifying the right leadership and are developing human resources for the team; obtaining key authorities, agreements, and processes; developing a shared understanding of the problem and vision of the goal; obtaining and managing resources through appropriate structures and processes; and ensuring host nation ownership.

In Malaya, Vietnam, and Afghanistan, having the right leader supported by the best team made all the difference. There have been several U.S. Government initiatives to improve the processes across all agencies of government for the selection and education of key personnel. Two of the principal initiatives are: the National Security Professionals, established by executive order in 2007 to develop a cadre of government-wide personnel to lead and execute coordinated, effective national security operations; and the Interagency Management System (IMS) established by presidential directive and approved by the Deputies Committee of the NSC in March 2007 to establish a means to successfully integrate the instruments of national power. Both have established educational and training programs open to all government agencies. There is even a proposed bill in committee, House Resolution 6249, submitted on September 29, 2010, by then Congressman Ike Skelton, former chairman of the House Armed Services Committee, to mandate a system to educate, train, and develop interagency nation security professionals across the government. If passed into law and funded, it will be a catalyst.[27]

However, these governmental initiatives are limited and the RAND Corporation has identified two problematic issues. First, the lack of civilian and military capacity to perform these stability tasks and second, the need for the United States to project a U.S. Government civilian face rather than a military one to support U.S. foreign policy goals. There is little slack or flexibility in the civil capacity of the U.S. Government. Unlike the military, the civilian organizations are fully committed all the time and have no excess capacity for training and preparation for emerging crises. This has been recognized and the Department of State's Coordinator for Reconstruction and Stabilization (S/CRS) has designed a Civilian Response Corps (CRC) to meet some of this need. Currently it is partially funded and slowly recruiting members. The DoD realized that it had limited capacity to advise the defense ministries of other countries and initiated the Civilian Expeditionary Workforce (CEW) to address that shortfall.

> While civilian agencies clearly have many of the capabilities required in [Security, Stability, Transition, and Reconstruction] SSTR operations, they lack capacity. The two primary DoD interagency partners, DoS and USAID, are relatively small organizations with limited surge capacity to support large-scale, complex SSTR operations. In fact, based on the numbers and availability of appropriate personnel, the organic capacity of the Army in stability operations (most of all, Civil Affairs) can dwarf the capacity of USAID and DoS. Moreover, numbers alone tell only a part of the story. There is a very different orientation between the civilian agencies and the military. The former's organizational focus is on the steady state, while the latter's focus is contingency response.[28]

The development of in-house expertise in the U.S. Government, both civil and military, will take time, and there is no certainty that the appropriate capacity or capability will be available when needed. As the contracting business has expanded, talent has shifted from the military, academic, and governmental agencies toward the contractors. Now the only place some of the expertise exists is in the private sector.

As all of these government agencies have increasingly relied on contractors for additional support so much so that we must now now consider contractors as part of the civil-military team. Contractors, many who use local nationals, can provide critical knowledge of the terrain, culture, language, social and political structures, as well as have special skills in the stability sectors. As Sam Meiss, a career Naval Officer and a contractor in Afghanistan and Iraq has observed:

> There is an inherent and growing core of talent available within the 'contractor' community—who possess a deep reservoir of realistic knowledge, skills, abilities with an inherent capacity to provide physical sustainment to the full range of tasks to be accomplished by not only the Theater Command, but [also by] other USG Agencies, Coalition Partners and relevant members of the International Community and contributing members of Non-Governmental Organizations [NGOs]. Against the backdrop of the urgent need for sustainable successes at all levels of the challenges in Iraq [and in Afghanistan], the role of a truly knowledgeable contractor base can and should be appropriately leveraged into this complex mix of challenges and imperatives. . . . The huge impact of a truly knowledgeable core of culture, language, social, political, economic structure of the environment are monumental in consequence to 'get it right' in the execution of the Theatre Campaign, from the contributing U.S./Coalition military, political, economic, health and development communities.[29]

The burden is on the contacting agency to ensure that the knowledge is indeed present and appropriate. This is especially the case if the contracting agency is directly supporting the host nation and its institutions. It is incumbent on the contracting agency to insist on getting that key expertise. The military and the other agencies of government must also be prepared to handle this contracting. As the Ganser Report, released in November 2007, and a number of other reports have stated, neither the Army nor other federal agencies were prepared to transition to an expanded contracting approach that, in the wake of Iraq and Afghanistan, increased their contracting work load by over 600 percent. These organizations need a cultural transformation on how to appropriately use contracting to accomplish their mission.[30]

Contracting agencies can provide the U.S. Government with more flexible options than can be achieved inside the federal system. Contractors will use best business practices that will emphasize the most efficient and effective methods, processes, and activities to accomplish the task. Contracts can be quickly adapted to changing circumstances, and packages of expertise can be tailored to meet situations to provide economy-of-force and force multiplier functions, if done properly. As needs become apparent, as they will in the fluid moments of a post conflict stability operation, the U.S. Government can reach back, using the correct contracting vehicle, obtain, and apply the expertise needed. USAID has recognized this for years, and the majority of their efforts are provided through implementing partners, be they private enterprise or NGOs.

However, there are factors that can make contracting inflexible. Unlike the case above, there are practices of using multiple agencies, multiple contractors, and multiple flows of money. These practices confuse unity of effort and obscure accountability. Contractors work for money and are motivated to maintain their contact even if it might not meet the client's needs or has ceased to embody best business practices. This can become counterproductive because it will have a direct effect on the people and the government of the host nation, thus affecting the development of capacity and legitimacy. The struggle over the training of the

Afghanistan Police is a case in point, where various agencies squabbled over who should have the lead and what the outcomes should be.[31]

Leaders need the authorities and processes to bring their programs into action. In 2007, as part of the presidential initiatives, the S/CRS developed a WoG reconstruction and stabilization planning and execution process to be applied at multiple levels, from the field to Washington, DC. This integrated planning process has been exercised by civil-military teams at Joint Forces Command and several combatant commands and is the basis for a planner's course, presented regularly in Washington, DC, that prepares civilians and military personnel to deploy into a crisis area. As a result of the response to the Haiti Earthquake, where this process was not used, this initiative is being reviewed and the DoD, the Department of State, and USAID are working on a Three Ds Planning Guide to codify what has been learned. The three agencies agree that getting the appropriate agreements, authorities, and approaches in place is essential but, as outlined in the examples provided above, institutional equities must be considered.[32]

Another key is to establish a unity of purpose based on a shared vision of what the problem is that needs to be addressed. In 2008, the Deputies Committee of the National Security Council endorsed the Interagency Conflict Assessment Framework (ICAF) as a key tool for all agencies to use in achieving an agreed upon assessment of the problem. This framework is a USAID product based on World Bank assessments. The ICAF is a framework that can be used to help people from different U.S. Government departments and agencies work together to reach a shared understanding of a country's conflict dynamics and reach a consensus on potential entry points for additional U.S. Government efforts. This assessment will provide for a deeper understanding of the underlying conflict dynamics in the host country or region.

Another tool that has been developed and is being used in Afghanistan is the District Stability Framework (DSF). It is a methodology designed for use, by both military and civilian personnel, to identify the underlying causes of instability and conflict in a region, devise programs to diminish the root causes of instability and conflict, and measure the effectiveness of programming. It is employed to gather information using the following lenses: operational environment; cultural environment; local perceptions; and, stability/instability dynamics. This information then helps identify, prioritize, monitor, evaluate, and adjust programming that is intended to diminish the causes of instability or conflict. It remains to be seen if these tools will be institutionalized.[33]

Early resources, judiciously applied, can produce quick and visible results and lead to increasing host nation ownership. Malaya solved the resource problem by centralizing management, but it has been a challenge in each of the other conflicts discussed in this chapter. CORDS had a uniformed resource flow, but the PRTs do not. Funding has been a source of division and contention that at times limits the impact of civil-military teams. In both Vietnam and Afghanistan, the other agencies of government have been reluctant to t relinquish their institutional prerogatives.

In 2007, the Interagency Management System for Reconstruction and Stabilization (R&S IMS) was created to provide an organizational structure for a WoG approach to crisis situations, not only to plan but also to manage the resources. It is an institutionalized system of interagency bodies that manages WoG stabilization and reconstruction planning and operations. However, although exercised in several combatant command exercises, the IMS, as such, has not been used as intended outside of the exercises. S/CRS has deployed parts of the IMS to provide key functions to the Country Team and the combatant command. For example, in 2008 in Afghanistan, S/CRS put together a civil-military team, the Integrated Civilian-Military Action Group (ICMAG), that served as a planning staff at the U.S. Embassy in Kabul. It was essential in developing the regional and provincial Civilian-Military plans in regional Command-East and South and also part of the ISAF team that developed the overall U.S. Government Civilian-Military Campaign Plan for Support of Afghanistan. In August 2009, ICMAG evolved within the Political-Military Affairs section of the U.S. Embassy into the Civilian-Military Plans and Assessments Sub-Section (CMPASS). These IMS structures and concepts provide opportunity to explore civil and military teaming, and with the publication of the Department of State's QDDR, the IMS has been reevaluated as not being flexible enough and will be revised.

At the tactical level, the PRTs have been a fixture of our approach for over 10 years, and some type of PRT concept has been used by many at least since the 1950s when the French developed the *Section Administrative Specialisee* (SAS) in Algeria.[34] The PRTs are still ad hoc organizations and, as of yet, have not been considered as a concept worthy of either force design or doctrine development. The structure, personnel, policy, and procedures have been created over time and published in various hand books and studies, but these lessons have not migrated into doctrinal publications.

By all studies and accounts, there is some utility to such an organization; therefore, the U.S. Government needs to look at Afghanistan and Iraq and project toward future needs. RAND has done several studies on the need to look at the PRTs and have recommended a civil-military teaming vision for the future.

The IMS conceived a type of civilian PRT called the Field Advance Civilian Teams (FACTs). FACTs are primarily local, on-the-ground operational and action entities whose tasks are to establish a U.S. presence, provide direct information about conditions on the ground, and support R&S operations conducted at a provincial and local level. They are flexible, scalable teams responsible for a range of operations in governance, security, rule-of-law, infrastructure, and economic stabilization to provide the Chief of Mission (CoM) with maximum capacity to implement R&S programs. As required, they may coordinate the field execution of projects that involve the activities and resources of not only the U.S. Government, but also foreign governments, the UN, other international governmental organizations (IGOs), NGOs, or host nations (HN). While remaining under CoM authority, FACTs may integrate with U.S. or foreign military forces to maintain unity of effort. In this regard, FACTs build upon the lessons learned from PRTs established for the conflicts in Afghanistan and Iraq, but their role in assessments, plan revisions, and sub-national field level planning is also important.

The FACT concept offers an opportunity to look beyond the PRTs of Iraq and Afghanistan and consider this as a WoG development that could be the basis for civil-military teaming at the implementation level. It is an opportunity to rationalize and formalize what has been ad hoc by conducting parallel force design force development with the other agencies of the U.S. Government. As the U.S. Government reorients itself in the wake of the QDDR with declining resources, it needs to look at some of the concepts that have been proposed and subject them to intense scrutiny.[35]

CONCLUSIONS

The three cases above demonstrate that without the HN taking ownership, there is no hope for success. While writing *The Guidelines for Stabilization and Reconstruction,* the USIP reviewed all of the literature and interviewed many practitioners around the world and all agreed that HN ownership was the key, cross-cutting principle. The international community can impose stability, but only the locals can achieve a sustainable peace. The civil-military team must understand the local context and craft programs and operations that are sensitive to that context. Even in Malaya, where the UK had been for years, the British initially did not appreciate the changes that had occurred as a result of World War II.

Without context, fostering ownership will be difficult, but that is the ultimate responsibility for the civil-military team. This means allowing local and national governments and civil society to lead and partner in the planning and implementation. This starts at the top, and General Petraeus and Ambassador Eikenberry state:

> Through the Kabul Process and Afghan National Priority Programs and other sector strategies, the Government of the Islamic Republic of Afghanistan (GIRoA) has articulated its priorities. The U.S. efforts in Afghanistan support those priorities, which are

> reflected throughout this document. The Plan, which incorporates Department of State, Department of Defense, and U.S. Agency for International Development, U.S. Forces-Afghanistan, and other U.S. agencies' priorities and strategies, integrates joint and interagency elements under one umbrella, oriented toward a common mission. The plan is also intended to communicate USG priorities to the international community and the Afghan Government.[36]

The challenge is in implementation. The PRTs are designed to have Afghans involved in their process, but a great deal depends on selecting the right people with the appropriate skills but, as we have seen, the recruiting and training programs coupled with the personal rotation policy are inadequate.

As long as the focus of the civil-military team is on the population, building legitimacy and local capacity to provide the population good governance, success is possible. Having a workable plan that establishes: a framework plan; developing structures and procedures that can execute that plan; providing a platform for all stakeholders, especially for the local nationals to be a part of the solution; and, selecting a leader with the appropriate understanding and personality along with adequate, resources and support from the National Government; are the minimum essential requirements for success.

ENDNOTES - CHAPTER 11

1. Secretary of State Hillary Clinton's QDDR Town Hall, updated on December 15, 2010, available from *http://secretaryclinton.wordpress.com/2010/12/15/secretary-of-state-hillary-clintons-qddr-town-hall/*.

2. Steven J Hadley *et al.*, *The QDR in Perspective: Meeting America's National Security Needs for the 21st Century, The Final Report of the Quadrennial Defense Review Independent Panel*, Washington, DC: USIP, 2010, p. 37.

3. *U.S. Army Field Manual* (FM) *3-07 Stability Operations*, Washington, DC: U.S. Department of the Army, October 2008, pp. 1-4.

4. William J Olson, "Interagency Coordination: The Normal Accident or the Essence of Indecision," in Gabriel Marcella, ed., *Affairs of State: The Interagency and National Security*, Carlisle, PA: Strategic Studies Institute, U.S. Army War College, December 2008, p. 223.

5. *Ibid.*, p. 229.

6. John A. Nagl, *Learning to Eat Soup with a Knife: Counterinsurgency Lessons from Malaya and Vietnam*, Chicago, IL: University of Chicago Press, 2005, p. 87.

7. The British Military Administration assigned Sir Harold MacMichael to gather the Malay state ruler's approval for the Malayan Union. They agreed, though most sources believed that their agreement was given very reluctantly and perhaps from fear they would be dethroned. The rulers (sultans) gave all powers to the British Crown except for religious matters. Ariffin Omar, *Mangsa Melayu: Malay Concepts of Democracy and Community, 1945-1950*, Kuala Lumpur, Malaysia: Oxford University Press, 1993.

8. Benjamin Grob-Fitzgibbon, "The Interagency Process and Malaya: The British Experience," *The U.S. Army and the Interagency Process: Historical Perspectives*, Ft. Leavenworth, KS: Combat Studies Institute (CSI), 2008, p. 95.

9. *Ibid.*, p. 102; Nagl, p. 74.

10. Joel Hamby, "Civil-Military Operations Joint Doctrine and the Malayan Emergency," *Joint Forces Quarterly*, Autumn 2002, p. 61; Nagl, p. 74.

11. Nagl, p. 166.

12. Thomas W. Scoville, *Reorganization for Pacification Support*, Washington, DC: U. S. Army Center of Military History, 1999, p. 23.

13. Major John Rogan, "Improving Interagency Coordination and Unity of Effort: An Organizational Analysis of the Contemporary Provincial Reconstruction Team," Ft. Leavenworth, KS: U.S. Army Command and General Staff College, 2010, p. 23; Scoville, p. 66.

14. Richard Weitz, "CORDS and the Whole of Government Approach: Vietnam, Afghanistan and Beyond," *Small Wars Journal*, February 4, 2010, p. 7; Scoville, pp. 67, 82.

15. Jeffrey Woods, "Counterinsurgency, the Interagency Process, and Vietnam: The American Experience," in Kendall Gott, ed., *The U.S. Army and the Interagency Process: Historical Perspectives*, Ft. Leavenworth, KS: Combat Studies Institute (CSI), 2008, p. 110.

16. *Ibid*.

17. Scoville, p. 83.

18. General David Petraeus, "Letter to the Soldiers, Sailors, Airmen, Marines, and Civilians of NATO's International Security Assistance Force," July 4, 2010.

19. William Flavin, *Civil Military Operations: Afghanistan, Observations on Civil Military Operations During the First Year of Operation Enduring Freedom*, Carlisle, PA: Peacekeeping and Stability Operations institute (PKSOI), 2004, p. ix.

20. CJCMOTF, "Provincial Reconstruction Team Concept," briefing slides, Kabul, Afghanistan, January 3, 2003. The detailed mission of PRTs is:

Assist in marginalizing causes of instability by:

Forming and facilitating information sharing bodies that support the Interim Transitional Government of Afghanistan (ITGA) thus stimulating and enhancing local, regional, and national reconstruction efforts. Create a more safe and secure environment by monitoring/assessing/reporting on military, political, civil reform efforts.

Facilitate negotiations to defuse local and inter-regional tensions.

Assist, as required, with regional development of Afghan National Army and local Afghan law enforcement/security sector authorities.

Facilitate information sharing between National/international/local organizations and agencies

ITGA Security sector and military (Afghan and Coalition).

Facilitate/strengthen/extend ITGA influence through interaction with political, military and community leaders.

Provide expert advice, as needed, to local leaders/officials in the province. Monitor local and regional situation via conducting frequent patrols in both civil and security sectors.

Monitor, assist, and report on United Nations Assistance Mission in Afghanistan-Disarmament, Demobilization, and Reintegration [UNAMA-DDR] process.

Report information on: Government operations, Infrastructure improvements, Intra-regional commerce, Health care/basic human needs, Security Operations, Economic improvement.

Afghan acceptance of the rule of law/ arbitration of disputes in a non-violent and peaceful manner.

Report on local/provincial leader's acceptance of the ITGA.

Handbook: Iraq Provincial Reconstruction Teams, Observations, Insights, Lessons, Ft. Leavenworth, KS: Center for Army Lessons Learned (CALL), November 2010, p. 5.

21. Lawner, pp. 22-23.

22. Center for Complex Operations (CCO), PRT Interagency Lessons Learned Project October 2010, Washington, DC: National Defense University (NDU) Press, October 2010, pp. 5-8.

23. *Ibid.*, pp. 18-24.

24. *Ibid.*, pp. 17-20; Flavin, p. 20; Lawner, p. 24.

25. Terrence Kelly, "PRT Lessons from IRAQ," in Christopher M. Schnaubelt, ed., *Operationalizing a Comprehensive Approach in Semi-permissive Environments,* Rome, Italy: NATO Defense College, June 2009, p.113.

26. CCO, p. 18.

27. Civilian Personnel Management Service Webpage, available from *www.cpms.osd.mil/lpdd/NSPD/NSPD_index.aspx;* U.S. Congress, House, Committee on Oversight and Government Reform, *Interagency National Security Professional Education, Administration, and Development System Act of 2010,* H.R. 6249, 111th Cong., as introduced by the House, September 29, 2010.

28. Thomas S. Szayna, Derek Eaton, James E. Barnett II, Brooke Stearns Lawson, Terrence K. Kelly, and Zachary Haldeman, *Integrating Civilian Agencies in Stability Operations,* Santa Monica, CA: RAND Arroyo Center, 2009, p. 20; see also Nora Bensahel, Olga Oliker, and Heather Peterson, *Improving Capacity for Stabilization and Reconstruction Operations,* Santa Monica, CA: RAND, 2009.

29. Sam Meese, "A Contractor on the Battlefield: Observations and Opportunities," Carlisle, PA: PKSOI, three unpublished research papers.

30. Dr. Jacques S. Gansler *et.al.*, "Urgent Reform Required: Army Expeditionary Contracting," Report of the Commission on Army Acquisition and Program Management in Expeditionary

Operations, Washington DC: Department of the Army, October 31, 2007, pp. 11, 18, 22.

31. Christine Spolar, "Military Training of Afghan National Police Mired in Contract Dispute," *Huffington Post Investigative Fund*, February 22, 2010, available from *www.huffingtonpost.com/2010/02/22/military-training-of-afgh_n_471519.html*; T. Christian Miller, Mark Hosenball, and Ron Moreau, "The Gang That Couldn't Shoot Straight," *Newsweek*, March 19, 2010, available from *www.newsweek.com/id/235221*.

32. *3D Planning Guide: Working Draft 2011*, Washington, DC: Department of State, Department of Defense, and U.S. Agency for International Development, 2011; D. Guha-Sapir, T. Kirsch, S. Dooling, and A. Sirois, *Earthquake Interagency Lessons Learned Workshop Report June 22, 2010*, Washington, DC: USAID, 2010.

33. *Joint Publication 3-07 Signature Draft Stability Operations*, Washington, DC: The Joint Staff, June 2011. Annex A explains the various assessment tools.

34. Alistair Horne, *A Savage War of Peace; Algeria 1954-1962*, New York: Viking Press 1977, pp. 108-109. The *Section Administrative Specialisee* (SAS) corps was created to take back the countryside. It consisted of 400 detachments of small teams led by an army captain who was an expert in Arabic and Arab affairs. The team was to deal with all aspects of life in the countryside from development to agriculture, to justice, to health, to building schools. They were successful in keeping the countryside out of the conflict and were seen by the National Liberation Front – Algeria (FLN) as a major threat.

35. *Handbook for Military Participation in the Interagency Management System for Reconstruction and Stabilization*, Suffolk, VA: U.S. Joint Forces Command, February 17, 2010, p. II-4; State Coordinator for Reconstruction and Stabilization, "Afghanistan: Continued Planning Support," Washington DC: Department of State, December 22, 2010, p. 2.

36. *United States Government Integrated Civilian-Military Campaign Plan for Support to Afghanistan*, Kabul, Afghanistan: U.S. Forces Afghanistan and U.S. Embassy Afghanistan, February 2011, p. i.

CHAPTER 12

ETHICAL LESSONS ON MAXIMIZING PRIVATE CONTRACTOR VALUE IN AFGHANISTAN AND IRAQ

Doug Brooks
Mackenzie Duelge

INTRODUCTION

Private sector contracting has become an integral part of modern international operations, and in Afghanistan and Iraq contracting has been largely fruitful, despite some well-publicized problems and the enormous difficulties inherent to reconstructions in the midst of violent conflicts. Casual observers may not perceive that the biggest problems faced by private contractors are not ethical problems of fraud or abuse, but rather are grander problems of waste. This waste stems from poor contract design and management, and is neither new nor unforeseen, but can be difficult and time intensive to address. The lessons learned from past experience in stability operations have not always been heeded, and the consequences of failing to heed those lessons have plagued reconstruction efforts in Afghanistan and Iraq. Furthermore, the government's contracting capacity has not always matched the ambitious goals set by the presidential administration in office at the time, and this mismatch has resulted in a lack of clarity and consistency. In spite of these problems, the level of support for the troops has been unmatched in history, and significant support, reconstruction, and development goals were achieved in the midst of war.

This generally positive perspective is not just an industry perspective; it is shared by government investigative and research organizations such as the Commission on Wartime Contracting (CWC), the Government Accountability Office (GAO), the Congressional Research Service (CRS), the Special Inspector General for Afghanistan Reconstruction (SIGAR), and the Special Inspector General for Iraq Reconstruction (SIGIR), who, while citing many failures and problems, are all largely in agreement that contracting in Afghanistan and Iraq has functioned reasonably well. When discussing private security contracting, problems are generally split into three categories: waste, fraud, and abuse. By far the biggest drain on stability operations in Afghanistan and Iraq has come as a result of waste.[1] Waste is a problem on the client-side of the process that includes failures of planning, coordination, contract oversight and management, flexibility, and communication. The greatest long-term value of all the commissions and investigative generals will be their influence on improving these structural aspects of future contingency operations that will be conducted by the U.S. Government and the larger international community.

This chapter examines the role of the private sector in reconstruction and stability operations through several lenses. First, the chapter reviews how the general attitude toward contractors has hindered the ability of the contractors to perform and how this attitude has interfered with the overall success of stability operations. Next, the chapter provides a discussion of the weaknesses of the government-private sector partnership. Then, the chapter outlines the future of private sector contractors in stability operations. Finally, an analysis is provided on how this role fits into the overall picture to recommend not only a course of action vis-à-vis contractors, but also the kind of overall structure that best utilizes all of the resources available in stability, peacekeeping, and military operations.

Most contingency contractors will agree that there is much that can be done to tackle fraud and abuse, but limiting waste requires structural improvements in the conduct of contingency operations. Political constraints, preferences for speed over efficiency, and interagency and interorganizational noncooperation hamper the ability of the actors to address and begin to solve the waste issue. As is the case in all international operations, private sector security operations are not the product of a single agency, organization, or government. Goals are set by one agency, budgets by another, and the ground rules for operations may be set by yet another. All of these requirements must then be met by the private contractor, whose future contracts may depend more on compliance than on success. The many facets of private sector-government collaborations mean that a new, successful, cooperative model cannot simply integrate governments and governmental agencies, but must also include those who work with the government, but who are not a part of it. While setbacks and failures can cost the stability operations industry millions of dollars and sometimes the lives of their employees, avoidable problems also cost the international community time, resources and ultimately human lives on a far more catastrophic scale.

The role of the private sector in Afghanistan and Iraq has been misunderstood by many analysts and journalists, and thus, predictably, it has also been mischaracterized by the media (albeit sometimes intentionally to ensure a sensational impact). There has been an improvement in recent coverage, especially since the heady days of 2004-08 when coverage of the industry was dominated by glaringly exaggerated accounts focused on Western private security companies (PSCs). Western employees of PSCs earned the majority of the media coverage while comprising a tiny percentage of the actual contractors (less than 3 percent)[2] working in Afghanistan and Iraq. It is no wonder that any subsequent analysis was skewed as a result.

Recently, it is interesting to note that while the proportion of contractors engaged in security operations has increased (to almost 20 percent in some places[3]), media coverage of the private sector has shifted focus to logistics, construction, demining, training, and other essential stability activities. It is possible that the shift to more positive (though only marginally so) coverage of private security is the result of a transition to more reconstruction-centric roles for the contractors.[4] These more mundane activities lead to stories that do not have quite the same flair, but they also represent the bulk of the industry operations and value, and comprise the largest potential for poor planning and waste. It seems then, that media coverage has shifted to topics where it has the greatest potential to help repair the most significant problem facing private security operations.

The problematic coverage of private sector stability operations in academia and the media has hampered constructive, rational discussion of the optimization of private sector actors' work in Afghanistan and Iraq. The discussion has long focused on issues of fraud and abuse and has failed to take on the more difficult questions of role definition for contractors in stability operations and waste minimization. The discussion going forward needs to determine where the private sector can provide the greatest value to stability operations, while ensuring ethical behavior at the same time. Serious analysts and academics have taken a long-term view of the role of the private sector in security operations; they have looked beyond Afghanistan and Iraq. Even accepting the realities of private security operations, the lessons learned from Afghanistan and Iraq have enormously positive potential to influence future international stability operations. Many laws, regulations and guidelines are being developed as a direct result of experiences in Afghanistan and Iraq, and if the wrong lessons or inappropriate rules are applied to future situations, then future contingency operations will be doomed before they even begin.

CONTRACT MANAGEMENT NEEDS AN ATTITUDE ADJUSTMENT

Many commentators have expressed concerns about the propriety of for-profit firms working in conflict or post-conflict environments. These concerns have in the past turned the issue of private sector work into an emotional debate. Contractors are sloppily called "mercenaries" by the press, and are routinely accused of profiting from war, destruction, and suffering.[5] This attitude ignores the fact that stability operations are essential if international efforts are to have any chance of success in the future, not just in Afghanistan and Iraq, but in places like Cote d'Ivoire, the Democratic Republic of Congo, Sudan, and even Haiti. There are roles that private sector firms are far better equipped to fill than are any other kind of organizations including governments and nongovernmental organizations (NGOs). The reality is that there are no practical substitutes for a central private sector role in undertaking the thousands of necessary tasks vital to success.[6]

Some have claimed that the inclusion of security firms in security operations has amounted to the privatization or the outsourcing of policy.[7] Obviously, it is not policies that are being privatized; it is execution of those policies. Private sector actors do not make the strategic decisions and in fact have little influence at the policy level. They are brought in to execute successfully those decisions, and often the means and preferences for carrying out the plan come from their government clients with surprisingly rigid requirements and little leeway for tactical flexibility. There has been much speculation that private firms are influencing political decisions about interventions, but there is a remarkable dearth of evidence that any such influence is being applied.[8] Often, criticism of the role of the for-profit industry misses its target because the real aim of the criticism is the larger policy of intervention, and the private sector is merely a convenient vehicle for such criticism.

The watchdog group, Taxpayers for Common Sense, has embraced a typical "blame the contractors" perspective. In their reports on contractors in Iraq, the group cited GAO reports to warn against contractor fraud and abuse.[9] While it is certainly important to work against fraud and abuse and the GAO does highlight certain concerns in those areas, the report also indicated that the most critical problem plaguing contractor involvement is waste, not fraud or abuse. According to the GAO report, waste costs accrue from poor planning, bad designs, poorly written government contracts, poor government management, and other similarly draining errors.[10] Indeed, Commissioner Clark Irwin of the CWC emphasized that point when he commented, "Waste is a bigger issue than fraud or abuse . . . bad planning, bad coordination—those are probably the biggest problems."[11] Fraud and abuse are the headline-grabbers, and no one is arguing that they should be ignored, but the larger problem cannot be ignored either. In fact, addressing some of the waste issues, especially those related to improving management and contractual flexibility will make it much harder for any contractor to get away with fraud or abuse. Sensationalistic rhetoric may be useful for high profile stories but it leaves the far larger and more costly issues unaddressed.

Serious researchers have indeed recognized that the private sector has always had a role in conflicts and especially in reconstruction operations. The United States has tapped into the capabilities of the private sector to support everyone of their military operations since the beginning of its existence. The data on contractors throughout American history shows that reliance on contractors has varied, depending on the nature of the conflict and the status and strength of the military of the time. Figure 12-1 clearly demonstrates this relationship:

Presence of Contractor Personnel During U.S. Military Operations

Conflict	Estimated Personnel (Thousands) Contractor[a]	Military	Estimated Ratio of Contractor to Military Personnel[a]
Revolutionary War	2	9	1 to 6
War of 1812	n.a.	38	n.a.
Mexican-American War	6	33	1 to 6
Civil War	200	1,000	1 to 5
Spanish-American War	n.a.	35	n.a.
World War I	85	2,000	1 to 24
World War II	734	5,400	1 to 7
Korea	156	393	1 to 2.5
Vietnam	70	359	1 to 5
Gulf War	9 [b]	500	1 to 55 [b]
Balkans	20	20	1 to 1
Iraq Theater as of Early 2008[c]	190	200	1 to 1

Source: Congressional Budget Office based on data from William W. Epley, "Civilian Support of Field Armies," *Army Logistician*, vol. 22 (November/December 1990), pp. 30–35; Steven J. Zamparelli, "Contractors on the Battlefield: What Have We Signed Up For?" *Air Force Journal of Logistics*, vol. 23, no. 3 (Fall 1999), pp. 10–19; Department of Defense, *Report on DoD Program for Planning, Managing, and Accounting for Contractor Services and Contractor Personnel During Contingency Operations* (October 2007), p. 12.

Figure 12-1. Presence of Contractor Personnel During U.S. Military Operations.

Obviously some previous conflicts have involved more contractors than do the current operations. Though the ratio of contractors to military personnel is at an all time high of 1:1, a ratio that was previously matched in the Balkans, the high ratio makes sense, considering the nature of the missions. Stability operations require significantly more reconstruction and development than do typical conflicts and thus favor a larger civilian role. It makes little economic and operational sense to have highly trained combat soldiers from the U.S. all-volunteer military building schools or guarding sewage plants when they have strategic military objectives to attend to. The lowest ratio (1:55) was in the First Gulf War, which involved virtually no reconstruction or infrastructure development at all.[12]

One of the results of the fear and hostility toward contractors is that contracting operations often suffer a "death by a thousand cuts." In the face of fear that contractors are taking advantage of the government or are wresting control from the government, representatives in Congress push executive departments for ever more detailed reports on contractor errors. In turn, the departments pressure their contract officers (those responsible for managing public-private contracts) who pressure their contract officer representatives (CORs) for the same minute reporting of issues. This intense scrutiny shifts the focus of the contractors and government managers alike away from the success of the mission and the policy and toward finding and preventing ever more harmless errors. Instead of spending time carrying out the mission, the contractors must watch their every move to ensure that they will not lose their contract over a single error, inappropriate personal action, or unverifiable cost, no matter how insignificant.[13]

This emphasis on minutiae to the overall detriment of the mission has been called "vengeance contract management."[14] This term comes from the idea that all too often, any deviation from the contract draws immediate reprisals against the contracting company, due to political hostility and suspicion toward the firm, the private sector in general, or even the larger geo-political mission itself. Any experienced organization working for a government expects multiple audits and sometimes micro-oversight on high-profile contracts; however, the nature of contingency operations means that circumstances on the ground can change quickly. The evolving realities in the field and the constantly fluctuating levels of risk can delay or frequently necessitate contract modifications. Unforeseeable problems will always arise in conflict and post-conflict situations, but unfortunately, in an era with this kind of vengeance contract management, the constant scrutiny can land these problems on the front page of the *New York Times*. Once public and government opinion has turned against the contractor, there may no longer be the time or ability to actually solve the problem. Perhaps worse yet, this vengeance contract management may go to its logical extreme and actually provide an incentive for concealing problems. When the emphasis is on blame rather than finding a solution, the operation, the taxpayer, the policies, and eventually, the local population in the area of operation, will suffer the consequences.[15]

FERRETTING OUT THE PROBLEM

As the saying goes, "where there's smoke, there's fire," even if the fire is a lot smaller than expected. So, while contracting operations have suffered from public and government scrutiny, the reality is, of course, that the scrutiny *has* revealed that all is not perfect in contracting operations. The goal, then, should be to determine the real problems and find ways to solve them, both in advance and in hindsight. A number of oversight agencies and investigators have identified the biggest problems suffered in contracting operations, and despite documented cases of fraud and/or abuse, the reports agree that the biggest problem is waste.

The Gansler Report of 2007 makes four key recommendations.[16] They include: improving the quality and prestige of the Army contracting community; improving the structure of contracting offices to facilitate control and responsibility; and, engaging the support of the legislature to ensure effectiveness. The report strives to identify the problems of military contracting, and to correct them for future engagements. Overall, the report emphasizes the continuing importance of private sector contractors to the military and post-conflict operations. In acknowledging this importance, the Gansler Report also indicates that contractors are not being effectively used. When identifying the problems with military contractors, the Gansler Report briefly mentions issues like fraud and abuse, but mainly focuses on issues of contract management, and treats contract management as a far bigger and more worthwhile problem to address. Not only does the report insist that contract management reform is immediately necessary, but it also cites the experiences of Afghanistan and Iraq as evidence of the changes that need to be made. The Gansler Report cites financial management, civil-military cooperation, contracting and contract management, and training and education, among other things, as the major problems between the military and the private sector in current operations.

In some senses, the Gansler Report, and the reforms that followed, rejected a WoG approach. The report recommended the consolidation of military contracting into a new, larger, and better trained office. Where it might have argued for more intense oversight, it instead argued for increased flexibility. The SIGIR, Stuart Bowen, has gone a step further and argued for a single government office to handle contingency contracting.[17] In fact, the Gansler Report grasped the unique nature of contingency operations and attempted to inject changes that are vital to effective contracting in conflict, post-conflict, and disaster relief operations.

The report insisted on the importance of putting contract officers on the ground to interact with the contractors. This is a kind of oversight that allows for rapid contractual modifications to address fast-changing events typical to conflict and reconstruction situations. While the segregation of contracting into its own office shows a general rejection of WoG principles, the report also talks about the importance of integrating contractors into the overall military and post-conflict operations of the government. The Gansler Report says that these operations depend on a variety of players who come from both the private and public sectors. The argument for greater cooperation and integration between the military, agencies, and contracting firms is actually one that embraces WoG principles. This seemingly conflicting perspective has some intriguing implications for WoG that we will explore in our conclusion.

The Gansler Report is not the only detailed report that attempts to discover the real problems with security contracting in Iraq, Afghanistan, and worldwide stability operations. In 2008, Congress established a Commission on Wartime Contracting (CWC). The CWC was essentially created in response to some of the more sensational reports of fraud and abuse cited above. After much investigation, the CWC largely agreed with the Gansler Report that contract management is the real problem plaguing contractors and the government alike.[18] While certainly fraud and abuse occur (as they do in nearly every business), it is waste that is the most stunning problem in regards to the work of the contractors. The CWC report points out that many contracts have been awarded without knowing if a contractor has the physical capacity to monitor and adequately bill for services performed. These companies lack the ability to record what they have done, what they have spent, and what their services are worth under their contracts. These business system deficiencies have led to at least $13 billion of disputed charges from contracting firms. Some were the result of simple errors, but others were true cases of waste where money was spent unnecessarily. As the report says, "Without pre□award audits, the risk grows that contracts will be awarded to unqualified bidders and that contract prices may be unreasonably high."[19]

Another factor that contributes to the problem of waste is the problem of absentee oversight, which is particularly severe in Afghanistan. More often than not, contracts in Afghanistan are monitored remotely, meaning that there is no contract officer on the ground to allow the contractors to adjust their mission or to reallocate their funds more effectively. CORs—often military officers quickly trained for the role—have been used to fill some gaps, but in reality they have limited experience and ultimately no authority. Changes, therefore, take time and cannot be effected as immediate responses to changing conditions. This means money is spent on objectives that are unnecessary, and once the money is spent, it cannot be unspent.[20]

Further supporting the notion that poor contract management is the biggest problem and a primary source of waste were significant findings of both the Gansler Report and the CWC Reports, and that fraud and abuse are largely the result of poor contract management. When oversight is provided at a distance and delayed, and enforcement is spotty, the opportunities for fraud and abuse increase. Effective contract management provides appropriate oversight as well as the flexibility needed to help minimize waste. In the end, while it is fraud and abuse that grabs the headlines, it is contract management that can actually ensure operational success.

WHERE DO CONTRACTORS FIT IN?

The whole point of utilizing the private sector is for the client to gain capacity and/or services faster, better or cheaper, or some combination of those traits. The Gansler Report explains:

> [T]imely and efficient contracting for materiel, supplies and services in support of expeditionary operations, and the subsequent management of those contracts, are and will be a key component of our achieving success in future military operations. Contracting is the nexus between our warfighters' requirements and the contractors that fulfill those requirements—whether for food service, interpreters, communications operations, equipment repair, new or modified equipment,

> or other supplies and services indispensable to warfighting operations. In support of critical military operations, contractor personnel must provide timely services and equipment to the warfighter; and the Army contracting community must acquire those services and equipment effectively, efficiently, and legally.[21]

Obviously, the private sector has much inherent strength that can be applied to stability operations. The ability to provide jobs and training, along with the know-how to increase the economic capacity of underdeveloped areas means that private contractors can make a real difference in complex and dangerous situations. The need for private sector services is obvious when one realizes that no government has all the skills and capacities in-house that are needed for even modestly-sized stability operations.

Although the U.S. Government has some of the most comprehensive procurement and contract management guidelines of any government in the world, it is still clear that the clients who make the most cost-effective utilization of private sector services are other private firms. Governments and government agencies do not have financial incentives for success and at the same time are bound by a number of strict, often arcane rules and operational limitations. Governmental contracting does not incentivize innovation or flexibility the way profit-centric private sector business does. In spite of these limitations, there are things that governments can do to ensure better, more efficient, and more ethical services.

As mentioned earlier, "where there's smoke, there's fire." The headlines tell us that there are some ethics issues, and the fact that there are huge projects that are never completed, or get completed but never used, tells us there are some waste issues as well.[22] But there are also some innovation issues. Too often government contracts not only outline the mission, but also dictate the precise manner in which the mission must be accomplished. This eliminates flexibility and also precludes innovation. Unfortunately, the default procurement method in U.S. contingency contracting is known as "lowest price, technically acceptable" (LPTA) contracting. LPTA contracting means that so long as the competing private firms meet the minimum requirements of the mission, the contract is by law awarded to the lowest bidder. The idea is to ensure that the government is not being cheated on the price of materials and services, but that is often not the only result. The award is made regardless of the quality of service that the firm can provide. In addition to rewarding lower-capability companies, LPTA forces more capable firms to cut elements out of their bids that would have added quality to their services. Things that get eliminated include: enhanced personnel vetting; more qualified hiring; improved equipment; and, a number of other things that help avoid operational problems. An alternative to LPTA is to use a "best value" determination. Best value determinations allow a procurement officer to select a proposal based on how well it meets the goals of the overall operation. Best value rewards firms who are better at ensuring quality and innovation and with more impressive historical track records. Best value contracting means that the government gets the best bang for its buck, rather than just the least possible bucks. In the larger picture, we should keep in mind that U.S. policies in contingency operations have very real political and humanitarian stakes that are put at enormous increased risk by entrusting policy implementation to the lowest bidders all of the time.

The CWC thought that this issue was important enough to issue a special report advocating for best value contracting, especially for private security services, but the concept should be expanded as it makes sense for all contingency services.[23] The Project on Government Oversight (POGO) and other government watchdogs disagreed with this recommendation, which is naturally in line with their mission of reducing the costs of government programs and waste. They continue to press for LPTA in service contracts, a stance that may be contributing to many of the complications handicapping U.S. efforts in Afghanistan and Iraq. Contractors are forced to strive to meet the very minimum requirements, because winning LPTA contracts requires that they need to be at least one dollar cheaper than their competitors.[24] Some in the industry describe this reality as a disastrous, government-induced, "race to the bottom," in quality scenario. Many of the well-publicized failures can be traced directly to quality issues, something confirmed in numerous and extensive private conversations with company executives of the firms that were highlighted in reports related to Afghanistan contracting and specifically in regards to the much derided Kabul embassy contract.[25] Most quality companies accept the reality of enhanced oversight, and willingly submit to nearly continual audits of their operations and progress.[26] Indeed, the point has frequently been made that good oversight and accountability rewards the better firms. Most established companies have entire departments focused on nothing except compliance, and alert clients will quickly eliminate low-end companies attempting to cut corners or use smoke and mirrors to mask capability flaws. Thus, effective oversight and accountability is beneficial to better companies and the industry as a whole. Oversight is not always easy in stability operations, but when done properly, oversight makes the client and contractor alike more effective and efficient. The contracting experience, however, can be damaged when the client, in this case the government, prefers low price to high quality, and demands high quality without the funding to backup the demand.

Holding companies (and individuals) accountable for violations rewards the more professional companies to an even more welcome degree and it is no coincidence that more than 50 companies have joined the International Stability Operations Association (ISOA) and agreed to abide by the ISOA Code of Conduct.[27] In fact, any reputable company should have no problem abiding by its terms. The ISOA Code of Conduct was first drafted in 2001 and is a living document originally created by NGOs, human rights organizations, and academics, and has been updated every few years to include clarifications and to address previously unforeseen concerns.[28] The private sector support for self-policing reveals both an interest by many in the industry to ensure an ethical industry, as well as recognition that ethics have market value to enlightened clients. Anyone can bring a complaint against an ISOA member company based on the Code of Conduct, and the complaint will be heard by the ISOA Standards Committee. As a trade group, the goal of the Code is not to remove errant member companies out of the Association (although the bylaws allow that kind of penalty should accused firms be unusually recalcitrant), but instead, the goal is to work with those firms to ensure they return to compliance. The ISOA Code and accountability mechanism can never replace governments and legal courts, but its robust utilization demonstrates that the industry can have a useful and effective role in self-policing operations in weak and failed states where normal legal structures are feeble or absent altogether.

Industry has supported additional accountability efforts as well, including support for the creation of the Montreux Document, an initiative led by the Government of Switzerland and the International Committee of the Red Cross.[29] The Montreux Document has been affirmed by more than 30 governments including Afghanistan, Angola, Iraq, South Africa, the United Kingdom (UK), and the United States. The Montreux Document clarified international law as it applies to international personnel working for contingency contractors. The final step was the International Code of Conduct for Private Security Providers (ICoC), a follow-up to the Montreux Document that focused specifically on private security companies.[30] What makes the ICoC so exciting is that the largest clients (U.S. and UK Governments) have both indicated that they will only hire firms who have signed the ICoC and agreed to the accountability system, which was still under construction as of September 2011. Once the ICoC accountability system is up and running, the incentive for both PSCs and international clients will be to provide higher quality services than ever before. The ICoC is intended to expand beyond just PSCs at some point in the future. The ICoC has far more international recognition than the ISOA Code, and already scores of PSCs have signed to indicate their acceptance of the ICoC. At some point the ICoC may even make the ISOA Code of Conduct redundant, but until that day comes, ISOA will continue to maintain, enforce, and upgrade their Code as well.

Finally, it should be noted that industry associations, especially ISOA, have been consistent in their support for improved accountability for civilians accused of crimes in conflict and post-conflict environments. ISOA has publically supported expansions to the Military Extraterritorial Jurisdiction Act (MEJA)[31]—the primary tool for holding civilian contractors accountable during contingency operations on scores of cases addressed by the U.S. Department of Justice since 2001—as well as the Civilian Extraterritorial Jurisdiction Act (CEJA) which has yet to be passed but will expand to fill some of the loopholes left by MEJA.[32]

Competition is healthy and useful; however, ensuring competition in contingency operations can be problematic. Contingency contracting involves operating in extreme environments: weak and failed states; in conflict and post conflict areas; and, in disaster relief operations.[33] Few companies have the capacity to fulfill such contracts and are prepared to do the liability management necessary for success. The pool of competitors is further diminished by non-mission requirements (i.e., past performance records, demonstration of certain accounting standards, etc.), and by arbitrary factors required by Congress including location of headquarters, nationality of personnel, or size of firm. Much has been done to diminish the competition even before we come to the issue of competitor capability and operational time constraints. For example, there are obvious benefits to hiring local companies; local companies will have a better working knowledge of the area, will be better able to attract the support of the local population, and perhaps most importantly, will be able to maintain programs and equipment vital to ongoing stabilization once the intervention has ended. Unfortunately, without mentoring, it is rare that local companies in impacted nations are able to adequately provide the necessary services and capabilities in the necessary scale and quality required. More often than not, local companies lack expertise and the technological capacity to adequately support many of the missions, and perhaps more significantly, they almost always lack the capability to adhere to the reporting and oversight requirements set by the U.S. Government. Indeed, while missions often favor local firms for contracts, ensuring proper observance of the thousands of rules, regulations, and guidelines on everything from sexual harassment to ethnic nondiscrimination, and an ability to provide the myriad reports and audits necessary is difficult indeed. This issue is often addressed through the utilization of Western prime contractors that then subcontract to local firms that they can mentor and guide through the complex contracting process. Nevertheless, there are already too many factors that limit the number of companies that are willing and able to support these missions with the visibility and capability that is often demanded.

The alternatives to continuously competitive contracts are the much derided sole-source contracts. These are contracts which are, by definition, "urgent and compelling," and for which only one contractor is qualified or immediately available, so the bidding process is skipped to save resources and especially time. Time is often critical in stability operations and to wait for a full-blown competitive bid process that can take months (or years!) when the training, medical clinic, road, or security for an ambassador is needed immediately could end in disaster for the mission. Sole-sourcing obviously has the potential to be abused, and the hostility that sole-sourcing has attracted has undermined the government's ability to carry out its policies and objectives. Indeed, the media has never quite understood which companies are actually sole-sourced and which are actually cost-plus.[34] More confusing, in Iraq quite a few contracts that were "sole-sourced" were actually existing contracts that needed to be rapidly expanded to support the operation. For example, if the original design of a facility turns out to be too small or otherwise inappropriate for the mission, the government could exercise the urgent and compelling tool to draw-up a larger contract so the company that won the original competition could build the facility in a hurry. Considering all the pressure to begin and then complete the reconstruction, it is hardly surprising that sole-sourcing was utilized instead of recompetition. Nevertheless, woe unto the government official involved in sole-source contract modifications months or years later when the auditors and investigators who are not familiar with the urgency of the issue at the time decide the contract may have been inappropriate.[35]

We have discussed what contractors can do, how best to choose a contractor, but there is still the issue of contractor compensation. There are two basic ways to contract with a firm: cost-plus and fixed price. Cost-plus contracts are awarded as the cost of the operation plus a certain profit percentage, generally between 1 and 10 percent, with a potential bonus of about 2 percent as an incentive for particularly quick or effective work. Cost-plus contracts have drawn much criticism, mainly focused on the Logistics Civil Augmentation Program (LOGCAP) III, the contract that provided logistical support to the U.S. Army from 2001 to 2010, and ended up being valued at more than $30 billion. Awarded to KBR in 2001 (a subsidiary to Halliburton at the time), it was perhaps the most criticized contract of the past decade. It faced endless allegations about war-profiteering, failure to deliver, and contract padding, among other accusations. It did not help that a former chief executive officer (CEO) of Halliburton was also the vice president, Dick Cheney, a lightning rod for liberal and anti-war dissent. There were accusations that KBR purchased more expensive fuel then necessary in order to pad its margins, that it served tens of thousands more meals than were necessary, and many other charges.[36] Most of the allegations proved to be meritless, and eventually much of the reality behind the headlines was revealed as bad policy executed according to bad contracts. [37] The contractors were easy targets to place blame for many problems simply because they were the executors, but also because they cannot and will not finger their government clients no matter how egregious the problem. There are two reasons no contractor will blame the government client. First, they are often constrained by contractual guidelines requiring written permission before publicizing any information; and second, because criticizing the largest client in the world is simply not good for their long-term business prospects.[38]

The LOGCAP III cost-plus contract had a profit margin of only 1 percent (with a potential bonus margin of 2 percent for speed or quality) and required KBR to tie up tens of millions of dollars to fund projects prior to monthly reimbursement.[39] In order to meet the obligations of the cost-plus contract, the company used its own funds in advance to be reimbursed at the end of the month. However, if costs were challenged, there could be a delay in repayment, and sometimes such repayments were left incomplete while further inquiries were conducted. Despite the size of the contract, it is questionable if there was much profit at all for KBR on this contract, especially considering the lost interest on advanced funds pending payment, which ate into the razor thin profit margin. It is rather revealing, and too often ignored, that Halliburton rid itself of KBR in the midst of the LOGCAP III contract—in fact, KBR had become a gigantic, high-risk, resource-intense operation that barely made a dime.[40] Various holds were put on government payments to the contractor due to allegations of fraud and abuse, something that is not unusual in chaotic conflict and post-conflict environments, but most were ultimately resolved. For example, in testimony to the CWC, the Defense Contract Audit Administration (DCAA) admitted that it had withheld $553 million on LOGCAP III payments, but eventually at least $439 million of the discrepancies were resolved and paid.[41] The failure of Congress to pass necessary spending legislation sometimes left KBR to go for weeks or months without payment. The company could legally have stopped working on the contract, which would have significantly hampered the policy effort in Iraq, but instead the company essentially loaned the government funds at no interest until the legislation was passed. A case could be made that the LOGCAP III contract was the best deal ever for American taxpayers, and certainly the quality of service for the troops was remarkable in light of the circumstances.[42]

Most companies actually prefer fixed price contracts to cost-plus contracts. Fixed price contracts give companies a higher profit margin, albeit with additional risk. Fixed price contracts are not always ideal in fluid contingency operations when risks and conditions are rapidly changing and often require expensive contract modifications to adjust to those changes. Fixed price contracts usually require a greater knowledge of conditions and costs then is generally available during contingency operations. Nevertheless, if the realities of contingency operations are understood well enough, fixed price contracts can be used successfully. Fixed price contracts in contingency operations may be ideal for concrete, specific operations, and where there is a fair understanding of variables, but if the risk is high, contractors have offset that by building in larger margins to deal with contingencies. Operations that are less defined or subject to great change due to circumstances make more sense to be prepared as a cost-plus contract.[43]

CONCLUSIONS – HOW TO MAKE IT WORK

International interventions of some form or another are going to continue, as we have seen in the past or currently in Libya or in Somalia. The international community continues to condone and support interventions in dire situations, though they remain controversial.[44] Clearly, some have been more beneficial than others, but the better, faster, and more effectively that the international community is able to engage in these interventions, the more positive the humanitarian and political results; thus the private sector is too valuable a tool to ignore. It would be hypocritical to recognize this yet not support high quality and professionalism among the contractors tasked to carry out the policies. Afghanistan and Iraq were operations on a scale rarely seen, and the role of the private sector was expanded and tested to a level never before imagined, while the size and capability of the oversight community lagged far behind.[45] While reconstruction and stability operations have been largely effective despite the enormous challenges that these missions faced, ultimately no level of effectiveness can overcome unresolved political complications and barriers. Nevertheless, if future operations embrace the lessons learned and include a focus on quality, best value, and improved oversight that rewards the better companies, then contractors will become a more reliable and valuable partner. Ultimately, contractors are not there to make policy decisions for the governments and international community, but they are there to make their policy decisions more effective and successful.

To be truly effective, contingency operations require a working partnership of the government and private sector. The nature of this partnership requires organization, oversight, cooperation, proper incentives, and transparency. This is why the question of private sector contracting is bound so tightly with questions of intervention management and WoG policy. It is obvious that the private sector is necessary to interventions like those in Afghanistan and Iraq, as well as less high-profile operations such as those in the Democratic Republic of Congo and Haiti. Those who argue for WoG approaches to international interventions claim that interagency redundancies and competition along with a lack of communication hamper the success of interventions. In some ways, then, it seems contrary to the Gansler Report recommendation to embrace a WoG approach to contracting. In truth, however, the struggles of the contracting world may provide insights into an overall balanced WoG approach.

The Gansler Report's recommendation to consolidate contract management government-wide is in many ways a classic WoG approach. The idea is to put contracting into the hands of those who are most qualified to manage contracts. Consolidation could help minimize one of the most severe problems in contracting: waste. However, the Gansler Report and others also recommend putting contract managers on the ground near interventions. The two recommendations together suggest a hybrid approach to contracting that may have other applications. Perhaps rather than a pure WoG approach, it would be better to unify communications and record keeping, while keeping the work on the ground divided among those most qualified to do it. Most writers either accept or reject WoG approaches, but the unique circumstances of private sector contracting suggest a third way that allows agencies and private companies the latitude to maintain their specialties, while also establishing better communications and a more unified policy and purpose. Under such a hybrid approach, the administrative functions, including communication and record keeping, between the various groups and agencies could be consolidated into a single unit. The administrative unit could serve as a hub for the more specialized agencies, groups, and companies which would continue to serve their on-the-ground functions, but could do so with a minimum of interagency politics. With all of the information thus consolidated, the sharing of information and changes in conditions could be communicated to the appropriate parties quickly. Of course, sharing would have to be subject to certain policies and rules, but it could be the job of the administrative hub to be experts on this element. The administrative hub would also be able to help prioritize the needs of the various agencies so that urgent matters do not get lost in a mountain of paperwork. This kind of hybrid approach could not only help eliminate waste, but it could also improve oversight, flexibility, and ethical behavior.

It may be years before we will see a return to the pragmatic and effective partnerships that existed in U.S. support for international peacekeeping prior to September 11, 2001 (9/11). Journalists and watchdog organizations make their reputations by ferreting out fraud and abuse while virtually ignoring the larger issues of waste, impairing the hope for rational, pragmatic improvements. It will be difficult to get the government-private sector relationship back on an even footing where the partnership focuses again on genuine policies and mission goals instead of the current reality of vengeance contract management. The examples of the ISOA Code of Conduct, the Montreux Document, and the ICoC are indicative of the tangible interest from the industry in tackling operational concerns head-on. This kind of self-policing should be taken seriously as an effort to eliminate the distractions of headline grabbing anecdotes. Industry criticism is welcome when it is constructive, but damning contingency contracting without an alternative is simply counterproductive to good policy.

The final report from the CWC[46] has added yet more ideas to the mix and fueled both contingency contractor champions and detractors. While highlighting that waste continues to be the largest drain on reconstruction budgets as opposed to fraud or abuse, it also makes crystal clear that the U.S. Government has no realistic option to using contractors in all of its future stability operations. It is also clear that most projects are, in fact, successful, but there is much that can be done to ensure less waste and more success. This is fully consistent with the conclusions of this chapter. Governmental support for quality and ethics in the contractors tasked with carrying out its policies will pay far more dividends than simply hiring the cheapest firms available no matter what the trade-off is in quality and professionalism. If effective policies mean shortening conflicts and less humanitarian suffering, then contractor quality should matter far more to the government than it has thus far in Afghanistan or Iraq.

ENDNOTES - CHAPTER 12

1. Although rarely highlighted in media reports, a general perusing of testimony emphasizes the dominant problem of waste over fraud and abuse. This issue was specifically raised by Naveed Bandali, "Improving Oversight of Contingency Operations: A Conversation with the SIGIR, Stuart W. Bowen, Jr.," *Journal of International Peace Operations,* Q&A Section, Vol. 6, No. 6, May-June 2011, p. 24.

2. The most comprehensive numbers for contractors in Afghanistan and Iraq come from the U.S. Department of Defense (DoD) Synchronized Predeployment and Operational Tracker (SPOT) database run by the Office of the Assistant Secretary of Defense, Program Support, available from *www.acq.osd.mil/log/PS/hot_topics.html.* The DoD employs the vast majority of contractors, although the Department of State and the U.S. Agency for International Development (USAID) also employ many which have not yet been incorporated into the SPOT database. Note that the numbers in the database have been challenged by some journalists and academics (notably T.X. Hammes at the National Defense University (NDU), see *csis.org/event/benefits-united-states-governments-employment-armed-contractors-iraq-and-afghanistan-outweigh-,* a debate where Colonel Hammes challenges the veracity of the database). While imperfect, the numbers seem to be reasonably accurate and the accuracy of the reports has been improved. Furthermore, there does not appear to be anything else with a better level of accuracy available at this time.

3. DoD contractors are tracked by the SPOT database, available from *www.acq.osd.mil/log/PS/hot_topics.html.*

4. See, for example, Bill Chappell, "Afghanistan's Ban on Security Firms May Halt Rebuilding, Relief Work," NPR Online, October 21, 2010, available from *www.npr.org/blogs/thetwo-way/2010/10/21/130735968/afghanistan-s-ban-on-security-firms-may-halt-rebuilding-relief-work.*

5. Even the once respected *New York Times* continues to use the derogatory "mercenary" label for contractors, a practice long discarded by other professional media sources and serious academics. For example, see Mark Mazzetti and Emily B. Hager, "Blackwater Founder Forms Secret Army for Arab State," *New York Times*, May 15, 2011. Academic Deborah Avant wrote in *Foreign Policy*, "The term 'mercenary' describes a wide variety of military activities, many of which bear little resemblance to those of today's private security companies," from "Think Again: Mercenaries," *Foreign Policy*, Vol. 1, July 2004. See also Volker Franke, "Service Versus Profit," *Journal of International Peace Operations*, Vol. 7, July-August 2011, available from *web.peaceops.com/*; Volker Franke and Marc von Boemcken, "Guns for Hire: Motivations and Attitudes of Private Security Contractors," *Armed Forces & Society*, forthcoming.

6. *At What Cost? Contingency Contracting in Iraq and Afghanistan*, Interim Report, Washington, DC: Commission on Wartime Contracting in Iraq and Afghanistan, June 2009; *Transforming Wartime Contracting: Controlling Costs, Reducing Risks*, Washington, DC: Commission on Wartime Contracting in Iraq and Afghanistan, August 31, 2011, available from *www.wartimecontracting.gov*.

7. Examples include Allison Stanger, *One Nation Under Contract: The Outsourcing of American Power and the Future of Foreign Policy*, New Haven, CT, and London, UK: Yale University Press, 2009; see also Laura A. Dickinson, *Outsourcing War & Peace: Preserving Public Values in a World of Privatized Foreign Affairs*, New Haven, CT, and London, UK: Yale University Press, 2010.

8. Stanger, *One Nation Under Contract.*

9. Laura Peterson, "Troop Surge Dollars Must be Watched," Taxpayers for Common Sense, December 3, 2009, available from *taxpayer.net/projects.php?action=view&category=&type=Project&proj_id=2982.*

10. Richard Lardner, "US oversight of war-zone contractors labeled weak," *Washington Post*, February 22, 2011, available from *www.washingtonpost.com/wp-dyn/content/article/2011/02/22/AR2011022205739.html*.

11. Scott Canon, "Black & Veatch's fog-of-war contract in Afghanistan," *Kansas City Star*, February 19, 2011.

12. Chappell's NPR article hints at the critical role of the private sector in reconstruction. This is particularly striking from a news outlet that has criticized private security in the past. See "Afghanistan's Ban on Security Firms May Halt Rebuilding, Relief Work," NPR Online, October 21, 2010.

13. For a more detailed essay on this concern, see Doug Brooks, "Vengeance Contract Management," *Journal of International Peace Operations*, Vol. 4, No. 6, May-June 2009, p. 4.

14. *Ibid.*

15. See Doug Brooks, "Shifting the Blame," *Journal of International Peace Operations*, Vol. 5, No. 6, May/June 2010.

16. "Urgent Reform Required: Army Expeditionary Contracting," *Report of the Commission on Army Acquisition and Program Management in Expeditionary Operations*, Washington, DC: U.S. Department of Defense, September 24, 2007. General Jacques Gansler was the chair of the authoring commission, and the report is most commonly referred to as the "Gansler Report."

17. Stuart W. Bowen, Jr., "Applying Lessons Learned from Iraq: A Proposal for a New Office for Contingency Operations," *Journal Of International Peace Operations*, July-August, 2010, available from *web.peaceops.com/archives/740#more-740*.

18. *At What Cost? Contingency Contracting in Iraq and Afghanistan; Transforming Wartime Contracting: Controlling Costs, Reducing Risks.*

19. *Ibid.*

20. For example, as cited in the Commission on Wartime Contracting (CWC) report, a new dining facility was contracted for in Iraq, despite the fact that the old dining facility was being repaired and only one project was necessary, but money was spent on both.

21. Gansler Report, p. 3.

22. For a summary of some of the most infamous examples of waste, fraud, and abuse, see Bruce Burton and Lauren McLean, "The Black and White of Fraud, Waste, and Abuse," *Defense AT&L*, March/April 2009.

23. "Special Report on Embassy Security Contracts: lowest-priced security not good enough for war-zone embassies," CWC Special Report 2, Washington, DC: Commission on Wartime Contracting, October 1, 2009, available from *www.wartimecontracting.gov/docs/CWC_SR2-2009-10-01.pdf.*

24. Danielle Brian, "CWC Findings on Embassy Guards Fiasco Amount to 'Blame Shifting'," Project on Government Oversight, October 6, 2009, available from *pogoblog.typepad.com/pogo/2009/10/cwc-findings-on-embassy-guards-fiasco-amount-to-blame-shifting.html.*

25. The CWC report cites a number of situations in which contractors lacked the suppliers, skills, or personnel to achieve the goals set in their contracts. The Burton and McLean article also hints at quality control issues.

26. In fact, companies in the industry undergo regular audits when working for the U.S. Government, and while these normally came from their contractor officers and maybe the Defense Contract Management Agency (DCMA) and Defense Contract Audit Administration (DCAA), as well as the inspectors general of the organization they work with (DoD, DoS, State, USAID, Corps of Engineers, etc.), since 2003, the audits and inspections have markedly increased with the creation of the CWC, Special Inspector General for Iraq Reconstruction (SIGIR), Special Inspector General for Afghanistan Reconstruction (SIGAR), and additional reports from the Government Accountability Office (GAO), Congressional Research Service (CRS), and numerous congres-

sional investigations. In fact, numerous, repetitive audits and inspections are recognized as part of the job and the cost of doing business with the U.S. Government.

27. The latest version is available on the International Stability Operations Association (ISOA) webpage, available from *www.stability-operations.org*.

28. Information on the origins of the ISOA Code of Conduct is available from *stability-operations.org/index.php*.

29. *Montreux Document*, Geneva, Switzerland: Federal Department of Foreign Affairs, 2011, available from *www.eda.admin.ch/psc*.

30. International Code of Conduct (ICoC) information is online, available from *www.icoc-psp.org/*.

31. For a good understanding of the origins of Military Extraterritorial Jurisdiction Act (MEJA), see Major Joseph R. Perlak, "The Military Extraterritorial Jurisdiction Act Of 2000: Implications For Contractor Personnel," *Military Law Review*, Vol. 169, September 2001.

32. Information on Civilian Extraterritorial Jurisdiction Act (CEJA) can be found on the Human Rights First website, "Senate Judiciary Committee Passes Bill on U.S. Civilian Contractor Accountability Abroad," June 23, 2011, available from *www.humanrightsfirst.org/2011/06/23/senate-judiciary-committee-passes-bill-on-u-s-civilian-contractor-accountability-abroad/*.

33. *Transforming Wartime Contracting: Controlling Costs, Reducing Risks*, p. 46.

34. "U.S. Wasting Billions While Tripling No-Bid Contracts After Decade of War in Iraq, Afghanistan," *Democracy Now*, September 2, 2011, transcript available from *www.democracynow.org/2011/9/2/us_wasting_billions_while_tripling_no*.

35. This information comes from numerous conversations and interviews with private sector management coming from operations in Iraq.

36. "DEFENSE CONTRACT MANAGEMENT: DOD's Lack of Adherence to Key Contracting Principles on Iraq Oil Contract Put Government Interests at Risk," GAO-07-839, Washington, DC: Government Accountability Office, July 2007. The report shows the complexities of contingency contracting and the fluid negotiations in a cost-plus contract. Few have read the KBR perspective on the meals issue, which was eventually, largely, accepted by the government. See, "Halliburton Says War-Time Conditions Make It Hard To 'Guess Who Is Coming To Dinner'," available from *www.halliburton.com/news/archive/2004/corpnws_020204.jsp*.

37. While the policy aspects are probably beyond the scope of this volume, a thorough reading of GAO and CWC reports reveal significantly more problems on the government contracting side than on the contractor side. See also Christopher Shays and Michael Thibault, "Reducing waste in wartime contracts," *Washington Post*, August 28, 2011.

38. More information on this can be found in Brooks, "Vengeance Contract Management," p. 4.

39. Russell Gold, "The Temps Of War: Blue-Collar Workers Ship Out For Iraq, Halliburton Jobs Pay Well, If You Don't Mind Danger; Camping—With Mortars," *Wall Street Journal*, February 5, 2004, p. 1.

40. Loren Steffy, "Halliburton Hasn't Been Making Out Like a Bandit," *Houston Chronicle*, August 22, 2006; see also "KBR Announces Separation from Halliburton and Appointment of New Board Members," *Houston Chronicle*, April 6, 2007.

41. April Stephenson, Director, Defense Contract Audit Agency, in testimony to the Commission on Wartime Contracting, May 14, 2009.

42. Steve Schooner, Professor of Government Procurement Law and Co-Director of the Government Procurement Law Program, George Washington University, interview, May 19, 2005, by Frontline, "Under the circumstances, I give KBR unbelievable marks." Transcript available from (quote not included in actual documentary) *www.pbs.org/wgbh/pages/frontline/shows/warriors/interviews/schooner.html*; also see Anthony Bianco and Stephanie Anderson

Forest, "Outsourcing War: an Inside Look at Brown and Root," *Business Week*, September 15, 2003.

43. A good analysis of contract types can be found in Patrick Cullen and Peter Ezra Weinberger, "Reframing the Defense Outsourcing Debate: Merging Government Oversight with Industry Partnership," Washington, DC: Peace Operations Institute, 2007.

44. Book review by Seth G. Jones, "How To Fight a War When It's Not Yours," Review of Rory Stewart and Gerald Knaus, *Can Intervention Work*, New York: Norton, 2011, *Washington Post*, September 4, 2011, p. B7.

45. Steven Kelman and Steven L. Schooner, "Scandal or Solution?" *Government Executive*, November 7, 2005.

46. *Transforming Wartime Contracting: Controlling Costs, Reducing Risks.*

CHAPTER 13

MULTIETHNIC CONFLICTS IN U.S. MILITARY THEATERS OVERSEAS: INTERCULTURAL IMPERATIVES

Gregory Paul P. Meyjes

We inhabit a multipolar world in which ethno-cultural tensions fester, in which "intercivilizational" strife lurks, and where local populations use destructive and communicative tools that compete with those of states. More often than not, intergroup controversies are based on language, religion, race, or ethnicity—perennial properties of poignant primacy for group meaning and identity. The conflicts that make headlines and cause headstones today are chiefly ethno-cultural in origin as predicted.[1] Whether current global trends weaken or motivate ethno-nationalism is vigorously debated, with two seemingly opposite processes, global homogenization and heterogenization, concurrently observed.[2] Despite the ubiquity of the globally dominant, minority populations persist in asserting themselves, often defying displacement and disadvantage against a backdrop of violence by man and/or nature. In the second millennium's waning years, armed clashes were largely state-internal,[3] especially in what are slightingly called "fragile" states, such wars carry serious international security connotations, including the spread of weapons of mass destruction (WMDs) and terror.[4] Those in strategic studies and international relations thus acutely feel the need to come to grips with ethno-cultural and related forms of communal friction. Yet, whether U.S. troops surge or dwindle in number, whether defense budgets wax or wane, whether a military or whole of government (WoG) approach is taken, the exorbitant U.S. interventions overseas and the policies that underpin them are only as viable as their conceptual underpinnings permit.

Post-Cold War grand theories of international relations have insufficiently accounted for the state of affairs discussed in the previous paragraphs. Fukuyama tells of a new world without ideological polarization, unified through *Pax Americana*, democracy, and international cooperation[5]—the end of "history" in the sense of Hegel's progressive dialectics.[6] In lieu of such globalized Occidentalism, "offensive realism" champion Mearsheimer presages conflict as usual—multipolar state rivalry for hegemony in the interest of national security.[7] Rejecting both Western universality and zero-sum state dominance, Huntington describes a world of "civilizational" tectonic rupture, where economic globalization need not imply Westernization, where democratization may serve indigenization, and where military intervention can fuel local resistance.[8] To explain and predict inter-ethnic conflict in global perspective—a precondition for evidence-based intervention strategies—social theory must grasp the nature of both ethnicity and inter-ethnic relations. The three influential theories identified above do not meet this standard. However dissimilarly applicable to geopolitics, they all offer but a bird's eye viewpoint of relations between countries, regions, and civilizations—failing to drill down to the heart of the matter, ethnicity at the local level at which it occurs. To rally our best collective judgment to comprehending and sustainably reducing ethnic conflict requires a multisectoral stance in which philosophical, empirical, and practical insights are harnessed across a number of disciplines. An expanded model is called for. To anticipate and respond to inter-ethnic hostilities, it must include a grasp of ethno-cultural reality *tout court*. Instead of a mere top-down view, it will also have to reflect ethnic, state, and global realities from the cultural ground up. This contribution is dedicated to such an eventual framework. Following this introduction, the first section ("What Culture?") briefly reviews the nature of culture and ethnicity. The next section ("What Competence?") looks at certain efforts by the U.S. armed services to acquire the requisite cultural skill. The remaining half is devoted to a handful of recommendations for progress in this vein ("What Imperatives?"), with concluding remarks ("What Next?").

WHAT CULTURE?

As the way in which human groups inwardly and outwardly represent their assumed inherited identity, "culture" is seen as that *ensemble* of properties, practices, and comportments through which their "genius," the essence of their particular way of collective life, is passed on. Of the physical, socio-institutional, and ideational elements of culture, it is the latter, its value set, that is deemed of greatest import.[9] Through it, each culture subliminally creates a group-mediated experience of the world. Thus understood, culture symbolizes social meaning at its most visceral. Like the acquisition of the native tongue, it is transferred through a largely subconscious process called *enculturation,*[10] as distinguished from *socialization,* defined as the conscious transmission of in-group know-how. In this sense, culture is both the prism through which we experience social life and the prison to group self-awareness we unwittingly inhabit. Typologically, the elitist distinction between "high" and "low" culture of the Eurocentric Romantic period[11] has made way for a recent revisiting of the contrast between "objective" and "subjective" culture.[12] The former refers to the positive, observable aspects of the distinctiveness of groups, the latter to the inner workings of cultures, the value orientations that motivate and define their social and physical attributes. *Ceteris paribus*, subjective culture so dictates human consciousness as to inhibit awareness of its workings and so determines a particular worldview as to essentially guarantee ethnocentrism. Hidden in plain sight, it forms the heart of all ethno-cultural groups, dominant and nondominant alike.

Awareness of the social construction of culture is rooted in centuries of thought. For instance, through the work of Herder, von Humboldt and other 19th-century German philosophers, language has come to be accepted as *primus inter pares* among cultural attributes, in part because of its link to cognition and worldview. Due to the critical role of language in creating cultural identity, failure to honor language rights or "linguistic human rights" is seen as "one of the important factors which can contribute to inter-ethnic conflict—and often does."[13] Similarly, the relation between religion and culture,[14] and between religion and war, has been the object of scholarly attention for centuries, if not millennia. Huntington regards religion as "a central defining characteristic of civilizations."[15] In the Middle East, sub-state religious ethnicities have attracted growing scholarly interest—for instance, in Shi'a resistance to Sunni dominance of post-Saddam-Hussein Iraq; in cyclical violence between Sunni, Shi'a, and various Christians in Lebanon; and in the mobilization of the Muslim Brotherhood and Copts against

Hosni Mubarak in Egypt during the "Arab Spring." Reviewing ethno-religious wars in light of Durkheim[16] and other theorists, Fox concludes that religion serves four social functions. "First, it provides an interpretative framework, or belief system, for understanding the world. Second, it contains rules and standards of behavior which guide the actions of believers. Third, religions are generally associated with institutions that transmit religious frameworks from one generation to the next. Finally, religion can legitimize all forms of action."[17] In concert, these factors all but guarantee the ethno-cultural relevance of religion. Religion can both foment and aid the resolution of conflicts[18]—ranging as it does from motivating violent extremism, to faith-based peacemaking,[19] to the preventive promotion of interfaith tolerance and equality.[20]

Largely overlapping with culture, the term "ethnicity" emphasizes belonging, kinship, ancestry, and identity.[21] Rather than objective truths, ethnicities are subjective, which makes them real whether based in myth or externally validated fact. Ethno-national conflicts need not be grounded on accurate information; they need only be culturally real. For instance, the long-standing tension between tens of millions of Urdu speakers and hundreds of millions of Hindi speakers is as ethno-nationally real as it is linguistically illusory, the distinction depending almost entirely on whether the same pre-Aryan language is written in the Nagari (Hindi) or the Arabic (Urdu) script for religious reasons.[22] However elusive, complex, or dynamic, ethnicity endures as a key meaning-giving reality. It can prevail even when the original ethnic markers have disappeared or been replaced.[23] Ethnicity is also acknowledged as a powerful vehicle for political mobilization. Moreover, it need not be undermined by mobility or inter-ethnic contact; it is often perpetuated through in- and exclusive practices.[24] That cultural differences tend to be inseparable from social disparities is often overlooked. Mainstream accounts habitually: (a) ignore the essence of ethnicity; (b) downplay its societal indicators; and/or, (c) deny the attitudes and practices that often inexorably link the two. Some authors reject ethnicity outright, deeming that economic, institutional, political, territorial, or material interpretations adequately explain the conflicts in question.[25] Others disavow the collective nature of ethnic identities, seeing them as merely demagogic channels for the ambitions of political leaders. On the whole, however, cultural minorities themselves are not thus confused. Especially for those in conflict, the stifling combination of difference and disparity lies at the heart of the matter. Minority ethnic groups choose conflict when motivated in the interest of self-preservation. Reductionist external accounts lack the cultural self-awareness to capture the essence of ethnic conflicts and provide adequate responses. On average, one out of two countries in the world currently faces ethno-cultural conflicts. Horowitz, pursuing a kinship-based theory of ethnic strife, describes dozens such conflicts in emerging and developing economies.[26] Given the approximately 100 cases worldwide where ethno-cultural minority groups are engaged in violent existential struggles today[27] and the grave security implications, we must consider ethno-cultural identities, and the conflicts to which they can lead, to be far from academic in nature. Their lacking recognition, consideration, and policy integration are critical omissions in international relations, the redress of which is of vital urgency and consequence. The following discussion flows from this position.

WHAT COMPETENCE?

As if to substantiate Winston Churchill's reported backhanded compliment that one "can always count on the Americans to do the right thing, after they have exhausted all the other possibilities," the U.S. armed services are pushing for the cultural knowledge they spent most of history neglecting. Anthropologists have been sporadically called upon in the past to provide information on U.S. enemies of war[28] – generally to their professional dismay.[29] Up to a decade or two ago, only members of U.S. armed services Psychological Operations (PSYOPS) units, tasked with public (dis)information of the enemy, were expected to understand foreign cultures. U.S. Armed Forces were usually neither asked to learn much about enemy cultures nor interact extensively with locals abroad. These days, the use of cultural outreach skills, e.g., General David Petraeus' counterinsurgency calling card both in Iraq and Afghanistan,[30] have become part of the "new normal." In the 21st century, foreign operations hinge in part on the inclusion on local knowledge and on protracted interaction with cultural groups as different as they are distant from those at home.[31]

Ethno-cultural issues are complex, interdisciplinary expertise is in short supply, and foreign interventions present a host of cross-cultural challenges. Merely at the level of an individual service member in organizational context, McDonald identifies many levels of cultural complexity: (a) the person's own cultural identity; (b) the home culture of the other U.S. team members; (c) the culture of the team itself; (d) that of the military, within which; (e) embedded civilians may not be attuned to military culture; (f) the institutional cultures of other agencies or armed services with which the individual interacts; (g) as well as the personal, institutional, and macro-social cultures of the international coalition partners in theater.[32] Such challenges are further compounded when, as in Afghanistan, armed interventions take place using blended international forces, across wide cultural distances and civilizational divides, in societies marked by ethno-cultural conflict, and with incongruous power disparity between "donor" and "host" society. This further begs the question as to whether, and if so where, to seek the relevant competencies with which to shorten foreign missions and boost their success. Language schools are, at best, reluctant newcomers to the field of cultural competence; diversity training is mostly concerned with the rights of individuals in Western organizations; and intercultural training is the traditional purview of study abroad and business-to-business etiquette training for expatriates. In matters of culture, how can the U.S. military achieve clarity of ends, ways, and means—if at all? Culturally, who could, or should, learn what to optimize for the success of such costly, extended, and highly unpredictable military missions overseas?

Urged by Washingtonian policymakers, the U.S. armed services have sought to innovate. As the Petreus counterinsurgency doctrine suggests,[33] the military has attempted to turn a corner from its traditional "boots on the ground," "shock and awe" national security stance, toward inclusion of the subtler, more socially-engaged human security approach that asymmetrical, irregular, and ethnic conflicts ostensibly dictate. Perplexity at the array of considerations and skills pertinent to the cultural marketplace may persist. Yet a host of avenues have been suggested, and some pursued, to rise to the cultural challenge. These range from phrase-based language warm-ups, via cultural profiling, immersion programs, to calls for a special civil-military force, appeals to assorted experts, new academic positions, publications, ministerial appointments, and so forth. For instance, the U.S. Joint Forces Command's (USJFCOM) Joint Knowledge Online (JKO) initiated an online training program to promote language and cultural understanding between Afghan and U.S./North Atlantic Treaty Organization (NATO) military troops. Participants are meant to acquire key certain words, phrases, and behaviors. To teach such skills like combining verbal greetings with a handshake, a "gesture wizard" and virtual coach were added. The efficacy of such advanced electronic enhancements over the old foreign-language phrasebook is yet to be determined. Going back via de Saussure[34] to von Humboldt and Herder, linguistics has known for over half a century[35] that natural language is communicated creatively—speech is based on the creative use of internalized rules—rather than on the repetition of memorized phrases. Human intelligence (HUMINT) in cross-cultural contexts requires sensitive rapport-building under conditions of violence, inequality, resistance, and distrust. While the services may not easily overcome their institutional propensity for "technology overmatch," to roll out "off-the-shelf" gadgetry in response to the complex cultural challenges at hand, is hardly an auspicious way to pursue policy and pay a pretty penny from the public purse—regardless of how cost-effective cultural expertise may be compared to military hardware.

When it was noted in the early 2000s that the U.S. war effort in Iraq suffered from poor local intelligence and that in Afghanistan insurgents were emphasized over the local society, a response was to create a small new experimental program. Five-person Human Terrain Teams (HTTs) consisting of linguists, anthropologists, political scientists, and other social scientists were assigned to Army and Marine units in embedded forward positions.[36] Compiling and interpreting data through interviews and observations and the like, HTTs were meant to provide field commanders with a better understanding of the local populace in order to augment military effectiveness and lessen conflict. With training in regional studies, language, Islam, army command structure, military culture, and counterinsurgency, HTTs can train brigade personnel and provide institutional memory when units are replaced. Along with program management, the experienced cultural advisors of the HTTs are supported by Reachback Research Centers (RRC) stateside to analyze data and supply maps and other technology (MAP-HT) back to the field. The HTTs also have access to an international network of social-scientists, human terrain analysis teams (HTAT), program development teams (PDTs), and an academic consortium.[37] The overall Human Terrain System (HTS) thus constructed represents a free-standing cultural intelligence system to some and a joint intelligence addition to traditional state and military intelligence services to others.[38] In theory, the model is relatively well-rounded. In practice, legion problems are reported, such as the constraints of practicing academic field work in wartime, communication between service personnel and social scientists, tensions between academic freedom and military secrets, ethical issues involving the use of research subjects overseas, and so forth.[39] Yet the perceived operational success of this $60 million HTS graduate-level warfare program led to its expansion as of 2007 in both the Iraqi and Afghan theaters.[40] With a few dozen combat brigades in theater, each with several thousand personnel, the question is whether to further expand the experimental proof-of-concept HTS or whether efforts of a different kind are also needed. In case of the latter, what else needs to be understood and done?

Whether military support assignments concur with the professional ethics and methodology of social scientists remains an open question. Despite their avowed interest in opponents' cultures and acquiring culture-general skills, there are limits to the support the services can expect from anthropologists. In the course of the 20th century, with the notable exception of the Third Reich, linguists resisted connecting the features of individual languages to a presumed hierarchy of cognitive abilities. Instead, they *en masse,* consider all language varieties cognitively equal. Likewise, anthropology has largely discarded the study of cross-cultural similarity and/or comparison, despite a few very notable exceptions,[41] since neither diffusion nor origination of cultural traits in multiple locations was found to adequately account for such similarities. Instead, through ethnography, the anthropological study of culture[42] has focused on particularity, which leads to cultural relativism rather than culture-general insight. Consequently, and:

> paradoxically, few anthropologists are in agreement as to what to include under the general rubric of culture. While it will be denied, much depends on the anthropologist's own culture, which exerts a deep and abiding influence not only over how anthropologists think but over where they draw the boundaries in such matters.[43]

It is inherently difficult to interrogate the ideational tools, including those enshrined in one's language, on which one relies for perception. One's subjective culture colors the view of others.[44] Whereas such engrained cultural myopia facilitates our in-group effectiveness it also limits communication between cultures—and prevents us from noticing this dilemma due to its subconscious nature. Anthropology being outward-looking, anthropologists, like enculturated adults in general, resist questioning their worldview in relationship to that of others. "Like everyone else, anthropologists use models, and some models are more fashionable than others."[45] Anthropological bias in favor of cultural specificity and humanity's subconscious ethnocentrism thus conspire to largely limit the development of models suited to meta-culturally informed interventions in foreign and inter-ethnically charged environs.

Military rhetoric in favor of cultural-general skills notwithstanding, its cultural competency model has essentially remained two-dimensional—us versus them. Culturally-specific skills and information about *them* are added to operations by *us* to raise the effectiveness of the latter and limit harm, especially to us. The adequacy of this two-tiered approach to cultural competency is questionable. The following are among the factors that make predominant reliance on culturally-specific knowledge problematic:

- Minority cultural identities are often ambiguous, multilayered, and/or unstable.[46] While this makes them no less relevant, it renders training in language phrases and gestures less than adequate. A two-dimensional approach merely creates the *illusion* of adequacy. Regardless of how much ethnographic data one amasses, one can never learn the detail needed to effectively operate in fluid, foreign, old, and complex areas of ethnic tension and resistance. A more profound approach is needed.

- Learning about the other without cultural self-scrutiny means learning objective detail rather than to penetrate the subjective core of the exchange. Service members are no ethnographers, and such "culture learning"[47] does not sufficiently critique the culture of the learners themselves who as a result are apt to perpetuate simplistic, laughable, or harmful stereotypes unlikely to truly build inter-ethnic trust.
- Deep ethnographic knowledge about individual cultures takes ethnographers, or teams of ethnographers, years to acquire. The time factor reduces its applicability to military interventions. With thousands of ethnicities worldwide,[48] the HTS effort would have to be exponentially expanded, over a great many years, with continual updates, to produce an endlessly detailed data bank of potential use to interventions in the ever-changing multiethnic societies of which virtually all of humanity is comprised. Even then, the effective use of such information would be operationally and politically demanding.
- An objective-culture approach to learning about its foes increases an occupying force's one-sided dependence on informants. The culturally-embedded attitudes of informants can be at cross-purposes, motivating them to disinform. Indeed, the often considerable power imbalance inherent in military interventions, in addition to the perspective of irrelevant or un-

wanted cultural imposition, can render reliance on local informants fallacious, exploitative, or both.

- To what does a culturally-specific approach aspire? Is it: (a) the managerial convenience of purchasing training modules; (b) the objectivity of measurable training outcomes; or, (c) real-life communication between members of different ethno-cultural traditions? If it is the latter, learning about the other and mimicking phrases is unlikely to yield desired results, since no deep communication can take place. If it is one of the former, the results are unlikely to lead to cultural competence that can neutralize destructive developments.

WHAT IMPERATIVES?

That the conflicts in the Middle East and Central Asia have been time-, resource-, and manpower-intensive to the Armed Forces of the United States and its allies is a platitudinous understatement. Made-for-media questions such as whether the war in Afghanistan represents the longest in U.S. history or whether Afghan forces will have taken effective control of security by 2014 are not the only concerns. Drawing on a deep well of civilizational, ethno-cultural, religious, and political variables, those who would thwart peace in Afghanistan on foreign terms remain far from neutralized. While coalition forces prevail in certain areas, in much, indeed in most, of Afghanistan the war is far from won. The country continues to be destabilized by terror attacks, including on U.S. interests and on the central government in Kabul. In Afghanistan, al-Qaeda may be sufficiently haunted by the Joint Special Operations Command (JSOC) to consider shifting its operations elsewhere under the direction of Osama Bin Laden's successor, al-Zawahiri. However, what does not kill it may strengthen the organization; its geographical spread has been linked to growing sophistication, adaptability, and threat. Meanwhile, perceptions of the Karzai government's relevance are waning, even as the Taliban once again gains in presence, its control moving ever closer to Kabul, as it levies its taxes and enforces its brand of justice as it goes. With the specter of military defeat looming over the allied forces, U.S. decisionmakers ever less subtly hint at the need for a negotiated settlement with the Taliban, if only to save face. Like British and Soviet interventions before, the U.S. alliance in Afghanistan is learning the limits of might in the face of cultural resistance. As argued above, the international community cannot anticipate, much less contain or resolve ethno-cultural conflict unless and until it acts on the basis of an appropriate model. The prevailing legal, political, and philosophical frame of reference remains state-centered, combined with inconsistent and uncritical attention to individual human rights. Without a deeper understanding of the role of culture, and a model to match, the international community cannot but remain unable to lastingly confront ethno-cultural conflict, despite the legitimacy of its security concerns. To address this, a host of imperatives can be identified, most of which defy discussion in this context. Four are outlined below.

Cultural Self-Awareness.

Any remedy will depend on our perception of the problems at hand. Whereas culturally-specific approaches focus on objective-culture information, experts agree that the first key to competency in cross-cultural matters is to develop an understanding of one's own culturally-mediated role, biases, values, and outlook. This stems from realization that cultural relativity *de facto* colors our perception of social matters, however unaware we may be of it. Hence we must first seek to escape the perceptual confinement of our cultural programming. Advanced cultural competency training thus first and foremost calls for the development of cultural self-awareness, recognition that and possibly how our inherited worldview is relative, and that what we perceive is not universally true. It is considered "a necessary precursor of intercultural learning, that involves recognizing cultural differences," since without "a mental baseline for their own culture(s)" those placed in cross cultural situations "will find it difficult to recognize and manage cultural differences."[49]

Most of the literature on cultural self-awareness is developmental, i.e., psychological, in nature. As levels of analysis it distinguishes; the individual, the institution, and the group,[50] whereby the latter refers to any groups, such as gender or generation, where individuals may be identified. By contrast, to apply a level-of-analysis approach to international military interventions in ethnically conflicted societies overseas would necessitate a sociological orientation. The introduction of *societal* entities is therefore indicated; notably the ethno-cultural group as the primary meaning-giving entity; the state as a legal-political institution; and, the international community. In social context, the following six possible levels can be posited:

1. Individual culture self-awareness (ICSA) at the personal level;[51]

2. Organizational culture self-awareness (OCSA) at the institutional level;

3. Ethno-cultural self-awareness (ECSA) at the group level;

4. Political culture self-awareness (PCSA) at country or state level;

5. Regional culture self-awareness (RCSA) at the area and/or civilizational level;

6. Global culture self-awareness (GCSA) at the worldwide level.

At the personal level, for instance, one should ask whether service personnel—if untrained in intercultural concepts and inexperienced in self-reflection on matters of culture—could employ self-searching cultural questions to the extent their military mission requires. Organizationally, one could question whether the services—their processes, policies, physical attributes, and principles—have been scrutinized for effectiveness in ethno-cultural context and adapted where possible or indicated. At the next level, is the central government ethno-culturally inclusive in that it pursues effective policies in that vein? Moreover, are there regional or civilizational forces at play—governmental or nongovernmental—that prejudice certain groups over others or that color relationships with foreign interventionists? Finally, does the international community, comprised of both civil society and governmental forces, recognize the primacy of ethnic identity, and work effectively on behalf of ethnically diverse populations to promote a global ecology of peaceful state and inter-ethnic relations rather than allow ethnic violence to fester internationally as it stands impotently by asking when it will end and where it is all heading? We cannot be sanguine in the face of such rhetorical questions, as scores of ethnopolitical conflicts attest.

Of the six levels identified above, the two criteria that do not refer to political culture, ICSA and OCSA, may be considered secondary—not only because both individual and institutional cultural training is currently part of HTTs, but because the focus here is on collective consciousness. Moreover, of the remaining four criteria, RCSA is problematic, since the concept of civilization[52] is politically tenuous. How, for instance, is one to engage the orthodox civilization politically, who would be the military point-of-contact for the Islamic family of cultures, or what entity represents cultural policy in matters of an African nature? As a result of the operational weakness of the civilizational concept RCSA, it is not further short-listed here. A cultural awareness model as it relates to society must thus include the following three levels most closely linkable to collective decisionmaking. First, any evaluation of international, state-level, and/or ethnic matters as they pertain to inter-ethnic peace and stability on the one hand and tension and violence on other presupposes self-awareness of one's ethno-culturally-based outlook. Dominant cultural groups, the normativity of whose worldview may appear to obviate the need for self-awareness, may find this particularly counterintuitive. Macro-cultural self-awareness, at the level of the society or country, is the next level. It includes macro-social societal attributes, processes, institutions, practices, and norms, with particular reference to the deferential inclusion of cultural groups in society. Third, there should be questioning of the lens applied to the international community of states, nations, and ethnicities, for instance, with regard to the role of English, the degree of Westernization, the sense of competition between what Huntington calls civilizations or regarding the status of sub-state ethno-cultural groups. Among other things, this requires a critical, culturally-aware reading of such seminal internationalization theories as modernization theory,[53] hegemony theory,[54] and globalization theory.[55] To claim concern for the international security implications of ethnic conflict without calling into question the lens through which the international community is being perceived will not do, if the desired result is to be the lessening of ethno-cultural tensions in the world. In sum, in this triple sense, the development of cultural self-awareness as it applies to political collectivity is the first imperative.

Intercultural Competence.

The success of the HTS, however modest, may bolster the view that any knowledge of local groups is better than none. Necessary, however, does not mean sufficient. Local information, while useful and seemingly adequate to the untrained eye, is the lesser of the elements needed. Greater economy, impact, depth, and competency require an additional tier or dimension of which the development of cultural self-awareness is but the beginning.

> Significantly more promising than such *culture* learning is what is called *intercultural* (emphasis in original) learning. Participants in the former may learn something about the target culture, but that kind of culture learning usually refers to the acquisition of knowledge about, and perhaps even skills in enacting a particular foreign culture. Such . . . knowledge is not necessarily related to general intercultural competence. . . . To acquire general intercultural competence, one needs to have learned some . . . culture-general categories for

recognizing and dealing with a wide range of cultural differences.[56]

Intercultural learning, also called meta-cultural, or culture-general learning,[57] entails the development of skills, abilities, and dispositions with which to navigate the dynamics between specific cultures.[58] This includes, for instance, negotiating the pitfalls of communication between cultures. The main objective of intercultural learning is to progressively develop master-key skill at bridging the myriad perceptive and communicative differences that divide cultural groups and define their relations. Significantly, it includes a keen understanding of the recurrent problems inherent in social disparities between groups. For, in contrast to culture learning, such competency speaks to the inner, subjective dimension of ethno-cultural identities and relations. Instead of the assembling of endless details about countless, often fluid, cultural identities, it focuses on the issues to which such details belong, on their significance, interaction, and the skills required for their resolution.

Whereas intercultural competency makes use of some culture-specific knowledge, it is less labor-intensive than cultural competency. For instance, the ability to anticipate ethnic tensions and conflicts is thought to facilitate early intervention and raise the chance of conflict reduction.[59] Compared to a two-dimensional cultural competency approach, intercultural competency—including knowledge of and skill in interethnic dynamics—is considered a lesser strain on human resources, less expensive to organizations, more transferable to new cultural demographics, and more likely to lead to sustainable success with stakeholders from a variety of cultural backgrounds. Intercultural competence, by extension, is more apt to allow groups to reach societal goals, facilitate the institutional attainment of organizational goals, and empower individuals to achieve personal goals. For instance, to design an intercultural competency training program in the context of institutional medical care, a 15-point scale has been proposed[60] comprised of cognitive and societal variables:

- Culture—to acknowledge culture and its impact on thinking and behavior.
- Self—to understand one's own cultural identity and worldview (i.e., self-awareness).
- Communication—to exchange thoughts and feelings with others.
- Prejudice—to recognize prejudice in ourselves and others and respond appropriately.
- Empathy—to experience the common humanity behind various cultural perspectives.
- Tolerance for ambiguity—to develop comfort with multiple perspectives.
- Power—to appreciate the relevance of power differences between groups.
- Conflict management—to address tensions in a constructive, fair, and inclusive manner.
- Diversity—to practice and promote cultural diversity throughout the workplace.
- Creativity—to seek solutions based on continuous dialogue and learning.
- Training—to challenge oneself through professional intercultural learning.
- Learning—to remain open to lifelong informal intercultural learning.
- Levity—to experience enthusiasm for learning and practicing intercultural competency.
- Structure—to create professional processes for intercultural competency.

- Integration—to continually align the variables identified above with community practices and relations.

In military environments, a less institutional, more streamlined, and empirically-validated framework may be preferable. From the relevant literature, for instance, nine cognitive development parameters were extracted and tested for cross-cultural competence (CCC), a term largely interpreted as intercultural competence.[61] They include: (1) self-efficacy; (2) ethno-cultural empathy; (3) openness to new experiences; (4) willingness to engage; (5) cognitive flexibility; (6) self-monitoring; (7) emotional self-regulation; (8) low need for cognitive closure; and, (9) tolerance for ambiguity.[62] It was noted, for instance, that less advanced performers displayed the need for more cognitive closure (i.e., more structure, predictability, and rigidity), and that they manifested lower tolerance for ambiguity (through ethnocentrism, dichotomous thinking, and a penchant for authoritarianism). After testing, a simpler 6-point scale was ultimately developed, comprising: (1) willingness to engage; (2) cognitive flexibility and openness; (3) emotional regulation; (4) tolerance of uncertainty; (5) self-efficacy; and, (6) ethno-cultural empathy. Along such a 6-point variable scale, armed services personnel could conceivably be tested and trained.

Service personnel, including high-level decision-makers who fall short of such intercultural competence, are prone to mistake their own outlook, reality, and practices as objective or universally valid—and that of others as inherently lacking in comparison. Such perceptions are inherently problematic when looking from one culture to the next. Cultural universals, to the extent that they exist, cannot be reliably perceived from within a particular cultural viewpoint. The underlying premise of intercultural competency is that no valid judgments, especially about the subjective aspect of other cultures, can be made without it. A three-dimensional approach is a *sine qua non*. Besides relatively trivial objective-culture learning about the enemy, the greater need is for self-awareness of one's own cultural viewpoint and above all that for training in meta-cultural concepts, culture-general issues, and intercultural communication skills. Though in part it overlaps with the first, intercultural learning in the broader sense constitutes the second imperative.

Collective Cultural Rights.

Failure to acknowledge ethno-cultural groups as primary, historically-grounded, collectively identified human aggregates are the most plausible explanation for the current global powerlessness in the face of ethnic conflicts. The blatant shortcomings of the global response to the conflict in the Darfur region of the Sudan may serve as example. Though tensions had been building long before, the international community was unable to conceive of and thus adequately respond to, the violence—with its pre-Islamic roots in three millennia of Kush Empire—as a state-sponsored ethno-Arabist "apartheid" war against Afro-ethnic groups in the South, notably the Zaghawa, Masalit, and the Furs from which Darfur derives its name. From the outset of hostilities in 2003, the global community has vacillated between: (a) exaggerated political deference to the central government, the very instigator of the atrocities; (b) overuse of military terms "civil war," "guerilla," "militia," and "rebel" which speak to the violence without denoting its ethno-cultural source; (c) unsuitably a-cultural economic arguments, since oil revenues have been used to fund the ethno-cultural war itself; and, (d) a feeble focus on the humanitarian calamity that inevitably resulted from the injustice. The conflict is undoubtedly complex in its ethno-cultural, religious, and historic dimensions. Still, in Darfur the world cannot competently unravel that of which it is not culturally aware, it cannot appropriately intervene in what it does not interculturally define, and it cannot effectively resolve what it will not politically confront.

An intercultural competency stance on ethnic tension may remind one of human-rights based approaches to international relations[63] or human-rights transnationalism.[64] There is a difference, however. Human rights are posited for individual human beings whereas group cultural rights are neither held by individual persons nor do they a priori apply across groups. By contrast, collective ethno-cultural rights are universal only in that they embody the fundamental human need for cultural identity, group membership, and shared values. Though not immune from occasional misuse to protect ethno-cultural elites, they are intended to protect indigenous and other sub-state minority populations within broader society.

It is only rather recently that the international community has sought to recognize cultural matters as meriting legal protection. From the 1948 Universal Declaration of Human Rights[65] onward, the 20th century saw a series of international attempts to formulate cultural rights, most limited to individual rights and seeking "protection" only against their violation. In earlier documents, such as United Nations (UN) General Assembly resolution 260, the 1948 Convention on the Prevention and Punishment of the Crime of Genocide, violence against entire ethno-cultural groups was repudiated—provided it was terminal. While focus has since shifted to a more precise and less fatalistic view of cultural rights than defense against outright collective annihilation, this has generally come at the cost of the rights of the group as a whole and of the entirety of its cultural capital. For instance, the Declaration on the Elimination of All Forms of Intolerance and of Discrimination Based on Religion or Belief,[66] the International Convention on the Elimination of All Forms of Racial Discrimination of 2000, and the 1998 U.S. International Religious Freedom Act were all designed to guard against violations of certain *elements* of minority culture as opposed to the overall culture, and only at the level of the individual rather than the group. With regard to "linguistic human rights," the Council of Europe's European Charter for Regional or Minority Languages[67] focused only on languages as forms of communication. Formulated in inanimate concepts such as "territories," "media," and other areas of societal concern, the document is entirely comprised of the public responsibilities of states without mention of the cultural rights of individuals or groups. When several years later the Council of Europe drafted its Framework Convention for the Protection of National Minorities,[68] frequent reference was made to abstractions such as pluralism, diversity, religion, history and the like, but provisions for cultural rights, freedoms, and protections were limited only to individual minority members. It was not until the latter 1990s that the concept of group rights gradually reemerged. When dozens of mostly nonstate experts and stakeholders convened in Barcelona, Spain, to draft the Universal Declaration of Linguistic Rights, they did so in explicit contrast to the age-old unifying tendency of the majority of states to reduce diversity and foster attitudes opposed to cultural plurality and linguistic pluralism. Claiming that states had impeded the recognition of group cultural rights, the resulting Declaration "takes language communities and not states as its point of departure," recognizing a language community as having "developed a common language as a natural means of communication and cultural cohesion among its members," and explicitly formulating linguistic rights as collective rights.[69]

Much remains unresolved. Regarding language rights, for instance, legion questions linger such as which countries will ratify the Declaration of Linquisitic Rights, which languages qualify for protection, how to define a language, what level of protection should be offered, and the like. More importantly, the validity of individual and especially collective cultural rights is far from universally accepted—in part due to perceived tensions between cultural rights and the interests of states and those who control them. Moreover, though ethnicity is usually based on a combination of factors self-attributed by groups,[70] holistic group cultural rights are as yet unprotected other than via genocide. Scholars also differ in opinion as to whether rights efforts ease or fan the flames of ethnic resistance, whether postmodernity has rendered the world more vulnerable to ethnic polarization, whether the global economy can afford to take a *laissez faire* attitude to ethnic war.[71] While it remains uncontroversial that the international order is strained by its current level of ethnic discord, the link to collective cultural rights is as yet insufficiently elaborated or established.

Both actual and conceptual crises must be addressed where they occur. In light of the definition of culture provided above, "the deliberate attempt to impose a culture directly and speedily, no matter how backed by good will, is an affront to the human spirit."[72] Many experts regard the recognition of collective cultural needs as being central to the promotion of ethnic peace. Given the fundamental role of group cultural subjectivity, collective rights cannot be ignored. Basic group needs require basic group rights. As an international community, we must come to terms with the realization that multiethnic societies can only stabilize by way of the reasonable satisfaction of their own value sets. As nearly 100 current conflicts show, the world is replete with ethno-cultural tensions that are often age-old, in countries with young, tentative, and/or culturally biased central governments; and with more or less porous borders. With or without foreign troops and/or humanitarian presence, it is futile to expect they will to stabilize on Western terms merely because foreign and central governments lavish billions of dollars and millions of tons of ordinance on them. "Whether treated to carrots or sticks," these so-called insurgencies "will resist and they will prevail—for such is the nature, and power, of culture."[73] Consequently, the outlook appears bleak for another Western effort, lacking in cultural self-awareness, at forcing itself on Afghanistan. For international actors to competently respond to the inter-ethnic conflicts of our age, they must recognize ethnic identity for what it is, including the issues that characterize relationships between minorities and mainstreams within and between countries—and do so with self-awareness and intercultural skill. Sustainable inter-ethnic peace depends less on the application of external force, or on political machinations, than on the internal perception of cultural justice,[74] i.e., justice in ethno-cultural perspective. While it may challenge our worldview and lead to a more diverse international order, we must therefore consider the international recognition of collective ethno-cultural rights the third imperative.

Sub-State Ethno-Nationalities.

Since the Allied invasions of Iraq and Afghanistan respectively dismantled the Saddam Hussein and Taliban regimes, the rationale of bringing democracy has been frequently evoked. Though the notion of externally-imposed democracy may be a contradiction in terms, even observationally the endeavor is difficult to construe as successful. With 75 percent of the Afghani electorate reportedly participating in the 2004 presidential elections, the subsequent 2009 elections were low in turnout and high in fraud, violence, and intimidation. At the 2010 parliamentary elections alleged vote-rigging was even more systemic than the year before.[75] Globally, the level of corruption in Afghanistan is considered third only to Somalia and Myanmar,[76] and the country ranks 150 out of 167 countries in the democracy index.[77] Iraq, a global fourth in corruption and 111th in democracy, rates similarly. Seen ethno-culturally, democracy appears particularly distant in Afghanistan. In southern Pashtun-dominated provinces such as Kandahar, the 2009 election turnout was so low that hundreds of polling stations never opened, even though the incumbent president was Pashtun. In the Tajik-dominated northern region, comprised of Kundun and seven other provinces, talk of secession is in part inspired by proximity to Pakistan's southwestern province, Baluchistan, an area of Baluch ethno-nationalist resistance. Scholars have long recognized that plural democracy is particularly challenging in multiethnic societies.[78] The combination of political and ethno-national plurality often creates disunity. The ethnicization of political parties, the existence of systemic "horizontal inequalities"[79] between ethnic groups, the risk of separatism on the part of aggrieved ethno-nationals, the polarization and sabotage of elections, and the mobilization of ethno-national violence, are among the recognized risk factors of multiethnic democracies.[80] It has been suggested that the risks of cyclical ethnic war may be too high a price for the erection of democracies in such diverse societies, especially given the youth of their often post-colonial central institutions. As the signatories to the Declaration of Linquisitic Rights recognized, states and collective sub-state rights are often at loggerheads, the former considering recognition of primordial nature of the latter anathema to their interests and ideology. Whereas a reconstituted Taliban may be more dreaded than welcomed by an Afghan populace longing for peace, it is doubtful that the imposition of ethno-culturally naïve Western-style democracy will bring about the country's security and stability. In lieu of the Eurocentric, economically liberalist view of democracy that currently dominates, a more flexible, complex, and cooperative model is needed that explicitly incorporates the basic rights of diverse cultural groups even if their values differ from the secular, materialist, late-modernist, putatively acultural model of major world powers. Since ethno-cultural rights are indispensable to the stability of the larger social order, peace in Afghanistan and other areas of the world is unrealistic without such an expanded view of the state commonwealth.

At the very heart of the tension between global homogeneity and ethno-cultural specificity lie questions about the nature of the state in relation to the nation, nationalism, and the nation-state as social constructs. Conceptualizations of these imagined communities,[81] and the nationalist sentiments and actions that drive them, vary across centuries, cultures, and ideologies, each stressing a variety of socio-psychological, economic, political, technological, or cultural factors.[82] Tensions abound between states as sovereign political structures, nation-states allegedly comprised of citizens united by cultural characteristics, and nations defined by ethno-cultural group identities that strain toward autonomy. Unlike states, the concepts of nation and nationalism can apply at both state- and sub-state levels. Therein lies part of the problem. In multiethnic countries, the issue is far from abstract. Whereas the world only comprises some 200 states, it contains many thousands of ethno-national entities, states' terminological appropriation of international matters and UN organizations notwithstanding. Eighty percent of the world's states are ethnically diverse,[83] and countries in which states and nations coincide, populated by a single ethno-culturally homogenous group, are virtually nonexistent. In all but a theoretical sense, the concept of the nation-state lacks worldwide applicability. The self-evident and self-serving way in which states—whether on their own reconnaissance or supported by other states—ignore sub-state nationalities and promote the illusion of cultural homogeneity contrasts with the perceived upward trend in global ethno-nationalism. Though it remains to be empirically demonstrated, the discrepancy is difficult to dissociate from the preponderance of ethnic wars currently in evidence. Peace in multiethnic states may prove elusive unless and until states abandon the largely inapplicable myth of the nation-state and meaningfully integrate the needs of sub-state ethno-national needs. This is particularly the case in so-called "fragile" states where lack of state control in the traditional sense is seen by dominant powers as a risk to international security, for instance with regard to human-rights abuses, nuclear proliferation, drug trafficking, disease, poverty, or terrorism. However, neither these risk factors nor their socio-political meaning are objective truths; all depend on cultural valuation. Any attempt to address them internationally presupposes cultural self-awareness and intercultural skill. The claimed "fragility" of states, too, remains a controversial concept, even in Western countries.[84] States described as fragile, while no doubt challenged in their own way, may be more grounded in diverse local culture, more dynamic and adaptable, and less prone to obfuscating the difference between state and nation. An expanded, more culturally flexible view of what constitutes a viable state may be called for. However defined, healthy states are needed for the promotion of peace. In global perspective, they will rarely be traditionally-defined "nation-states."

Many theorists assert that culture is not directly relevant to states, which they perceive as comprised of neutral governments and more or less politicized individuals. Not only do claims of a priori inter-ethnic neutrality justifying state control smack of rationalizations, states are rarely ethnically neutral, as demonstrated the world over.[85] Not only do ethnic groups compete for resources, political privileges, and cultural rights; their struggle is rarely equal. Rather than practicing neutral impartiality, states tend to standardize the cultural agenda of their dominant ethnicities, whose speech varieties become official, whose worldview becomes generalized, and whose implicit control of the state apparatus becomes normative. In a variety of ways, states pursue one of three strategies vis-à-vis nondominant ethnicities: assimilation; extermination; or, integration. Assimilation policies that affect, for instance, the Sami in Scandinavia, the Roma in Eastern Europe, or the Aborigines of Australia are well-documented. State ethnic cleansing policies that practice the disappearing of ethno-cultural minorities in favor of the dominant group's hold over the state also remain in evidence around the world. Many states pursue integration along ethno-cultural lines—whereby nonimmigrant minority groups are given some control over their affairs, whether through federation, regionalization, or other political accommodations—to co-opt ethnic leadership, or otherwise forestall or resolve conflict or secession. Attempts have been made to classify approaches to managing inter-ethnic conflict. Ranging from consociationalism,[86] via federalization, arbitration, integration, to assimilation, secession, ethnic cleansing and genocide, certain scholars focus on state actions[87] while others foreground the experience of sub-state groups, e.g., indigenization, accommodation, assimilation, acculturation, population transfer, boundary alteration, genocide, and ethnic suicide.[88] Many countries are challenged by a rise in ethno-nationalism. Democracy is considered in global decline,[89] and in light of the information age the demise of the state itself has been increasingly debated,[90] though social media are primarily the purview of individuals. The degree to which the issues of inter-ethnic disparity, of inter-ethnic dominance, and repression from the perspective of cultural justice, drive today's ethno-nationalism remains much underappreciated. The inapplicability of the nation-state concept, the inevitability of ethno-national accommodation, the need for cultural self-awareness, and intercultural skill, contribute to a new state reality. At the central government level, the equitable inclusion of ethnicities as collectivities with the framework of the state appears crucial. State-level commitment to, recognition of, and reasonable legal and or legislative accommodations for the cultural needs of sub-state nondominant ethno-national groups is therefore the fourth imperative before us.

WHAT NEXT?

Scores of military, paramilitary, and post-conflict operations around the world—from Afghanistan to Algeria, Burma to Burundi, Columbia to Congo, and so on through the alphabet—have accentuated the dearth of an adequate framework. The business of forcibly intervening in the affairs of other countries is always very delicate. Article 2, Section 4 of the UN Charter precludes it, stipulating that members "shall refrain in their international relations from the threat or use of force against the territorial integrity or political independence of any state."[91] Among justifiable exceptions to this maxim, armed responses to humanitarian crises rank more highly, while preemptive strikes remain controversial, and preventive wars are generally considered less than acceptable. Regardless of cultural context, the absence of internationally recognized norms, the inherently patronizing nature of forced interventions, and the challenges of post-conflict rebuilding further compound the precariousness of armed interventions.[92] The question as to what to do about inter-ethnic conflict requires an international framework, standards of international law that include a cultural, a state-level, and an international dimension. Such a global charter, one that that takes the ethno-cultural minority group as its point of departure, that includes due regard for the prerogatives and responsibilities of states, and that also outlines international standards of engagement is to be detailed in future research. It will need to be ethno-cultural in its substance, political in framework, and in its practical application can combine diplomacy, the military, and a WoG approach—a multi-sectoral grouping for which the shorthand, "The Three Ds" (development, defense, and diplomacy), is often employed.

In theory, a whole of society approach (WoS), whereby civil society organizations (CSOs), including nongovernmental organizations (NGOs) and community-based organizations (CBOs), work alongside governmental agencies, could broaden the set of capabilities deployed in the interest of peace and stability,[93] providing access to more relevant tools and experts. In the long term, WoG approaches have also been shown to yield substantial fiscal savings over traditional enemy-centric military interventions. On the other hand, variability in state WoG approach contexts and commitments,[94] as well as differences in organizations and political systems, along with the greater logistical complexities, and greater personal safety risks[95] can challenge the efficacy of such broad collaborations. Moreover, international comparisons of WoG approaches have not explicitly focused on culture or intercultural matters,[96] implying that even under a WoG/WoS approach lacking cultural self-awareness could be of concern. Invasion by the world's most dominant countries inherently raise questions of cultural self-awareness. Not only is ethnocentrism endemic to the human condition, power may be directly proportional to the illusion of value self-evidence. It thus seems no coincidence that the WoG approach of the world's only superpower reportedly compares poorly in coherence, motivation, funding, and level of activity to those of, for instance, Canada, Australia, or the United Kingdom.[97] In short, though the requisite expertise may most easily be found in civil society, WoG/WoS approaches the breadth of which carries its own liabilities, is no guarantee for intercultural competency. With or without it, to confront multiethnic strife in Central Asia or elsewhere requires cultural self-awareness and intercultural competence.

In contrast to human security, autonomous unmanned aerial vehicles (UAVs) and unmanned ground vehicles (UGVs) have rapidly become standard features of asymmetrical warfare in the post-bin Laden era. Along with Measurement and Signatures Intelligence (MASINT) and Signals Intelligence (SIGINT), drone technology has improved exponentially and, with it, its use in theater. It may appear oddly Luddite to emphasize matters of culture, security so "soft," it is largely intangible. Yet nostalgia for the U.S. military's overreliance on technology at the expense of human skills that previously undermined its intelligence capabilities is counterindicated. No societal matter escapes some degree of cultural valuation. Drone warfare, for instance, may be popular stateside since it satisfies the value of putting fewer U.S. lives in harm's way. To think that members of all cultures and societies share this value is to lack cultural self-awareness. Drone warfare may adversely affect our ability to win hearts and minds overseas because it is often seen as cowardly by those whose value set, for instance, places a premium on sacrifice, martyrdom, or personal courage. Moreover, the collateral damage caused by drones is particularly unpalatable overseas, its political tenability precarious, and its recent tactical successes likely to invigorate anti-U.S. attitudes. In volatile ways, any of these factors can cause grave long-term security risks for the United States. In a world where a landmine costs less than a Starbucks coffee and an improvised explosive device (IED) has come down to the cost of a McDonald's meal, those who would foment ethnic strife are at an advantage over those who would contain it. Not even a drone-assisted military is up to the task. The solution is to truly engage the values that motivate others and broker a culturally just peace.

In the U.S. military, the cultural outreach model has hitherto been two-dimensional, i.e., to tentatively complement national security efforts with objective cultural information in theater. Though the HTS has presumably made some deployed units more professional at this approach, it is neither qualitatively nor quantitatively adequate. Though neither HUMINT nor a WoG/WoS approach is as fiscally burdensome as traditional warfare, a different quality of effort, three-dimensional in nature, is indispensable. Of the four imperatives reviewed here: (1) to acquire cultural self-awareness; (2) develop intercultural competence; (3) recognize collective cultural rights; and, (4) protect sub-state ethno-nationalities, myriad details remain to be determined. Essentially, however, these challenges revolve around: (a) the inevitability of ethno-cultural justice as the key to societal peace and stability and, by extension, to international security; and, (b) the insights, capabilities, and processes essential to meeting the demands of peace and security in a world greatly jeopardized by ethnic conflict. Regardless of its outcome, the war in Afghanistan thus presents the impetus for more sustainable international conflict management through the imperative establishment of ecological relations between the world's ethno-cultural groups.

REFERENCES

Allport, Gordon. *The Nature of Prejudice*. Cambridge, MA: Perseus Books. 1954.

American Anthropological Association, Commission on the Engagement of Anthropology with the U.S. Security and Intelligence Communities (AAA). *Final Report on The Army's Human Terrain System Proof of Concept Program*. Washington, DC: American Anthropological Association. 2009.

Anderson, Benedict. *Imagined Communities*. London, UK: Verso. 1965.

Arnold, Matthew. *Culture and Anarchy: An Essay in Political and Social Criticism*. New Haven, CT: Yale University Press. 1974.

Asamoah, Yvonne. *Innovations in Delivering Culturally Sensitive Social Work Services: Challenges for Practice and Education*. New York: Routledge. 1997.

Avruch, Kevin, Peter W. Black, and Joseph Scimecca. "Conflict Resolution: Cross-cultural Perspective." in *Aggressive Behavior*, Vol. 19, No. 4. New York, NY: Greenwood Press, 1993, pp. 313-315.

Barber, Benjamin and Schulz, Andrea. *Jihad versus McWorld: How the Planet is Both Falling Apart and Coming Together*. New York: Ballantine Books. 1996.

Baker, James A., and Hamilton H. Lee. *The Iraq Study Group Report*. New York: First Vintage Book. 2006.

Barth, Fredrik, ed. *Ethnic Groups and Boundaries: the Social Organization of Culture Difference*. Oslo, Norway: Universitetsforlaget. 1969.

Barthes, Roland. *Elements of Semiology*. Bel Air, CA: Hill and Wang. 1977.

Benedict, Ruth. *The Chrysanthemum and the Sword*. Peabody, MA: Mariner Books. 2005.

Bennett, Milton. "Current Perspectives on Intercultural Communication." in Milton J. Bennett, ed. *Basic Concepts of Intercultural Communication: Selected Readings*. Boston, MA, and London, UK: Intercultural Press. 1998.

Bennett, Milton J. "Defining, Measuring, and Facilitating Intercultural Learning: A Conceptual Introduction to the IJIE Special Issue." *Intercultural Education,* Vol. 20, 2009, pp. S1-S15.

Binsbergen, Wim M. J. "Cultures do not exist: exploding self-evidences in the investigation of interculturality." in *Intercultural Encounters: African and Anthropological Lessons Towards a Philosophy of Interculturality*. Münster, Germany: LIT Verlag, 2003, pp. 459-522.

Boas, Franz. "Scientists as Spies." *The Nation,* December 20, 1919; *Small Wars Journal*, Vol. 7. 2007.

Brown, Michael E., ed. *Ethnic Conflict and International Security*. Princeton, NJ: Princeton University Press. 1993.

Bucher, Richard D. and Patricia L. Bucher. *Building Cultural Intelligence (CQ): Nine Megaskills*. Upper Saddle River, NJ: Pearson. 2008.

Coakley, John. "The Resolution of Ethnic Conflict: Towards a Typology." *International Political Science Review,* Vol. 13, No. 4, 1992, pp. 343-358.

Chomsky, Noam. *Aspects of the Theory of Syntax*. Cambridge, MA: MIT Press. 1965.

Coffey, Heather. *Culturally Relevant Teaching*. Learn NC. Chapel Hill, NC: University of North Carolina. 2008.

Coulmas, Florian Dua. *Sprache und Staat: Studien zur Sprachenplanung und Sprachpolitik.* Berlin, Germany: Walter de Gruyter. 1985.

Council of Europe (COE). *European Charter for Regional or Minority Languages.* Strasbourg, France: Council of Europe. 1992.

Council of Europe (COE). *Framework Convention for the Protection of National Minorities.* Strasbourg, France: Council of Europe. 1995.

Creveld, Martin van. *The Rise and Decline of the State.* New York, NY: Cambridge University Press. 1999.

Diller, Jerry V. and Moule, Jean. *Cultural Competence: A Primer for Educators.* Belmont, CA: Thomason Learning. 2005.

Dunaway, Wilma A. "Ethnic Conflict in the Modern World-System: The Dialectics of Counter-Hegemonic Resistance in an Age of Transition." *Journal of World Systems Research,* Vol. IX, No. 1, 2003, pp 3-16.

Durkheim, Emile. *Durkheim on Religion.* Atlanta, GA: American Academy of Religion. 1994.

Economist Intelligence Unit, The (EIU). *Democracy Index 2010: Democracy in Retreat.* London, UK: The Economist Intelligence Unit. 2010.

Edwards, John. *Multilingualism.* London/New York: Routledge. 1994.

Epstein, Leon. *Culturally Appropriate Health Care by Culturally Competent Health Professionals: International Workshop Report.* Hashomer, Israel: The Israel National Institute for Health Policy. 2007.

Ethier, Kathleen A. and Deaux, Kay. "Negotiating Social Identity when Contexts Change: Maintaining Identification and Responding to Threat." *Journal of Personality and Social Psychology,* Vol 67, No. 2, August 1994, pp. 243-251.

Fantini, A.E. *87 Assessment Tools of Intercultural Competence.* Brattleboro, VT: School for International Training. 2006.

Fishman, Joshua A. "Summary and Interpretation: Post-Imperial English 1940-1990." in Joshua Fishman et al., eds. *Post Imperial English. Status Change in Former British and American Colonies 1940- 1990.* Berlin/New York: Mouton de Gruyter. 1996.

Foucault, Michel. *Society Must be Defended.* New York, NY: Picador, 2003, pp. 6-7.

Fox, Jonathan. *Ethno-religious Conflict in the Late Twentieth Century.* Lanham, MD: Lexington. 2002.

Fukuyama, Francis. "The End of History." *The National Interest,* No. 16. 1989, pp. 3-18.

Fukuyama, Francis. *The End of History and the Last Man.* New York, NY: Free Press. 1992.

Gay, G. *Culturally Responsive Teaching: Theory, Research, & Practice.* New York, NY: Teachers College Press. 2000.

Gellner, E. *Nations and Nationalism.* Oxford, UK: Basic Blackwell. 1983.

Geertz, Clifford. *The Interpretation of Cultures.* New York, NY: Basic Books. 1973.

Grimes, Barbara F. *Ethnologue.* Dallas, TX: Summer Institute of Linguistics. 1996.

Green, James. *Cultural Awareness in Human Services: A Multi-Ethnic Approach.* Upper Saddle River, NJ: Allyn & Bacon. 1998.

González, Roberto. *American Counterinsurgency: Human Science and the Human Terrain.* Chicago, IL: University of Chicago & Prickly Paradigm. 2009.

Gudykunst, W. B., and M. R. Hammer. "Dimensions of Intercultural Effectiveness: Culture Specific or Culture General?" *International Journal of Intercultural Relations,* Vol. 8, 1984, pp. 1-10.

Gurr, Ted R. *The Ethnic Basis of Political Action in the 1980s and 1990s*. Working Paper, Minorities at Risk Project. Baltimore, MD: Center for International Development and Conflict Management, University of Maryland. 1999.

Gusterson, Hugh. "The Seven Deadly Sins of Samuel Huntington." in Bestemont, Catherine and Hugh Gusterson, eds. *Why America's Top Pundits are Wrong: Anthropologists Talk Back*. Berkeley, CA: University of California Press. 2004.

Herder, Johann Gottfried. *Herder: Philosophical Writings*, Michael N. Forster, trans. Cambridge, UK/MA: Cambridge University Press. 2002.

Herskovits, Melville J. *Man and his Works, the Science of Cultural Anthropology*. New York, NY: Knopf. 1948.

Hobsbawm, E. J. *Nations and Nationalism Since 1780: Programme, Myth, Reality*. Cambridge, UK: Cambridge University Press. 1990.

Horowitz, Donald. *Ethnic Groups in Conflict*. Berkeley, CA: University of California Press. 2000.

Humboldt, Friedrich Wilhelm Christian Karl Ferdinand von. *On the Diversity of Human Language Construction and its Influence on the Mental Development of the Human Species (Über die Verschiedenheit des menschlichen Sprachbaus und seinen Einfluss auf die geistige Entwicklung des Menschengeschlechts,1836)*. Michael Losonsky, ed. Cambridge UK/MA: Cambridge University Press. 2005.

Huntington, Samuel P. "The Clash of Civilizations?" *Foreign Affairs*, Vol. 72, No. 3, 1993, pp. 22-49.

Huntington, Samuel P. *The Clash of Civilizations and the Remaking of World Order*. New York, NY: Simon & Shuster. 1997.

Jandora, John W. "War and Culture: A Neglected Relation." *Armed Forces & Society*, Vol. 25, No. 4. Sage, 1999, pp. 541-556.

Jandora, John W. "Military Cultural Awareness: From Anthropology to Application." *Landpower Essay*, Vol. 06, No. 3. Arlington, VA: Association of the United States Army. November 2006.

Kallen, Evelyn. *Ethnicity and Human Rights in Canada*. New York: Oxford University Press. 1995.

Kaplan, Robert D. "The Coming Anarchy." *The Atlantic Monthly*, Vol. 273, No. 2, 1994, pp. 44-76.

Keohane, Robert O. with Joseph S. Nye. *Power and Interdependence: World Politics in Transition*. Oxford, UK: Blackwell Publishing. 1977.

Khan, Abdul Jamil. *Urdu/Hindi: An Artificial Divide*. New York, NY: Algora. 2006.

King, Charles. "The Myth of Ethnic Warfare: Understanding Conflict in the Post-Cold War World." *Foreign Affairs*, Vol. 80, No. 6, 2001, pp. 165-170.

King, Christopher. "Managing Ethical Conflict on a Human Terrain Team." *Anthropology News*, Vol. 50, No. 6, 2009, p. 16.

Köchler, Hans C. *Terrorism and Human Rights: Reflections on the Global War on Terror*. Vienna, Austria: International Progress Organization. 2008.

Köchler, Hans C. "World order: vision and reality." *Studies in International Relations*, Vol. XXXI. David Armstrong, ed. New Delhi, India: Manak, 2009, pp. xxiii-564.

Knowlson, James S. *Universal Language Schemes in England and France, 1600-1800*. Toronto, Ontario, Canada: University of Toronto Press, 1975.

Krauss, Robert M. and Ezequiel Morsella. "Communication and conflict." in M. Deutch and P.Coleman, eds. *The Handbook of Constructive Conflict Resolution: Theory and Practice*. San Francisco, CA: Jossey-Bass Publishers. 2006, pp. 144-156.

Kimmel, Paul. "Culture and conflict." in Morton Deutsch and Peter T. Coleman, eds. *The Handbook of Conflict Resolution: Theory and Practice.* San Francisco, CA: Jossey-Bass Publishers, 2000, pp. 453-474.

Lerner, D. *The Passing of Traditional Society: Modernizing the Middle East.* Glencoe IL: The Free Press. 1958.

Lijphart, A. *Democracy in Plural Societies: A Comparative Exploration.* New Haven, CT: Yale University Press. 1977.

Maersheimer, John. *The Tragedy of Great Power Politics.* New York: W. W. Norton & Co. 2003.

McDonald, Daniel P. *A Brief Note on the Multi-layered Nature of Cross-Cultural Competence.* Patrick Air Force Base, FL: Defense Equal Opportunity Management Institute. 2008.

McGarry, John and Brendan O'Leary. "Introduction: The macro-political regulation of ethnic conflict." in John McGarry and Brendan O'Leary, eds. *The Politics of Ethnic Conflict Regulation: Case Studies of Protracted Ethnic Conflicts.* London, UK: Routledge, 1993, pp. 1-40.

Merry, Sally and Mark Goodale. *The Practice of Human Rights: Tracking Law Between the Global and the Local.* Cambridge, UK: Cambridge University Press. 2007.

Meyjes, Gregory Paul P. "Plan 'C' is for Culture: Out of Iraq, Opportunity." *Landpower Essay,* Vol. 07, No. 4. Arlington, VA: Association of the United States Army. June 2007.

Meyjes, Gregory Paul P. "Language and Universalization: a 'Linguistic Ecology' Reading of Bahá'í Writ." *The Journal of Bahá'í Studies,* Vol. 9, No. 1, 1999, pp. 51-63.

Meyjes, Gregory Paul P. "*A Guide to Intercultural Health Care: Serving African Americans.*" Unpublished manuscript. Denver, CO: Kaiser Permanente, African American Center of Excellence. 2010.

Meyjes, Gregory Paul P. "English beyond our borders: reflections on the risks, rewards, and responsibilities of TESOL." *TESOL in Action,* Vol. 23, No. 1, 2011, pp. 3-23.

Mitrany, David. *The Functional Theory of Politics.* New York: St Martin's Press. 1975.

Moix, Bridget. "Matters of Faith: Religion, Conflict, and Conflict Resolution." in Morton Deutsch and Peter T. Coleman, eds. *The Handbook of Conflict Resolution: Theory and Practice.* San Francisco, CA: Jossey-Bass Publishers. 2006, pp. 582-601.

Monnet, Jean. "The First Statesman of Interdependence." *Foreign Affairs*, Vol. 74, No. 2, 1995, pp. 154-155.

Morgenthau, Hans and Thompson, Kenneth. *Politics Among Nations: 6th Edition.* New York: McGraw-Hill, 1985, pp. 165-ff.

Müller, Johannes U. "Nationalism and modernity." In *EUI Working Paper HEC No. 99/1.* Stråth, Bo ed. Florence, Italy: European University Institute, 1995, pp. 1-69.

Ochola, Robert L. "The Acholi Religious Leaders' Peace Initiative in the Battlefield of Northern Uganda: An example of an integrated, inculturated, and ecumenical approach to pastoral work in a war situation." Unpublished Diploma Thesis. Innsbruck, Austria: Theology, University of Innsbruck. 2006.

Organization for Economic Co-operation and Development (OECD). *Whole of Government Approaches to Fragile States.* Paris, France: OECD. 2006.

Ortiz, Fernando. *Contrapunteo Contrapunteo Cubano Del Tobacco y el Azúcar. (Cuban Counterpoint: Tobacco and Sugar).* Durham, NC: Duke University Press. 1995.

Patrick, Stewart and Kaysie Brown. *Greater than the Sum of Its parts? Assessing "Whole of Goverment" Approaches to Fragile States.* New York: International Peace Academy. 2007.

Pederson, Paul. "Multicultural Conflict Resolution." in Morton Deutsch and Peter T. Coleman, eds. *The Handbook of Constructive Conflict Resolution: Theory and Practice.* San Francisco, CA: Jossey-Bass Publishers. 2006, pp. 144-156.

Phillip, Conrad. *Window on Humanity*. New York: McGraw-Hill. 2005.

Philipson, Robert, Mart Rannut, and Tove Skutnabb-Kangas. "Introduction." in Tove Skutnabb-Kangas and Robert Philipson, eds. *Linguistic Human Rights: Overcoming Linguistic Discrimination*. Berlin, Germany: Mouton De Gruyter, 1995, pp. 1-19.

Price, David. *Anthropological Intelligence: The Deployment and Neglect of American Anthropology in the Second World War*. Durham, NC: Duke University Press. 2008.

Priest, Dana and William M. Arkin. *Top Secret America: The Rise of the New American Security State*. New York: Little, Brown and Company. 2011.

Recchia, Stephano. "Just and Unjust Postwar Reconstruction: How much external interference can be morally justified? " *Ethics & International Affairs*, Vol. 23, Issue 2, 2009, pp. 165–187.

Robertson, Roland. *Globalization: Social Theory and Global Culture*. London, UK: Sage Publications Ltd. 1992.

Roosevelt, Eleanor *et al*. *Universal Declaration of Human Rights*. Bedford, MA: Applewood Books. 2000.

Rosecrance, Richard N. and Arthur A. Stein, eds. *No More States? Globalization, National Self-determination, and Terrorism*. Rowman & Littlefield Publishers. 2004.

Ross, Karol G., Carol A. Thomson, Daniel P. McDonald, and Meagan C. Arrastia. *The Development of the CCCI: The Cross-Cultural Competence Inventory*. Patrick Air Force Base, FL: Defense Equal Opportunity Management Institute. 2009.

Safran, William. "Non-Seperatist Policies Regarding Ethnic Minorities: Positive Approaches and Ambiguous Consequences." *International Political Science Review*, Vol. 15, No. 1, 1994, pp. 61-80.

Sapir, Edward. "Culture, Genuine and Spurious." *The American Journal of Sociology*, Vol. 29, No. 4. 1924, pp. 401–429.

Saussure, Ferdinand de. *Course in General Linguistics*. London, UK: Duckworth. 1983.

Schirch, Lisa. "Where does Whole of Government meet Whole of Society?" Chap 5 of the present volume. 2011.

Sewall, Sarah, John A. Nagl, David H. Petraeus, and James F. Amos. *The U.S. Army/Marine Corps Counterinsurgency Field Manual*. Chicago, IL: University of Chicago Press. 2007.

Smith, Anthony D. *Myths and Memories of the Nation*. Oxford, UK: Oxford University Press. 1999.

Smith, Daniel A. "Trends and causes of armed conflicts." in Alexander Austin, Martina Fischer, and Norbert Ropers, eds. *Berghof Handbook for Conflict Transformation*. Berlin, Germany: Berghof Research Centre for Constructive Conflict Management. 2003, pp. 1-16.

Smith, George W, Jr. "Avoiding a Napoleonic Ulcer: Bridging the Gap of Cultural Intelligence (or, have we focused on the wrong transformation?)." In *Chairman of the Joint Chiefs of Staff Strategy Essay Competition: Essays 2004*. Washington, DC: National Defense University Press. 2004, pp. 21-22.

Stearns, Peter N. "Nationalisms: An Invitation to Comparative Analysis." *Journal of World History*, Vol. 8, No. 1, 1997, pp. 57-74.

Stewart, F., ed. *Horizontal Inequalities and Conflict: Understanding Group Violence in Multiethnic Societies*. Basingstoke, UK: Palgrave Macmillan. 2008.

Transparency International (TI). *Corruption Perception Index*. Berlin, Germany: Transparency International. 2010.

Tully, James. *Strange Multiplicity: Constitutionalism in an Age of Diversity*. Cambridge, UK: Cambridge University Press. 1995.

Tyler, Edward. *Primitive Culture*. New York: J.P. Putnam's Sons. 1920.

United Nations Educational Scientific and Cultural Organization (UNESCO). *Universal Declaration of Linguistic Rights.* Paris, France: UNESCO. 1996.

United Nations High Commissioner on Refugees (UNHCR). *Statistical Yearbook 2006.* Geneva, Switzerland: United Nations High Commissioner on Refugees. 2007.

United Nations Organization (UNO). *Charter of the United Nations and Statute of the International Court of Justice.* New York: UNO. 1978.

United Nations Organization (UNO). *Declaration on the Elimination of All Forms of Intolerance and of Discrimination Based on Religion or Belief.* UN General Assembly. Resolution 36/55. New York: UNO. 1981.

Universal House of Justice (UHJ). *The Message to the World's Religious Leaders.* London, UK: Bahá'í Publishing Trust, UK. Haifa, Israel: Bahá'í World Centre. 2002.

U.S. Department of Defense (DoD). *Human Terrain Teams Preliminary Assessment.* Washington, DC: U.S. Department of Defense. 2007.

U.S. Department of Defense (DoD). *Quadrennial Defense Review Report.* February 2010.

Waltz, Kenneth N. *Theory of International Politics.* New York: McGraw-Hill. 1979.

Wear, D. "Insurgent Multiculturalism: Rethinking How and Why We Teach Culture in Medical Education." *Academic Medicine,* Vol. 78, 2003, pp.549–554.

Welsh, David. "Domestic Politics and Ethnic Conflict." *Survival,* Vol. 35, No. 1, 1993, pp. 63-80.

Wendt, Alexander. *Social Theory of International Politics.* Cambridge, MA: Cambridge University Press. 1999.

Worden, Scott. "Afghanistan: An Election Gone Awry." *Journal of Democracy,* Vol. 21, No. 3, 2010, pp. 11-25.

Zinni , Anthony C. "Non-Traditional Military Missions: Their Nature, and the Need For Cultural Awareness and Flexible Thinking." in Joseph L. Strange, ed. *Capital "W" War: A Case for Strategic Principle of War*. Quantico, VA: U.S. Marine Corps War College, 1998, pp. 267-ff.

ENDNOTES - CHAPTER 13

1. Samuel P. Huntington, "The Clash of Civilizations?" *Foreign Affairs*, Vol. 72, No. 3, 1993, pp. 22-49; Robert D. Kaplan, "The Coming Anarchy," *The Atlantic Monthly*, Vol. 273, No. 2, 1994, pp. 44-76.

2. For example, Benjamin Barber, and Andrea Schulz, *Jihad versus McWorld: How the Planet is Both Falling Apart and Coming Together*, New York: Ballantine Books, 1996; Joshua A. Fishman, "Summary and Interpretation: Post-Imperial English 1940-1990," in Joshua Fishman *et al.*, eds., *Post Imperial English. Status Change in Former British and American Colonies 1940-1990*, Berlin, Germany/New York: Mouton de Gruyter, 1996, p. 639.

3. Dan Smith, "Trends and causes of armed conflicts," in Alexander Austin, Martina Fischer, and Norbert Ropers, eds., *Berghof Handbook for Conflict Transformation*, Berlin, Germany: Berghof Research Centre for Constructive Conflict Management, 2003, p. 3; Ted R. Gurr, *The Ethnic Basis of Political Action in the 1980s and 1990s*, Working Paper, Minorities at Risk Project, Baltimore, MD: Center for International Development and Conflict Management, University of Maryland, 1999.

4. *Quadrennial Defense Review Report (QDR)*, Washington, DC: U.S. Department of Defense, February 2010, p. iv. (Hereafter QDR.)

5. Francis Fukuyama, "The End of History," *The National Interest*, No. 16, 1989, pp. 3-18; Francis Fukuyama, *The End of History and the Last Man*, New York, NY: Free Press, 1992.

6. Georg Wilhelm Friedrich Hegel, *The Philosophy of History*, Mineola, NY: Dover Publications, 1956.

7. John Maersheimer, *The Tragedy of Great Power Politics*, New York: W. W. Norton & Co., 2003.

8. Samuel P. Huntington, "The Clash of Civilizations?" in *The Clash of Civilizations and the Remaking of World Order*, New York: Simon & Schuster, 1997.

9. Edward Sapir, "Culture, Genuine and Spurious," *The American Journal of Sociology*, Vol. 29, No. 4, 1924.

10. Melville J. Herskovits, *Man and His Works: The Science of Cultural Anthropology*, New York: Knopf, 1948, p. 39ff.

11. See, for example, Matthew Arnold, *Culture and Anarchy: An Essay in Political and Social Criticism*, New Haven, CT: Yale University Press, 1974.

12. See, for example, Milton J. Bennett, "Defining, Measuring, and Facilitating Intercultural Learning: A Conceptual Introduction to the IJIE Special Issue," *Intercultural Education*, Vol. 20, 2009, pp. 2-4.

13. Robert Phillipson and Tove Skutnabb-Kangas, eds., *Linguistic Human Rights: Overcoming Linguistic Discrimination*, Berlin, Germany: Mouton De Gruyter, 1995, p. 7.

14. Clifford Geertz, *The Interpretation of Cultures*, New York: Basic Books, 1973, pp. 87-125.

15. Huntington, *The Clash of Civilizations and the Remaking of World Order*, p. 4.

16. Emile Durkheim, *Durkheim on Religion*, Atlanta, GA: American Academy of Religion, 1994.

17. Jonathan Fox, *Ethnoreligious Conflict in the Late Twentieth Century*, Lanham, MD: Lexington,. 2002, p. 29.

18. Bridget Moix, "Matters of Faith: Religion, Conflict, and Conflict Resolution," in Morton Deutsch and Peter T. Coleman, eds., *The Handbook of Conflict Resolution: Theory and Practice*, San Francisco, CA: Jossey-Bass Publishers, 2006.

19. Robert L. Ochola, *The Acholi Religious Leaders' Peace Initiative in the Battlefield of Northern Uganda: An Example of an Integrated, Inculturated, and Ecumenical Approach to Pastoral Work in a War Situation*, Unpublished Diploma Thesis, Innsbruck, Austria: Theology, University of Innsbruck, 2006.

20. Universal House of Justice (UHJ), *The Message to the World's Religious Leaders*, London, UK: Bahá'í Publishing Trust, 2002.

21. The three predominant theories of ethnicity are: (a) primordialism, and its corollary essentialism, which claims that ethnicity is historically defined via given existential markers such as place or race; (b) perennialism holds that ethnicities are historically defined and thus subject to constant change; and, (c) constructivism denies a basis in externality and sees it as a strictly negotiable social construct. "Geertz primordialism," moreover, holds that the elements of identity need not truly be "primordial," as long as they are so defined by groups. Anthony D. Smith, *Myths and Memories of the Nation*, Oxford, UK: Oxford University Press. 1999, p. 13.

22. Abdul Jamil Khan, *Urdu/Hindi: An Artificial Divide*, New York: Algora, 2006.

23. See, for example, Kathleen A. Ethier and Kay Deaux, "Negotiating Social Identity when Contexts Change: Maintaining Identification and Responding to Threat," *Journal of Personality and Social Psychology*, Vol. 67, No. 2, August 1994.

24. Fredrik Barth, ed., *Ethnic Groups and Boundaries: The Social Organization of Culture Difference*, Oslo, Norway: Universitetsforlaget, 1969, p. 9.

25. See, for example, Charles King, "The Myth of Ethnic Warfare: Understanding Conflict in the Post-Cold War World," *Foreign Affairs*, Vol. 80, No. 6, 2001.

26. Donald Horowitz, *Ethnic Groups in Conflict*, Berkeley, CA: University of California Press, 1985.

27. Dan Smith.

28. See, for example, Ruth Benedict, *The Chrysanthemum and the Sword*, Peabody, MA: Mariner Books. 2005; David Price, *Anthropological Intelligence: The Deployment and Neglect of American Anthropology in the Second World War*, Durham, NC: Duke University Press, 2008.

29. Franz Boas, "Scientists as Spies," *The Nation*, December 20, 1919; Marc W. D. Tyrrell, Ph.D., "Why Dr. Johnny Won't go to War: Anthropology and the Global War on Terror," *Small Wars Journal*, Vol. 7, February 2007; Roberto González, *American Counterinsurgency: Human Science and the Human Terrain*, Chicago, IL: University of Chicago & Prickly Paradigm, 2009.

30. Sarah Sewall, John A. Nagl, David H. Petraeus, and James F. Amos, *The U.S. Army/Marine Corps Counterinsurgency Field Manual*, Chicago, IL: University of Chicago Press, 2007.

31. See, for example, John W. Jandora, "War and Culture: A Neglected Relation," *Armed Forces & Society*, Vol. 25, No. 4, 1999, pp. 541-556; Anthony C. Zinni, "Non-traditional Military Missions: Their Nature, and the Need for Cultural Awareness and Flexible Thinking," in Joseph L. Strange, ed., *Capital "W" War: A Case for Strategic Principles of War*, Quantico, VA: U.S. Marine Corps War College, 1998, pp. 267-ff.

32. Daniel P. McDonald, *A Brief Note on the Multi-layered Nature of Cross-Cultural Competence*, Patrick Air Force Base, FL: Defense Equal Opportunity Management Institute, 2008.

33. Sewall *et al.*

34. Ferdinand de Saussure, *Course in General Linguistics*, London, UK: Duckworth, 1983.

35. See, for example, Noam Chomsky, *Aspects of the Theory of Syntax*, Cambridge, MA: MIT Press, 1965.

36. González.

37. See American Anthropological Association (AAA), Commission on the Engagement of Anthropology, with the U.S. Security and Intelligence Communities (AAA), *Final Report on The Army's Human Terrain System Proof of Concept Program*, Washington, DC: American Anthropological Association, 2009.

38. Priest and Arkin argue that the post-9/11 intelligence construct—comprising in excess of 1300 facilities, close to 2000 private companies, and close to a million individuals with "Top Secret" security status—has become a "fourth branch" of government far too unsurveyable, lacking in transparency, dependent on contractors, and too expensive to be efficient, reliable, or even effective. Dana Priest and William M. Arkin, *Top Secret America: The Rise of the New American Security State*, New York: Little, Brown and Company, 2011.

39. AAA.

40. *Human Terrain Teams Preliminary Assessment*, Washington, DC: U.S. Department of Defense, 2007. (Hereafter HTT.)

41. Geertz, 1973.

42. See, for example, Edward Tyler, *Primitive Culture*, New York: J. P. Putnam's Sons, 1920.

43. *Ibid.*

44. See, for example, Gordon Allport, *The Nature of Prejudice*, Cambridge, MA: Perseus Books, 1954.

45. Edward T. Hall, *Beyond Culture*, New York: Doubleday, 1977.

46. See, for example, William Safran, "Non-seperatist Policies Regarding Ethnic Minorities: Positive Approaches and Ambiguous Consequences," *International Political Science Review*, Vol. 15, No. 1, 1994, pp. 61-80.

47. Bennett, "Defining, Measuring, and Facilitating Intercultural Learning."

48. The number of attested ethnolinguistic traditions in the world—not counting religious or racial-phenotypal groups—varies considerably, i.e., from around 3,000 (Florian Dua Coulmas, *Sprache und Staat: Studien zur Sprachenplanung und Sprachpolitik*, Berlin, Germany: Walter de Gruyter, 1985) to approximately 5,000 (John Edwards, *Multilingualism*, London, UK/New York: Routledge, 1994) to between 6,000 and 7000 (Phillipson and Skutnabb-Kangas) to exactly 6,703 (Barbara F. Grimes, *Ethnologue*, Dallas, TX: Summer Institute of Linguistics, 1996). Paradoxically, despite the record cases of language death reported, languages appear to be increasing in number as traditional distinctions between languages and dialects are fine-tuned.

49. Bennett, "Defining, Measuring, and Facilitating Intercultural Learning," p. S4.

50. *Ibid.*, pp. S3-S4.

51. Only the ethno-cultural identity to which individuals subscribe is intended here.

52. Huntington, *The Clash of Civilizations and the Remaking of World Order*, 1997.

53. D. Lerner, *The Passing of Traditional Society: Modernizing the Middle East*, Glencoe, IL: The Free Press, 1958.

54. Antonio Gramsci, *Selections from the Prison Notebooks*, London, UK: Lawrence and Wishart, 1971.

55. Roland Robertson, *Globalization: Social Theory and Global Culture*, London, UK: Sage Publications Ltd., 1992.

56. Bennett, "Defining, Measuring, and Facilitating Intercultural Learning," p. S4.

57. W. B. Gudykunst and M. R. Hammer, "Dimensions of Intercultural Effectiveness: Culture Specific or Cultural General?" *International Journal of Intercultural Relations*, Vol. 8, No. 1, 1984, pp. 1-10.

58. Sources alternatingly refer to cultural, cross-cultural (Bennett, 1998), multi-cultural (James Green, *Cultural Awareness in Human Services: A Multi-Ethnic Approach*, Upper Saddle River, NJ: Allyn & Bacon, 1998), insurgent multicultural (D. Wear, "Insurgent multiculturalism: Rethinking How and Why We Teach Culture in Medical Education," *Academic Medicine*, Vol. 78, 2003, pp. 549–554), trans-cultural (Fernando Ortiz, *Contrapunteo Cubano Del Tobacco y el Azúcar (Cuban Counterpoint: Tobacco and Sugar)*, Durham, NC: Duke University Press, 1995), intercultural (A. E. Fantini, *87 Assessment Tools of Intercultural Competence*, Brattleboro, VT: School for International Training, 2006), culturally responsive (G. Gay, *Culturally Responsive Teaching: Theory, Research, & Practice*, New York: Teachers College Press, 2000), culturally relevant (Heather Coffey, *Culturally Relevant Teaching*, Chapel Hill, NC: University of North Carolina, 2008), culturally sensitive (Yvonne Asamoah, *Innovations in Delivering Culturally Sensitive Social Work Services: Challenges for Practice and Education*, New York: Routledge, 1997), culturally appropriate (Leon Epstein, *Culturally Appropriate Health Care by Culturally Competent Health Professionals: International Workshop Report*, Hashomer: The Israel National Institute for Health Policy and Health Services Research Health Services Research, 2007); and/or, culturally competent (Jerry V. Diller and Jean Moule, *Cultural Competence: A Primer for Educators*, Belmont, CA: Thomason Learning, 2005) initiatives. Such a perplexing range of formulations may flummox the most well-intended armed services professional.

59. Michael E. Brown, ed., *Ethnic Conflict and International Security*, Princeton, NJ: Princeton University Press, 1993, p. 10.

60. Gregory Paul P. Meyjes, *A Guide to Intercultural Health Care: Serving African Americans*, Unpublished manuscript, Denver, CO: Kaiser Permanente, African American Center of Excellence, 2010. Also, see Richard D. Bucher and Patricia L. Bucher, *Building Cultural Intelligence (CQ): Nine Megaskills*, Upper Saddle River, NJ: Pearson, 2008.

61. Karol G. Ross, Carol A. Thomson, Daniel P. McDonald, and Meagan C. Arrastia, *The Development of the CCCI: The Cross-Cultural Competence Inventory*, Patrick Air Force Base, FL: Defense Equal Opportunity Management Institute, 2009.

62. *Ibid.*

63. See, for example, Hans C. Köchler, "World Order: Vision and Reality," in David Armstrong, ed., *Studies in International Relations,* Vol. XXXI, New Delhi: India, Manak, 2009, pp. xxiii-564.

64. See, for example, Sally Merry and Mark Goodale, *The Practice of Human Rights: Tracking Law Between the Global and the Local,* Cambridge, UK: Cambridge University Press, 2007.

65. Eleanor Roosevelt, *Universal Declaration of Human Rights,* Bedford, MA: Applewood Books, 2000.

66. *Declaration on the Elimination of All Forms of Intolerance and of Discrimination Based on Religion or Belief,* United Nations General Assembly, Resolution 36/55, New York: United Nations Organization, 1981.

67. *European Charter for Regional or Minority Languages,* Strasbourg, France: Council of Europe, 1992.

68. *Framework Convention for the Protection of National Minorities,* Strasbourg, France: Council of Europe, 1995.

69. United Nations Educational Scientific and Cultural Organization (UNESCO), *Universal Declaration of Linguistic Rights,* Paris, France: UNESCO, 1996.

70. Six very general categories have been cited for defining an "ethnic community:" 1. a name; 2. a belief in common ancestry; 3. historical memories; 4. a shared culture; 5. attachment to a past or current territory; and, 6. self-identification as a group, Anthony D. Smith as quoted in Brown, p. 5; Kallen's distinction between the right of the group as a category, the cultural rights of the group, and the right to national collectivity may also prove useful, Evelyn Kallen, *Ethnicity and Human Rights in Canada,* New York: Oxford University Press, 1995.

71. See, for example, Wilma A. Dunaway, "Ethnic Conflict in the Modern World-System: The Dialectics of Counter-Hegemonic Resistance in an Age of Transition," *Journal of World Systems Research,* Vol. IX, No. 1, 2003, pp. 3-16.

72. Sapir, p. 328.

73. Gregory Paul P. Meyjes, "Plan 'C' Is for C ulture: Out of Iraq, Opportunity," *Landpower Essay*, Vol. 7, No. 4, Arlington, VA: Association of the United States Army, June 2007.

74. Gregory Paul P. Meyjes, "Language and Universalization: a 'Linguistic Ecology' Reading of Bahá'í Writ," *The Journal of Bahá'í Studies*, Vol. 9, No. 1, 1999, pp. 51-63.

75. Scott Worden, "Afghanistan: An Election Gone Awry," *Journal of Democracy*, Vol. 21, No. 3, 2010, pp. 11-25.

76. TI, *Corruption Perception Index*, Berlin, Germany: Transparency International, 2010.

77. *Democracy Index 2010: Democracy in Retreat*, London, UK: The Economist Intelligence Unit, 2010.

78. Brown, p. 9.

79. F. Stewart, ed., *Horizontal Inequalities and Conflict: Understanding Group Violence in Multiethnic Societies*, Basingstoke, UK: Palgrave Macmillan, 2008.

80. See, for example, Donald Horowitz, *Ethnic Groups in Conflict*, Berkeley, CA: University of California Press, 1985, pp. 681-684.

81.Benedict Anderson, *Imagined Communities*, London, UK: Verso, 1965.

82. See, for example, E. Gellner, *Nations and Nationalism*, Oxford, UK: Basic Blackwell, 1983; E. J. Hobsbawm, *Nations and Nationalism since 1780: Programme, Myth, Reality*, Cambridge, UK: Cambridge University Press, 1990; Peter N. Stearns, "Nationalisms: An Invitation to Comparative Analysis," *Journal of World History*, Vol. 8, No. 1, 1997, pp. 57-74; James Tully, *Strange Multiplicity: Constitutionalism in an Age of Diversity*, Cambridge, UK: Cambridge University Press, 1995.

83. David Welsh, "Domestic Politics and Ethnic Conflict," *Survival*, Vol. 35, No. 1, 1993, pp. 63-80.

84. Stewart Patrick and Kaysie Brown report that internationally:

> the concept is most popular among development ministries, which use it to describe a subset of poor countries where weak governance and state capacity are impediments to pro-poor growth. Foreign and defense ministries tend to be more skeptical, finding the term a distraction from concrete challenges of crisis response and post-conflict reconstruction. Foreign ministries are especially sensitive to the potential diplomatic fallout of publicly labeling particular sates as 'fragile.'

Stewart Patrick and Kaysie Brown, *Greater than the Sum of Its parts? Assessing "Whole of Goverment" Approaches to Fragile States*, New York: International Peace Academy, 2007, pp. 128-129.

85. Meyjes, "Plan 'C'," 2007:

> Governments often claim that overbearing policies are necessary to avoid inter-ethnic strife, but rarely are they disinterested. Consequently, minority issues fester, only to reappear later. The . . . Iraqi government concedes that its partisanship, including regarding its security forces and sectarian violence, has aggravated the instability of the society it represents. To leave certain minorities seriously aggrieved is to plant the seeds of revenge. It leaves them little choice but resistance, and it can lead to centuries of cyclical conflict.

86. A. Lijphart, *Democracy in Plural Societies: A Comparative Exploration*, New Haven, CT: Yale University Press, 1977.

87. John McGarry and Brendan O'Leary, "Introduction: The Macro-Political Regulation of Ethnic Conflict," in John McGarry and Brendan O'Leary. eds., *The Politics of Ethnic Conflict Regulation: Case Studies of Protracted Ethnic Conflicts*, London, UK: Routledge, 1993, pp. 1-40.

88. John Coakley, "The Resolution of Ethnic Conflict: Towards a Typology," *International Political Science Review*, Vol. 13, No. 4, 1992, pp. 343-358.

89. *Democracy Index 2010: Democracy in Retreat.*

90. See, for example, Martin van Creveld, *The Rise and Decline of the State*, New York: Cambridge University Press, 1999; Richard N. Rosecrance and Arthur A. Stein, eds., *No More States? Globalization, National Self-determination, and Terrorism*, Rowman & Littlefield Publishers, 2006.

91. *Charter of the United Nations and Statute of the International Court of Justice*, New York: United Nations Organization, 1978.

92. See, for example, Stephano Recchia, "Just and Unjust Postwar Reconstruction: How Much External Interference Can Be Morally Justified?" *Ethics & International Affairs*, Vol. 23, Issue 2, 2009, pp. 165–187.

93. Lisa Schirch, "Where Does Whole of Government Meet Whole of Society?" In this volume.

94. *Whole Government Approaches to Fragile States*, Paris, France: Organization for Economic Cooperation and Development, 2006.

95. Schirch.

96. *Whole Government Approaches to Fragile States*, pp. 7-11.

97. Patrick and Brown.

ABOUT THE CONTRIBUTORS

FOUZIEH MELANIE ALAMIR is an independent consultant for governance, peace and security. She is a political scientist who has been working on issues of regime transformation, international conflict and crisis management, peace building, and governance for more than 15 years in different functions. Her previous assignments have been at the University of the German Armed Forces and the Armed Forces Staff and Command College as a research associate and lecturer from 1997-2002, as a desk officer in the Military Policy Division of the German Federal Ministry of Defense, a Program Manager at the German Agency for Technical Cooperation (a development organization), and as Head of Comprehensive Security at IABG, a private high technology and consulting enterprise with focus on security and defense. In 2011, Dr. Alamir established her own consultancy company offering research, consulting, and training services in the thematic field of governance, peace, and security, serving clients from ministries, the armed forces, and the police, as well as several other security, emergency response, and development agencies. Her international deployments covered Afghanistan, Azerbaijan, China, Ghana, and Indonesia, among others. Dr. Alamir is familiar both with military and civilian thinking and approaches to peace building, conflict and crisis management, combining academic perspectives with experience in governmental agencies and in private business from the politico-strategic to the project/tactical field level.

MICHAEL ASHKENAZI has been a Project Leader and Senior Researcher at the Bonn International Center for Conversion (BICC) since 2004. At BICC, he has led the TRESA program to design and publish universal training materials on small arms and light weapons (SALW) control. Prior to coming to work for BICC, Dr. Ashkenazi was professor of Anthropology and Deputy Academic Dean (Regents College, London), Senior Lecturer (Gyosei College, Reading University), Research Fellow (Japan Centre, University of Birmingham), Visiting Fellow (NASA-Ames), Visiting Professor (Department of Anthropology/School of Management, University of Calgary), and Senior Lecturer (Hebrew University). He previously served in the U.S. Army, reaching the rank of captain; his Army duties included posts as infantry platoon, and company commander and in field and staff positions. Dr. Ashkenazi is Associate Editor of *Encyclopaedia of Ground Warfare* (ABD-Clio). He has taught and supervised graduate and undergraduate students, and is author and editor of several academic volumes, as well as scholarly papers.

DOUG BROOKS is President of International Stability Operations Association (ISOA), a nongovernmental, nonprofit, nonpartisan association of service companies dedicated to providing ethical services to international peacekeeping, peace enforcement, humanitarian rescue, stabilization efforts, and disaster relief. Mr. Brooks has worked as a teacher in Kambuzuma Township in Harare, Zimbabwe, at the Library of Congress, at the National Archives, and the Institute of International Education (IIE). Previous to founding ISOA, he was an academic fellow at the South African Institute for International Affairs in 1999-2000. Mr. Brooks holds a B.A. in history from Indiana University and an M.A. in history from Baylor University, with additional doctoral studies at the Graduate School of

Public and International Affairs, University of Pittsburgh.

ROBERT H. "ROBIN" DORFF joined the Strategic Studies Institute in June 2007 as Research Professor of National Security Affairs where he currently holds the General Douglas MacArthur Chair of Research. He previously served on the U.S. Army War College (USAWC) faculty as a Visiting Professor (1994-96) and as Professor of National Security Policy and Strategy in the Department of National Security and Strategy (1997-2004), where he also held the General Maxwell D. Taylor Chair (1999-2002) and served as Department Chairman (2001-04). He has been a Senior Advisor with Creative Associates International, Inc., in Washington, DC, and served as Executive Director of the Institute of Political Leadership in Raleigh, NC (2004-06). Dr. Dorff is the author or co-author of five books, and numerous journal articles and book chapters. Dr. Dorff holds a B.A. in political science from Colorado College and an M.A. and Ph.D. in political science from the University of North Carolina-Chapel Hill.

CHARLES J. DUNLAP, JR., is a Visiting Professor of the Practice at Duke Law School and the Associate Director of its Center on Law, Ethics and National Security. Prior to retiring from the U.S. Air Force as a major general in June of 2010, General Dunlap assisted in the supervision of more than 2,500 military and civilian attorneys worldwide. His 34-year career included tours in both the United Kingdom and Korea, and he deployed for military operations in Africa and the Middle East. Totaling more than 120 publications, his writings address a wide range of topics including various aspects of national security law, airpower, counterinsurgency, cyberpower, civil-military relations, and leadership. General Dunlap speaks frequently at professional conferences and at numerous institutions of higher learning, including Harvard, Yale, MIT, UVA, and Stanford, as well as National Defense University and the Air, Army, and Navy War Colleges. He serves on the Board of Advisors for the Center for a New American Security. General Dunlap received his undergraduate degree from St. Joseph's University (PA), a law degree from Villanova University, and is a distinguished graduate of the National War College.

MACKENZIE DUELGE is a member of the Georgia Bar Association. Her research interests include counterterrorism, the education/conflict nexus, and the role of contractors in international interventions. Ms. Duelge holds a J.D. from Emory University and an M.A. in International Affairs from the Catholic University of America. She is working on a Ph.D. in international conflict management at Kennesaw State University.

WILLIAM FLAVIN became the Directing Professor of the Doctrine, Concepts, Training and Education Division at the U.S. Army Peacekeeping and Stability Operations Institute (PKSOI), located at the U.S. Army War College in Carlisle, PA, in July 2007. Before this assignment, he was a senior foreign affairs analyst with Booz Allen Hamilton on contract to assist the PKSOI for doctrine development. From 1995 to 1999, he was a colonel in the U.S. Army serving as the Deputy Director of Special Operations for the Supreme Allied Commander Europe at the Supreme Headquarters, Allied Powers Europe. Colonel Flavin holds a B.A. in history from the Viginia Military Institute (VMI) and an M.A. in history from Emory University. He was a senior fellow at the Center for Strategic and International Studies for his Army War College year and then taught at the Army War College.

VOLKER C. FRANKE is Associate Professor of Conflict Management and Director of the Ph.D. program in International Conflict Management at Kennesaw State University. From 2006-08, he served as Director of Research at the BICC, one of Germany's premier peace and conflict research and capacity building institutes. From 1998-2007, he was Director and Managing Editor of the National Security Studies Case Studies Program at Syracuse University's Maxwell School of Citizenship and Public Affairs. Dr. Franke is the author of *Preparing for Peace: Military Identity, Value-Orientations, and Professional Military Education* (Praeger, 1999) and more than 30 journal articles, book chapters, case studies, and research reports on issues related to peace and security studies, conflict management, civil-military relations, development policy, and social identity. He is also the editor of *Terrorism and Peacekeeping: New Security Challenges* (Praeger, 2005) and *Security in a Changing World: Case Studies in U.S. National Security Management* (Praeger, 2002). Dr. Franke holds an M.A. in political science and sociology from Johannes Gutenberg University in Mainz, Germany, a Master of Public Administration degree from North Carolina State University, and a Ph.D. in political science from Syracuse University's Maxwell School.

MARY HABECK is an Associate Professor in Strategic Studies at Johns Hopkins School of Advanced International Studies (SAIS), where she teaches courses on military history and strategic thought. Before coming to SAIS, she taught American and European military history at Yale University from 1994 to 2005. Dr. Habeck was appointed by President George Bush to the Council on the Humanities at the National Endowment for the Humanities (2006-12), and in 2008-09 she was the Special Advisor for Strategic Planning on the National Security Council staff. Dr. Habeck holds a B.A. in international studies, Russian, and Spanish from Ohio State University and an M.A. in international relations and a Ph.D. in history from Yale University.

CHRISTOPHER HOLSHEK, Colonel (retired), U.S. Army (Reserve) Civil Affairs, has 25 years of civil-military operations experience at the strategic, operational, and tactical levels in joint, interagency, and multinational settings across the full range of operations. He commanded the first U.S. Army Civil Affairs battalion to deploy in support of Operation IRAQI FREEDOM. His final tour of duty prior to retirement after 30 years in the Army was as the Military Representative at the U.S. Agency for International Development's Office of Military Affairs for U.S. European Command/Supreme Headquarters Allied Powers Europe. He has served with the United Nations (UN) in military capacities, such as the Senior U.S. Military Observer and Chief, Civil-Military Coordination at UN Mission in Liberia from January 2008 to July 2009. He also served in civilian capacities with the UN as a logistics officer with the UN Transitional Administration in Eastern Slavonia and with the UN Mission in

Kosovo as Political Reporting Officer. In more recent years, he has been a consultant associated with DynCorp International, Creative Associates, the Institute for Defense Analyses, and the Naval Postgraduate School's Center for Civil-Military Relations. He is currently a Senior Associate with the Project on National Security Reform and the Liberia country project manager for the Defense Institution Reform Initiative.

ROBERT KENNEDY, a former senior government official, is a Professor in the Sam Nunn School of International Affairs, Georgia Institute of Technology, Atlanta, GA, since January 2003. His previous assignments include director of the joint German-American George C. Marshall European Center for Security Studies in Germany; Civilian Deputy Commandant, NATO Defense College, Rome, Italy; Dwight D. Eisenhower Professor of National Security Studies at the U.S. Army War College; researcher at the U.S. Army Strategic Studies Institute; and Foreign Affairs Officer, U.S. Arms Control and Disarmament Agency. Dr. Kennedy was an enlisted man in the Army and a command pilot on active duty with the U.S. Air Force and later with the reserve forces.

JACK A. LeCUYER, a retired U.S. Army Colonel, is a Distinguished Professor holding a Minerva Chair at the U.S. Army War College Strategic Studies Institute in Carlisle, PA. His previous assignments have been as a Distinguished Fellow with the Project on National Security Reform (PNSR) with lead responsibility for PNSR's efforts in design of the new National Security Staff, alignment of strategy and resources, and design of the Next Generation State Department. Colonel LeCuyer has been a strategic planner and Special Assistant to the Supreme Allied Commander, Europe; the Commander-in-Chief, United States Southern Command; and two Army Chiefs of Staff. He played a major role in the post-Vietnam transformation of the Army into today's world class organization. He served as an Olmsted Scholar in Florence, Italy; White House Fellow with duty in the White House Office of Intergovernmental Affairs; Army Fellow at the Atlantic Council of the United States; Senior Army Fellow at the Brookings Institution; and Executive Director of the White House Fellows Foundation and Association.

GREGORY PAUL P. MEYJES is Associate Professor of Linguistics in the Department of Inclusive Education at Kennesaw State University, and President of Solidaris Intercultural Services LLC, an intercultural and international consulting firm with a focus on language, religion, and race/ethnicity. Previous assignments included Professor of foreign languages at North Carolina State University (1990-2001); Fulbright Lecturer/Researcher in Sociolinguistics at the University of Conakry in Guinea, West Africa (1998-2000); and Visiting Professor for Intercultural Education and Internationalization at Middle Tennessee State University (2007-08). Dr. Meyjes holds a doctorate in linguistics from the University of North Carolina at Chapel Hill, NC, and graduate credentials in political science, socio and applied linguistics, and international relations from the Universities of Heidelberg (Germany), Lancaster, Oxford, Essex (United Kingdom), and the Netherlands Universities Foundation for International Cooperation (Netherlands).

LISA SCHIRCH is the founding director of the 3P Human Security, a partnership for peacebuilding policy; and Research Professor at the Center for Justice and Peacebuilding at Eastern Mennonite University. 3P Human Security Initiative is a policy voice for civil society to foster peacebuilding through more extensive diplomatic initiatives, smarter development strategies, and human security-oriented defense strategies. A former Fulbright Fellow in East and West Africa, Dr. Schirch has worked in Afghanistan, Lebanon, Iraq, Taiwan, Ghana, Kenya, Brazil, and 15 other countries. She is a frequent public speaker and has TV and radio experience discussing U.S. foreign policy. Dr. Schirch is the author of 5 books on peacebuilding and conflict prevention. She holds a B.A. in international relations from the University of Waterloo, Canada, and an M.S. and Ph.D. in conflict analysis and resolution from George Mason University.

JAMES STEPHENSON is the Senior Advisor for Stabilization and Reconstruction at Creative Associates International, Inc. Dr. Stephenson is a retired Senior Foreign Service Officer with the U.S. Agency for International Development (USAID). His USAID assignments included 13 months as Mission Director in Iraq; Senior Advisor to the State Department's Coordinator for Reconstruction and Stabilization; Mission Director in Serbia/Montenegro and Lebanon; and in various positions in Egypt, Barbados, Grenada, El Salvador, the Philippines, and Washington, DC. He frequently lectures at the military service colleges and various universities, and trains deploying units in counterinsurgency. Before joining USAID, Mr. Stephenson practiced law in Columbia, SC. He holds a bachelor's honors degree in English literature and a juris doctorate from the University of South Carolina.